Praise for *The Invention of the Jewish People*

"Zionism's quest for a historical homeland is brilliantly excavated by Shlomo Sand in his recent *The Invention of the Jewish People*."

Alex Cockburn, *The Nation*

"Shlomo Sand, historian and author of *The Invention of the Jewish People*—much reviewed and rebutted, and recently translated into English—is provoking the international community by arguing that Jews have never been genetically or otherwise 'a people' … Sand's larger point, that Israel needs to become more like other Western democracies and less obsessed with ethnic purity, is welcome."

Newsweek

"Shlomo Sand's *The Invention of the Jewish People* is both a welcome and, in the case of Israel, much needed exercise in the dismantling of nationalist historical myth and a plea for an Israel that belongs equally to all its inhabitants. Perhaps books combining passion and erudition don't change political situations, but if they did, this one would count as a landmark."

Eric Hobsbawm, *Observer*, Books of the Year

"The translated version of his polemic has sparked a new wave of coverage in Britain and has provoked spirited debates … The book has been extravagantly denounced and praised."

Patricia Cohen, *New York Times*

"A formidable polemic against claims that Israel has a moral right to define itself as an explicitly and exclusively Jewish society, in which non-Jews, such as Palestino-Israelis, are culturally and politically marginalised."

Max Hastings, *Sunday Times*

"I am one of many Jews who would agree with Sand that a decisive factor in the future of Israel will be its capacity to be far more attentive to the narratives and rights of its Palestinian and other non-Jewish citizens."

Jonathan Wittenberg, *Guardian*

"[Shlomo Sand's] quiet earthquake of a book is shaking historical faith in the link between Judaism and Israel."

Rafael Behr, *Observer*

"A string of firecrackers."

Independent, Book of the Week

"It is certainly one of the bravest [books of the year]."

Terry Eagleton, *Times Literary Supplement*

"Sand takes on a formidable tradition in claiming that moral validity in the Middle East needs good history, and no discussion of the region any longer seems complete without acknowledgement of his book."

Independent on Sunday, Best History Books of 2009

"No serious reader who is interested in Zionism or Israel—whatever their personal views—can avoid being shaken up ... by Sand's impressive redrawing of the major religious and 'racial' boundaries that are usually taken for granted in most discussions of these subjects."

Bertell Ollman, *MR Zine*

"[Sand's] conclusion is that Israel has to become a democratic state of all its citizens, including the 20 per cent who are Muslims and Christians, not a state of all the Jews. This book must be as seen as a milestone on that road."

The National

"His latest academic work has spent 19 weeks on Israel's bestseller list and that success has come to the history professor despite his book challenging Israel's biggest taboo."

Jonathan Cook, *Al Jazeera*

"Sand makes a very strong case against the neo-biblical story of the Jews that has been used by both Christians and modern Jews, and forms the religious underpinning of Zionism."

Colorlines

"His book is a trip through a landscape of illusions which Sand aims to explode, leaving the scenery freer for a Middle East built ... from the hard bricks of truth."

Simon Schama, *Financial Times*

The Invention of the Jewish People

Shlomo Sand

Translated by Yael Lotan

VERSO
London • New York

English edition first published by Verso 2009
© Verso 2009
Translation © Yael Lotan
This paperback edition published by Verso 2010

The Invention of the Jewish People was first published as
Matai ve'ekh humtza ha'am hayehudi?
[When and How Was the Jewish People Invented?]
© Resling 2008
All rights reserved

7 9 10 8 6

Verso
UK: 6 Meard Street, London W1F 0EG
US: 20 Jay Street, Suite 1010, Brooklyn, NY 11201
www.versobooks.com

Verso is the imprint of New Left Books

ISBN-13: 978-1-84467-623-1

British Library Cataloguing in Publication Data
A catalogue record for this book is available from the British Library

Library of Congress Cataloging-in-Publication Data
A catalog record for this book is available from the Library of Congress

Typeset in Minion by Hewer Text UK Ltd, Edinburgh
Printed in the US by Maple Vail

To the memory of the refugees who reached this soil
and those who were forced to leave it.

Contents

viii

Preface to the English-Language Edition

This book was originally written in Hebrew. My mother tongue is actually Yiddish, but Hebrew has remained the language of my imagination, probably of my dreams and certainly of my writing. I chose to publish the book in Israel because initially my intended readers were Israelis, both those who see themselves as Jews and those who are defined as Arabs. My reason was simple enough: I live in Tel Aviv, where I teach history.

When the book first appeared in early 2008, its reception was somewhat odd. The electronic media were intensely curious, and I was invited to take part in many television and radio programs. Journalists, too, turned their attention to my study, mostly in a favorable way. By contrast, representatives of the "authorized" body of historians fell on the book with academic fury, and excitable bloggers depicted me as an enemy of the people. Perhaps it was this contrast that prompted the readers to indulge me—the book stayed on the bestseller list for nineteen weeks.

To understand this development, you have to take a clear-eyed look at Israel and forgo any bias for or against. I live in a rather strange society. As the closing chapter of the book shows—to the annoyance of many book reviewers—Israel cannot be described as a democratic state while it sees itself as the state of the "Jewish people," rather than as a body representing all the citizens within its recognized boundaries (not including the occupied territories). The spirit of Israel's laws indicates that, at the start of the twenty-first century, the state's objective is to serve Jews rather than Israelis, and to provide the best conditions for the supposed descendants of this *ethnos* rather than for all the citizens who live in it and speak its language. In fact, anyone born to a Jewish mother may have the best of both worlds—being free to live in London or in New York, confident that the State of Israel is theirs, even if they do not wish to live under its sovereignty. Yet anyone who did not emerge from Jewish loins and who lives in Jaffa or in Nazareth will feel that the state in which they were born will never be theirs.

Yet there is a rare kind of liberal pluralism in Israel, which weakens in times of war but functions quite well in peacetime. So far it has been possible in Israel to express a range of political opinions at literary events, to have Arab parties take part in parliamentary elections (provided they do not question the Jewish nature of the state), and to criticize the elected authorities. Certain liberal freedoms—such as freedom of the press, of expression and of association—have been protected, and the public arena is both variegated and secure. That is why it was possible to publish this book, and why its reception in 2008 was lively and aroused genuine debate.

Furthermore, the tight grip of the national myths has long been loosened. A younger generation of journalists and critics no longer echoes its parents' collectivist ethos, and searches for the social models cultivated in London and New York. Globalization has sunk its aggressive talons into the cultural arenas even of Israel and has, in the process, undermined the legends that nurtured the "builders' generation." An intellectual current known as post-Zionism is now found, though marginally, in various academic institutions, and has produced unfamiliar pictures of the past. Sociologists, archaeologists, geographers, political scientists, philologists, and even filmmakers have been challenging the fundamental terms of the dominant nationalism.

But this stream of information and insights has not reached the plateau on which resides a certain discipline, called "The History of the Israelite People" in Hebrew academies. These institutions have no departments of history as such, but rather departments of general history—such as the one I belong to—and separate departments of Jewish (Israelite) history. It goes without saying that my harshest critics come from the latter. Aside from noting minor errors, they chiefly complained that I had no business discussing Jewish historiography because my area of expertise is Western Europe. Such criticism was not leveled against other general historians who tackled Jewish history, provided they did not deviate from the dominant thinking. "The Jewish people," "the ancestral land," "exile," "diaspora," "aliyah," "Eretz Israel," "land of redemption" and so forth are key terms in all reconstructions within Israel of the national past, and the refusal to employ them is seen as heretical.

I was aware of all this before I began writing this book. I expected my attackers to claim that I lacked a proper knowledge of Jewish history, did not understand the historical uniqueness of the Jewish people, was blind to its biblical origin, and denied its eternal unity. But it seemed to me that to spend my life at Tel Aviv University amid its vast collection of volumes and documents about Jewish history without taking time to read and tackle them would have been a betrayal of my profession. Certainly it is pleasant, as a well-established professor, to travel to France and the United States to gather material about Western culture, enjoying the power and tranquility of academe. But as a historian taking part in shaping the collective memory of the society I live in, I felt it was my duty to contribute directly to the most sensitive aspects of this task.

Admittedly, the disparity between what my research suggested about the history of the Jewish people and the way that history is commonly understood—not only within Israel but in the larger world—shocked me as much as it shocked my readers. Generally speaking, educational systems teach you to begin writing after you have finished your thinking—meaning that you should know your conclusion before you start writing (that was how I obtained my doctoral degree). But now I found myself being shaken repeatedly as I worked on the composition. The moment I began to apply the methods of Ernest Gellner, Benedict Anderson and others, who instigated a conceptual revolution in the field of national history, the materials I encountered in my research were illuminated by insights that led me in unexpected directions. I should emphasize that I encountered scarcely any new findings—almost all such material had previously been uncovered by Zionist and Israeli historiographers. The difference is that some elements had not been given sufficient attention, others were immediately swept under the historiographers' rug, and still others were "forgotten" because they did not fit the ideological needs of the evolving national identity. What is so amazing is that much of the information cited in this book has always been known inside the limited circles of professional research, but invariably got lost en route to the arena of public and educational memory. My task was to organize the historical information in a new way, to dust off the old documents and continually reexamine them. The conclusions to which they led me created a radically different narrative from the one I had been taught in my youth.

Unfortunately, few of my colleagues—the teachers of history in Israel— feel it their duty to undertake the dangerous pedagogical mission of exposing conventional lies about the past. I could not have gone on living in Israel without writing this book. I don't think books can change the world, but when the world begins to change, it searches for different books. I may be naive, but it is my hope that the present work will be one of them.

Tel Aviv, 2009

Introduction: Burdens of Memory

A Nation … is a group of persons united by a common error about their ancestry and a common dislike of their neighbors.
—Karl Deutsch, *Nationality and Its Alternatives*, 1969

I do not think I could have written the book on nationalism which I did write were I not capable of crying, with the help of a little alcohol, over folk songs.
—Ernest Gellner, "Reply to Critics," 1996

This book is a work of history. Nonetheless, it will open with a number of personal stories that, like all biographical writing, required a liberal amount of imagination to give them life. To begin like this is less strange than readers may at first imagine. It is no secret that scholarly research is often motivated by personal experiences. These experiences tend to be hidden beneath layers of theory; here some are proffered at the outset. They will serve the author as the launch pad in his passage toward historical truth, an ideal destination that, he is aware, no one ever truly reaches.

Personal memory is untrustworthy—we do not know the color of the ink with which it was written—and thus one should view the depiction of the following encounters as inexact and partly fictitious, though no more so than any other type of biographical writing. As for their possibly troublesome connection with the central thesis of this book, readers will discover it as they proceed. True, their tone is sometimes ironic, even melancholic. But irony and melancholy have their uses, and might jointly be suitable attire for a critical work that seeks to isolate the historical roots and changing nature of identity politics in Israel.

IDENTITY IN MOVEMENT

The First Story—Two Immigrant Grandfathers

His name was Shulek. Later, in Israel, he was called Shaul. He was born in Lodz, Poland, in 1910. At the end of the First World War his father died of the Spanish flu, and his mother went to work as a laborer in a textile plant near the city. Two of her three children were put up for adoption with the help of the local Jewish community; only Shulek, the youngest, remained at home. He attended a heder for a few years, but his mother's straitened circumstances forced him out into the streets at an early age, and he began to do various jobs associated with the processing of textiles. That's how it was in Lodz, Poland's center of textile production. The young man shed his parents' ancient faith for fairly ordinary reasons. As his mother had been impoverished by his father's death, the local synagogue ordered her to sit in the back rows of the congregation. Hierarchy ruled in this traditional society. The reduction of financial capital almost always led to a rapid reduction in symbolic capital, and so the mother's distance from respectable social status was mirrored in her distance from the holy Torah. Her son, carried along by the momentum of exclusion, found himself cast out of the house of prayer. Loss of faith among the young in the Jewish quarters of major cities was becoming widespread. Overnight young Shulek, too, found himself without a home and without a faith.

But not for long. He joined the Communist Party, as was the fashion, which brought him in line with the cultural and linguistic majority of Polish society. Soon Shulek became a revolutionary activist. The socialist vision filled his imagination and strengthened his spirit, prompting him to read and think in spite of the demanding work he did for a living. The party became a haven. Before long, however, this warm and lively shelter also got him thrown in prison for political sedition. He spent six years there, and while he never finished school, his education was considerably broadened. Though unable to assimilate Marx's *Das Kapital*, he became familiar with the popular writings of Friedrich Engels and Vladimir Ilych Lenin. He who never finished his heder education, and did not fulfill his mother's hope that he would enter a yeshiva, became a Marxist.

One cold December day in 1939, Shulek saw three Jews hanged in Lodz's central avenue—a stunt by some German soldiers who'd been drinking in a nearby beer hall. A few days later, he and his young wife and her sister were swept up with a flood of displaced people rushing eastward toward the Red Army, which had occupied half of Poland. Shulek did not take his mother along. Later he would say she was old and frail; in fact, she was then fifty years old. She was similarly old and also indigent when the ghetto dwellers—and she among them—began to be eliminated in slow and cumbersome gas trucks, the primitive extermination technology that preceded the more efficient gas chambers.

When the refugees reached the Soviet-occupied area, Shulek knew better than to reveal that he was a Communist: Stalin had recently eliminated the leaders of Polish Communism. Instead Shulek crossed the German-Soviet boundary bearing an old-new identity: that of an avowed Jew. At the time, the USSR was the only country willing to accept Jewish refugees, although it sent most of them to its Asian regions. Shulek and his wife were fortunate in being sent to distant Uzbekistan. His sister-in-law, who was educated and spoke several languages, enjoyed the privilege of being allowed to remain in civilized Europe, which, sadly, had not yet been dubbed Judeo-Christian. So it was that in 1941 she fell into the hands of the Nazis and was dispatched to a crematorium.

In 1945, Shulek and his wife returned to Poland, but even in the absence of the German army the country continued its rejection of the Jews. Once again the Polish Communist was left without a homeland (unless we count Communism, to which, despite all his troubles, he remained loyal). He and his wife and two small children found themselves in a camp for displaced persons in the mountains of Bavaria. There he met one of his brothers, who, unlike Shulek, disliked communism and favored Zionism. History looked on their fates with an ironic smile: the Zionist brother got a visa to emigrate to Montreal, where he remained for the rest of his life, while Shulek and his little family were transferred by the Jewish Agency to Marseilles, whence at the end of 1948 they sailed to Haifa.

In Israel, Shulek lived for many years as Shaul, though he never became a real Israeli. Even his identity card did not classify him as such. It defined him as Jewish by nationality and religion—since the 1960s, the state had recorded a religion for all citizens, including confirmed unbelievers—but he was always much more of a Communist than a Jew, and more of a Yiddishist than a Pole. Though he learned to communicate in Hebrew, he did not much care for the language, and continued to speak Yiddish with family and friends.

Shulek was nostalgic for the 'Yiddishland' of Eastern Europe and the revolutionary ideas that had seethed and fermented there before the war. In Israel he felt he was stealing other people's land; though it wasn't his doing, he continued to regard it as robbery. His obvious alienation was not from the native-born Sabras, who looked down on him, but from the local climate. The hot breath of the Levant was not for him. It only intensified his longing for the heavy snows that blanketed the streets of Lodz, the Polish snow that slowly melted in his memory until his eyes finally closed. At his graveside, his old comrades sang "The Internationale."

Bernardo was born in Barcelona, Catalonia, in 1924. Years later he would be called Dov. Bernardo's mother, like Shulek's mother, was a religious woman her entire life, although she attended a church rather than a synagogue. His father, however, had early on abandoned any intensive preoccupation with the soul and, like many other metalworkers in rebellious Barcelona, become an anarchist. At the beginning of the Spanish Civil War, the anarcho-syndicalist cooperatives supported the young leftist republic and for a while actually ruled Barcelona. But the right-wing, Francoist forces soon reached the city, and young Bernardo fought alongside his father in the final retreat from its streets.

Bernardo's conscription into Franco's military, a few years after the end of the Civil War, did not soften his feelings about the new regime. As an armed soldier in 1944, he deserted to the Pyrenees, where he helped other opponents of the regime cross the border. Meanwhile he waited eagerly for the American forces to arrive and bring down the cruel ally of Mussolini and Hitler. To his dismay, the democratic liberators did not even try. Bernardo had no choice but to cross the border himself and become a stateless person. He worked as a miner in France, then stowed away on a ship in hope of reaching Mexico. But he was caught in New York and sent back to Europe in shackles.

Thus in 1948 he, too, was in Marseilles, working in one of the shipyards. One evening in May, he met a group of enthusiastic young men in a dockside café. The young metalworker, still dreaming of the human beauty of Barcelona's revolutionary cooperatives, became convinced that the kibbutz in the new state of Israel was their natural successor. Without the slightest connection to Judaism or Zionism, he boarded an immigrant ship, arrived in Haifa and was promptly sent to the battlefront in the valley of Latrun. Many of his companions fell during combat, but he survived and immediately joined a kibbutz, just as he had dreamed of doing that spring day in Marseilles. There he met the woman of his life. Along with several other couples, they were married by a rabbi in a speedy ritual. In those days, the rabbis were still happy to provide this service and asked no superfluous questions.

The Ministry of the Interior soon discovered that a serious error had been made: Bernardo, now known as Dov, was not a Jew. Although the marriage was not annulled, Dov was summoned to a formal meeting to clarify his true identity. In the government office to which he was directed sat an official wearing a large black skullcap. At that time, the religious-Zionist party Mizrahi, which ran the Ministry of the Interior, was cautious and hesitant. It was not yet insistent about "national" territories or the politics of identity exclusion.

The exchange between the two men went more or less as follows:

"You are not a Jew, sir," said the official.

"I never said I was," replied Dov.

"We shall have to change your registration," the official said casually.

"No problem," Dov agreed. "Go right ahead."

"What is your nationality?"

"Israeli?" Dov suggested.

"There is no such thing," stated the official.

"Why?"

"Because there is no Israeli national identity," the ministry official said with a sigh. "Where were you born?"

"In Barcelona."

"Then we'll write 'nationality: Spanish.'"

"But I'm not Spanish. I'm a Catalan, and I refuse to be categorized as Spanish. That's what my father and I fought about in the 1930s."

The official scratched his head. He knew no history, but he did respect people. "So we'll put 'nationality: Catalan.'"

"Very good!" said Dov.

Thus Israel became the first country in the world to officially recognize the Catalan nationality.

"Now, sir, what is your religion?"

"I'm a secular atheist."

"I can't write 'atheist.' The State of Israel does not recognize such a category. What was your mother's religion?"

"The last time I saw her, she was still a Catholic."

"Then I shall write 'religion: Christian,'" the official said, relieved.

But Dov, normally a calm man, was growing impatient. "I won't carry an identity card that says I'm a Christian. It's not only opposed to my principles; it offends the memory of my father, who was an anarchist and set fire to churches in the Civil War."

The official scratched his head some more, weighed the options, and found a solution. Dov left the ministry office with a blue identity card that declared both his nationality and his religion to be Catalan.

Over the years, Dov took pains not to let his national and religious identity adversely affect his daughters. He knew that Israeli schoolteachers often referred to "us Jews," despite the fact that some of their pupils, or the pupils' parents, might not be among that group. Since Dov was antireligious, and his wife was opposed to his being circumcised, conversion to Judaism was not on the cards. At some point he searched for some imaginary link to the Marranos (forced converts) of Spain. But when his daughters grew up and assured him that his being a non-Jew did not trouble them, he abandoned the search.

Fortunately for him, the graveyards of kibbutzim do not bury gentiles outside the fence or in Christian cemeteries, as all other Israeli communities do. Dov, therefore, is buried in the same plot of land as the other members of the kibbutz. His identity card, however, has disappeared, though he could hardly have taken it with him on his final journey.

In due time, the two immigrants, Shulek and Bernardo, shared Israeli granddaughters. Their father was a friend of two men whose stories begin here.

The Second Story—Two "Native" Friends

Mahmoud One (both protagonists in this story are named Mahmoud) was born in Jaffa in 1945. In the 1950s there were still some Arab neighborhoods whose inhabitants had not fled to Gaza during the fighting and were permitted go on living in their native city. This Mahmoud grew up in the impoverished alleys of the city, which was almost entirely settled by Jewish immigrants. Unlike the population in the Sharon Plain and the Galilee, the Palestinians of Jaffa had been left depleted and orphaned; too few of the city's original inhabitants remained to carry forward an independent culture, and the immigrant society refused to become involved or integrated with them.

One outlet from the small, narrow ghetto of Arab Jaffa was the Israeli Communist party. Young Mahmoud joined its youth movement, in which he met Israelis his own age. The movement also enabled him to learn Hebrew well and to travel in and become familiar with "Eretz Israel," which was still quite small. Moreover, the movement took him beyond the scanty education he had received at the Arab school, and, like Shulek of Poland, he studied Engels and Lenin and tried to read Communist writers from around the world. His Israeli youth guides liked him, and he was always willing to help his comrades.

Mahmoud befriended an Israeli boy a year younger than he was. They shared an outlook, and Mahmoud helped his friend cope with the intense, challenging street life of Jaffa. His physical strength made the younger lad feel safe, while the latter's sharp tongue sometimes served Mahmoud well. They grew very close. They told each other their deepest secrets. The friend learned that Mahmoud dreamed of being called Moshe and of being accepted as one of the boys. Some evenings as they wandered about the streets, Mahmoud introduced himself as Moshe and succeeded in convincing peddlers and shopkeepers of his Jewishness. But he could not maintain the other identity for long, and always reverted to Mahmoud. Nor did his pride allow him to turn his back on his family.

One advantage Mahmoud enjoyed as an Arab was exemption from military service. His friend, however, received a conscription notice, which threatened to separate them. One weekend in 1964, they sat on Jaffa's beautiful beach and speculated about the future. Fantasizing freely, they resolved that as soon as Mahmoud's friend completed his military service they would travel the world, and perhaps, if they were lucky, would not have to come back to Israel. To cement this fateful resolution, they carefully cut their palms and pressed them together and, like a pair of silly little boys, swore to make the great journey together.

Mahmoud waited for the younger man to complete his national service. It lasted more than two and a half years. But the friend came back changed—in love, emotionally shackled, confused. Though he remembered their pact, he became hesitant. Tel Aviv's vibrancy attracted him. Its abundant temptations were too great to resist. Mahmoud waited patiently but finally had to admit that his friend was very attached to the excitement of Israeliness and would not be able to break away from it. So Mahmoud gave up, saved his money, and left. He crossed Europe slowly, putting Israel farther and farther behind him, until he reached Stockholm. Despite Sweden's unfamiliar cold and blinding white snow, he tried hard to adapt. He began working for an elevator company and became an expert installer.

But during the long northern winters he still dreamed of Jaffa. When he wanted to marry, he returned to the place that had once been his homeland but that history had decided, when he was three, would not be his. He found a suitable woman, took her back to Sweden, and raised a family with her there. Somehow the Palestinian from Jaffa became a Scandinavian, and his children grew up speaking Swedish. They taught their mother their native tongue. Long ago, Mahmoud stopped wishing his name were Moshe.

The other Mahmoud was born in 1941 in a small village, now long extinct, near Acre. In 1948 he became a refugee when his family fled the fighting to Lebanon, and his birthplace was erased. A thriving Jewish village rose on its ruins. One moonless night, a year after the war, Mahmoud and his family quietly crossed back across the border and made their way to the house of relatives in the village of Jadida, in the Galilee. In this way, Mahmoud came to be included among those who for many years were classified as "present absentees"— refugees who remained in their country of birth but had lost their land and possessions. This second Mahmoud was a dreamy, gifted child who used to amaze his teachers and friends with his eloquence and imagination. Like the first Mahmoud, he joined the Communist Party and soon became famous within its ranks as a journalist and poet. He moved to Haifa, which was then the biggest mixed Jewish-Arab city in Israel. There he met young Israeli men and women, and his poetry attracted a growing public. His bold poem "Identity Card," written in 1964, excited an entire generation of young Arabs, both inside Israel and beyond its borders. The poem opens with a proud challenge to an official of the Israeli Ministry of the Interior:

> Record!
> I am an Arab
> And my identity card number is fifty thousand
> I have eight children
> And the ninth is coming after the summer
> Will you be angry?

Israel compelled its indigenous non-Jewish citizens to carry an identity card in which their nationality was listed neither as Israeli nor Palestinian, but as Arab. Paradoxically, it thus became one of the very few countries in the world that recognized not only Catalan but Arab nationalities. Early on, the poet foresaw that the growing number of non-Jewish residents in Israel would begin to worry the authorities and politicians.

Mahmoud was soon labeled seditious. In the 1960s, Israel still feared poets more than *shaheed*s (martyrs). He was repeatedly detained, sentenced to house arrest, and in quiet periods forbidden to leave Haifa without a police permit. He suffered the persecution and restrictions with a stoical, rather than a poetical, sangfroid, and took comfort in the friends who made the pilgrimage to his flat in Haifa's Wadi Nisnas neighborhood.

Among his distant associates was a young Communist from Jaffa. This comrade knew no Arabic, but Mahmoud's poems in Hebrew translation fired his imagination and tempted him to try his hand at writing. Once discharged from the army, he would travel to Haifa from time to time to visit the poet. Their talk not only strengthened his faith in the struggle, but was also a useful deterrent against writing puerile verse.

At the end of 1967 the young man again visited Haifa. While taking part in the conquest of East Jerusalem, he had had to shoot at the enemy and intimidate terrified inhabitants. Israelis were intoxicated with victory; Arabs were sick with humiliation. Mahmoud's young friend felt bad and smelled bad with the stink of war. He longed to abandon everything and leave the country. But he also wanted a final meeting with the poet he admired.

During the fighting in the Holy City, Mahmoud was manacled and taken to prison through the streets of Haifa. The soldier saw him after his release. They passed a sleepless, drunken night immersed in the fumes of alcohol beside windows made dim by cigarette smoke. The poet tried to persuade his young admirer to remain and resist, rather than flee to alien cities and abandon their common homeland. The soldier poured out his despair, his revulsion with the general air of triumphalism, his alienation from the soil on which he had shed innocent blood. At the end of the night, he vomited his guts out. At midday, the poet woke him with a translation of a poem he had written at first light, "A Soldier Dreaming of White Lilies":

> understanding
>   as he told me
> that home
> is drinking his mother's coffee
> and coming back safely at evening.

> I asked him:
>   and the land?
> He said:
>   I don't know it

In 1968, a Palestinian poem about an Israeli soldier capable of feeling remorse for his violence and for having lost his head in battle, of feeling guilty about taking part in a conquest of the land of others, was perceived by the Arab world as a betrayal—surely such Israeli soldiers did not exist. The Haifa poet was roundly chastised, even accused of cultural collaboration with the Zionist enemy. But this did not last. His prestige continued to grow, and he soon became a symbol of the proud resistance of the Palestinians in Israel.

Eventually the soldier left the country, but the poet had left before him. He could no longer bear being suffocated by the police, subjected to continual persecution and harassment. The Israeli authorities quickly abrogated his questionable citizenship. They never forgot that the cheeky poet was the first Arab in Israel to issue his own identity card, when he wasn't supposed to have an identity at all.

The poet traveled from one capital to another, his fame growing all the while. Finally, during the ephemeral Oslo Initiative thaw, he was allowed to return and settle in Ramallah, on the West Bank. But he was forbidden to enter Israel. Only when a fellow writer died did the security authorities relent and allow Mahmoud to set his eyes on the scenes of his childhood, if only for a few hours. As he did not carry explosives, he was subsequently permitted to enter a few more times.

The soldier, meanwhile, spent many years in Paris, strolling its beautiful streets and studying. Finally he weakened. Despite the alienation, he was overcome by longing for the city in which he had grown up, and so he returned to the painful place where his identity was forged. His homeland, claiming to be the "State of the Jewish people," received him willingly.

As for the rebellious poet who had been born on its soil, and the old friend who had dreamed of being Moshe—the state was too narrow to include them.

The Third Story—Two (Non-)Jewish Students

Named Gisèle, after her grandmother, she was born and brought up in Paris. She was a lively, impetuous girl whose first response was always, No. Yet despite the stubborn no, or perhaps because of it, she was an excellent student, though barely tolerated by her teachers. Her parents indulged her in every way, even when she suddenly decided to study the Holy Tongue. They had hoped she would be a scientist, but she made up her mind to live in Israel. She studied philosophy at the Sorbonne and learned Yiddish and Hebrew at the same time. Yiddish she chose because it was the language spoken by her grandmother, whom she never knew, and Hebrew because she wanted it to be the language of her future children.

Her father had been imprisoned in the camps. Owing mainly to the help of German fellow prisoners, he was saved, and thus was fortunate enough to return to Paris after the war. His mother, Gisela, who was taken with him in the summer of 1942, was sent directly from Drancy to Auschwitz. She did not survive. He joined the French socialist party and there met his future wife. They had two daughters, one of whom was named Gisèle.

By the time she was in secondary school, Gisèle was already a wild anarchist, associating with the remnants of the legendary groups of May '68. When she turned seventeen, she abruptly announced she was a Zionist. At the time, there were not yet many books in French about the fate of the French Jews during the Nazi occupation, and Gisèle had to be content with general writings about the period, which she read avidly. She knew that many of those who survived the death camps had gone to Israel, but that her grandmother Gisela had perished. Gisèle sought out Jewish women who resembled her, and prepared to undertake "aliyah."

In the winter of 1976 she took an intensive Hebrew course given by the Jewish Agency in the heart of Paris. Her teacher was an irritable, sensitive Israeli. She annoyed him with her questions and did not hesitate to correct him on tricky verb declensions. Although her critical remarks displeased him, she intrigued him and he did not strike back: she was the best student in the class, and he could not help but respect her.

Before the end of the year, however, Gisèle suddenly stopped attending the course. The Hebrew teacher wondered if he had unwittingly offended her during one of their disputes in class. A few weeks later, as the course was coming to an end, she suddenly turned up, haughtier than ever but with a touch of melancholy in her eyes. She informed him that she had decided to stop studying Hebrew.

Gisèle had been to the Jewish Agency to arrange her travel to Israel. There she was told that she could study at the Hebrew University in Jerusalem and could receive the usual immigrant benefits, but that she would not be considered Jewish unless she converted. Gisèle, who always insisted she was a Jew and was proud of her typically Jewish surname, had known that her mother, despite her wholehearted identification with her husband, was a gentile. She also knew that in the Jewish religion the child's religious identity is derived from the mother's, but she had considered this only a minor bureaucratic detail. Being young and impatient, and also convinced that the history of her father's family provided sufficient grounds for her self-identification, she had expected these matters to be easily resolved.

Impertinently, in French, she had asked the Jewish Agency official if he was a believer. No, he replied. Then she asked him how a nonreligious person who regarded himself as a Jew could advise another nonreligious person who regarded herself as a Jew to convert in order to join the Jewish people and their country? The representative of the Jewish people replied drily that this was the law, adding that in Israel her father would not have been able to marry her mother, as only religious marriage was allowed. Suddenly Gisèle understood that she was, so to speak, a national bastard. Though she thought of herself as a Jew, and since becoming a Zionist was also seen by others as a Jew, she was not enough of a Jew to satisfy the State of Israel.

Gisèle refused to consider conversion. She could not bear clerics of any persuasion, and having heard about the embarrassment and hypocrisy involved in conversion to orthodox Judaism, she recoiled in disgust. There were still traces of radical anarchism in her personality, and she promptly eliminated Israel from her list of desirable destinations. She decided not to migrate to the state of the Jewish people, and gave up learning Hebrew.

Having conducted her final talk with her Israeli teacher in French, she ended it by saying, in strongly accented Hebrew, "Thanks for everything, so long and perhaps good-bye."

The teacher thought he could discern a Yiddishist intonation in her voice. She had, after all, learned Yiddish. He never heard from her again. Years later, he came across her name in a respected Paris newspaper. She'd written an article about Israel's conduct in the occupied territories; beneath her name, it was noted that she was a psychoanalyst. No doubt many French Jews immediately classified her as a self-hating Jew, while the anti-Semites probably thought hers was a typically Jewish profession.

The other student, whose name was Larissa, was born in 1984 in a small town in Siberia. Soon after the collapse of the Soviet Union, in the early 1990s, her parents migrated to Israel, where they were sent to a so-called development town in the Upper Galilee. There Larissa was brought up amid a balance of immigrant and Israeli children, and appeared to integrate well. She began to speak Hebrew like a Sabra and was content with herself and with daily life in Israel. Sometimes she was upset when called a Russian and teased because of her golden hair, but that was how local youngsters treated newly arrived children.

In the year 2000, at age sixteen, she went to the Ministry of the Interior office to obtain her first identity card. She was received cordially by a woman clerk and given an application form to complete. When it came to the question of nationality, she asked, naively, if she could write "Jewish." The clerk looked through the information she had already entered and explained, apologetically, that she could not. She would be in the same category as her mother, and thus bear the taunting title "Russian." Later she would say at that moment she felt the same pain as when she began to menstruate—something that occurs in nature and can never be got rid of.

Larissa was not the only girl in the town who bore this mark of Cain. At school they even formed a sorority of non-Jewish girls. They shielded each other and tried to smudge the nationality information on their identity cards to make it illegible, but that didn't work and they had to continue to carry the incriminating document. At seventeen they all hastened to get a driver's license, as that did not detail nationality and could substitute for an identity card.

Then came the school's "Roots" trip to the death camps in Poland. A problem arose. To obtain a passport, Larissa had to bring her identity card to school. Fear that the entire class would discover her secret, as well as her parents' limited means, made her forgo the trip. So she didn't get to see Auschwitz, which has gradually been replacing Masada as the site of formative memory in modern Jewish identity. She was, however, conscripted into national military service, and although she tried to use her Russian national status to avoid the draft—even writing a long letter to the recruiting office about it—her request was turned down.

Military service actually did Larissa some good. Fumbling for the Bible during the swearing-in ceremony, she trembled and even shed tears. For a moment she forgot the little cross she had received from her maternal grandmother upon leaving Russia as a little girl. Once in uniform, she felt she belonged, and was convinced that from now on she would be taken for an Israeli in every way. She turned her back on the detested, faltering Russian culture of her parents, choosing to date only Sabras and avoiding Russian men. Nothing pleased her more than to be told she did not look Russian, despite the suspicious color of her hair. She even considered converting to Judaism. Indeed, she went so far as to seek out the military rabbi, but then desisted at the last moment. Though her mother was not devout, Larissa did not want to abandon her to an isolated identity.

After her military service, Larissa moved to Tel Aviv. Fitting into the lively, carefree city was easy. She had a new feeling that the nationality detailed on her identity card was insignificant, and that her persistent sense of inferiority was merely a subjective invention. Yet sometimes at night, when she was in love with someone, a worry nagged at her: What Jewish mother would want non-Jewish grandchildren from a gentile daughter-in-law, a *shickse*?

She began to study history at the university. She felt wonderful there, and liked to spend time in the student cafeteria. In her third year she signed up for a course called "Nations and Nationalism in the Modern Age," having heard that the lecturer was not too strict and that the work was not difficult. Later she realized that something else, too, had attracted her curiosity.

During the first class the teacher asked if any of the students in the room were registered as something other than Jewish by the Ministry of the Interior. Not a hand was raised. She feared that the lecturer would stare at her, but he only looked slightly disappointed and said nothing more about it. The course appealed to her, though the lessons were sometimes boring and the professor tended to repeat himself. She began to understand the unique nature of Israeli identity politics. Unwrapping situations she'd experienced while growing up, she saw them in a new light; she understood that in her mind, if not in her lineage, she was in fact one of the last Jews in the State of Israel.

Later in the semester, obliged to choose a subject for a term paper, she quietly approached the professor.

"Do you remember the question you asked in the first class?"

"What do you mean?"

"You asked if any student present was not classified as Jewish. I should have raised my hand, but I couldn't bring myself to do it." Then she added, with a smile, "You might say I once again failed to come out of the closet."

"Well, then," he said. "Write a term paper about what made you 'pretend.' Maybe it will spur me to start writing a book about a confused nation pretending to be a wandering people-race."

Her paper received a high mark. It was the final push that broke the barrier of anxiety and mental struggle.

By now, you may have guessed that Larissa's history teacher in Tel Aviv was also Gisèle's Hebrew teacher in rainy Paris. In his youth, he was a friend of Mahmoud the elevator installer, as well as of the Mahmoud who became the Palestinians' national poet. He was the son-in-law of Bernardo, the Barcelona anarchist, and the son of Shulek, the Lodz Communist.

He is also the author of the present troublesome book—written, among other reasons, so that he can try to understand the general historical logic that might underlie these personal stories of identity.

CONSTRUCTED MEMORIES

Undoubtedly, personal experience can sway a historian's choice of research topic, probably more so than for a mathematician or a physicist. But it would be wrong to assume that personal experience dominates the process and method of the historian's work. Sometimes a generous grant directs a researcher to a particular field. At other times, if less often, findings rise up and compel a scholar to take a new direction. Meanwhile, everything that originally alerted the scholar to the central issues with which he or she is preoccupied continues to engage the mind. Other factors, too, of course, help shape any intellectual endeavor.

Over and above all these components is the fact that the historian, like other members of society, accumulates layers of collective memory well before becoming a researcher. Each of us has assimilated multiple narratives shaped by past ideological struggles. History lessons, civics classes, the educational system, national holidays, memorial days and anniversaries, state ceremonies—various spheres of memory coalesce into an imagined universe representing the past, and it coalesces well before a person has acquired the tools for thinking critically about it. By the time a historian has taken the first steps in his career, and begun to understand the unfolding of time, this huge universe of culturally constructed "truth" has taken up residence in the scholar's mind, and thoughts cannot but pass through it. Thus, the historian is the psychological and cultural product not only of personal experiences but also of instilled memories.

When, as a young child in nursery school, the author stamped his feet during Hanukkah festivities and sang enthusiastically, "Here we come with fire and light / darkness to expel!" the primary images of "us" and "them" began to take shape in his mind. We, the Jewish Maccabees, became associated with the light; they, the Greeks and their followers, with the dark. Later, in primary school, Bible lessons informed him that the biblical heroes had conquered the land that had been promised him. Coming from an atheistic background, he doubted the promise, yet in a natural sort of way he justified Joshua's warriors, whom he regarded as his ancestors. (He belonged to a generation for whom history followed a path directly from the Bible to national revival, unlike the elision made in later years from the exile to the Holocaust.) The rest is known— the sense of being a descendant of the ancient Jewish people became not merely a certainty but a central component of his self-identity. Neither studying history at university nor becoming a professional historian could dissolve those crystallized historical "memories." Although historically the nation-state arose in the world before compulsory mass education, only through this system could it consolidate its position. Culturally constructed memories were firmly entrenched at the upper levels of state education; at their core was national historiography.

To promote a homogeneous collective in modern times, it was necessary to provide, among other things, a long narrative suggesting a connection in time and space between the fathers and the "forefathers" of all the members of the present community. Since such a close connection, supposedly pulsing within the body of the nation, has never actually existed in any society, the agents of memory worked hard to invent it. With the help of archaeologists, historians, and anthropologists, a variety of findings were collected. These were subjected to major cosmetic improvements carried out by essayists, journalists, and the authors of historical novels. From this surgically improved past emerged the proud and handsome portrait of the nation.[1]

Every history contains myths, but those that lurk within national historiography are especially brazen. The histories of peoples and nations have been designed like the statues in city squares—they must be grand, towering, heroic. Until the final quarter of the twentieth century, reading a national history was like reading the sports page in the local paper: "Us" and "All the Others" was the usual, almost the natural, division. For more than a century, the production of Us was the life's work of the national historians and archaeologists, the authoritative priesthood of memory.

Prior to the national branching-out in Europe, many people believed they were descended from the ancient Trojans. This mythology was scientifically adjusted at the end of the eighteenth century. Influenced by the imaginative work of professional students of the past—both Greeks and other Europeans— the inhabitants of modern Greece saw themselves as the biological descendants of Socrates and Alexander the Great or, alternatively, as the direct heirs of the Byzantine Empire. Since the end of the nineteenth century, influential textbooks have transformed the ancient Romans into typical Italians. In the schools of the French Third Republic, Gallic tribes who rebelled against Rome in the time of Julius Caesar were described as true Frenchmen (though of a not-quite-Latin temperament). Other historians chose King Clovis's conversion to Christianity in the fifth century as the true birth of the almost eternal French nation.

The pioneers of Romanian nationalism drew their modern identity from the ancient Roman colony of Dacia; given this exalted origin, they called their new language Romanian. During the nineteenth century, many Britons began to view Queen Boudicca, leader of the Celtic tribe of Iceni, who fiercely

---

1 For the invention of a fictional past see E. Hobsbawm and T. Ranger (eds.), *The Invention of Tradition*, Cambridge: Cambridge University Press, 1983.

resisted the Roman conquerors, as the first Englishwoman; a glorified statue of her stands in London. German authors seized eagerly on Tacitus's account of Arminius leading the ancient tribe of the Cherusci, and depicted him as the father of their nation. Even Thomas Jefferson, the third president of the United States and owner of many black slaves, insisted that the state seal of the United States bear the images of Hengist and Horsa, who led the first Saxon invaders of Britain during the century in which Clovis was baptised. The reason he gave was that it was they "from whom we claim the honor of being descended, and whose political principles and form of government we have assumed."[2]

Much the same went on in the twentieth century. After the collapse of the Ottoman Empire, the inhabitants of the new Turkey found that they were white Aryans, the descendants of the Sumerians and the Hittites. Arbitrarily mapping the boundaries of Iraq, a lazy British officer drew a dead straight line; those who had overnight become Iraqis soon learned from their authorized historians that they were the descendants of the ancient Babylonians as well as of the Arabs, descendants of Saladin's heroic warriors. Many Egyptian citizens had no doubt that their first national state had been the ancient pagan pharaonic kingdom, which did not stop them from being devout Muslims. Indians, Algerians, Indonesians, Vietnamese and Iranians still believe that their nations always existed, and from an early age their schoolchildren memorize long historical narratives.

For Israelis, specifically those of Jewish origin, such mythologies are far-fetched, whereas their own history rests on firm and precise truths. They know for a certainty that a Jewish nation has been in existence since Moses received the tablets of the law on Mount Sinai, and that they are its direct and exclusive descendants (except for the ten tribes, who are yet to be located). They are convinced that this nation "came out" of Egypt; conquered and settled "the Land of Israel," which had been famously promised it by the deity; created the magnificent kingdom of David and Solomon, which then split into the kingdoms of Judah and Israel. They are also convinced that this nation was exiled, not once but twice, after its periods of glory—after the fall of the First Temple in the sixth century BCE, and again after the fall of the Second Temple, in 70 CE. Yet even before that second exile, this unique nation had created the Hebrew Hasmonean kingdom, which revolted against the wicked influence of Hellenization.

They believe that these people—their "nation," which must be the most ancient—wandered in exile for nearly two thousand years and yet, despite this prolonged stay among the gentiles, managed to avoid integration with,

---

2   Quoted in Patrick J. Geary, *The Myth of Nations: The Medieval Origins of Europe*, Princeton: Princeton University Press, 2002, 7. This brilliant work exposes the fallacy of "ethnic" labeling as applied in most modern, national histories dealing with the Middle Ages.

or assimilation into, them. The nation scattered widely, its bitter wanderings taking it to Yemen, Morocco, Spain, Germany, Poland, and distant Russia, but it always managed to maintain close blood relations among the far-flung communities and to preserve its distinctiveness.

Then, at the end of the nineteenth century, they contend, rare circumstances combined to wake the ancient people from its long slumber and to prepare it for rejuvenation and for the return to its ancient homeland. And so the nation began to return, joyfully, in vast numbers. Many Israelis still believe that, but for Hitler's horrible massacre, "Eretz Israel" would soon have been filled with millions of Jews making "aliyah" by their own free will, because they had dreamed of it for thousands of years.

And while the wandering people needed a territory of its own, the empty, virgin land longed for a nation to come and make it bloom. Some uninvited guests had, it is true, settled in this homeland, but since "the people kept faith with it throughout their Dispersion" for two millennia, the land belonged only to that people, and not to that handful without history who had merely stumbled upon it. Therefore the wars waged by the wandering nation in its conquest of the country were justified; the violent resistance of the local population was criminal; and it was only the (highly unbiblical) charity of the Jews that permitted these strangers to remain and dwell among and beside the nation, which had returned to its biblical language and its wondrous land.

Even in Israel these burdens of memory did not appear spontaneously but rather were piled layer upon layer by gifted reconstructors of the past, beginning in the second half of the nineteenth century. They primarily collected fragments of Jewish and Christian religious memories, out of which they imaginatively constructed a long, unbroken genealogy for "the Jewish people." Before then, there had been no organized public "remembering," and remarkably enough, it has not changed much since then. Despite the academization of Jewish history studies—with the founding of universities in British-ruled Jerusalem and later in Israel, and the opening of Jewish studies courses throughout the West—the idea of the Jewish past has remained generally unchanged, retaining its unified, ethnonational character to this day.

Different approaches have, of course, been employed in the extensive historiography of Judaism and Jews. There has been no shortage of polemic and disagreement in the highly productive field of the "national past." But, so far, hardly anyone has challenged the fundamental concepts that were formed and adopted in the late nineteenth and early twentieth centuries. Neither the important processes that profoundly changed the study of history in the Western world in the late twentieth century, nor the significant paradigm changes in the study of nations and nationalism, have affected the departments of the "History of the People of Israel" (aka Jewish history) in Israeli universities. Nor, amazingly, have they have left their imprint on the ample output of Jewish studies departments in American or European universities. When occasional findings threatened the picture of an unbroken, linear Jewish history, they were rarely cited; when they did surface, they were quickly forgotten, buried in oblivion. National exigencies created an iron-jawed vise that prevented any deviation from the dominant narratives. The distinctive frameworks within which data about the Jewish, Zionist, and Israeli past is produced— namely, those exclusive departments of Jewish history that are completely isolated from the departments of general and Middle Eastern history—have also contributed much to the astonishing paralysis and stubborn refusal to open up to new historiography that would soberly investigate the origin and identity of the Jews. From time to time the question "Who is a Jew?" has stirred up the public in Israel, chiefly because of the legal issues it entails. But it has not perturbed the Israeli historians. They have always known the answer: a Jew is a descendant of the nation that was exiled two thousand years ago.

The dispute of the "new historians," which began in the 1980s and for a short while looked set to shake the structure of Israeli memory, involved almost none of the "authorized" historians. Of the small number of individuals who took part in the public debate, most came from other disciplines or from outside the academy. Sociologists, political scientists, Orientalists, philologists, geographers, scholars of literature, archaeologists, even a few independent essayists, voiced new reservations about Jewish, Zionist, and Israeli history. Some had doctorates in history from outside Israel but had not yet found positions in the country. Departments of Jewish history, however, which should have been the main sources of breakthrough research, contributed only uneasy, conservative responses framed in apologetic, conventional rhetoric.[3]

In the 1990s, the counterhistory dealt mainly with the stages and outcomes of the 1948 war, focusing especially on its moral implications. This debate was certainly of great significance in the morphology of memory in Israeli society. What one might call the 1948 syndrome, which troubles the Israeli conscience, is important for the future politics of the State of Israel but perhaps even essential for its future existence. Any meaningful compromise with the Palestinians, if it ever materializes, would have to take into account not only the history of the Jews, but the recent history of the "others."

---

3   To understand this controversy, see Laurence J. Silberstein, *The Postzionism Debates: Knowledge and Power in Israeli Culture*, New York: Routledge, 1999, and also my book *Les mots et la terre: Les intellectuels en Israël*, Paris: Fayard, 2006, 247–87.

Yet this significant debate has yielded limited achievements in the area of research, and its presence in the public mind has been marginal. The older, established generation has utterly rejected all the new findings and evaluations, unable to reconcile them with the strict morality it believes guided its historical path. A younger generation of intellectuals might have been willing to concede that sins were committed on the road to statehood, but many among that group possessed a relative and flexible morality that was willing to allow for exceptions: How bad was the Nakba compared with the Holocaust? How can anyone liken the short and limited Palestinian refugee situation to the agonies of a two-thousand-year exile?

Sociohistorical studies that concentrated less on "political sins" and more on the long-term processes of the Zionist enterprise received less attention. And though written by Israelis, they were never published in Hebrew.[4] The few Hebrew works that tried to question the paradigms that underpin the national history were met with general indifference. These include Boas Evron's bold *Jewish State or Israeli Nation?* and Uri Ram's intriguing essay "Zionist Historiography and the Invention of Modern Jewish Nationhood." Both issued a radical challenge to the professional historiography of the Jewish past, but such challenges scarcely disturbed the authorized producers of this past.

The present work was written after the breakthroughs of the 1980s and early 1990s. Without the challenging writings of Evron, Ram and other Israelis,[5] and above all the contributions of non-Israeli scholars of nationalism such as Ernest Gellner and Benedict Anderson,[6] it is doubtful if it would have occurred to this author to question anew the roots of his identity and to extricate himself from the many layers of memory that, since childhood, had been heaped upon his own sense of the past.

Where national history is concerned, it is not merely hard to see the wood for the trees. A momentary glance at the encompassing woodland reveals a forest canopy of intimidating size. Professional specialization sequesters

---

4   Two works mainly: Baruch Kimmerling, *Zionism and Territory: The Socio-Territorial Dimensions of Zionist Politics*, Berkeley: University of California Press, 1983, and Gershon Shafir, *Land, Labor and the Origins of the Israeli-Palestinian Conflict, 1882–1914*, Cambridge: Cambridge University Press, 1989.

5   See Boas Evron, *Jewish State or Israeli Nation?*, Bloomington: Indiana University Press, 1995; and Uri Ram, "Zionist Historiography and the Invention of Modern Jewish Nationhood: The Case of Ben Zion Dinur," *History and Memory* 7:1 (1995), 91–124. The intellectuals of the "Canaanite" movement were the first Israelis to challenge the classical paradigms of Zionist historiography, but they did so with the aid of highly tenuous mythologies.

6   See Benedict Anderson, *Imagined Communities: Reflections on the Origin and Spread of Nationalism*, London: Verso, 1991; and Ernest Gellner, *Nations and Nationalism*, Oxford: Blackwell, 1983.

scholars in specific portions of the past. Narratives grow toward inclusiveness, but for a heretical metanarrative to take shape, it is necessary that historical research be conducted in a pluralistic culture, free from the tension of armed national conflict and from chronic anxiety about its identity and sources.

In light of Israeli reality in 2008, such a statement may justifiably be called pessimistic. In the sixty years of Israel's existence, its national history has hardly developed, and there is no reason to expect it to attain maturity anytime soon. The author has few illusions about the reception of this book. He does, nevertheless, hope that a small number of readers will be willing to risk a more radical re-evaluation of the past, and thus help to erode the essentialist identity that permeates the thoughts and actions of almost all Jewish Israelis.

Though the present work was composed by a professional historian, it takes risks not usually permitted or authorized in this field of endeavor. The accepted rules of academe demand that the scholar follow prescribed pathways and stick to the field in which he is supposedly qualified. A glance at the chapter headings of this book, however, will show that the spectrum of issues discussed herein exceeds the boundaries of a single scientific field. Teachers of Bible studies, historians of the ancient period, archaeologists, medievalists and, above all, experts on the Jewish People will protest that the author has encroached on fields of research not his own.

There is some truth in this argument, as the author is well aware. It would have been better had the book been written by a team of scholars rather than by a lone historian. Unfortunately, this was not possible, as the author could find no accomplices. Some inaccuracies may therefore be found in this book, for which the author apologizes, and he invites critics to do their best to correct them. He does not see himself as an Israeli Prometheus, stealing the fire of historical truth for the Israelis. So he does not fear an omnipotent Zeus, in the shape of the professional corporation of Jewish historiography. He seeks only to draw attention to a well-known phenomenon—that venturing outside a specific field, or walking on the fences between several of them, may occasionally yield unexpected insights and uncover surprising connections. At times, thinking beside, rather than thinking within, can fertilize historical thought, despite the drawbacks of being a nonspecialist and of exercising a high degree of speculation.

Because the recognized experts in Jewish history are not in the habit of confronting simple questions that at first glance may seem surprising yet are fundamental, it may be worthwhile doing it for them. For instance, has a Jewish nation really existed for thousands of years while other "peoples" faltered and disappeared? How and why did the Bible, an impressive theological library (though no one really knows when its volumes were composed or edited), become a reliable history book chronicling the birth of a nation? To what extent was the Judean Hasmonean kingdom—whose diverse subjects did not all speak one language, and who were for the most part illiterate—a nation-state? Was the population of Judea exiled after the fall of the Second Temple, or is that a Christian myth that not accidentally ended up as part of Jewish tradition? And if not exiled, what happened to the local people, and who are the millions of Jews who appeared on history's stage in such unexpected, far-flung regions?

If world Jews were indeed a nation, what were the common elements in the ethnographic cultures of a Jew in Kiev and a Jew in Marrakech, other than religious belief and certain practices of that belief? Perhaps, despite everything we have been told, Judaism was simply an appealing religion that spread widely until the triumphant rise of its rivals, Christianity and Islam, and then, despite humiliation and persecution, succeeded in surviving into the modern age. Does the argument that Judaism has always been an important belief-culture, rather than a uniform nation-culture, detract from its dignity, as the proponents of Jewish nationalism have been proclaiming for the past 130 years?

If there was no common cultural denominator among the communities of the Jewish religion, how could they be connected and set apart by ties of blood? Are the Jews an alien "nation-race," as the anti-Semites have imagined and sought to persuade us since the nineteenth century? What are the prospects of defeating this doctrine, which assumes and proclaims that Jews have distinctive biological features (in the past it was Jewish blood; today it is a Jewish gene), when so many Israeli citizens are fully persuaded of their racial homogeneity?

Another historical irony: there were times in Europe when anyone who argued that all Jews belong to a nation of alien origin would have been classified at once as an anti-Semite. Nowadays, anyone who dares to suggest that the people known in the world as Jews (as distinct from today's Jewish Israelis) have never been, and are still not, a people or a nation is immediately denounced as a Jew-hater.

Dominated by Zionism's particular concept of nationality, the State of Israel still refuses, sixty years after its establishment, to see itself as a republic that serves its citizens. One quarter of the citizens are not categorized as Jews, and the laws of the state imply that Israel is not their state nor do they own it. The state has also avoided integrating the local inhabitants into the superculture it has created, and has instead deliberately excluded them. Israel has also refused to be a consociational democracy (like Switzerland or Belgium) or a multicultural democracy (like Great Britain or the Netherlands)—that is to say, a state that accepts its diversity while serving its inhabitants. Instead, Israel insists on seeing itself as a Jewish state belonging to all the Jews in the world, even though they are no longer persecuted refugees but full citizens of the countries in which they choose to reside. The excuse for this grave violation of a basic principle of modern democracy, and for the preservation of an unbridled ethnocracy that grossly discriminates against certain of its citizens, rests on the active myth of an eternal nation that must ultimately forgather in its ancestral land.

It is difficult to formulate a new Jewish history while looking through the dense prism of Zionism—the light that traverses it keeps breaking into sharply ethnocentric colors. Please note: the present work, which proposes that the Jews have always comprised significant religious communities that appeared and settled in various parts of the world, rather than an *ethnos* that shared a single origin and wandered in a permanent exile, does not deal directly with history. Given that its main purpose is to criticize a widespread historiographic discourse, it cannot avoid suggesting alternative narratives. The author began with the question posed by the French historian Marcel Detienne—"How can we denationalize national histories?"—echoing in his mind.[7] How can we stop trudging along roads paved mainly with materials forged in national fantasies?

Imagining the nation was an important stage in the development of historiography, as indeed in the evolution of modernity. It engaged many historians from the nineteenth century onward. But toward the end of the twentieth century the dreams of national identity began to disintegrate. More and more scholars began to dissect and examine the great national stories, especially myths of common origin, that had hitherto clouded the writing of history. It goes without saying that the secularization of history took place under the hammer blows of cultural globalization, which continually takes unexpected forms throughout the Western world.

Yesterday's nightmares of identity are not tomorrow's identity dreams. Just as every personality is composed of fluid and diverse identities, so is history, among other things, an identity in motion. This book seeks to illuminate this dimension, both human and social, that is inherent in the passage of time. Though this lengthy plunge into the history of the Jews differs from the usual narratives, it may not be free of subjectivity, nor does the author claim to be free of ideological bias. He intends to present some outlines for a future counterhistory that may promote a different kind of culturally constructed memory—a memory that is aware of the relative truth it contains, and that aspires to help forge emerging local identities and a critical, universal consciousness of the past.

---

7   Marcel Detienne, *Comment être autochtone*, Paris: Seuil, 2003, 15. It is worth mentioning here that my conversations with the French historian Marc Ferro provided material and inspiration for this book. See his article "Les Juifs: tous des sémites?" in *Les Tabous de l'Histoire*, Paris: Nil éditions, 2002, 115–35.

CHAPTER ONE

Making Nations: Sovereignty and Equality

> *No nation possesses an ethnic base naturally, but as social formations are nationalized, the populations included within them, divided up among them or dominated by them, are ethnicized—that is, represented in the past or in the future as if they formed a natural community.*
> —Étienne Balibar, "The Nation Form: History and Ideology"

> *Nationalism was the form in which democracy appeared in the world, contained in the idea of the nation as a butterfly in a cocoon.*
> —Liah Greenfeld, *Nationalism: Five Roads to Modernity*

Thinkers and scholars have struggled for more than a hundred years with the issue of nationalism but have not come up with an unambiguous and universally accepted definition. A widely accepted description will probably be achieved only after the age of the nation has ended, when Minerva's owl takes flight and we see past this overarching collective identity that so powerfully shapes modern culture.[1]

But it is only proper that a historical work, particularly one likely to cause controversy, should begin its explorations with a look, however brief, at the basic concepts that it will employ. In any event, this is sure to be a challenging, even exhausting, voyage, but a lexicon that consists of explanations of the conceptual apparatus employed in this book may prevent superfluous wandering and frequent stumbling.

European languages use the term "nation," which derives from the late Latin *natio*. Until the twentieth century, this term denoted mainly human groups of various sizes and with internal connections. For example, in ancient Rome it commonly referred to aliens (as well as to species of animals). In the Middle Ages it could denote groups of students who came from afar. In England at the start of the modern era it denoted the aristocratic strata. Now and then it was used in reference to populations of a common origin, sometimes a group speaking a particular language. The term was used in diverse ways throughout the nineteenth century, and its precise significance remains a subject of controversy to this day.

---

1 Please note that the term "nationalism" when used this book should not immediately be equated with an extremist ideology.

The great French historian Marc Bloch said that "to the great despair of historians, men fail to change their vocabulary every time they change their customs."[2] We might add that one source of anachronism in historiographical research (though not the only one) is human laziness, which naturally affects the creation of terminology. Many words that have come down to us from the past and, in a different guise, continue to serve us in the present are sent back, charged with a new connotation. In that way, distant history is made to look similar, and closer, to our present-day world.

A close reading of historical and political works, or even of a modern European dictionary, reveals a constant migration of meanings within the boundaries of terms and concepts, especially those devised to interpret changing social reality.[3] We can agree that the word "stone," for instance, though context-dependent, does correspond more or less to a specific and agreed object. Like many other abstract terms, however, concepts such as "people," "race," ethnos, "nation," "nationalism," "country," and "homeland" have, over the course of history, been given countless meanings—at times contradictory, at times complementary, always problematic. The term "nation" was translated into modern Hebrew as le'om or umah, both words derived, like so many others, from the rich biblical lexicon.[4] But before taking the discussion to the crucial "national" issue, and trying to define "nation," which still very reluctantly submits to an unequivocal definition, we should stop to consider two other problematic concepts that keep tripping up the clumsy feet of professional scholars.

LEXICON: "PEOPLE" AND ETHNOS

Almost all history books published in Israel use the word am (people) as a synonym for le'om (nation). Am is also a biblical word, the Hebrew equivalent of the Russian Narod, the German Volk, the French peuple, and the English "people." But in modern Israeli Hebrew, the word am does not have a direct

---

2   Marc Bloch, *The Historian's Craft*, Manchester: Manchester University Press, 1954, 28. Nietzsche had already written, "Wherever primitive men put down a word, they thought they made a discovery. How different the case really was! ... Now, with every new piece of knowledge, we stumble over petrified words and mummified conceptions, and would rather break a leg than a word in doing so." Friedrich Nietzsche, *The Dawn of Day*, New York: Russell & Russell, 1964, 53.
3   On connotations of this term and their evolution, see the essays in S. Remi-Giraud and P. Retat (eds.), *Les Mots de la nation*, Lyon: Presses Universitaires de Lyon, 1996.
4   For example, "Two nations [le'umim] *are* in thy womb, and two manner of people [goyim] shall be separated from thy bowels," Gen. 25:23; and "Come near, ye nations [le'umim], to hear; and hearken, ye people," Isa. 34:1.

association with the word "people" in a pluralistic sense, such as we find in various European languages; rather it implies an indivisible unity. In any case, the *am* in ancient Hebrew, as well as in other languages, is a very fluid term, and its ideological use, which has unfortunately remained very sloppy, makes it difficult to include it in any meaningful discourse.[5]

The best way to define a concept is to follow its history, but as it is not possible to expand on the evolution of the term *am* in such a short chapter, the present discussion will confine itself to a number of comments on the history of the meanings it acquired in the past.

Most of the agrarian societies that preceded the rise of modern society in eighteenth-century Europe developed statewide supercultures that influenced their surroundings and gave rise to various collective identities among the elite. Yet in contrast to the image that a good many history books continue to peddle, these monarchies, principalities and grand empires never sought to involve all the "people" in their administrative superculture. They neither needed such participation nor possessed the necessary technological, institutional or communications systems with which to foster it. The peasants, the absolute majority in the premodern world, were illiterate, and continued to reproduce their local, unlettered cultures without hindrance. Where they resided in or near a ruling city, their dialects more closely resembled the central administrative language. These subjects represented what was then called "the people," but for those who cultivated the soil in outlying regions, far from the political centre, the connection between their dialects and the language of the central administration was quite weak.[6]

So long as human societies were dominated by the principle of divine kingship, rather than by the will of the people, rulers did not need their subjects'

---

5   The word *am*, which is translated as "people," appears frequently in the Old Testament with a variety of meanings. It can mean a clan, or a throng gathered in the city center, or even a fighting force. See for example, "So Joshua arose, and all the people [am] of war, to go up against Ai," Josh. 8:3; "And the people of the land [am ha'aretz] made Josiah his son king in his stead," 2 Chron. 33:25. It can also indicate the "holy community," namely, the People of Israel, chosen by God. For example, "For thou *art* an holy people [am] unto the Lord thy God: the Lord thy God hath chosen thee to be a special people [am] unto himself, above all people that *are* upon the face of the earth," Deut. 7:6.

6   Exceptions to this model include certain Greek polis cities, as well as some aspects of the early Roman republic. In both, the formation of small groups of citizens bears a slight resemblance to modern "peoples" and nations. But the Greek concepts of "demos," "ethnos" and "laos," and the Roman "populus," which arose in the early stages of the Mediterranean slave-owning societies, did not have the mobile and inclusive dimension of modern times. They did not include the entire population—e.g., women, slaves and foreigners—and equal civil rights were granted only to locally born, slave-owning men, meaning they were strictly limited social groups.

love. Their principal concern was to ensure they had enough power to keep people afraid. The sovereign had to secure the loyalty of the state's administration in order to preserve the continuity and stability of the government, but the peasants were required simply to pass along the surplus agricultural produce and sometimes to provide the monarchy and nobility with soldiers. Taxes were of course collected by force, or at any rate by its constant implicit threat, rather than by persuasion or efforts at consensus. Nevertheless, it must not be forgotten that the existence of this power also gave the valued producers of food a physical security, an added value granted them by the very presence of authority.

The state apparatuses, occupied in collecting taxes and recruiting troops, subsisted mainly thanks to the integrated interests of the upper strata—the nobility and the politically powerful. The continuity and relative stability of these apparatuses—not only the crowning of a sovereign, but the invention of dynastic monarchies—had already been achieved by means of certain ideological measures. The religious cults that flourished around the centers of government reinforced the loyalty of the upper levels of the hierarchy through unearthly legitimation. This is not to say that the polytheistic or, later, the monotheistic religions came into being as direct functions of government (the circumstances of their rise were more complex), for otherwise they would have been unnecessary, but that they almost always, though not invariably, served to reproduce power.

The consolidation of belief around the ruling power created a slender, though important, social stratum that grew within the administrative apparatus, sometimes merging with it and later competing with it. This stratum, composed of priests, court scribes, and prophets—and later clergymen, bishops, and the ulema—was dependent on the political centers but acquired its most important symbolic capital through both its privileged connections and its direct dialogues with the deity. In early agrarian societies its power and its methods of organizing the religion varied in time and place, but since its principal strength sprang from belief, it constantly sought to widen the demographic base of its following. Like the administrative state apparatuses, it did not have the means to create a broad, homogeneous mass culture, but it did develop a strong ambition to reach an ever-growing number of convinced subjects, and it succeeded in this aim.

Neither the strategy of creating dominant collectives around the apparatuses of state power in agrarian societies nor the sophisticated technology employed by religious institutions resembled the identity politics that began to develop with the rise of nation-states at the end of the eighteenth century.

However, as stated before, laziness in coining new terms, along with the ideological and political interests that paralleled this terminological slackness, completely blurred the profound differences between past and present, between the ancient agrarian universes and the new commercial, industrial worlds in which we still live.

In premodern writings, historical and otherwise, the term "people" was applied to a variety of groups. They might be powerful tribes, populations of tiny kingdoms or principalities, religious communities of various sizes, or low strata that did not belong to the political and cultural elites (in Hebrew these were called, in antiquity, "the people of the land"). From the "Gallic people" in late antiquity to the "Saxon people" in the Germanic area at the start of the modern era; from "the people of Israel" when the Bible was written to "God's people" or the *peuple de Dieu* in medieval Europe; from peasant communities speaking a particular dialect to rebellious urban masses—the term "people" was casually attached to human groups whose identity profile was elusive and far from stable. In fifteenth-century Western Europe, with the rise of the city and the beginning of more advanced forms of transportation and communication, firmer boundaries began to appear between broad linguistic groups, and the term "people" began to be applied mainly to these.

With the rise of nationalism at the end of the eighteenth and early nineteenth centuries, this ideology and overarching identity, which in modern times embraces all cultures, has made constant use of the term "people," especially to stress the antiquity and continuity of the nationality it sought to construct. Since the fundamentals of nation building almost always included some cultural components, linguistic or religious, that survived from earlier historical phases, clever engineering contrived to make them into hooks on which the history of nations could be skillfully hung. The people became a bridge between past and present, thrown across the deep mental chasm created by modernity, a bridge on which the professional historians of all the new nation-states could comfortably parade.

To complete the analysis of the term "people," it is necessary to add some caveats. In the nineteenth century, national cultures often tied the soft "people" to the rigid and problematic "race," and many regarded the two words as intersecting, supporting, or complementary. The homogeneous collective origin of "the people"—always, of course, superior and unique, if not actually pure— became a kind of insurance against the risks represented by fragmentary though persistent subidentities that continued to swarm beneath the unifying modernity. The imagined origin also served as an efficient filter against undesirable mixing with hostile neighboring nations.

The murderous first half of the twentieth century having caused the concept of race to be categorically rejected, various historians and other scholars enlisted the more respectable concept of *ethnos* in order to preserve the intimate contact with the distant past. *Ethnos*, meaning "people" in ancient Greek, had served even before the Second World War as a useful alternative to, or a verbal intermediary between, "race" and "people." But its common, "scientific" use began only in the 1950s, after which it spread widely. Its main attraction lies in its blending of cultural background and blood ties, of a linguistic past and a biological origin—in other words, its combining of a historical product with a fact that demands respect as a natural phenomenon.[7]

Far too many authors have used this concept with intolerable ease, sometimes with astonishing intellectual negligence, though some of them do apply it to some premodern historical entity, some mass of shared cultural expressions from the past, that despite its dissolution persists in a different form. The ethnic community is, after all, a human group with a shared cultural-linguistic background, not always well defined but capable of providing crucial materials for a national construction. Yet a good many other scholars cling to *ethnos* as though to bring in by the back door the essential primevalism, the racial concept that in the nineteenth and twentieth centuries bolstered the promoters of the fragile national identity.

Thus *ethnos* has become not merely a historical and cultural unit but an ambiguous entity of ancient origin, at whose heart lies a subjective sense of closeness that it inspires in those who believe in it, much as race did in the nineteenth century. Committed scholars argue that this identity belief should not be challenged, because it carries a powerful sense of origin that should not only be taken into account during critical analysis and dissection—a legitimate, even essential process—but should even be adopted as a whole, and as a positive historical fact that need not be questioned. These scholars admit that the idea that the modern nation sprang from the *ethnos* may be unverifiable. Nevertheless, we have no choice but to live with it; attempting to question it is pointless and ultimately undesirable.

Blurring the categories of ancient social groupings, as these scholars have helped to do, apparently seemed to them a necessary condition for the preservation of unstable identities in the present. Anthony D. Smith, who became one of the most active scholars in the field of nation studies, made a significant contribution to this process. At a relatively late stage in his work, he

---

7   See the comments on the loose usage of this term in an important work by Dominique Schnapper, *La Communauté des citoyens: Sur l'idée moderne de nation*, Paris: Gallimard, 2003, 18.

decided to grant the ethnic principle a decisive role in his research, and even described his approach as "ethno-symbolic." The term "symbolic" helps soften the essentialist resonance of the phrase while supplying the desired ambiguity. For Smith, "an ethnic group, then, is distinguished by four features: the sense of unique group origins, the knowledge of a unique group history and belief in its destiny, one or more dimensions of collective cultural individuality, and finally a sense of unique collective solidarity."[8]

The diligent British scholar, it seems, considers that the *ethnos* is no longer a linguistic community with a common way of life; that the *ethnos* does not inhabit a particular territory but needs only to be associated with one; that the *ethnos* need not have an actual history, for ancient myths can continue to serve this function equally well. The shared memory is not a conscious process moving from the present to the past (since there is always someone around who can organize it) but rather a "natural" process, neither religious nor national, which flows by itself from past to present. Smith's definition of *ethnos*, therefore, matches the way Zionists see the Jewish presence in history—it also matches the old concept of pan-Slav identity, or that of the Aryans or Indo-Europeans, or even of the Black Hebrews in the United States—but is quite unlike the accepted connotation among the traditional community of anthropologists.[9]

Toward the end of the twentieth century and in the early twenty-first, "ethnicity"—which Étienne Balibar rightly described as entirely fictitious—has experienced a resurgence in popularity. This French philosopher has reiterated that nations are not ethnic, and that even what is deemed to be their ethnic origin is dubious. It is in fact nationalization that creates a sense of ethnic identity in societies—"represented in the past or in the future *as if* they formed a natural community."[10] Unfortunately, this critical approach, which warns against ethnobiological or ethnoreligious definitions, has not had sufficient impact. Various theoreticians of nationality, like nationality-supporting historians, continue to thicken their theories and hence their narratives with essentialist, ethnicist verbiage. The relative retreat of the classic sovereign

8 Anthony D. Smith, *The Ethnic Revival*, Cambridge: Cambridge University Press, 1981, 66; and see also by Smith, *The Nation in History: Historiographical Debates about Ethnicity and Nationalism*, Hanover, NH: University Press of New England, 2000. See also a very similar definition in John Hutchinson, *Modern Nationalism*, London: Fontana Press, 1994, 7.

9 No wonder that Smith has been a godsend to Zionist historians seeking to define the Jewish nation. See, for example, Gideon Shimoni, *The Zionist Ideology*, Hanover, NH: Brandeis University Press, 1995, 5–11.

10 Étienne Balibar, "The Nation Form: History and Ideology," in *Race, Nation, Class*, Étienne Balibar and Immanuel Wallerstein, London: Verso, 1991, 96.

nationalism in the Western world in the late twentieth century and the beginning of the twenty-first has not weakened this trend; indeed, in some ways it has strengthened it.

Be that as it may, if the present work sometimes errs and occasionally uses the term "people"—though not the term *ethnos*, on account of its biological resonances—it will be pointing very cautiously to a fairly fluid human community, usually a premodern one and especially one in the early stages of modernization. The cultural and linguistic structures held in common by such a group have never been very strong, but arose because of a particular administrative communication that gradually blended, under kingdoms or principalities, with "lower" cultures. The "people" is therefore a social group that inhabits a defined territory and exhibits at least the outlines of shared norms and secular cultural practices (related dialects, foods, clothing, music, and so on). Such linguistic and ethnographic features, which predate the nation-states, were not rigidly consolidated, and the boundary between them and the comparable features of other groups was not essential or unequivocal. It is precisely the accidental history of interstate relations that in many cases determined the location of the barrier between "peoples."

Sometimes, as has already been stated, such a "people" has served as the Archimedean point for the launching of a new nation—a point that has often been worn down in the nationalizing enterprises of modern culture. The culture of the English "people" became hegemonic in Britain much as the culture of the Île-de-France and the administrative language of the Bourbon monarchs came to dominate their realm. By contrast, the Welsh "people," the Breton, Bavarian, Andalusian, even the Yiddish "people," have been almost entirely shredded in the process.

Constructing a nation can also lead to the opposite outcome. Cultural-linguistic minorities, which had not been sharply defined before the era of nationalism, begin to acquire—owing to hasty engineering dictated from the center, or to alienating discrimination—a new, distinguishing sense of identity (modernization can intensify subtle differences). In such cases the reaction, especially among the intellectual elites of the group excluded from the hegemon, can harden, turning amorphous distinctions into an essentialist basis for a struggle for self-rule—namely, for national separation. (This issue will be more fully addressed below.)

Another comment, of special relevance to the present work: Where the common denominator of a premodern human group consisted solely of religious norms and practices (cults, rituals, precepts, prayers, religious symbols, and the like), the terms used here will be "religious congregation," "religious community," or "religious civilization." I may as well add that, prior to the national era, "peoples" both emerged and disappeared, just as kingdoms did, in the unfolding of history. (Again, I shall return to this matter below.) Religious communities, on the other hand, usually persisted in the *longue durée*, to use the well-known term coined by Fernand Braudel, because they preserved and reproduced tradition-minded intellectual strata.

At times, even religious cultures—when weakened yet still relatively stable, or even when disintegrating—served, much as did popular folklore or the language of state administration, as valuable raw material for the forging of nations. Belgium, Pakistan, Ireland and Israel, despite manifold differences, serve as good illustrations. In all these cases, we find a common denominator in the form of national construction, even when the starting point was a religious community or "people." Despite the major importance of religious elements in the ways a nation is created, we must not forget that nationality has helped define the contours of the emergent modern religious temperament. There must, therefore, be a significant decline in the intensity of religious fatalism when large human groups, mainly their political and intellectual elites, take control of their destiny and begin to make national history.[11]

Peoples, populations, native populaces, tribes and religious communities are not nations, even though they are often spoken of as such. To be sure, as cultural building materials they have been vital in the fashioning of the new national identities, but they lack the decisive characteristics that total modernity, falling upon them like a raptor, carries below its wings.

THE NATION: BOUNDARIES AND DEFINITIONS

Much has been written about the fact that the issue of nationality did not produce its own Tocqueville, Marx, Weber or Durkheim on the social thinking behind it. "Class," "democracy," "capitalism," and even "state" were quite closely diagnosed, but "nation" and "nationalism" have been neglected—starved of theoretical calories. The main, though not sole, reason for this is that "nations," as a synonym for "peoples," were perceived as primary, almost natural, entities— in existence since time immemorial. A good many authors, including scholars of history, noted the developments that had taken place in the human groups

---

11 Paradoxically, even the extreme case of the Islamic Republic in Iran does not entirely contradict this position. The Islamic revolution sought to bring the message of Islam to the whole world, but in fact succeeded primarily in "nationalizing" the Iranian masses (much as Communism had done in other areas in the Third World). On nationalism in Iran, see Haggay Ram, "The Immemorial Iranian Nation? School Textbooks and Historical Memory in Post-Revolutionary Iran," *Nations and Nationalism* 6:6 (2000), 67–90.

designated as nations, but these were perceived as minor changes in entities regarded as primeval.

Most of these thinkers lived in emerging national cultures, so they tended to think from within them and were unable to examine them from outside. Moreover, they wrote in the new national languages, and were thus held captive by their principal working tool: the past was made to conform closely to the linguistic and conceptual structures molded in the nineteenth century. As Marx, seeing the social realities of his time, assumed that history was essentially a vast supernarrative of class struggles, so most of the others, principally the historians, imagined the past as the constant rise and fall of eternal nations, and their mutual conflicts thickly and solemnly packed the history books. The new nation-states naturally encouraged and generously funded such imagery and writing, thereby helping to reinforce the contours of the new national identities.

Reading the works of the British philosopher John Stuart Mill or the French philosopher Ernest Renan, we encounter some divergent insights, unusual for their time. As early as 1861, Mill wrote:

> A portion of mankind may be said to constitute a Nationality, if they are united among themselves by common sympathies, which do not exist between them and any others—which make them co-operate with each other more willingly than with other people, desire to be under the same government, and desire that it should be government by themselves or a portion of themselves, exclusively.[12]

Renan, on the other hand, declared in 1882:

> A nation's existence is, if you will pardon the metaphor, a daily plebiscite, just as an individual's existence is a perpetual affirmation of life … The nations are not something eternal. They had their beginnings and they will end. A European confederation will very probably replace them.[13]

Though both brilliant thinkers were capable of contradictions and hesitations, their awareness of the democratic core in the formation of a nation showed that they understood they were dealing with a modern phenomenon. There was a good reason that these two liberal writers, who viewed mass culture with

---

12   John Stuart Mill, *Considerations on Representative Government*, Chicago: Gateway, 1962, 303. Regarding Mill and the national question, see also Hans Kohn, *Prophets and Peoples: Studies in Nineteenth-Century Nationalism,* New York: Macmillan, 1946, 11–42.

13   See "What Is a Nation?" available at *www.cooper.edu/humanities/core/hss3/e_ renan.html*.

some trepidation, nevertheless accepted in principle the idea of government by the people.

Unfortunately, neither writer went on to publish extensive, methodical inquiries into nationhood. The nineteenth century was not ready for this. Such famous thinkers on this subject as Johann Gottfried Herder, Giuseppe Mazzini and Jules Michelet did not fully fathom the cunning of national reason, which they mistakenly considered to be ancient or even, at times, eternal.

The first to deal with this issue in terms of theory were Marxists of the early twentieth century. For ideologues such as Karl Kautsky, Karl Renner, Otto Bauer, Vladimir Ilyich Lenin and Joseph Stalin, nationalism was a sucker punch. In its presence, history, the permanent proof of their rightness, seemed to betray them. They had to contend with the strange phenomenon that the prognosis of the great Marx failed to envision. A wave of national demands in Central and Eastern Europe forced them to engage in a discussion that produced intricate analyses as well as hasty conclusions that were always subjected to immediate party exigencies.[14]

The Marxists' significant contribution to the study of the nation was to call attention to the close connection between the rise of the market economy and the crystallization of the nation-state. They argued that the advance of capitalism destroyed autarkic markets, severed their specific social links and opened the way to the development of new species of relations and consciousness. "Laissez faire, laissez aller," the first war cry of capitalist commerce, did not in its early stages lead to sweeping globalization, but enabled the conditions for the rise of market economies within the framework of the old state structures. These economies formed the basis for the rise of nation-states, with their uniform language and culture. Capitalism, the most abstract form of property control, required, above all, a system of law that sanctified private property, as well as the state power that ensured its enforcement.

Significantly, the Marxists did not ignore the psychological aspects of the national changes. From Bauer to Stalin, they involved psychology in their central polemics, though in simplistic terms. For Bauer, the famous Austrian socialist, "the nation is the totality of men tied by the community of destiny to the community of character."[15] Stalin, on the other hand, summed up the discussion in more definite terms:

---

14   For more on Marxists and the nation, see Horace Davis, *Nationalism and Socialism: Marxist and Labor Theories of Nationalism to 1917*, New York: Monthly Review Press, 1967; and Ephraim Nimni, *Marxism and Nationalism: Theoretical Origins of a Political Crisis*, London: Pluto Press, 1991.

15   Quoted in G. Haupt, M. Lowy, and C. Weil, *Les Marxistes et la question nationale, 1848–1914*, Paris: Maspero, 1974, 254.

A nation is a historically constituted, stable community of people, formed on the basis of a common language, territory, economic life, and psychological make-up manifested in a common culture.[16]

This definition is undoubtedly too schematic and not especially well phrased. Nevertheless, this attempt to characterize the nation on the basis of an objective historical process, though not entirely satisfactory, remains intriguing. Does the lack of one element prevent the formation of a nation? And, as is no less relevant to our discussion, is there no dynamic political dimension that accompanies and shapes various stages in the process? The Marxists' devotion to the theory that holds class struggle to be the key to understanding all of history, as well as their bitter rivalry with national movements in Central and Eastern Europe, which were rapidly outflanking them, prevented their producing more on the national issue than the simplistic rhetoric whose main purpose was to confront rivals and recruit followers.[17]

Other socialists who might not have significantly advanced the discussion used their sharp senses to discern the attraction and promise of popular democracy in the formation of the nation. It was they who discovered the seductive symbiosis between socialism and nationalism. From the Zionist Ber Borochov and the Polish nationalist Josef Pilsudski to the red patriots Mao Zedong and Ho Chi Minh, the formula of "nationalized" socialism proved triumphant.

In the field of pure research there have been discussions about the nation, as we shall see, but only in the 1950s do we encounter fresh intellectual efforts to deal with the social dimension in the rise of a nation. It was no accident that it was an immigrant who revived the debate. While Marxist thought provided, as it were, a lens through which to observe the nation from the outside, the experience of migration—of being uprooted from one's birthplace—and of living as an "alien," a subject minority in a dominant culture, proved an almost indispensable condition for the more advanced methodological tools of observation. Most of the leading researchers in the field of national ideology were bilingual in their childhood or youth, and many were children of immigrant families.

Karl Deutsch fled from the Czech Sudetenland region with the coming of the Nazis, and in time found a place in the American academic world. Although his book *Nationalism and Social Communication* did not attract

16   Joseph Stalin, *Marxism and the National Question*, first published in *Prosveshcheniye* 3–5 (1913).
17   On the Marxist approach to the issue of nationalism, see also John Breuilly, *Nationalism and the State*, New York: St. Martin's Press, 1982, 21–8.

much attention, it was a significant stage in the further discussion of the concept of the nation.[18] Deutsch had insufficient data, and his methodological apparatus was awkward, but he showed extraordinary intuition in discerning the socioeconomic processes of modernization that underlie the formation of the nation. The need for a new kind of communication for the alienated urban masses, uprooted from the array of agrarian forms of communication, prompted the integration or disintegration of national groupings. Mass democratic politics, he argued, completed the consolidation. In Deutsch's second work on the nation, published sixteen years later, he continued to develop the thesis in a historical description of social, cultural and political aggregations that underlay the process of nationalization.[19]

Three decades passed after Deutsch's first book before another breakthrough was made in this field of research. The rapid communications revolution in the final quarter of the twentieth century, and the gradual conversion of human labor in the West into an activity of symbols and signs, provided a congenial setting in which to reexamine the old issue. It is possible, too, that the first signs of the declining status of classical nationalism, in precisely the territory that had first produced national consciousness, contributed to the appearance of the new paradigms. Two landmark books on the subject appeared in Britain in 1983: Benedict Anderson's *Imagined Communities* and Ernest Gellner's *Nations and Nationalism*. From then on, the issue of nationalism would be examined primarily through a sociocultural prism. The nation became an unmistakable cultural project.

Anderson's life, too, was one of wandering across large cultural-linguistic expanses. Born in China to an Irish father and an English mother, he was taken to California as a child but was educated mainly in Britain, where he graduated with a degree in international relations, a discipline that led him to divide his time between Indonesia and the United States. His life story resonates in his book on national communities, which critically rejects any position that smacks of Eurocentrism. This attitude led him to assert, though not very convincingly, that the pioneers of national consciousness in modern history were the Creoles—the locally born offspring of settlers in the Americas.

For the present purpose, it is the original definition that he offers in his book that is most significant: "the nation … is an imagined political community— and imagined as both inherently limited and sovereign."[20] Indeed, every

---

18 Karl W. Deutsch, *Nationalism and Social Communication*, New York: MIT Press, 1953.
19 Karl W. Deutsch, *Nationalism and Its Alternatives*, New York: A. A. Knopf, 1969.
20 Anderson, *Imagined Communities*, 6.

community that is bigger than a tribe or a village is imagined, because its members do not know one another; such were the great religious communities before modern times. But the nation has new tools for people's imaginary belonging to it that were unavailable to the old societies.

Anderson reiterates that the advent of the capitalism of printing in the fifteenth century began to dissolve the long historical distinction between the high sacred languages and the various local vernaculars used by the masses. The language of administration in the European kingdoms also expanded significantly with the advent of printing, laying the groundwork for the future formation of the national territorial languages we know today. The novel and the newspaper were the first players in the new world of communications that began to demarcate the rising national boundaries. The map, the museum, and other cultural amenities would later complete the task of national construction.

For the contours of the nation to harden, the religious commonwealth and the dynastic kingdom—the two long-standing historical frameworks that preceded the nation—had to be significantly downgraded, both institutionally and conceptually. Not only had the status of the great imperial systems and the church hierarchies been relatively weakened, but a significant break had occurred in the religious perception of time, which also affected traditional belief in the divine right of kings. The citizens of the nation, as distinct from the subjects of kingdoms or the tenant farmers in principalities, began to see themselves as equals and, moreover, as rulers of their own destinies—as sovereigns, in other words.

Ernest Gellner's *Nations and Nationalism* may be read as largely complementing Anderson's project. In his writings, too, the new culture is depicted as the principal catalyst in the creation of the nation, and he also viewed the processes of modernization as the source of the new civilization. But before we proceed to Gellner's ideas, we may note that the rule of the "outsider," of "writing from the margins," applies to him as well. Like Deutsch, he was a young refugee compelled to leave Czechoslovakia with his family on the eve of the Second World War. His parents settled in Britain, where he grew up and became a successful British anthropologist and philosopher. All his writings include the comparative analysis of cultures that marked all his intellectual endeavours. His brilliant, concise book opens with a double definition:

1. Two men are of the same nation if and only if they share the same culture, where culture in turn means a system of ideas and signs and associations and ways of behaving and communicating.
2. Two men are of the same nation if and only if they *recognize* each other as

belonging to the same nation. In other words, *nations maketh man*; nations are the artifacts of men's convictions and loyalties and solidarities.[21]

The subjective aspect must, therefore, complement the objective one. Together they describe an unfamiliar historical phenomenon that had not existed prior to the emergence of the new bureaucratic, industrialized world. Agrarian societies contained discrete cultures that existed side by side for hundreds or thousands of years. The more advanced division of labor, however— in which human activity is less physical and more symbolic, and occupational mobility keeps increasing—undermined the traditional partitions. The world of production demanded for its actual operation homogeneous cultural codes. The new occupational mobility, both horizontal and vertical, shattered the insularity of the higher culture and forced it to become an ever-expanding mass culture. Universal primary education and literacy were the essential conditions for a developed, dynamic industrial society. And this, according to Gellner, was the great secret of the political phenomenon known as the nation. Thus the formation of a national group is an unmistakable sociocultural process, although it can take place only in the presence of some state apparatus, local or alien, whose presence facilitates or stimulates the awakening of a national consciousness, the construction of a national culture, and their continuation.

Many scholars expressed reservations about certain premises in Gellner's thesis.[22] Did nationalism always wait for complete industrialization before hoisting its flags and symbols? Had there been no national feelings—no aspirations for sovereignty—in early capitalism, before the rise of a complex, developed division of labor? Some of the criticism was persuasive, but it did not detract from Gellner's important philosophical achievement in determining that the advanced consolidation of a nation is closely connected with the formation of a unified culture, such as can exist only in a society that is no longer agrarian and traditional.

To define the term "nation" in light of Anderson's and Gellner's theoretical propositions, as well as some working hypotheses of scholars who followed in their footsteps, it might be suggested that the "nation," though its historical rise is multifaceted and fluid, is distinguished from other social groupings in history by several features:

---

21 Gellner, *Nations and Nationalism*, 7.
22 See the following largely supportive but critical essay collection: John A. Hall (ed.), *The State of the Nation: Ernest Gellner and the Theory of Nationalism*, Cambridge: Cambridge University Press, 1998.

1. A nation is a human group wherein universal education gives rise to a homogeneous mass culture that claims to be common and accessible to all its members.
2. The nation gives rise to a perception of civil equality among all who are seen and who see themselves as its members. This civil body regards itself as sovereign, or demands political independence in cases where it has not yet achieved that independence.
3. There must be a unifying cultural-linguistic continuum—or at least some general idea of such a continuum—between the actual representatives of the sovereign power, or those aspiring to it, and every last citizen.
4. In contrast to the subjects of past rulers, the citizenry that identifies with the nation is conscious of belonging to it, or aspires to be a part of it, with the aim of living under its sovereignty.
5. The nation has a common territory about which the members feel and assert that they are its sole owners, and any attack on it is felt to be as powerful as a threat to their personal property.
6. The aggregate economic activity within the boundaries of this national territory, after the achievement of its sovereignty, was more closely interconnected, at least until the late twentieth century, than its relations with other market economies.

This is, of course, an ideal depiction in the Weberian sense. We have already implied that there are scarcely any nations that do not harbor or coexist with cultural and linguistic minorities, whose integration in the dominant super-culture has been slower than that of other groups. Where the principle of civil equality has been slow to apply to them, it has led to constant friction. In exceptional cases, such as Switzerland, Belgium and Canada, the national state has formally maintained two or three dominant languages that had developed separately and remained unbridgeable.[23] Furthermore, in contrast to the proposed model, certain productive and financial sectors have eluded the rule of the dominant national market and have been subjected directly to global supply and demand.

But it should be reiterated that only the post-agrarian world, with its altered division of labor—its distinctive social mobility and thriving new communications technologies—has produced conditions conducive to linguistic and cultural homogeneity, leading to an identity and self-awareness

---

23   This has been done while combining other cultural elements, and with a high degree of decentralization and citizen involvement in politics. On the Swiss example, see Hans Kohn's old book, *Nationalism and Liberty: The Swiss Example*, London: Allen & Unwin, 1956; and also the new work of Oliver Zimmer, *A Contested Nation: History, Memory and Nationalism in Switzerland, 1761–1891*, Cambridge: Cambridge University Press, 2003.

not confined to narrow elites or groups, as was always the case in the past, but now broadly manifest among the productive masses. Whereas earlier, in the era of the great empires, through the nature of the feudal and religious fabric, human societies had always been marked by definite cultural-linguistic divisions and strata, henceforth all the people—high and low, rich and poor, educated or not—would feel they belonged to a particular nation and, what is no less meaningful, would be convinced they belonged to it in equal degree.

The consciousness of legal, civil and political equality—produced mainly by social mobility in the era of commercial, and later of industrialized, capitalism—created an umbrella under which everyone could share an identity. Whoever was not covered or included by it could not be a member of the national body, an immanent aspect of equality. It is this equality that underlies the political demand that construes "the people" as a nation that warrants full self-government. This democratic aspect—"the rule of the people"—is utterly modern and clearly distinguishes nations from the older social formations, such as tribes, peasant societies under dynastic monarchies, religious communities with internal hierarchies, even premodern "peoples."

No premodern human community manifested an inclusive sense of civil equality or a persistent desire for self-rule that was felt by the entire populace. But when people begin to see themselves as sovereign creatures, there arises the consciousness, or illusion, that enables them to believe they can rule themselves through political representation. This is the attitudinal core of all national expressions in the modern age. The principle of self-determination, accepted since the end of the First World War as a guiding principle in international relations, is to a large extent a universal translation of this process of democratization, demonstrating the sway of the new masses in modern politics.

The birth of the nation is undoubtedly a real historical development, but it is not a purely spontaneous one. To reinforce an abstract group loyalty, the nation, like the preceding religious community, needed rituals, festivals, ceremonies and myths. To forge itself into a single, firm entity, it had to engage in continual public cultural activities and to invent a unifying collective memory. Such a novel system of accessible norms and practices was also needed for the overarching consciousness, an amalgamating ideological consciousness: namely, nationalism.

FROM IDEOLOGY TO IDENTITY

For a long time, scholars—especially historians—regarded nations as an ancient, indeed primeval, phenomenon. Reading their writings today, one sometimes gets the impression that history began with the rise of national groups. These thinkers stirred together past and present, and projected their contemporary, homogeneous and democratic cultural world onto perished civilizations. They based their arguments on historical documents produced by the higher political and intellectual powers of traditional societies, translated them into standard contemporary languages, and adapted them to their own conceptualized national world. Because in their view, nations have always existed, they regarded as a new phenomenon the rise of nationalism as a formulated idea.

Gellner's theoretical land mine shook most scholars. "It is nationalism which engenders nations, and not the other way round," he declared with his trenchant radicalism, forcing everyone, even the reluctant, to reevaluate the issue.[24] Economic, administrative and technological modernization had created the infrastructure and the need for the nation, but the process was accompanied by deliberate ideological practices for steering—or wishing to steer, where the state system had yet to achieve power—the language, education, memory and other cultural elements that create and define the nation's contours. The supreme reasoning uniting all these ideological practices required that "the political and the national unit should be congruent."[25]

Gellner was prominently followed by Eric Hobsbawm, whose book *Nations and Nationalism since 1780* examined how and when political systems, or movements that sought to found states, produced national entities out of blends of existing cultural, linguistic and religious materials. But Hobsbawm appended a warning to Gellner's theoretical audacity, writing that nations are "dual phenomena, constructed essentially from above, but which cannot be understood unless also analysed from below, that is in terms of the assumptions, hopes, needs, longings and interests of ordinary people."[26]

It is not easy to discover what "ordinary people" thought in historical times, because they left almost no written sources, the supposedly trustworthy testimonies on which historians base their work. But the willingness of citizens of the new nation-states to join armies and fight in wars that became all-out

---

24   Gellner, *Nations and Nationalism*, 55.
25   Ibid, 1.
26   Eric Hobsbawm, *Nations and Nationalism since 1780*, Cambridge: Cambridge University Press, 1992, 10–11.

confrontations, the masses' intoxicating enthusiasm for international sports events, their eagerness during state occasions, their political preferences in the most decisive elections throughout the twentieth century—all of these tend to demonstrate that nationalism has been a captivating success story.

And rightly so, since only in the national democratic state are the citizens both formally and mentally the legitimate proprietors of the modern state. Historical kingdoms belonged to the monarchs, princes and nobility, not to the societies that bore these persons on their productive backs. Modern democratic political entities, by contrast, are perceived by the masses to be their collective property. The imagined ownership of the new state is also seen as proprietorship of the national territory. Printed maps, which were not of course available in premodern times, familiarize people with the exact dimensions of their state, the boundaries of their common and "eternal" property. Hence the appearance of, among other things, passionate mass patriotism and the impressive willingness to kill and be killed, not only for the abstract homeland but for every inch of its ground.

It is true that nationalism has spread in different ways through different social classes, and it has certainly not fully erased earlier collective identities, but its victorious hegemony in the modern era is beyond question.

The assumption that it was national ideology that created, invented or shaped the forms of identity and the envisioning of the nation does not imply that this ideology was the accidental invention or the whim of evil rulers and thinkers. We are not dealing here with a dark world of conspiracies, nor even with an industry of political manipulation. Although ruling elites did foster the development of a national identity by the masses, primarily in order to maintain their loyalty and obedience, nationalism is an intellectual and emotional phenomenon that exceeds modernity's basic power relations. It springs from the intersection of various historical processes that began in the developing capitalist West about three centuries ago. It is both ideology and identity, embracing all human groupings and providing them with an answer to a variety of needs and expectations.

If identity is a lens through which the individual makes sense of the world, and is in fact a condition of subjecthood, national identity is a modern lens through which the state makes sense of a diverse population, making it feel it is a homogeneous and unique historical subject.

The early stages of modernization—the destruction of agrarian dependency relations, the collapse of the associated traditional communal connections, and the decline of the religious beliefs that had provided comforting frameworks of identity—already presented conceptual breaches through which nationalism could enter at an accelerating rate. The breakdown in the forms of solidarity and identity of the small human communities in the villages and towns—caused by occupational mobility and urbanization, and by the abandonment of extended-family homes and of familiar objects and spaces—produced cognitive lacerations that only a total identity politics, such as nationalism, could heal, through powerful abstractions given shape by the dynamic new means of communication.

We find the early buds of national ideology, though still hidden in religious foliage, beginning to flower in the political spring of the Puritan revolution in seventeenth-century England. (Perhaps they had been pollinated by the new Church of England, in its break with the Roman papacy.)[27] Following that upheaval, these buds proceeded to open and then spread east and west, along with the process of modernization. The revolutionary period of the late eighteenth century saw their fullest flowering. A national consciousness was beginning to flourish among North American and French revolutionaries, hand in hand with the idea of "the people's sovereignty," the mighty war cry of the new era.

The famous phrase "No taxation without representation!" taken up against Britain by the bold settlers of America, already presented this advancing entity's Janus face of nationalism and democracy. When the Abbé Sieyès wrote his famous essay in 1789, "What is the third estate?," the still virginally shy national-democratic ideology could be glimpsed between the lines. Three years later, it was borne aloft through the turbulent streets of France. The cult of the national state, with its rituals, festivals and anthems, began to seem natural and obvious in the eyes of the Jacobin revolutionaries and their successors.

Napoleon's conquests undermined the traditional monarchist structures and accelerated the spread of what might be described as the central ideological virus of political modernity. The national-democratic bug entered the hearts of France's soldiers when they came to believe that each one of them might be carrying a marshal's baton in his knapsack. Even the circles that sought to oppose the Napoleonic conquests, even the democratic movements that began to challenge the traditional kingdoms, soon became nationalistic. The historical logic of this spreading phenomenon was plain to see: "government by the people" could only be realized in the national state.

There was more. Old, enfeebled dynastic empires—the Prussian and the Austro-Hungarian and, later, the Tsarist Russian—were also obliged to adopt, cautiously and incrementally, the national innovation, in hopes of extending

---

27   For a further discussion on the later nationalism in England, see Krisham Kumar, *The Making of English National Identity*, Cambridge: Cambridge University Press, 2003.

their own survival. In the course of the nineteenth century, nationalism triumphed almost everywhere in Europe, although it would mature only with the passage of the law of compulsory education and, toward the end of the century, the universal franchise. These two major projects of mass democracy also helped shape the national structures.

Nationalism was further invigorated in the twentieth century. The repressive enterprises of colonialism produced many new nations. From Indonesia to Algeria, Vietnam to South Africa, national identity became universal.[28] There are few human beings today who do not see themselves as members of a defined nationality, and do not aspire to complete self-governance for their home country.

It was the American historian Carlton Hayes, arguably the first academic investigator of nationalism, who as early as the 1920s compared its force to that of the great traditional religions.[29] Hayes, who was probably a religious believer, assumed that nations had existed for a long time, but he also emphasized the inventive aspect and the structure of modern nationalism, and drew a comprehensive comparison between faith in the supreme deity and passionate belief in the supremacy of the nation. Although he was chiefly concerned with the history of ideas, Hayes argued that nationalism was a great deal more than simply another political philosophy expressive of a socioeconomic historical process, because its potential for destruction is immense. He wrote his first book with the images of the First World War, and its millions of new, highly nationalistic casualties, filling his mind's eye.

As Hayes saw it, the decline of Christianity in eighteenth-century Europe did not reflect a complete disappearance of the ancient and persistent human belief in transcendental powers. Modernization merely replaced the former objects of religion. Nature, science, humanism and progress are rational categories, but they also incorporate powerful external factors to which human beings are subject. The climax of the intellectual and religious transformation in the late eighteenth century was the advent of nationalism. Arising as it did from the heart of Christian civilization, it exhibited certain distinctive features from the start. Just as the church organized the faith during the medieval era in Europe, the national state regiments it in the modern era. This state sees itself

---

28   On nationalism outside the European sphere, see the two books by Partha Chatterjee, *Nationalist Thought and the Colonial World*, Tokyo: Zed Books, 1986; *The Nation and Its Fragments: Colonial and Postcolonial Histories*, Princeton: Princeton University Press, 1993.
29   Carlton J. H. Hayes, "Nationalism as a Religion," in *Essays on Nationalism*, New York: Russell, [1926] 1966, 93–125; and *Nationalism: A Religion*, New York: Macmillan, 1960.

as performing an eternal mission; it demands to be worshipped, has substituted strict civil registration for the religious sacraments of baptism and marriage, and regards those who question their national identity as traitors and heretics.

Hayes's ideas were taken up by many who viewed nationalism as a sort of modern religion. Benedict Anderson, for example, saw it as a type of faith that confronts the finality of death in a novel way.[30] Others defined nationalism as a species of religion that succeeds, amid modernity's fracturing upheavals, in endowing human life with new meaning. Giving meaning to constantly changing reality was one of the main functions of the new secular religion. Still other scholars diagnosed nationalism as a modern religion whose function was to construct a permanent cultic scaffolding for the social order and the class hierarchy. However, if we accept these or other assumptions about nationalism's religious nature, we are left with a double question that is yet to be answered: Does nationalism really provide what may be described as a genuine metaphysics of the soul, and will it last as long as the monotheistic religions?

There are significant differences between nationalism and the traditional religions. For example, the universalistic and proselytizing aspects that characterize a good part of the transcendental religions differ from the contours of nationalism, which tends to enclose itself. The fact that the nation almost always worships itself, rather than a transcendental deity, also affects the manner of rallying the masses for the state—not a permanent feature of the traditional world. Nevertheless, there is no doubt that nationalism is the ideology that most closely resembles the traditional religions in successfully crossing class boundaries and fostering social inclusion in a common system of relationships. More than any other worldview or normative system, nationalism has shaped both a personal and a communal identity, and despite its high degree of abstraction, has succeeded in bridging the gap and strengthening the union between the two. Identities of class, community or traditional religion have not been able to resist it for long. They have not been erased, but their continued existence became possible only if they integrated into the symbiotic interconnections of the newly arrived identity.

Other ideologies and political movements have likewise been able to flourish only insofar as they negotiated with the new national idea. This was the fate of all varieties of socialism, as well as of Communism in the Third World, in occupied Europe during the Second World War and in the Soviet Union itself. We must not forget that fascism and National Socialism, before they became an oppressive answer to the conflict between capital and labor, were

---

30 Anderson, *Imagined Communities*, 10–12.

specific varieties of radically aggressive nationalism. The modern colonialism and imperialism of the liberal nation-states were almost always supported at the center by popular national movements, and nationalist ideology served them as the principal source of emotional and political credit in financing every stage of their expansion.

So nationalism is a worldwide concept, born of the sociocultural process of modernization and serving as a leading answer to the psychological and political needs of the immense human masses rushing into the labyrinth of a new world. Nationalism might not have literally invented nations, as Gellner asserted, but neither was it invented by them, or by the "peoples" who preceded them. Without nationalism and its political and intellectual instruments, nations would not have come into being, and nation-states would certainly not have arisen. Every step in defining the outline of the nation and determining its cultural profile was taken deliberately, creating and managing the apparatus for its implementation. The national project was, therefore, a fully conscious one, and the national consciousness took shape as it progressed. It was a simultaneous process of imagination, invention, and actual self-creation.[31]

The forms of imagination and invention varied from place to place, hence also the boundaries of the new human divisions. Like all ideological and political phenomena, they depended on their particular histories.

FROM ETHNIC MYTH TO CIVIL IMAGINARY

Hans Kohn, a Zionist of Czech-German background who began to despair of Jewish nationalism, left Mandatory Palestine for the United States at the end of the 1920s. There he became, along with Carlton Hayes, one of the fathers of the academic study of nationalism. His youth in Eastern Europe, where he had fought in the First World War, along with his experiences and disillusion in the Zionist colonialist enterprise and his migration to New York, equipped him with more valuable firsthand data than his colleague Hayes possessed.[32] He, too, was a captive of the essentialist premise that peoples and nations had always existed, and he, too, assumed that only the national consciousness was a novel phenomenon that had to be interpreted in the context of modernization.

---

31   The self-construction of nations is not the same as the self-creation of a modern working class, but the dismantling of the essentialist approach to the two "things"—nation and class—has much in common. See E. P. Thompson, *The Making of the English Working Class*, London: Penguin, [1963] 2002.

32   On his fascinating life and the development of his thought, see Ken Wolf, "Hans Kohn's Liberal Nationalism: The Historian as Prophet," *Journal of the History of the Ideas* 37:4 (1976), 651–72.

Thus, much of his writing belongs to the "history of ideas," though it includes a cautious attempt to make use of sociopolitical history as well. His crucial contribution to the study of nationalism was his pioneering effort to map its different expressions.

Kohn began writing on the issue of nationalism back in the 1920s, but it was only in his comprehensive study *The Idea of Nationalism*, published in 1944, that he formulated his famous theory of dichotomy, which won him many supporters as well as many opponents.[33] If the First World War pointed him toward the study of nationalism, it was the Second World War that determined his political and ideological sensibilities and, in effect, determined his scholarly achievement. Kohn saw nationalism as made up of two dominant categories: Western nationalism, with an essentially voluntarist approach, which developed on either side of the Atlantic Ocean, bounded on the east by Switzerland; and the organic national identity that spread eastward from the Rhine, encompassing Germany, Poland, the Ukraine and Russia.

Nationalism in the West, except in Ireland, is an original phenomenon that sprang from autochthonous sociopolitical forces, without outside intervention. In most cases it appears when the state, which is engaged in modernization, is well established or is being established. This nationalism draws its ideas from the traditions of the Renaissance and the Age of Enlightenment, and its principles are based on individualism and liberalism, both legal and political. The hegemonic class that engenders this national consciousness is a powerful, secular bourgeoisie, and it constructs civil institutions with political power that play a decisive role in the formation of liberal democracy. It is a self-confident bourgeoisie, and the national politics it fosters tend generally toward openness and inclusiveness. Becoming a citizen of the United States, Britain, France, the Netherlands or Switzerland depends not only on origin and birth but also on the will to join. For all the differences between national perceptions, anyone naturalized in these countries is seen, legally and ideologically, as a member of the nation, with the state as the common property of the citizenry.

According to Kohn, the nationalism that developed in Central and Eastern Europe (the Czech case being something of an exception) was, by contrast, a historical product catalyzed principally from outside. It came into being during Napoleon's conquests and began to take shape as a movement of resistance against the ideas and progressive values of the Enlightenment. In these countries, the national idea arose before, and in fact unconnected with,

---

33 Hans Kohn, *The Idea of Nationalism*, New York: Collier Books, [1944] 1967. His early, pioneering work, *A History of Nationalism in the East*, New York: Harcourt, 1929, remains notable.

the consolidation of a modern state apparatus. In these political cultures the middle classes were weak, and the civil institutions they founded were deferential toward the central and aristocratic authorities. The national identity they embraced was hesitant; it lacked confidence. As a result, it rested on kinship and ancient origin, and defined the nation as a rigid, organically exclusive entity.

The national philosophies that flourished in the lands of the future state of Germany, of Poland-to-be, and of Russia, exclusive property of the tsars, were reactionary and irrational. They foreshadowed the political tendencies that would develop in these regions. The mystique of blood and soil characterized German nationalism, much as conservative romanticism animated the national ferment in the Slav countries of Eastern Europe. Henceforth it would be impossible to join the emerging nations, because they were perceived as exclusive ethnobiological or ethnoreligious entities. The boundaries of the nation were congruent with the "ethnic" boundaries, which could not be entered at will. Such was the unmistakable historical product of this identity politics.

Kohn's dichotomic theory, broadly sketched above without its finer nuances, was without doubt fundamentally normative and born chiefly in reaction to the rise of Nazism. The immigrant, who had already passed through several cultures and national movements, regarded the collective superidentity of the United States, his final refuge, as the highest realization of the universalistic aims that animated Western culture. By contrast, Germany and the East represented the terminus of all the myths and legends about ancient collectives, organic and ethnicist.[34]

Certainly Kohn's idealization of the American concept of citizenship and Anglo-Saxon nationalism in general does not withstand present-day criticism, and so not unexpectedly found a good many opponents. But the criticism of Kohn's theory may be broadly classified as of two kinds. One noted his excessively schematic division and pointed out empirical weaknesses in its historical descriptions but did not reject the essential elements of his analysis; the other entirely rejected the fundamental basis of his distinction between political-civil and ethnic-organic nationalisms, with implicit apologetics for the latter.[35]

---

34 See also Hans Kohn, *Nationalism, Its Meaning and History*, Princeton: Van Nostrand, 1955, 9–90; *The Mind of Germany: The Education of a Nation*, London: Macmillan, 1965; and Hans Kohn and Daniel Walden, *Readings in American Nationalism*, New York: Van Nostrand, 1970, 1–10.

35 See Taras Kuzio, "The Myth of the Civic State: a Critical Survey of Hans Kohn's Framework for Understanding Nationalism," *Ethnic and Racial Studies* 25:1 (2002), 20–39.

In reality, an analysis of the development of Western societies, which Kohn classified as civil, voluntarist, inclusive nations—the United States, Britain, France, the Netherlands—reveals tensions and struggles among diverse tendencies. Throughout the nineteenth century, Protestant Anglo-Saxon identity formed the principal focus of American nationalism, so that Native Americans, Asian and Eastern European immigrants, and black African slaves often experienced hostility and strong identity anxieties. In the 1940s, when Kohn was writing his pioneering book, black citizens had not yet been "imagined" as an immanent part of the great democratic nation.[36]

Although the British have always been proud of their mixed origins (Norman, Scandinavian, and so on), at the height of the liberal British Empire political thinkers and leaders saw the inborn English character as the source of its greatness, and their attitude toward the inhabitants of the colonies was always contemptuous. Many Britons took pride in their Anglo-Saxon heritage, and viewed the Welsh and the Irish "of pure Celtic origin" as their inferiors, races alien to the "chosen Christian people." In the course of the nineteenth century, during which national identity crystallized throughout the West, there were always Frenchmen who described themselves as direct descendants of the Gallic tribes, bolstering their hostility toward the Germans within the framework of the eternal struggle against the Frankish tribes invading from the east.

At the same time, we find in Central and Eastern Europe not a few thinkers, currents and movements that sought to devise an open, inclusive identity politics, bounded not by ethnobiological or ethnoreligious but by cultural and political boundaries. In Germany, the central object of Kohn's dichotomic model, there was not only the ethnocentric national tradition whose outstanding ideologists were Heinrich von Treitschke and Werner Sombart; there were also cosmopolitan writers such as Friedrich von Schiller and Johann Wolfgang von Goethe, national liberals such as Theodor Mommsen and Max Weber, as well as the great social-democratic mass movement that viewed Germanity as a hospitable culture and saw all who lived within its territory as its inherent parts. Similarly, in Tsarist Russia it was not only the various socialist movements that took the inclusive political position that anyone who saw oneself as a Russian must be regarded as such, but also liberal currents and broad intellectual strata that regarded Jews, Ukrainians and Belorussians as integral parts of the great nation.

---

36 On nationalism in the US, see the interesting article by Susan-Mary Grant, "Making History: Myth and the Construction of American Nationhood," in *Myths and Nationhood*, G. Hoskin and G. Schöpflin (eds.), New York: Routledge, 1997, 88–106.

Nevertheless, Kohn's primary intuition was correct and to the point. In the early phases of every Western nation—indeed in every emerging national ideology—ethnocentric myths surround the dominant cultural and linguistic group revered as the original people-race. But in Western societies, for all their subtle variations, these myths fade, though they are never quite extinguished, slowly giving way to a complex of ideas and sensibilities that hold every citizen and naturalized immigrant to be integral parts of the nation. At some point, the hegemonic culture comes to see itself as belonging to all members of the nation, and the dominant identity aspires to encompass them all. This inclusive democratization is not an unbroken process—it experiences regressions and deviations, as well as political upheavals in times of instability and crisis. Yet despite such setbacks, all the liberal democracies have given rise to an imagined citizenship in which the future is more significant than the past. This imagined concept has been translated into legal norms and eventually permeates the state educational systems.

This took place through the nineteenth and twentieth centuries in the Anglo-Saxon countries, the Low Countries, France and Switzerland. Not that racism vanished from these societies, or that contempt and conflict between different sectors within them ceased. But the processes of integration—sometimes through the absorption of divergent parts, sometimes by their suppression—were perceived as necessary, even as desirable. If hypocrisy is the tribute that vice pays to virtue, then citizenship nationalism is the relatively open culture in which the racist, or the excluding ethnicist, is always forced to apologize.

By contrast, in Germany, Poland, Lithuania, the Ukraine and Russia, despite considerable movements supporting a definition of national identity on the political basis of citizenship, it was the groups that continued to cultivate myths about an ancient homogeneous origin that carried the day. Such old concepts about a rigid ethnic entity that remained unchanged through history, a genealogy of a primeval and unique "people," effectively barred anyone from joining the nation or, for that matter, from quitting it—hence, Germans or Poles and their offspring in the United States would remain forever, in the eyes of nationalists, members of the German or the Polish nation.

The Gallic tribes were depicted in the French educational system as a kind of historical metaphor—even the children of immigrants repeated at school that their ancestors were Gauls, and their teachers took pride in these new "descendants"[37]—whereas the Teutonic knights, or the ancient Aryan tribes,

---

37   On the consciousness that France is not "Gaul's descendant," see the testimony

increasingly became toward the end of the nineteenth century the idealized forebears of the modern Germans. Whoever was not considered a descendant of theirs was not regarded as a true German. Similarly, in the Poland that arose after the First World War, whoever had not been conceived in a purely Catholic womb, who happened to be the child of Jews, Ukrainians or Ruthenians, even if a citizen, was not regarded as a member of the noble, long-suffering Polish nation.[38] Likewise, to many Slavophiles, subjects who had not been born within the bosom of the Orthodox Church and were not authentic Slavs were therefore not part of the holy Russian people and were not to be included within Greater Russia.

The life of linguistic or religious minorities in these countries was immeasurably harder than in the West, even if we leave to one side for the moment the pogroms against Jews in Russia and the murderous campaigns of the Nazis. It is enough to look at the character of the national entities that arose after the collapse of Yugoslavia, and the fragile criteria for membership in them, to perceive the connection between ethnoreligious definitions and the outburst of intercommunal xenophobia. These entities resorted to almost extinct "religion" in order to assert their national *ethnos*, which had never had much of an existence. It was only the use of ancient (and utterly fictitious) myths that made it possible to set "Catholic" Croatians against "Orthodox" Serbs, and these in an especially vicious way against "Muslim" Bosnians and Kosovars. Following the failure of the former Communist regime's integrative policies, minute cultural and linguistic differences turned into exclusionary walls.[39]

Until the final decade of the twentieth century, Germany and Eastern Europe remained dominated by persistent ethnicist nationalism. Cultural and linguistic minorities, even when in possession of citizenship, were still not included in the dominant public consciousness within the national boundaries. Locally born second- and even third-generation immigrants were not granted citizenship. Yet "ethnic Germans" who had lived for generations in the East, in some cases since the Middle Ages, and who had lost all cultural and linguistic connection with any kind of "Germanity," still had the privilege of becoming

---

of Ernest Lavisse, the "pedagogic father" of French national historiography, in the book of Claude Nicolet, *La Fabrique d'une nation: La France entre Rome et les Germains*, Paris: Perrin, 2003, 278–80.

38   On the nature of Polish nationalism, see Brian Porter, *When Nationalism Began to Hate: Imagining Modern Politics in Nineteenth-Century Poland*, Oxford: Oxford University Press, 2003.

39   On nationalism in the Balkans and elsewhere at the end of the twentieth century, see the interesting book by Michael Ignatieff, *Blood and Belonging: Journeys in the New Nationalism*, New York: Farrar, 1993.

German citizens anytime they wished. Only as the European Community grew, and traditional nationalism somewhat declined, did ethnocentric identities begin to weaken in Central and Eastern Europe, as it silently submitted to the requirements of full democratic citizenship in the new, unified Europe. It must not be forgotten that ethnicist nationalism meant that democracy—namely, government representing the entire population equally—was always imperfect because not all citizens were held to be legitimate members of the national body.

The historical origin of this difference lies in the unresolved division between the process that matured into a political nationalism based on citizenship, which one could call citizenship nationalism, as opposed to a nationalism based on an allegiance to ethnicity, which one could call ethnic nationalism. Unfortunately, Hans Kohn's explanations were not entirely satisfactory. For example, Italy's unification came late, paralleling that of Germany, and, as in Germany, the weak middle class did not accelerate its nationalization. In both countries national movements arose some time before actual unification, and in both it was the monarchies, rather than bourgeois strata with mass support, that created the states. Yet in Germany it was the ethnic, or ethnobiological, version of nationalism that triumphed, while in Italy by the end of the nineteenth century the political citizenship version had won.

The difficulty in understanding this contrast can be further highlighted by comparing the later movements—German National Socialism and Italian fascism. Both were strongly nationalistic, and among their various projects was popular unification, which had not been fully accomplished by the monarchies. Both movements were authoritarian, both viewed the nation as a collective greater than the sum of its parts (the individuals of which it was composed), and both despised Western individualism. But National Socialism adopted the ethnobiological heritage on which it had been nurtured from the start, whereas Italian fascism continued to draw, at least until 1938, on the inclusive political nationalism of Italy's legendary founders, Giuseppe Mazzini and Giuseppe Garibaldi. German speakers in northern Italy, Jews in the urban centers, and Croatians annexed by war were all perceived as parts of the Italian nation, or future members of it.

Even the historian Hobsbawm's interesting chronological classification is only partially convincing. He noted that the nationalist phenomenon had two hues: the first appeared during the revolutionary era of the late eighteenth and early nineteenth centuries, bearing liberal-democratic characteristics; the latter surged in a new form at the end of the nineteenth, based on reactionary ethnolinguistic and racist markers.[40] While it is true that toward the end of that century the processes of urbanization and migration in Eastern Europe intensified, and the friction between them produced resentment and racism, Hobsbawm's analysis cannot account for the German development. Moreover, Greece, which attained national independence in the first half of the nineteenth century and won the sympathy of all the democrats and liberals in Europe at that time, preserved almost to the end of the twentieth century its rigid ethnoreligious nationalism. By contrast, the nature of Italian nationalism, which matured later, was quite political and citizen-focused. Likewise, Czech nationalism—resulting in a nation-state, together with the Slovaks, that was attained only after the First World War—displayed a certain inclusiveness (though not toward German-speakers), which was quite rare among the other nationalities that arose with the fall of the Hapsburgs.

Liah Greenfeld, a noted scholar in the field of nationalism—as a child she emigrated from the USSR to Israel, and then left it to further her academic career in the United States—has tackled the issue with the tools of comparative sociology borrowed from Max Weber.[41] She accepted in broad terms the division between citizenship and ethnic nationalism, but chose to include the collectivist touchstone: if Britain and the United States are individualistic states, the state of France—born from the great Revolution—linked civil identity with reverence for the body politic. Hence its culture is more homogeneous and less tolerant and liberal toward resident minorities than that of its Western neighbors. However, the countries between the Rhine and Moscow developed a more problematic nationalism, being both collectivist and ethnicist. In these countries the nation is seen as an unchangeable primeval body, to which people can belong only by virtue of genetic inheritance.

For Greenfeld, the difference between the strategies of national identity formation was caused principally by the character of the historical subject responsible for them. In the West, broad social strata adopted and internalized the national consciousness—in England, it was the minor aristocracy and the fairly literate urban population; in North America, the generality of settlers; and in France, the strong bourgeoisie. In the East, however, quite narrow strata led the way in the adoption of nationalism—in the Germanic

---

40   Hobsbawm, *Nations and Nationalism since 1780*, 101–130.

41   See Liah Greenfeld, *Nationalism: Five Roads to Modernity*, Cambridge, MA: Harvard University Press, 1992; and also her article "Nationalism in Western and Eastern Europe Compared," in *Can Europe Work? Germany and the Reconstruction of Postcommunist Societies*, S. E. Hanson and W. Spohn (eds.), Seattle: University of Washington Press, 1995, 15–23.

cultural world it was small circles of intellectuals who sought a rise in status at the heart of the conservative social hierarchy, while in Russia it was the weak aristocracy that adopted a new modern identity through which it hoped to preserve its remaining privileges. The prolonged isolation of the groups who created "Eastern" nationalism was largely responsible for its exclusivity and its persistent attachment to a mythological past.

Other scholars have proposed further explanations for the disparate kinds of national temperament that produced such different histories in Europe and worldwide. According to Gellner, in the West it did not take many broken eggs to make the national omelette—thanks to the long existence of a high culture, only a few moderate corrections were needed to define the national boundaries. But the "East," given its general disarray, had no such long-standing high culture, hence the need felt by a particular cultural and linguistic group to forcibly modify the body politic through the use of exclusion, expulsion, even the physical annihilation of other cultural groups.[42] Here, too, Gellner's analysis, like Hobsbawm's, fails to fit the Germanic world: although it had a high culture ever since the Reformation, outright ethnocentric nationalism ultimately won.

Rogers Brubaker, an American sociologist who conducted a thorough methodical comparison between the development of nationhood in France and in Germany, also concluded that the complex mosaic of, and sharp frictions between, cultural-linguistic groups on the Germanic-Slavic frontiers were among the main causes of their differences. For a long time, there had not been a strong nation-state capable of "Germanizing" Poles and others who lived among speakers of German dialects. Nor did a revolutionary regime arise, as in France, capable of unifying all the "ethnic Germans" surrounded by other linguistically defined cultures.[43]

To this day, no agreed synthesis has been proposed that accounts for the spectrum of national expressions and for their development over the past two centuries. Socioeconomic, psychological and demographic factors, geographic location, even political and historical contingencies—the explanations remain partial and incomplete. Nor has a satisfactory answer been found thus far to the question of why certain nations preserved ethnocentric myths for a long time and used these in their self-definition, while other nations grew up rela-

---

42   Gellner, *Nations and Nationalism,* 100.

43   Rogers Brubaker, *Citizenship and Nationhood in France and Germany,* Cambridge, MA: Harvard University Press, 1992, 5–11. Brubaker later rejected the conceptual distinction between civil and ethnic nationalism, preferring to distinguish between "state-framed" and "counter-state" nationalism. See "The Manichean Myth: Rethinking the Distinction Between 'Civic' and 'Ethnic' Nationalism," in Hanspeter Kries, et al. (eds.), *Nation and National Identity: The European Experience in Perspective,* Zürich: Rüegger, 1999, 55–71.

tively fast and so succeeded in establishing mature democracies. It appears that further research is required, as well as additional empirical findings.

A primeval ancestral identity, an image of a biological genealogy, and the idea of a chosen people/race did not spring up in a vacuum. For the consolidation of a national consciousness, civil or ethnocentric, it was always necessary to have a literate elite. To enable the nation to "remember" and consolidate its historical imagery, it required the services of scholarly producers of culture, masters of memory, creators of laws and constitutions. While diverse social strata utilized or derived various advantages from the rise of the nation-state, the central agents in the formation of national entities—those who perhaps derived the greatest symbolic profit from them—were, above all, the intellectuals.

THE INTELLECTUAL AS THE NATION'S "PRINCE"

Carlton Hayes, who painstakingly researched national ideas in the classic texts of modern thought, had concluded in the 1920s that "the upshot of the whole process is that a nationalist theology of the intellectuals becomes a nationalist mythology for the masses."[44] To this Tom Nairn, a much later scholar, no less original and, significantly, a Scot, added, "The new middle-class intelligentsia of nationalism had to invite the masses into history; and the invitation-card had to be written in a language they understood."[45]

These two working hypotheses can stand, insofar as we succeed in shaking off the long scholarly tradition of viewing the ideas of its leading thinkers as the causes, or points of departure, for the actual historical development. Nationalism is not a theoretical product that germinated in scholars' studies and was then adopted by the masses yearning for ideology, thereby becoming a way of life.[46] To understand the way nationalism spread, we must define the role of intellectuals in this phenomenon, and perhaps begin by considering their differing sociopolitical status in traditional and in modern societies.

There has never been an organized society, except perhaps in the early tribal stages, that did not produce intellectuals. While the noun "intellectual" is a fairly late one, born at the end of the nineteenth century, the most basic divisions of labor had already seen the rise of individuals whose main activity or livelihood was the production and manipulation of cultural

---

44   Hayes, *Essays on Nationalism*, 110.
45   Tom Nairn, *The Break-Up of Britain: Crisis and Neo-Nationalism*, London: New Left Books, 1977, 340.
46   Elie Kedourie's classic, *Nationalism* (London: Hutchinson, 1960), embodies this approach.

symbols and signs. From the sorcerer or shaman, through the royal scribes and priests, to the church clerics, court jesters and painters of cathedrals, cultural elites emerged in all agrarian societies. These elites had to be capable of providing, organizing and disseminating words or images in three major areas: first, the accrual of knowledge; second, the development of ideologies that would preserve the stability of the social order; and third, the provision of an organizing metaphysical explanation for the seemingly magical cosmic order.

Most of these cultural elites, as noted earlier, were in some ways dependent on and entangled with the politically and economically dominant strata. The dependence could be lesser or greater; here and there, a measure of autonomy—and even, given a solid economic basis, a degree of independence—was achieved. Nor was the dependence one-sided: political power, which in traditional societies intermeshed with the web of economic production differently than it does in modern societies, needed cultural elites in order to maintain control.

By combining the explanation given by Antonio Gramsci for the various ways in which intellectuals exist in the world of production with Gellner's theory of modernization, we gain further insight into their role in the formation of nationalism and the nation. According to the Italian Marxist,

> Every social class, coming into existence on the original basis of an essential function in the world of economic production, creates with itself, organically, one or more groups of intellectuals who give it homogeneity and consciousness of its function.[47]

To retain control for a long time, it is not enough to possess visible power; it is necessary to produce ethical and legal norms. An educated stratum provides a hegemonic consciousness to underpin the class structure, so that it will not need to keep defending that structure by violent means. In the premodern world the traditional intellectuals were the court scribes, artistic protégés of a prince or a king, and the various agents of religion. Above all it was the clergy in historical societies who helped consolidate a consensual ideology. Gramsci, in his time, admitted that it was still necessary to investigate the rise of the intellectuals in the feudal and classical world, and indeed his writing on the subject is tentative and rather disappointing. Gellner, on the other hand, ventured a more interesting hypothesis.

---

47 Antonio Gramsci, "The Formation of Intellectuals," in *The Modern Prince and Other Writings*, New York: International Publishers, 1957, 118.

As stated earlier, before the invention of printing, court scribes and priests did not have the means of communication to reach the masses, nor did they need them. The divine right of royalty conveyed ideological legitimacy primarily to the administrative circles and landed aristocracy, and these groups controlled the territory. It is true that the religious elite slowly began its effort to reach the generality, namely, the peasant population, but it also avoided close contact with it. Gellner gives a good description of the intellectual mechanism in agricultural societies:

> The tendency of liturgical languages to become distinct from the vernacular is very strong: it is as if literacy alone did not create enough of a barrier between cleric and layman, as if the chasm between them had to be deepened, by making the language not merely recorded in an inaccessible script, but also incomprehensible when articulated.[48]

Unlike the relatively small priestly circles in the polytheistic royal courts around the ancient Mediterranean, the spreading monotheism gave rise to broader intellectual strata. From the ancient Essenes through the missionaries, monks, rabbis and priests, to the ulema, there were increasing numbers of literate individuals who had extensive and complex contact with the masses of agricultural producers—one reason that the religions survived through the ages while empires, kingdoms, principalities and peoples rose and fell. Religious bodies that did not fully blend with secular authorities acquired varying degrees of autonomy vis-à-vis the political and social classes. They cultivated lines of communication and were always perceived to be the servants of society as a whole, hence the impressive survival of the beliefs, cults and icons they disseminated. Another reason for the longevity of religions was that the value of the spiritual merchandise they provided to the masses must have been more meaningful than the earthly (and exploitative) security provided by the political powers: "divine providence" secured for believers the purity, grace and salvation of the next world.

We might add that the autonomy of religious bodies in the premodern world was achieved not only thanks to their reputation and widespread universal message, but also to the direct material support they received from the devout producers of food. Moreover, many literate individuals combined physical labor with their spiritual occupations, and those who belonged to the upper reaches of the establishment became in time a socioeconomic class and even a judicial establishment—for example, the Catholic Church.

---

48   Gellner, *Nations and Nationalism*, 11.

Despite the growing popularity of religious elites in the agrarian world, and their devotion to the human flock, they took good care of the working tool that enabled them to maintain their authority. Reading and writing, as well as the sacred tongue, were preserved by the "book people," and there was neither the will nor the means to propagate these practices throughout the populace. Anderson puts it well: "the bilingual intelligentsia, by mediating between vernacular and Latin, mediated between earth and heaven."[49] Not only did the religious elites know the sacred languages and, in some cases, the language of the administration, but they were also familiar with the peasant dialects. This mediating function of bilingual or trilingual intellectuals gave them a power they would not readily give up.

But the process of modernization—the decline in the power of the church, the shrinking of the religious communities, the disappearance of the patron-protégé relations that had sustained the medieval producers of culture, and the formation of a market economy in which almost everything might be bought and sold—inevitably contributed to the transmutation of all cultural morphologies, leading to major alterations in the place and status of the intellectuals.

Gramsci repeatedly emphasized the links between these new literati and the rising bourgeoisie. These intellectuals, whom he described as "organic," were not large capitalists but came mainly from the urban and rural middle strata. Some became skilled experts who administered production, while others followed the free professions or became public officials.

At the top of the pyramid Gramsci placed the "creators in the various fields of knowledge: philosophy, art, etc.,"[50] but he used the term "intellectual" broadly, including in effect the politicians and bureaucrats—that is, most of the modern state's organizers and directors. In fact, although he does not say so, for him the new state apparatus as an intellectual collective replaced the rational "Prince," the famous, idealized autocrat depicted by Niccolò Machiavelli. But unlike that mythological figure, the modern prince is not a single and absolute ruler, but rather a corps of intellectuals who control the apparatus of the nation-state. This body does not express its own interests but is supposed to represent the totality of the nation, for which purpose it produces a universal discourse claiming to serve all its members. In bourgeois society, Gramsci argued, the political-intellectual prince is a dependent partner of the property-owning classes that control production. Only when the party of workers comes to power—a new intellectual prince—will the universal dimension be realized in society's upper political spheres.[51]

49   Anderson, *Imagined Communities*, 15–16.
50   Gramsci, *The Modern Prince and Other Writings*, 125.
51   Actually Gramsci applied the term "prince" to a political organism seeking to seize

It is not necessary to believe in Gramsci's political utopia—designed to justify his work as an intellectual in a workers' party—to appreciate his theoretical achievement in analyzing the intellectual function that characterizes the modern state. Unlike the powers that ruled agrarian societies, modernization and the division of labor required that the political apparatus perform diverse, ever-multiplying intellectual functions. While the majority of the populace remained illiterate, this apparatus expanded and cultivated within it the bulk of the literate population.

Which social classes produced these first "intellectuals" in the growing state bureaucracy? The answer might help solve the question of the historical differences in the formation of civil and ethnic nationalisms. In Britain, after the Puritan revolution, the state apparatus was staffed by members of the new minor aristocracy and commercial bourgeoisie. In the United States the staff came mainly from wealthy farming families and prosperous city dwellers. In France it was mainly educated members of the commercial class and the petty bourgeoisie who filled the ranks of the "gown nobility," while the upheavals of the Revolution continued to inject new social elements into the body politic.

In Germany, on the other hand, the Prussian imperial state system was made up principally of conservative members of the Junker class, their offspring, and their associates, and things did not immediately change when Prussia became part of the German Reich after 1871. In Russia, too, the Tsarist state drew its public servants from the traditional nobility. In Poland, the first social class that aspired and struggled for a national state were the aristocrats. Without revolutions to introduce educated, dynamic elements and members of the new mobile classes, the early stages of state formation did not include intellectuals who were commoners in the political game or, therefore, in the dominant protonational ideologies.

The French thinker Raymond Aron wondered whether racism is not, among other things, the snobbery of the poor.[52] This observation not only diagnoses a familiar mental state of the modern mass; it can also point to the historical sources of the concept of "blood ties," which dictated the boundaries of certain national groups. Before the modern age it was the nobility that marked blood as the measure of kinship.[53] Only the aristocrats had blue blood

---

the state structure in the name of the proletariat. I apply here the concept to the entire state apparatus.

52   Raymond Aron, *Les Désillusions du progrès: Essai sur la dialectique de la modernité*, Paris: Calmann-Lévy, 1969, 90.

53   In the ancient Jewish world, it was mostly the priesthood that demarcated its identity by blood, and in the late Middle Ages it was, strangely, the Spanish Inquisition.

in their veins, which they inherited from their precious ancestral seed. In the old agrarian world, biological determinism as the criterion for human classification was perhaps the most important symbolic possession of the ruling classes. It was the basis of the legal customs that served as the infrastructure of its prolonged, stable power over the land and the realm. As Alexis de Tocqueville observed in his time, upward mobility during the Middle Ages was possible only in the church: it was the only system not based exclusively on genealogy and was thus the source of modern egalitarianism.[54]

The dominant presence of members and associates of the declining nobility among the new intellectuals in the government systems of Central and Eastern Europe apparently affected the direction of the future national identities that were then developing. When the Napoleonic wars forced the kingdoms east of France to don national costumes, their loyal and conservative literate circles sowed the ideological seeds that exchanged the horizontal concept of blue blood for a vertical one, and the reversal of aristocratic identity initiated the hesitant beginnings of a protonational identity. This identity, assisted by later intellectuals, soon led to the ideological and legal principle defining the membership of the "ethnic" nationality as blood-based (*jus sanguinis*). The national membership granted in the West on grounds of birth in the territory (*jus soli*) was entirely absent in the nation-states of Eastern Europe.

Yet here, too, the Italian example flies in the face of overconfident schematization. Why did civil-political nationalism succeed here at such an early stage? Surely the first intellectuals of the state apparatus throughout the future Italy also derived from the traditional aristocracy? A possible, if inadequate, explanation for the relative restraint of ethnicism in the consolidation of Italian identity could be the tremendous weight of the papacy and the Catholic universalism that it imbued in all the strata from which the Italian bureaucracy arose. Perhaps also the clearly political myth of the ancient Roman republic and empire helped immunize this unusual civil identity; moreover, the marked differences between northern and southern Italians could have prevented a dubious ethnic nationalism.

Or we may ditch all of Gramsci's analyses and choose a firmer basis on which to clarify the role of the intellectuals in national modernization. We can limit the term "intellectuals" to the producers, organizers and propagators of culture in the modern state and its extensions in civil society. With this approach, it will still be possible to discover how indispensable they were for the consolidation of nationalism and the formation of nation-states.

---

54 See Alexis de Tocqueville, *Democracy in America*, London: Oxford University Press, 1946.

As Anderson pointed out, one of the major developments leading up to the age of nationalism was the printing revolution that began in Western Europe at the end of the fifteenth century. This technocultural revolution weakened the status of the sacred languages and helped spread the languages of state administration that would eventually become national languages. The position of the clergy, whose use of the sacred languages was their main symbolic possession, declined. The clerics, who had attained their status and even earned their living thanks to their bilingualism, lost their historical role and were forced to seek other sources of income.[55]

The symbolic properties inherent in the national languages offered an expanding market of fresh opportunities. Flourishing book production required new specializations and new intellectual endeavors. Philosophers, scientists, and, before long, writers and poets abandoned Latin and turned to French, English, German and other vernaculars. The next stage, the rise of journalism, would hugely increase the number of readers, and thus the corps of writers catering to the public. But the real catalyst of national language and culture was the state, whose nature kept evolving. To promote production and compete with other national economies, the state apparatus had to take on the task of educating the populace and turn it into a national enterprise.

Universal education and the creation of agreed cultural codes were preconditions for the complex specializations demanded by the modern division of labor. Therefore every state that became "nationalized," whether authoritarian or liberal, made elementary education a universal right. No mature nation failed to declare education compulsory, obliging its citizens to send their children off to school. This institution, which became the central agent of ideology—rivaled only by the military and by war—turned all subjects into citizens, namely, people conscious of their nationality.[56] If Joseph de Maistre maintained that the executioner was the mainstay of social order in the state, Gellner's provocative insight was that the decisive role in the state belonged to none other than the educator.[57] More than to their rulers, the new national citizens became loyal to their culture.

Yet Gellner's argument that this has turned the modern state into a

---

55   On the rise and consolidation of national languages, see Michael Billing, *Banal Nationalism*, London: Sage Publications, 1995, 13–36.

56   There are not enough empirical studies of the nationalization of the masses in the Western nations. One exception is the relatively early book by Eugen Weber, *Peasants into Frenchmen: The Modernization of Rural France, 1870–1914*, Stanford: Stanford University Press, 1976.

57   Gellner, *Nations and Nationalism*, 34.

community made up entirely of priests/scribes is imprecise.[58] Though literacy has become universal, there is a new division of labor in the nation—between those who create and disseminate literacy and make their living doing so, and those who consume its products and make use of it. From the elected minister of culture through the university scholar and lecturer to the schoolteacher, a hierarchy of intellectuals serves the state, filling the roles of director and playwright, and even leading actors in the immense cultural spectacle called the nation. Agents of culture from the fields of journalism, literature, theater and, later, cinema and television form the supporting cast.

In the kingdoms that preceded the consolidation of nations, notably those in Western Europe, the agents of culture constituted an efficient corps that worked in tandem with administrative officialdom, the judiciary, and the military, and collaborated with them in the nation-building project. Among minority groups—cultural-linguistic or religious, and generally defined as ethnic—that had suffered discrimination under the supranational kingdoms and imperial powers, the intelligentsia were almost the only midwives of the new, rapidly rising nations.

Within the broad boundaries of the Austro-Hungarian, Tsarist Russian and Ottoman empires, and later the British, French, Belgian and Dutch colonies, there arose small circles of vigorous intelligentsia characterized by an acute sensitivity to cultural discrimination, linguistic repression, or exclusion on religious grounds. These groups arose only when the nationalist ferment was already seething in the metropolitan center—still weak and fictive in the crumbling kingdoms, but authentic and hegemonic in the new empires. These circles were familiar with the high culture that was taking shape and spreading in the centers of power, but still felt inferior to it, because they had come in from the margins and were constantly reminded of that fact. Since their working tools were cultural and linguistic, they were the first to be affected and thus formed the vanguard of the nationalist revolt.

These dynamic groups started a long campaign to lay the foundations for the emerging national movements that would claim sovereignty over the nations they represented while, at the same time, bringing them into being. Some of these intellectuals retrained to become the political leaders of the new mass movements. Others clung to their intellectual occupations and passionately continued to delineate the contours and contents of the new national culture. Without these early literati, nations would not have proliferated, and

---

58   Ibid., 32.

the political map of the world would have been more monochromatic.[59]

These intellectuals had to utilize popular or even tribal dialects, and sometimes forgotten sacred tongues, and to transform them quickly into new, modern languages. They produced the first dictionaries and wrote the novels and poems that depicted the imagined nation and sketched the boundaries of its homeland. They painted melancholy landscapes that symbolized the nation's soil[60] and invented moving folktales and gigantic historical heroes, and weaved ancient folklore into a homogeneous whole.[61] Taking events related to diverse and unconnected political entities, they welded them into a consecutive, coherent narrative that unified time and space, thus producing a long national history stretching back to primeval times. Naturally, specific elements of the various historical materials played a (passive) part in shaping the modern culture, but it was principally the intellectual sculptors who cast the image of the nation according to their vision, whose character was formed mainly by the intricate demands of the present.

Most of them did not see themselves as the midwives of the new nation but as the offspring of a dormant nation that they were arousing from a long slumber. None wanted to see themselves as a baby left on a church doorstep without an identifying note. Nor did the image of the nation as a sort of Frankenstein's monster, composed of organs from different sources, especially disturb its devotees. Every nation had to learn who its "ancestors" were, and in some cases its members searched anxiously for the qualities of the biological seed that they propagated.

Genealogy gave added value to the new identity, and the longer the perceived past, the more the future was envisioned as unending. No wonder, then, that of all the intellectual disciplines, the most nationalistic is that of the historian.

The rupture caused by modernization detached humanity from its recent past. The mobility created by industrialization and urbanization shattered not only the rigid social ladder but also the traditional, cyclic continuity between past,

---

59   On the stages in the development of national minority movements in Eastern and Central Europe, see the important empirical work by the Czech scholar Miroslav Hroch, *Social Preconditions of National Revival in Europe*, New York: Columbia University Press, 2000. The author himself attributed the book's awkward title and its obsolete terminology to the fact that its first version appeared back in the early 1970s.

60   On the visual depiction of nations, see Anne-Marie Thiesse's excellent, *La Création des identités nationales: Europe xviiie-xxe siècle*, Paris: Seuil, 1999, 185–224.

61   On why and how national heroes are created, see P. Centlivres, et al. (eds.), *La Fabrique des héros*, Paris: Maison des sciences de l'homme, 1998.

present and future. Previously, agrarian producers had no need for the chronicles of kingdoms, empires and principalities. They had no use for the history of large-scale collectives, because they had no interest in an abstract time unconnected to their concrete existence. Lacking such a concept of development, they were content with the religious imagination that comprised a mosaic memory devoid of a tangible dimension of progressive movement. The end became a beginning, and eternity bridged life and death.

The secular, upsetting modern world, however, turned time into the main artery through which symbolic and emotional imagery entered social consciousness. Historical time became inseparable from personal identity, and the collective narrative gave meaning to the national existence, whose consolidation required heavy sacrifices. The suffering of the past justified the price demanded of citizens in the present. The heroism of the receding world prophesied a brilliant future, perhaps not for the individual but certainly for the nation. With the help of historians, nationalism became an essentially optimistic ideology. This, more than anything else, was the secret of its success.

CHAPTER TWO

Mythistory: In the Beginning, God Created the People

From what has been said, it is thus clearer than the sun at noonday that the Pentateuch was not written by Moses, but by someone who lived long after Moses.

—Baruch Spinoza, *A Theologico-Political Treatise*, 1670

The Land of Israel was the birthplace of the Jewish people. Here their spiritual, religious and political identity was shaped. Here they first attained to statehood, created cultural values of national and universal significance and gave to the world the eternal Book of Books.

—The Declaration of the Establishment of the State of Israel, May 14, 1948

Antiquities of the Jews, the fascinating work by Flavius Josephus, was written in the late first century CE. It may be the first work by a known author who sought to reconstruct a general history of the Jews—or, more precisely, Judeans— from their "beginning" to his own time.[1] Josephus was a Hellenized Jew and a believer, and boasted he was of the chosen "priestly seed." So he opened his book with the words: "In the beginning God created the heaven and the earth. But when the earth did not come into sight, but was covered with thick darkness, and a wind moved upon its surface, God commanded that there should be light ... And this was indeed the *first* day. But Moses said it was *one* day."[2]

The ancient historian was certain that the Pentateuch (the first five books of the Old Testament) was dictated by God to Moses, and he took for granted that the history of the Hebrews and Judeans ought to start with the creation of the world, since this was how the Scriptures present it. The Scriptures, therefore, served as his only source for the opening of his work. Josephus tried now and then to bring in other sources to add verisimilitude to his history, but with little effect. From the story of the Creation through the appearance of Abraham the Hebrew and the Exodus from Egypt to the adventures of the

---

1   Josephus's *Antiquities of the Jews* says very little about the proliferating communities of Jewish believers outside Judea. See Shaye J. D. Cohen, "Ioudaios, Iudaeus, Judaean, Jew," in *The Beginnings of Jewishness: Boundaries, Varieties, Uncertainties*, Berkeley: University of California Press, 1999, 69–106.

2   Flavius Josephus, *Antiquities of the Jews*, 1, 1, 1.

pious Esther, he copied the biblical tales without commentary or doubt, except for some noticeable stylistic changes and a small number of tactical additions and deletions. Only in the final part of Josephus's work, when the historian proceeded to relate the story of the Judeans following the end of the biblical narrative, did he resort to more secular sources, which he strenuously adapted so as to create a continuous, coherent narrative.

The believing Jewish author at the end of the first century CE deemed it reasonable to investigate the genealogy of his Jewish contemporaries for the history of Adam and Eve and their offspring, as well as the story of the Deluge and Noah's ark. He continued to intertwine God's actions with the deeds of men, without any separation or mediation. He openly glorified the Judeans by describing their origin from earliest times—antiquity being a virtue in Rome—and mostly praised their religious laws and the omnipotent deity that guided them. Josephus lived in Rome, but he felt at his back the wind of monotheism blowing into the cultural halls of the great pagan world, and it impelled his missionarizing writing. Ancient history, as he copied it from the Old Testament, was to him above all an "exemplary philosophy," as defined by the Greek historian Dionysus of Halicarnassus, whose writing on the antiquities of the Romans served the Jewish historian as a model.[3]

The ancient myths were still pervasive in the first century, and the human deeds related in them could be seasoned with otherworldly events. At the beginning of the nationalist era in our time, however, there was a remarkable realignment. Divinity was kicked off its pedestal; thenceforth, truth came to be confined to the biblical stories that dealt with the deeds of humanity. But how did it happen that the miraculous works of Providence were suddenly rejected as untrue, while the human story that was closely intertwined with them was upheld as historical fact?

It should be remembered that the distilled biblical "truth" was not a universal narrative about the history of humanity, but the story of a sacred people whom a secularized modern reading turned into the first nation in human history.

THE EARLY SHAPING OF JEWISH HISTORY

Between Flavius Josephus and the modern era there were no attempts by Jewish authors to write a general history of their past. Although Jewish monotheism was born encased in theological-historical myth, no Jewish historiography was produced during the long period called the Middle Ages. Neither

---

3 See Dionysius of Halicarnassus, *Roman Antiquities*, Loeb Classical Library edn. Cambridge, MA: Harvard University Press, 1937.

Christianity's highly developed tradition of chronicles nor Islamic historical literature appealed to rabbinical Judaism, which, with rare exceptions, refused to examine either its near or distant past.[4] The chronological sequence of events in secular time was alien to exilic time—a condition of constant alertness, attuned to the longed-for moment when the Messiah would appear. The distant past was a dim memory that ensured his coming.

Some sixteen centuries would pass before Jacques Basnage, a Normandy-born Huguenot theologian who settled in Rotterdam, undertook to continue the project of the Judean-born historian who had settled in Rome. *The History of the Jews from Jesus Christ to the Present Time, Being a Supplement and Continuation of the History of Josephus* was written in the early eighteenth century by this Protestant scholar, mainly as an attack on the detested Church of Rome.[5] In this work, as in that of Josephus, writing about the past was designed to serve moral and religious purposes; it was not a work of research in the modern sense, and uses scarcely any Jewish documents.

Designed to extend the work of Josephus, Basnage's book does not begin with Genesis, though obviously as a devout theologian he did not doubt the veracity of that biblical prologue. Indeed, following Martin Luther in the sixteenth century, it was the Protestants who gave the Old Testament the greater importance and prestige, noticeable especially in the Anglican Church and its dissidents. But like most critics of the Catholic Church, Basnage did not draw an unbroken line from the ancient Hebrews to the Jewish communities of his time. He thought that the Old Testament belonged to all the offspring of the "Children of Israel," a term that embraced the Christians no less, and perhaps more, than the Jews, inasmuch as Christendom was the "true Israel." While applying the term "nation" to the Jews, he did not intend its modern connotation, and he discussed their history mainly as a sect persecuted for its refusal to accept Christ as the savior. Basnage, who wrote about them with

---

4   Chronicles similar to that of Josephus generally began with the Creation, the rise of King David and the reign of Josiah, then proceeded to Jesus and the Apostles, going on to the rise of the Christianized Frankish kings. See, for example, Gregory of Tours, *The History of the Franks*, London: Penguin Classics, 1976. It is worth noting that a work imitating that of Josephus appeared in the tenth century CE, *Sefer Yosiphon*, Jerusalem: Bialik, 1974 (in Hebrew). Rabbi Ahimaaz's genealogy, *Megillat Ahimaaz* (Jerusalem: Tarshish, 1974 [in Hebrew]), appeared in the eleventh century. Shorter chronicles describing the tribulations of the Jews began to appear in the twelfth century. On the lack of Jewish historiography, see also Yosef Hayim Yerushalmi, *Zakhor: Jewish History and Jewish Memory*, Washington, University of Washington Press, 2005.

5   Jacques Basnage, *Histoire de la religion des juifs, depuis Jésus-Christ jusqu'à present: Pour servir de supplément et de continuation à l'histoire de Josèphe*, Den Haag: Henry Scheurleer, 1706–7.

some sympathy, saw the Jews as having been, throughout the Middle Ages, the chosen victims of the corrupt papacy. Only the progress of enlightened Protestant reform would eventually lead the Jews to salvation—namely, the great day when they would at last convert to Christianity.[6]

About a hundred years later, when the German-Jewish historian Isaak Markus Jost sat down to write a history of the Jews, he used Basnage's writing as his model. Although he also criticized it, he preserved the structure of the Protestant historian's work. The first of the nine volumes of Jost's pioneering work—*A History of the Israelites from the Time of the Maccabees to Our Time*[7]—appeared in 1820. The term "Israelites" was adopted by German and French persons "of the religion of Moses," who preferred it to "Jews," a term charged with negative connotations.

This work would surprise today's readers, because this first modern attempt to tell the complete history of the Jews, written by a historian who saw himself as a Jew, skipped over the biblical period. Jost's long story opens with the kingdom of Judea under the Hasmoneans, followed by monographs reconstructing the histories of various Jewish communities up to modern times. This is a nonconsecutive narrative, broken into numerous stories, but its most memorable aspect is the fact that it lacks the "beginning" that would later be viewed as integral to the history of Jews in the world. By the latter half of the nineteenth century, the time of nationalist formation, which saw the "restoration" of the Bible to many Jewish literati in Europe, this historiographic feature must have seemed strange.

To understand this first methodical study of the history of Jews through the ages, we must remember that its gifted author was not yet a national historian or, more precisely, not a national Jew. We have to look over Jost's shoulder and appreciate his sensitivities as part of the new mental fabric of the young intelligentsia emerging from the old Jewish world. During the first two decades of the nineteenth century, the self-perception of German-Jewish intellectuals—even those who were "very Jewish"—was largely cultural and religious. At that time, the young Germany was not so much a political entity as a cultural-linguistic concept. This society of speakers of various dialects of German—a society of which the Jews constituted 1 percent—had recently begun the relative unification imposed by the French invader. Most of the intellectuals, whether of Jewish or of Christian background, had not yet fully responded to the political seduction of nationalism, though a few of them,

6 See the article by Jonathan M. Elukin, "Jacques Basnage and the History of the Jews: Anti-Catholic Polemic and Historical Allegory in the Republic of Letters," *Journal of the History of Ideas* 53:4 (1992), 603–30.

7 Isaak Markus Jost, *Geschichte der Israeliten seit der Zeit der Makkabäer bis auf unsere Tage: Nach den Quellen bearbeitet*, 9 vols., Berlin: Schlesinger'sche Buch, 1820–28.

including Jost, were already aware of its first hammer-blows. Most literati of Jewish background were gripped by the project of emancipation, namely, the process of achieving equal civil rights, that had begun to be implemented in part in various German principalities and kingdoms in the second decade of the century, and was a crucial element in the nationalization of politics. Everyone was hoping that the longed-for German state would break away from its clerical foundations and completely privatize all its religions.

Jost was born in Bernburg in central Germany, two years before the founder of critical historiography, Leopold von Ranke. He started his literary career as a typical Enlightenment liberal. He was raised as a Jew, attended a rabbinical school, and continued to cherish certain aspects of Jewish religious culture. Nevertheless, he favored the rising tide of reform, and believed that his life and the life of his community could be harmonized with the emerging historical-political vision of German citizenship.

With a number of friends and colleagues, all of Jewish background, he took part for a short while in creating a "science circle," out of which would emerge the important current that would come to be known as "the science of Judaism"—*Wissenschaft des Judentums*, in German. This movement influenced all Jewish studies in modern times. The members of the circle and their successors were quite conflicted about their identity, and experienced some distress over this issue.[8] These literati belonged to the first generation of German Jews to study at the universities, although their "exceptional" religious background barred them from academic posts. They subsisted as teachers, journalists or Reform rabbis and worked on their philosophical or historical studies in their spare time. As intellectuals whose symbolic capital lay principally in their Jewish heritage, they were unwilling to forgo their cultural distinction and sought to preserve whatever was best in it. At the same time, they longed to be integrated into the emerging Germany. They therefore set out on a complex and difficult intellectual journey, believing that to research the Jewish past and highlight its positive aspects would help build a bridge that could enable the Jewish community to participate in this future Germany.

Thus, at the early stages of writing Jewish history in modern times, the project was not characterized as a national discourse, which accounts for the writers' ambivalence about including biblical history as part of that history. For Jost, as for Leopold Zunz, the second important historian in the early days

---

8   On this intellectual movement, see Maurice-Ruben Hayoun, *La Science du judaïsme*, Paris: Presses Universitaires de France, 1995. See also Paul Mendes-Flohr (ed.), *Modern Jewish Studies: Historical and Philosophical Perspectives*, Jerusalem: Zalman Shazar, 1979 (in Hebrew).

of the science of Judaism, Jewish history began not with the conversion of Abraham, or the Tablets of the Law on Mount Sinai, but with the return of the exiles from Babylonia. It was only then, they argued, that historical-religious Judaism began, its culture having been forged by the experience of exile itself. The Old Testament had nurtured its birth, but it then grew into a universal property that would later inspire the birth of Christianity.[9]

Besides aspiring to civil emancipation, Jost, Zunz and, later, Abraham Geiger, and indeed most nineteenth-century supporters of reform, were guided by the non-Jewish biblical research that was gaining impetus at this time. Jost had been a pupil of Johann Gottfried Eichhorn, one of the gifted pioneers of this critical trend, and was familiar with the new philological criticisms, most of which he willingly adopted.[10] He knew that the Scriptures were written fairly late by various authors and, in addition, lacked external evidence that could substantiate them. This does not mean he doubted the truth of the myth about the rise of the Hebrews and the later consolidation of their kingdom. But he assumed that the period in question was too obscure to serve as the basis for a meaningful historical study. Moreover, the Hebrews in Canaan, despite having the laws of Moses imposed upon them, did not differ from the surrounding pagan peoples. Until their exile to Babylonia, they persistently rejected the divine commandments, which were followed only by a narrow stratum of priests and prophets. The Bible became the work that shaped identity and belief after it was edited and disseminated among a faithful public that truly needed it. "When the Children of Israel came out of Egypt they were primitive and ignorant," writes Jost. "The Jews in Persia studied and learned from the Persians a new religious outlook, a civilized life, language and science."[11] Hence, it was the period of exile, in the broadest sense, that ought to represent the start of Jewish history. The breach between ancient Hebraism and Jewish history came to be the underlying concept for most of the German pioneers of the science of Judaism.[12]

Every historical corroboration depends on ideology, whether overt or hidden. Jost's approach was consistently fair. His great work sought to convince German readers, Jewish and Christian alike, that despite the distinct faith of the "Israelites," they were not an "alien" people in their far-flung habitations. Long before the destruction of the Second Temple, their forefathers

9 On Zunz and the Bible see Reuven Michael, *Historical Jewish Writing*, Jerusalem: Bialik, 1993 (in Hebrew), 207.

10 On Jost's position on the Bible, see Ran HaCohen's gripping work, *Reviving the Old Testament*, Tel-Aviv: Hakibutz Hameuhad, 2006 (in Hebrew), 54–77.

11 Quoted in Michael, *Historical Jewish Writing*, 220.

12 On this subject see Nathan Rotenstreich, *Jewish Thought*, Tel Aviv: Am Oved, 1966 (in Hebrew), 43.

preferred to live outside the Holy Land, and despite their traditional religious self-isolation, they were always an integral part of the peoples among whom they lived. "They remained Jews, although also members of other nations," Jost reiterates. "They loved their brethren in Jerusalem and wished them peace and prosperity, but they cherished their new homeland more. They prayed with their blood brothers, but they went to war with their country brothers. They were friendly toward their blood brothers, but they shed their blood for their homeland."[13]

In the distant past, their homeland had been Babylonia or Persia, whereas then it was mainly post-Napoleonic Germany. Jost was well aware of the early signs of German nationalism and, like most literate individuals of Jewish origin, looked for indirect ways to join it. This accounts for the creation of a historiographic work of amazing scope and originality, which remains utterly unlike all the Jewish histories that followed. In the nineteenth century, a person setting out to write a history of the collective of which he regarded himself to be a member usually did so from nationalist motives. Jost, however, was impelled by quite different intellectual and mental stimuli to reconstruct his history of the Israelites. His premise was that the Jews might share a common origin, but the different Jewish communities were not separate members of a single body. The communities differed widely from place to place in their cultures and ways of life, and were only linked by their distinctive deistic belief. No supra-Jewish political entity separated Jews from non-Jews; hence in the modern world they were entitled to the same civil rights as all the other communities and cultural groups that were rushing to enter the modern nation.

Writing to a friend when his first volume appeared, Jost revealed the political thinking that underlay and motivated his historiographic work:

> The state cannot recognize Jews as legitimate as long as they will not marry the inhabitants of the country. The state exists only by virtue of its people and its people must constitute a unity. Why should it elevate an association whose main principle is that it alone possesses the truth and therefore must avoid all integration with the inhabitants of the country? ... This is the way our children will reason and they will gladly abandon a coercive church to gain freedom, a sense of belonging to the Volk, love of the fatherland and service to the state—the highest possessions of earthly man.[14]

---

13   Quoted in Reuven Michael, *I. M. Jost: Founder of Modern Jewish Historiography*, Jerusalem: Magness Press, 1983 (in Hebrew), 24–5.

14   This letter appeared in Ismar Schorsch, *From Text to Context: The Turn to History in Modern Judaism*, Hanover, NH: Brandeis University Press, 1994, 238.

These plain statements show that Jost clearly identified the basic principles of his time's surging nationalism. But he had doubts about the possibility of a symbiosis between Jews and non-Jews in the emerging German nation, and these doubts would intensify following the wave of conservatism during the 1830s with all its anti-Jewish currents.

The later writings of this pioneering historian show a number of developments. German identity politics would undergo a conceptual upheaval after midcentury, but the first signs of it were discernible even before the revolutions of 1848, and they affected the early reconstruction of the Jewish past. Already in his *General History of the Israelite People*, Jost's short second book that appeared in 1832, the biblical period occupies a larger portion of the story, while the Jews are presented as a unit with a tighter historical sequence.[15] From here on, the tone is rather political, though not yet nationalistic, and the Old Testament becomes a more legitimate source in the narrative of "the Israelite people." In the following years Jost's political opinions became more cautious and hesitant, and he also began to retreat from the biblical criticism he had followed in his first book. This change became manifest in the relative length of the eras he assigned to the early Hebrews and later Jews.

Thus, right from the start, there was a close connection between the perception of the Old Testament as a reliable historical source and the attempt to define modern Jewish identity in prenationalist or nationalist terms. The more nationalistic the author, the more he treats the Bible as history—as the birth certificate attesting to the common origin of the "people." Some of the reformists were interested in the Bible for quite different reasons, such as opposition to the Orthodox rabbinical attachment to the Talmud, or in imitation of Protestant fashions. But from Isaak Jost, through some of the intellectuals who joined the second stage of the science of Judaism, to the appearance of the great innovator Heinrich Graetz, the Old Testament came to serve as the point of departure for the first historiographical exploration into the fascinating invention of the "Jewish nation," an invention that would become increasingly important in the second half of the nineteenth century.

THE OLD TESTAMENT AS MYTHISTORY

Jost's *History of the Israelites*, the first Jewish history composed in modern times, was not very popular in its day, and it is no accident that the work was never translated into other languages, not even into Hebrew. While it suited

---

15 I. M. Jost, *Allgemeine Geschichte des Israelitischen Volkes*, Karlsruhe: D. R. Marx, 1836 (1832).

the outlook of the German-Jewish intellectuals, secular or not, who were involved in the emancipation movement, most of them did not wish to look for their roots in misty antiquity. They saw themselves as German, and insofar as they continued to believe in a providential deity, they described themselves as members of the Mosaic religion and supported the lively Reform current. For most of the literate heirs to the Enlightenment in Central and Western Europe, Judaism was a religious community, certainly not a wandering people or an alien nation.

The rabbis and the traditional religious figures—that is, the "organic" intellectuals of Jewish communities—did not yet have to examine history in order to affirm their identity, which for centuries had been taken for granted.

The first volumes of the *History of the Jews from the Oldest Times to the Present*, by Heinrich Graetz, began to appear in the 1850s. It was very successful, and parts of it were relatively soon translated into Hebrew, as well as into several other languages.[16] This pioneering work, written with impressive literary flair, remained a presence in national Jewish history throughout the twentieth century. It is hard to measure its impact on the rise of future Zionist thought, but there is no question of its significance and centrality. Though this expansive work is short on descriptions of Jewish history in Eastern Europe (Graetz, who was born in Poznań, then part of Germany, and whose mother tongue was Yiddish, refused to have his book translated into his parents' "shameful dialect"), the early nationalist intellectuals in the Russian empire embraced it enthusiastically. We can still find traces of his bold declarations in all their recorded dreams of the "ancient homeland."[17] His work fertilized the imagination of writers and poets eagerly seeking new fields of historical memory that were no longer traditional but nonetheless continued to draw on tradition. He also fostered secular, if not quite atheistic, interest in the Old Testament. Later the first Zionist settlers in Palestine used his work as their road map through the long past. In today's Israel there are schools and streets named after Graetz, and no general historical work about the Jews omits mention of him.

---

16   Heinrich (Hirsch) Grätz, *Geschichte der Juden von den ältesten Zeiten bis auf die Gegenwart*, Leipzig: O. Leiner, [1853–1876] 1909. Parts of the book were translated into Hebrew back in the 1870s, but the (almost) complete translation was done in the twentieth century. In English, it began to appear in the 1860s, and the complete work appeared in London in the 1890s. I used the following edition, Heinrich Graetz, *History of the Jews*, Philadelphia: JPS, 1891–98.

17   According to Shmuel Feiner, Graetz's work became the national history textbook of the Hovevei Zion organization (the Hovevei Zion were the forerunners of the Zionist movement). See *Haskalah and History: The Emergence of a Modern Jewish Historical Consciousness*, Oxford: Littman Library of Jewish Civilization, 2002, 347.

The reason for this massive presence is clear: this was the first work that strove, with consistency and feeling, to invent the Jewish people—the term "people" signifying to some extent the modern term "nation." Although he was never a complete Zionist, Graetz formed the national mold for the writing of Jewish history. He succeeded in creating, with great virtuosity, a unified narrative that minimized problematic multiplicity and created an unbroken history, branching but always singular. Likewise, his basic periodization—bridging chasms of time, and erasing gaps and breaches in space—would serve future Zionist historians, even when they renovated and reshaped it. Henceforth, for many people, Judaism would no longer be a rich and diverse religious civilization that managed to survive despite all difficulties and temptations in the shadow of giants, and became an ancient people or race that was uprooted from its homeland in Canaan and arrived in its youth at the gates of Berlin. The popular Christian myth about the wandering Jew, reproduced by rabbinical Judaism in the early centuries of the Common Era, had acquired a historian who began to translate it into a prenational Jewish narrative.

To create a new paradigm of time, it was necessary to demolish the "faulty and harmful" previous one. To begin the construction of a nation, it was necessary to reject those writings that failed to recognize its primary scaffolding. It was for this reason that Graetz accused his predecessor Jost of "tearing holes" in the history of the Jews:

He tore to shreds the heroic drama of thousands of years. Between the old Israelites, the ancestors and contemporaries of the Prophets and Psalmists, and the Jews, the disciples of the rabbis, Jost hollowed out a deep chasm, making a sharp distinction between them, as if the latter were not the descendants of the former, but of entirely different stock.[18]

What stock produced so many Jews? The next chapter will address this question. For now, it should be noted that a nationalist history—or, strictly speaking, a prenationalist one, since the platform in this case did not include an unambiguous call for political sovereignty—does not tolerate lacunae or perverse aberrations. Graetz sought to mend the unbearable gash that he claimed Jost, Zunz, Geiger and others had caused by their "blindness," and that

---

18 Graetz, *History of the Jews*, vol. 5, 595. Graetz's anger against Jost foreshadows Gershom Scholem's nationalist annoyance with Leopold Zunz and the other historians of the early Science of Judaism, who "have no idea where they are standing, and whether they wish to build up the Jewish nation and the Jewish people, or to help bring them down." See *Explications and Implications: Writings on Jewish Heritage and Renaissance*, Tel Aviv: Am Oved, 1975 (in Hebrew), 388.

prevented them from seeing the ancient kingdom as a legitimate chapter in Jewish history—thereby condemning the Jews to continue seeing themselves as members of a mere religious civilization rather than as an eternal people or tribe (*Volksstamm*).

Graetz's sharp criticism doesn't appear in the early part of this work but toward its end, in the volume about the modern era, which he wrote several years after Jost's death in 1860. When Graetz began publishing his immense oeuvre in 1853, he too, like Basnage and Jost, began the Jewish narrative after the biblical period, and the first volume covered the time of the Mishnah and Talmud, after the fall of the Temple. Shortly afterward, he returned to the period of the Hasmonean kingdom, but only twenty years later—that is, after the rise of the Second Reich and the unification of Germany by Bismarck's Prussia, with nationalism triumphantly increasing throughout Central and Southern Europe—did Graetz's protonationalist position achieve its final, mature form.[19] Only after he had summed up the history of the Jews in his time, and concluded his book with the mid-nineteenth-century present, in a defiant and bitter tone, did Graetz retreat chronologically in order to reconstruct the birth of the "chosen moral people." It was no accident that what was presented as the first national-historical epic ever written about the Jews should culminate with the biblical era.

For there to be a national consciousness, a modern collective identity, both mythology and teleology are required. The foundation myth was, of course, the textual cosmos of the Old Testament, whose narrative, historical component became a vibrant mythos in the latter half of the nineteenth century, despite the philological criticisms aimed at it.[20] For Graetz, the teleology was nurtured by a vague and not yet wholly nationalist assumption that the eternal Jewish people were destined to bring salvation to the world.

The centuries-old Jewish communities never thought of the Old Testament as an independent work that could be read without the interpretation and mediation of the "oral Torah" (the Mishnah and Talmud). It had become, mainly among the Jews of Eastern Europe, a marginal book that could be understood only through the Halakhah (religious law) and of course its authorized commentators. The Mishnah and Talmud were the Jewish texts in regular use; passages from the Torah (the Pentateuch) were introduced, without any narrative continuity, in

---

19   On the background to this book's writing, see Reuven Michael, *Hirsch (Heinrich) Graetz: The Historian of the Jewish People*, Jerusalem: Bialik, 2003 (in Hebrew), 69–93 and 148–60.

20   For example, *The Love of Zion* (London: Marshall Simpkin, 1887), the first novel written in biblical Hebrew, by Abraham Mapu, published in 1853, clothes the Kingdom of Judah in nationalist-romantic glory.

the form of a weekly section read aloud in the synagogues. The Old Testament as a whole remained the leading work for the Karaites in the distant past and for Protestants in modern times. For most Jews through the centuries, the Bible was holy scripture and thus not really accessible to the mind, just as the Holy Land was barely present in the religious imagination as an actual place on earth.

Mostly products of rabbinical schools, educated Jews who were feeling the effects of the secular age and whose metaphysical faith was beginning to show a few cracks longed for another source to reinforce their uncertain, crumbling identity. The religion of history struck them as an appropriate substitute for religious faith, but for those who, sensibly, could not embrace the national mythologies arising before their eyes—mythologies unfortunately bound up with a pagan or Christian past—the only option was to invent and adhere to a parallel national mythology. This was assisted by the fact that the literary source for this mythology, namely the Old Testament, remained an object of adoration even for confirmed haters of contemporary Jews. And since their putative ancient kingdom in its own homeland presented the strongest evidence that Jews were a people or a nation—not merely a religious community that lived in the shadow of other, hegemonic religions—the awkward crawl toward the Book of Books turned into a determined march in the imagining of a Jewish people.

Like other national movements in nineteenth-century Europe that were searching for a golden age in an invented heroic past (classical Greece, the Roman Republic, the Teutonic or Gallic tribes) so as to show they were not newly emerged entities but had existed since time immemorial, the early buds of Jewish nationalism turned to the mythological kingdom of David, whose radiance and power had been stored across the centuries in the batteries of religious belief.

By the 1870s—after Darwin and *The Origin of Species*—it was not possible to begin a serious history with the story of Creation. Graetz's work, therefore, unlike Josephus's ancient history, opened with the "settlement of Israel in the land and the start of their becoming a people." The early miracles were omitted to make the work more scientific. Reducing the tales of the patriarchs and the Exodus from Egypt to brief summaries was, oddly, supposed to make the work more nationalistic. Graetz describes Abraham the Hebrew succinctly, and Moses in a couple of pages. To him it was mother earth, the ancient national territory—rather than migration, wandering, and the Torah—that bred nations. The land of Canaan, with its "marvelous" flora and fauna and distinctive climate, produced the exceptional character of the Jewish nation, which in infancy took its first bold, precocious steps in that setting. The nature of a people is determined in the very beginning, and thereafter will never change:

And if when this nation was still in its infancy, the spiritual seeds were already burgeoning in its spirit, and its heart felt, though dimly, that it was destined to do great deeds, which would distinguish it from the other peoples and make it superior, and if its teachers and mentors instructed it till that dim feeling grew into a mighty faith—then it was not possible that such a nation in such a setting would not develop special qualities that would never be expunged from its heart.[21]

Having made this statement, Graetz begins to follow the biblical story closely, highlighting in fine literary language the heroic deeds, the military prowess, the sovereignty of the kingdom, and above all the moral vigor of the "childhood of the Jewish nation." While he voices some cautious reservations about the later books of the Old Testament, he presents the story following the conquest of Canaan as a solid block of unquestionable truth, a position he upheld to his dying day. To him, "the Children of Israel" who cross the river and conquer the land of Canaan, which had been willed to their forefathers, were the descendants of a single primeval clan.

Graetz strives to provide rational explanations for the miracles, but he also demotes them from central narrative to addenda. The prophecies he leaves intact, however, though it was human action that made them decisive. Thus the actions of the heroic judges and the triumph of young David over Goliath, for example, are related in some detail, and the rise of the redheaded young man to power and the consolidation of his kingdom fill many pages. Although David was quite a sinner, God and Graetz forgive the bold king, who became a paragon in Judaism "on account of his great deeds," which were always done for the people. The kingdom of Solomon also receives a whole chapter, because it was "a vast and mighty realm that could rival the greatest kingdoms on earth." Graetz estimates its population as some four million; its division into two kingdoms marked the beginning of its decline. The sinful kingdom of Israel caused its own destruction, and eventually the same fate overtook the last kings of Judah.

The story of the sad fate of the children of Israel is bound up with the religious concept of sin, but greater blame is placed on the daughters of Israel: "It is a striking fact that Israelitish women, the appointed priestesses of chastity and morality, displayed a special inclination for the immoral worship of Baal and Astarte."[22] But fortunately, the ancient children of Israel also had prophets, who struggled with all their might to guide the people to a high, sublime morality, a unique ethos known by no other people.

---

21   Graetz, *History of the Jews*, vol. 1, 7.

22   Ibid., 213. See Heinrich Graetz, *Essays–Memoirs–Letters*, Jerusalem: Bjalik, 1969 (in Hebrew), 131.

Graetz remains faithful to the central narratives and is always full of awe for the Old Testament; when he runs into contradictions in biblical ideology, he sometimes presents the different approaches without trying to reconcile them. For example, parallel with the isolationist policy of Ezra, leader of the returnees from Babylonian exile, Graetz describes the life of Ruth the Moabite, King David's gentile great-grandmother. Skillfully, he reconstructs the moral and political contrasts between the two, and for a moment it seems as if he cannot decide between them. Graetz clearly understood the significance of annulling mixed marriages and expelling gentile women along with their children. He writes:

> Ezra held this to be a terrible sin. For the Judean or Israelitish race was in his eyes a holy one, and suffered desecration by mingling with foreign tribes, even though they had abjured idolatry ... That moment was to decide the fate of the Judean people. Ezra, and those who thought as he did, raised a wall of separation between the Judeans and the rest of the world.[23]

Graetz does not hesitate to add that this move provoked hatred for the Jews for the first time. This may be the reason for the emphasis he places on the story of Ruth—aware that it was a universalist challenge to the concept of "holy seed," held by the returnees from Babylonia. Ultimately, however, he throws his full support behind the invention of an exclusive Judaism and the rigid demarcation of its boundaries as laid down by its pioneers, Ezra and Nehemiah.

A romantic conception based on an ethnoreligious foundation had already guided Graetz in the earlier volumes, but not so forcefully. He was, after all, a historian of ideas, and his earlier volumes about the history of the Jews recounted their literary heritage and focused primarily on its moral and religious content. At the same time, the hardening of German nationalist definitions based on origin and race, especially in the formative years after the failure of the national-democratic Spring of the Nations in 1848, stirred new sensitivities among a small group of intellectuals of Jewish descent. Graetz, for all his doubts and hesitations, was one of them. The sharpest senses belonged to Moses Hess, a leftist and a man of intellectual boldness, a former friend of Karl Marx, whose book *Rome and Jerusalem: The Last Nationalist Question* had appeared in 1862.[24] This was an unmistakable nationalist manifesto, perhaps the first of its kind in being quite secular. Since his position was fairly decisive in shaping Graetz's Jewish history, we should consider briefly the relations between the two.

---

23   Graetz, *History of the Jews*, vol. 1, 367–8.
24   Moses Hess, *Rome and Jerusalem: A Study in Jewish Nationalism*, New York: Bloch Publishing Company, 1918.

RACE AND NATION

In the foreword to *Rome and Jerusalem*, Hess quotes Graetz with enthusiasm. The Jewish historian's work (volume five) had informed him that even with the Talmud, the history of the Jews "still possesses a national character; it is by no means merely a creed or church history."[1] This striking revelation was the answer to the mental struggles of the weary revolutionary, whose daily encounters with anti-Jewish expressions, political and philosophical, in Germany drove him to discover his "national being." Throughout his work he makes no effort to hide his dislike of the Germans and does not cease to berate them. He prefers the French, and still more the "authentic" Jews.

Driven out of Germany, Hess moved to France. The failure of the revolutions in Europe caused him, he said, to retire temporarily from politics and to concentrate on natural science. His intense pseudoscientific reading introduced him to the racist theories that began to simmer in the 1850s.

It was in 1850 that the Scotsman Robert Knox published his well-known book *The Races of Man*; two years later, James W. Redfield's book *Comparative Physiognomy, or, Resemblances between Men and Animals*, appeared in the United States. In 1853 Carl Gustav Carus's *Symbolism of the Human Form* appeared in Germany, as well as the first volume of the Frenchman Arthur de Gobineau's *Essay on the Inequality of the Human Races*.[2] These works were followed by other "scientific" books, and some of the leading thinkers in the second half of the nineteenth century began to paddle happily in the swamp of racist and Orientalist conventions. The fashion spread, gathering support among both the political left and prominent academics. Thinkers from Karl Marx to Ernest Renan published prejudiced writings about Jews, Africans or the peoples of the Orient, which very quickly became the norm.

To account for the popularity of race theory in the centers of Western culture, we must consider the European sense of superiority based on rapid industrial and technological development in the West and center of the Continent, and how this was interpreted as reflecting biological and moral ascendancy. Furthermore, the progress made in the developmental sciences gave rise to comparative

---

1   Ibid., 39.
2   Robert Knox, *The Races of Men*, London: Beaufort Books, 1950; James W. Redfield, *Comparative Physiognomy or Resemblances between Men and Animals*, Whitefish, MT: Kessinger Publishing, 2003; Carl Gustav Carus, *Symbolik der Menschlichen Gestalt*, Hildescheim: G. Olms, 1962; Joseph-Arthur de Gobineau, *The Inequality of Human Races*, New York: Howard Fertig, 1999. Significantly, Johannes Nordmann's groundbreaking book, *Die Juden und der Deutsche Staat*, Berlin: Nicolai, 1861, appeared a year before *Rome and Jerusalem*, and was perhaps the first to set anti-Jewishness on a racial basis.

fantasies linking the life sciences with social studies and history. Racial theory came to be almost unquestioned and unchallenged until the 1880s.

Hess devoured the new literature, and his sharp senses—which had previously made him a communist, perhaps the first in Germany—now led him to a new conclusion: "that behind the problems of nationality and freedom there is a still deeper problem which cannot be solved by mere phrases, namely, the race question, which is as old as history itself and which must be solved before attempting the solution of the political and social problems."[27]

Past history consisted entirely of continuing stories of racial conflicts and class wars, but racial conflicts predominated. Until these bloody struggles come to an end, contends Hess, the Jews—at least those in Eastern Europe—should return to their place of origin, meaning the Holy Land. Hess concluded that the reason Jews were in conflict with gentiles was that they had always been a distinct racial group. The beginning of this ancient and persistent race could be found in Egypt. The murals in the tombs of the pharaohs depicted, among the builders of the temples and palaces, human types whose physiognomy was identical with that of modern Jews. "The Jewish race is one of the primary races of mankind that has retained its integrity," writes Hess, "in spite of the continual change of its climatic environment, and the Jewish type has conserved its purity through the centuries." He continues: "Jews and Jewesses endeavor, in vain, to obliterate their descent through conversion or intermarriage with the Indo-Germanic and Mongolian races, for the Jewish type is indestructible."[28]

What accounts for the marvelous longevity of this nation? Hess reiterates throughout the book that the answer is, above all, its religion and faith. He disdains the reformists as much as he mocks the followers of emancipation in Germany. The Jewish religion is a national tradition that prevented the assimilation of the Jewish people. Assimilation was impossible to begin with, however. Make no mistake—for all its importance, religion was not alone in preserving the Jewish identity:

> Thus it is not theory that forms life, but race; and likewise, it is not doctrine that made the Biblical-patriarchal life, which is the source of Jewish cult, but it is the patriarchal life of the Jewish ancestors that is the creative basis of the religion of the Bible, which is nothing else but a national historical cult developed out of family traditions.[29]

---

27 Hess, *Rome and Jerusalem*, 40.
28 Ibid., 59, 61.
29 Ibid., 85. For apologetic writing on Hess, see Shlomo Avineri, *Moses Hess: Prophet of Communism and Zionism*, New York: New York University Press, 1985.

Much of this basic position about "national origin-religion" is implied in the foreword to the first volume of Graetz's *History of the Jews*. Whereas Graetz's concept of history had until then tended to be dualistic, wavering between the spiritual and the material, Hess's racial "materialism" helped shift it to a still harder essentialist and nationalist position. By 1860 and the fifth (early) volume, which Hess praised in *Rome and Jerusalem*, Graetz depicted Jewish history before and even after the exile as made up of two essential elements. On the one hand, the apparently immortal Jewish tribe was the body, while the Jewish religion, no less eternal, was the soul. But from the late 1860s onward, Graetz's history presented the body as more decisive in the definition of the Jews, although divine Providence continued to hover over them through history.

Graetz read *Rome and Jerusalem* before meeting its author. That meeting began their close friendship and extensive correspondence, which went on till Hess's death in 1875. The two even planned to journey together to the old "ancestral land," but eventually the historian traveled there on his own. A year after the appearance of Hess's book, Graetz published a fascinating essay of his own, entitled "The Rejuvenation of the Jewish Race."[30] This is largely an unstated dialogue with Hess, and though it suggests some doubts and hesitations, it also reveals a partial acceptance of the ideological breakthrough of which Hess was one of the catalysts. The "Rejuvenation" reveals not only the means by which the Jewish people are invented in Graetz's writing, but also the historian's acute consciousness of the nationality issue roiling many circles of European intelligentsia.

What gives a human community the right to present itself as a nation, Graetz wonders, and replies that it is not a racial origin, because sometimes different racial types join up to form one people. Nor is language necessarily the common denominator, as shown by Switzerland, for instance. Even a unified territory is not enough for a national formation. Do historical memories unify peoples, asks Graetz, and responds with a sharp and prescient historical observation—that until the modern era the peoples did not take part in political history, but passively viewed the deeds of leaders and rulers. Was it, then, high culture that provided the basis for a nationality? No, because it, too, is new, and has not yet been acquired by the entire people. The existence of nations is a mystery, and there seems to be no single way to account for them.

As Graetz puts it, there have obviously been mortal peoples that vanished in history and others that are immortal. Nothing is left of the Hellenic and Latin races, which have dissolved into other human divisions. By contrast, the Jewish race has succeeded in preserving itself and surviving, and is about to

---

30   In Graetz, *Essays–Memoirs–Letters*, 103–109.

renew its marvelous biblical youth. Its revival after the Babylonian exile and the return to Zion revealed its potential for renewal. Thus, the people are an organic body with a miraculous capacity for rebirth, which distinguishes them from ordinary biological organisms. The existence of the Jewish race had been unique from the start, which is why its history is a marvel. It is, in fact, a "messianic people" that will eventually save all of mankind. For Graetz, the teleology of the chosen people is more moral than political, retaining some dusty remnants of a crumbling traditional belief.

Like all nation-fostering historians in the nineteenth century, Graetz assumed that the history of his nation was sublime and not to be compared with any other national history. We shall come across echoes of this (admittedly unoriginal) thesis in the final parts of the *History of the Jews*, written in the second half of the 1860s and early 1870s. The national aspect is especially prominent in the volume devoted to Jewish history in modern times (up to the 1848 revolutions) and even more so, as noted earlier, in the final two volumes of the work, in which the historian sought to reconstruct the biblical genealogy of the Jews. The conceited tone of these volumes provoked the ire of another historian.

A HISTORIANS' DISPUTE

In the 1870s Heinrich von Treitschke was a well-known historian holding a respected chair at the University of Berlin. His highly praised work *The History of Germany in the Nineteenth Century* began to appear in 1879, and that year the prestigious magazine *Prussian Yearbooks,* of which he was coeditor, published an important essay of his. The essay was entitled "One Word about Our Jewry" and was arguably the first academic legitimation of scholarly revulsion for the Jewish identity.

The respected historian's chief anxiety was demographic. Waves of Jewish immigrants from Eastern Europe had enlarged the Jewish presence in Germany, which was perceived as a threat to the German nation's very existence. These immigrants, Treitschke argued, did not in the least resemble Jews of Spanish origin. The latter had lived in a tolerant society and therefore became well integrated into their host nations in Western Europe. But Polish Jews had suffered from Christianity's heavy hand, which left them deformed and alien to the superior German culture, so that their integration might give rise to a mongrel German-Jewish culture. These Jews would have to make a tremendous effort to assimilate into the German nation, which was still barred to them. But this hoped-for development was far from being achieved, because they were being led by scholars who preached self-segregation, notably the impertinent historian Heinrich Graetz. Treitschke had read *History of the Jews*, or at any rate its final volumes, and was enraged:

> Do read Graetz's *History of the Jews*: what zealous rage against the "age-old enemy," Christianity, what deadly hatred for purest and grandest representatives of the German nation, from Luther to Goethe and Fichte! And what overblown, hollow and offensive pride! ... Nor is this rigid hatred for the German "gentiles" by any means confined to the mind of a single zealot.[31]

Graetz was not intimidated by Treitschke's high standing, and wrote a closely argued response to the anti-Jewish critique. But he could not resist concluding his article with a provocative quote from Benjamin Disraeli:

> You cannot destroy a pure Caucasian race. This is a psychological fact, a law of nature, that dismayed the kings of Egypt and Assyria, Roman emperors and Christian inquisitors. No punitive system, no physical torture, can cause a superior race to be consumed or destroyed by an inferior one.[32]

Faced with such nationalist "obstinacy," Treitschke heightened the tone and bared his historiographical teeth: "A full merger of Jewry with the peoples of the West will never be achieved. It may only be possible to soften the opposition, since it is rooted in ancient history."[33] Moreover, he discerned in Graetz an aspiration to have Jewry acknowledged as a nation within the German nation, an aspiration that every "authentic" German had to reject out of hand. He went on to charge Graetz with nationalist Jewish conceit, and wondered at length if the latter saw himself as a German in any way. No, he concluded, Graetz was an alien in his accidental homeland, an Oriental "who neither understands nor wants to understand our nation; he and we have nothing in common, except that he possesses our citizenship and uses our mother tongue—though only in order to curse and swear at us." Then the Prussian historian let rip:

> But if this racial conceit becomes public, if Jewry even demands recognition of its national status, it demolishes the legal foundation of emancipation. There is only one way to fulfill these aspirations: emigration, the creation of a Jewish state somewhere outside our country, and then it will see if it can win the recognition of other nations. There is no room for dual nationhood

---

31   Ibid., 213–14. A large part of this debate appeared in Hebrew in this volume. See also Michael A. Meyer, "Heinrich Graetz and Heinrich von Treitschke: A Comparison of Their Historical Images of the Modern Jew," *Modern Judaism* 6:1 (1986), 1–11.

32   Graetz, *Essays–Memoirs–Letters*, 218.

33   Ibid., 222.

on Germany's soil. It took thousands of years of toil to construct the German states, and Jews had no part in that.[34]

Treitschke's detestation of Jews' "origin in the East" would grow more extreme. For now, it was a middle-of-the-road position between civil nationalism and outright racial nationalism. Unlike more vulgar anti-Semites, such as Wilhelm Marr or Adolf Stoecker, he did not rule out the possibility of Jews "joining" the German nation. But his long-term historical contrast between a Jewish people and a German people revealed his essentialist tendency to regard Jewishness and Germanity as two contradictory, hence irreconcilable, identities. Treitschke's nationalism was suffused with an ethnicist-essentialist outlook, in which the Jew remained a Jew even if his culture and language were purely German. In this he was, in fact, not very different in principle from Graetz, who in the final chapters of his book presented similar, even identical, positions.

While Graetz was not yet a full-fledged nationalist historian, his entire opus is imbued with an abstract, if ambiguous, longing for state sovereignty. Though he was one of the first thinkers who helped construct a new secular link between the Jews and their "ancient homeland," he remained, unlike his opponent Treitschke or his friend Hess, skeptical about Jewish migration to that homeland. Despite his association with Hess, and his brief but emotional visit to the ancestral land, he was not actually a Zionist. That is why in his second response to Treitschke's challenge he retreated, evaded and disingenuously denied that he had ever defined Judaism as a nationality. In the heat of the debate, and possibly in view of the harsh reactions of most German-Jewish intellectuals, Graetz momentarily saw himself again as a thorough German who demanded nothing but equal rights. And since Treitschke disparaged Graetz's non-German origin, the author of *History of the Jews* repaid the Berlin historian with the same toxic currency: Is not Treitschke a Slavic name?

The clash of the two ethnocentric historians exposed the significant inner struggle in the consolidation of German nationalism. For both Graetz and Treitschke, the nation was principally a matter of descent, the product of an ancient, linear and prolonged history, supported by, respectively, Germanic mythology or the Old Testament. The nation is in effect a "people-race," originating in the distant past, whose weight determines and outlines collective identities in the present. Both historians were imbued with a *völkisch* national outlook, whence their doubts about the possibility of symbiosis between Germans of Jewish background and Germans of Christian origin. Neither

---

34   Ibid., 226–7.

believed that there was much point in trying to bolster such interrelations, since in the imagined national roots of both groups there had never been a divorce between "Jews" and "Germans," as there had never been a marriage.

It should be noted that more than a few German intellectuals of non-Jewish origin disputed this pessimistic and deterministic position. As pointed out in the first chapter, it is a mistake to assume that all the proponents of German nationalism were of the *völkisch* persuasion or anti-Semitic. Many liberals, as well as most social democrats, believed in the inclusive republican identity, of which the German Jews were an integral part. Similarly, the German-Jewish intelligentsia, which was naturally appalled by Treitschke's hostility, was sharply at odds with Graetz's national-ethnicist position. From Moritz Lazarus, a professor of philosophy at Berlin University, through Harry Bresslau, his colleague in the history department, to Hermann Cohen, Graetz's former student who became a well-known neo-Kantian philosopher at the University of Marburg, all were strongly critical of Graetz. They all agreed that there could not be two nationalities in a single state, but also maintained that there should be diversity within the unifying nation. Germanity itself was a historical product of various cultural elements, they argued, and it was flexible enough to continue absorbing them. The Jews, like other subjects of the empire, Protestants and Catholics, were first of all Germans and only second-arily Jews. No doubt some of the intellectuals of Jewish background believed in their distinct racial origin, but almost all decided that what mattered was the future national-cultural project, and that project was German.

The problem was that the elevated dispute among the historians was taking place in a murky atmosphere of low-level anti-Semitism that had spread through various parts of society. A series of economic crises during the 1870s, while it did not block the accelerating forces of industrialization, created a sense of economic insecurity that was immediately translated into anxieties of identity, a historical phenomenon that would become familiar in the twentieth century. The decisive victory of 1870 and the unification of the Reich "from above" soon lost their unifying glory, and the people blamed for the crises were, as always, the "others"—the religious and "racial" minorities. The progress of mass democracy also stimulated the rise of political anti-Semitism—an effective means of rallying mass support in modern times. From the streets through the press to the corridors of imperial power, venomous propaganda was aimed at the "Orientals" who had come from the East and "claimed to be Germans." There were open calls to repeal the emancipation. It was in this suffocating atmosphere that a public petition appeared in 1880, signed by seventy-five intellectuals and liberal public figures of non-Jewish origin, seeking to defuse and thwart the renewed wave of anti-Semitism. One of the most prominent and prestigious signatories was Theodor Mommsen.

This great historian of ancient Rome was not content merely to append his signature; he chose to get involved in the debate about the "Jewish question." He clearly understood that the issue was not just the status of the Jews, but the nature and quality of German nationality. A few months after the petition, he published a fascinating essay entitled "Another Word about Our Jewry."[35] It was a direct reply to his colleague Treitschke, and from then on, the debate of the historians involved three leading spokesmen.

Make no mistake: both as a historian and a citizen, Mommsen was a nationalist. He supported the unification of Germany and even its forcible annexation of Alsace-Lorraine. But he was worried by the growing ethnicization of German nationalism in the 1870s, which prompted him to write, ironically:

> We shall soon have a situation in which a full citizen will be only one who can look back on his origins and see himself as a descendant of one of the three sons of Mannus; secondly, who believes in the Gospels only as a priest interprets them; thirdly, who is skilled at plowing and sowing.[36]

To construct a modern nation in the light of Tacitus's writings about ancient Germany would mean leaving out not only the German Jews but a good many other inhabitants of the Reich. The author of *History of Rome*, who had been a revolutionary republican in his youth, always held to a civil concept of nationalism. Like all nineteenth-century historians, Mommsen assumed, naively, that nations and nationalism had existed since antiquity. But if Treitschke saw the origin of the German nation in the Teutonic kingdoms, and Graetz saw the source of the Jewish nation in the kingdom of David and Solomon, for Mommsen the supreme historical model was Rome in the time of Julius Caesar, with its open and flexible concept of citizenship. His imagined nation evolved from the dual source of his political past and his historiographic work. He detested the isolationism inherent in ancient identities, just as he despised the modern racism in his own political present. His knowledge of the ancient history of Judea came mostly through imperial Roman sources, although the first page of the chapter entitled "Judah and the Jews" in his *History of Rome* suggests that he was also well acquainted with Jost's writing. Mommsen did not think that the Judeans were necessarily the spiritual successors of the ancient

35 Theodor Mommsen, *Auch ein Wort über unser Judenhtum*, Berlin: Weidmannsche Buchhandlung, 1881.

36 Ibid., 4.

Hebrews, and assumed that most of the Jews throughout the Roman Empire were not direct biological descendants of the inhabitants of Judea.[37]

His anti-essentialist historical view of the development of nations came to the fore in the Treitschke-Graetz dispute. To Mommsen, the Jews were not an alien people-race but one of the tribes or communities integral to the new Germany. They were no different, in principle, from the people of Schleswig-Holstein, Mommsen's birthplace, or the population of Hanover or Hesse. A modern nation is the result of the blending of diverse cultural components from different sources. He felt that the Jews should indeed integrate into their surroundings—shedding, to the best of their consciousness and ability, a significant degree of their isolationist distinctiveness—but that they ought to do so just as any of Germany's other tribes had to forgo some elements of their premodern local culture. The Jews had entered the German nation through a different gate than Germany's other tribes, but this entrance gave them a distinctive quality:

> Without doubt, just as the Jews in the Roman Empire were an element that dismantled nations, they are an element dismantling tribalism in Germany. We ought to be pleased that in Germany's capital, where these tribes have gathered more than elsewhere, the Jews occupy an enviable position. I see no harm at all in the fact that the Jews have been efficiently working this way for ages. Altogether, it seems to be that God understood much better than Mr. Stoecker why it took a certain percentage of Jews to temper the German steel.[38]

It is clear that Mommsen regarded the Jews, who had functioned as dismantlers of prenational provincialisms, not merely as Germans but as the promising first agents of the new Germanity. The Jews were relatively urban and bourgeois, had a prominent presence in the educated classes, and made a major contribution to the spread of High German, which had become the national language.

As we know, this liberal attitude of Mommsen and other German national liberals would lose out in the long run. Not only was their model of civil nationalism defeated in the first half of the twentieth century but, ironically, in 1933, at the conference of the National Socialist German Workers' Party, the scholarly Joseph Goebbels praised the great Mommsen's "dismantling element" as

---

37   Theodor Mommsen, *Römische Geschichte*, VII, München: Deutscher Taschenbuch Verlag, 1976, 188–250 (English translation, *The History of Rome*, New York: Meridian Books, 1958). The next chapter discusses this outlook extensively.

38   Mommsen, *Auch ein Wort*, 9–10. See a comparison between Mommsen's and Treitschke's approaches in Hans Liebeschütz, "Treitschke and Mommsen on Jewry and Judaism," *Leo Baeck Institute Yearbook*, vol. 7, 1962, 153–82.

a model anti-Jewish position—similar, in his view, to Richard Wagner's idea of the Jew.[39] Treitschke and Graetz did not respond publicly to Mommsen's intervention, though obviously neither one welcomed a third position that dismantled such a "natural and logical" ethnonational discourse. Graetz's entire oeuvre was directed against the historiography notably represented by Jost in the early nineteenth century and Mommsen in the later nineteenth. He regarded this position as anti-Jewish because it firmly rejected the continuity and eternity of a Jewish people-race—paralleling that of the German *Volk*—which, in the biblical narrative, had been born in earliest times and then scattered throughout the world.

A PROTONATIONALIST VIEW FROM THE EAST

Beside his historiographic work, Graetz devoted much of his time in the last years of his life to the study of the Old Testament, which had in the meantime become the book of the Jewish national revival. He willingly accepted the principle of biblical philological critique, and even offered various suggestions as to when some of the late books were composed, but to his dying day continued to rebut any historical challenges to it. He was especially committed to the trustworthiness of the Pentateuch and totally rejected the many attempts to date its composition to several different periods. For example, he regarded Spinoza's hypothesis that the Old Testament, or parts thereof, was written by Ezra to be idiotic.[40] For Graetz, the Pentateuch was written not long after the events it described, and all that it recounted was historically accurate. The overwhelming proof was that the late prophets reiterated precisely the biblical stories "written" hundreds of years earlier. The idea that those stories could have been composed in that same late period did not even cross his mind.

In 1882 the well-known biblical scholar Julius Wellhausen published his *Prolegomena to the History of Israel*, which became the most authoritative work of biblical commentary of its time.[41] Wellhausen summarized and developed, by an ingenious and complex synthesis, a century of research that had attempted to date the composition of different parts of the ancient work. A brilliant philological analysis led him to doubt the historicity of some of the

39   Joseph Goebbels, "Rassenfrage und Weltpropaganda," in *Reichstagung in Nürnberg 1933*, Julius Streicher (ed.), Berlin: Vaterländischer Verlag C. A. Weller, 1933, 131–42.

40   See for example his article "Judaism and the critic of the Bible," *Essays–Memoirs–Letters*, 238–40.

41   Julius Wellhausen, *Prolegomena*, Charleston: BiblioBazaar, 2007. See also Ernest Nicholson, *The Pentateuch in the Twentieth Century: The Legacy of Julius Wellhausen*, Oxford: Oxford University Press, 2002.

biblical stories and to conclude that certain key passages were written long after the events they described. As he saw it, the Jewish religion had developed in stages, and every layer in the Pentateuch indicated a different date of composition. Graetz launched a furious attack on this "anti-Jewish" work (and, as we shall see, almost all the Jewish-nationalist historians would follow his example). He was especially incensed by Wellhausen's idea that the Priestly Codex, a major part of the Old Testament, was written after the return from the Babylonian exile. This meant that the narrative of the ancient history of the Jews was not the culture of a mighty and superb nation but that of a tiny sect, which he described as "bloodless," that returned from Babylonia. This opened the way to challenge the veracity of the heroic stories about the origin of the Jewish nation. In the eyes of the first protonationalist Jewish historian, this exposed Wellhausen as an ignoramus motivated mainly by hatred for the Jews ("He pours his hatred for the Jewish nose on Abraham, Moses and Ezra"). For that matter, the well-known French philologist and historian Ernest Renan, author of the *History of Israel*, also came in for fierce criticism from Graetz, who regarded him as no less ignorant and anti-Semitic than his German colleague Wellhausen. As far as Graetz was concerned, a scholar who was not a Jew could not understand the unique significance of Jewish history.

When Graetz died in 1891, Simon Dubnow, a native of Belorussia who had been educated in a rabbinical school but was otherwise self-taught, published a moving obituary in his honor. The young Dubnow even undertook to translate into Russian the biblical chapters from Graetz's last work, *Popular History of the Jews*.[42] Although published, this book had been condemned and destroyed by the Russian censors, because the Pravoslav church viewed Graetz's would-be biblical-national revisionism as an offense against "sacred history." It was this labor of translation, as well as an early and enthusiastic reading of, oddly enough, the first volume of Renan's *History of Israel*,[43] that prompted Dubnow to devote himself to the Jews and compose their history from the time they "emerged from the desert" to the modern era.

It was no accident that Graetz's successor was a product of the Yiddish-speaking population of Eastern Europe rather than an academic historian in a prestigious scholarly center in Berlin or Paris. Unlike the German empire, the Russian empire contained a vast Jewish population whose language differed from that of the majority. While the religion that had held it together for

---

42   Heinrich Grätz, *Volkstümliche Geschichte der Juden*, 3 vols., Leipzig: O. Leiner, 1889–1908.

43   See Simon Dubnow, *La Livre de ma vie: souvenirs et réflexions, matériaux pour l'histoire de mon temps*, Paris: Cerf, 2001, 289.

generations was weakening, it had a thriving secular culture of its own. Such a modernizing process had never taken place among the Jews of Central and Western Europe. The rise of nationalism in the surrounding societies—Russian, Ukrainian, Polish and others—in addition to the systemic discrimination in the Tsarist realm, worsened the situation of the growing Yiddishist community, whose more dynamic element was driven to migrate westward. The nationalist feelings that began to simmer in the remaining communities, especially after the wave of pogroms in the early 1880s, had no parallel in any contemporary Jewish community. There arose intellectuals and movements that were both prenationalist and nationalist—from the numerous supporters of autonomy to the handful of early Zionists—all searching for an independent collective expression with which to scale the walls of discrimination, exclusion and alienation presented by most of their neighbors.

In this situation, it was not surprising that Graetz's book became popular, indirectly prompting another impressive enterprise: the invention of a collective national past. It was somewhat unexpected that the author of this literary project was an "autonomist" though not a supporter of a national state. Dubnow, like Graetz, devoted his entire life to the presentation of an unbroken narrative of Jewish existence in history. Like his predecessor, Dubnow may be defined as a prenationalist historian, yet not a Zionist. He did not believe it was possible, or appropriate, to transfer a large human mass to Palestine to build a state of its own there. But he did call for the creation of a fully autonomous space for the Jewish people, whose situation was "anomalous." Most proponents of autonomy did not regard themselves as members of a race that was alien in Europe, and delineated their identity in keeping with the norms and mores of the lively, popular Yiddishist culture in which they lived. Dubnow was the exception: his prenationalist sensibility led him to look to the past in order to carve out a memory that would provide a firmer identity for a collective existence, which he feared had become too fragile and problematic.

Dubnow's theoretical assumptions were a kind of synthesis between the Frenchman Renan and the Germans Herder and Fichte. From Renan he took the subjective elements in the definition of nationalism—will and consciousness setting the boundaries of the collective—and from Herder and Fichte he took a large dose of their swollen ethnospiritual romanticism. Race, he thought, was just the first stage in the formation of a nation, which goes on to develop slowly and become a single cultural-historical entity. But neither the race, nor the language, nor the territory determines the final shape of the nation in history. Nations are characterized as bearers of a long-term spiritual culture that reproduces itself and passes from generation to generation.

But what was the secular superculture common to all the communities of the "world-people" (Dubnow's term for the Jews)? The Russian-Jewish historian found it difficult to answer this question. Hence, despite his consistent secularism and his sharp criticism of the faith, he could not avoid pointing to the preservation of the Jewish religion as an essential condition for the secular "national culture."[44] The trend toward pragmatism, which later in Zionist historiography would make religious faith wholly instrumental in the definition of national identity, had found its first historian in Dubnow.

But Dubnow felt uneasy about using a religious culture to define a modern nation, and this drove him to follow German Romanticism in search of a boundless and indefinable spirituality, beyond time and place, that rises like a mighty echo from an ancient source. As a subject of the vast Russian empire, which could hardly become a nation-state, he never fully understood the role of the modern state in the creation of a national culture. Thus he could describe himself as an autonomist, leaning expressly on Herder's well-known populist essentialism:

> It should be kept in mind that the state is an outward social alliance, whose purpose is to secure the needs of its members, whereas the nation is an inward and natural association. The former, by its very nature, is accustomed to change, while the latter is fixed and unchanging. A nation that has lost its political liberty owing to a historical disaster should not also lose its national selfhood.[45]

For Dubnow as for Graetz, the nation-state was not the definite, immediate goal for the realization of a stable, secular Jewish identity. This longed-for identity existed beyond the concrete political reality and, for the time being, needed to be fostered and preserved. A look at the mosaic of Jewish cultures in modern times was misleading, and certainly could not provide a suitable answer to the definition of the Jews as a "united spiritual nation." Hence the best way to preserve the nation's unchanging essence was to foster the consciousness that knew and recognized it, a consciousness that could be achieved by developing the study of history and expanding knowledge of the shared origin. For Dubnow, in the absence of political sovereignty, the historian ought to replace the rabbi as the agent of memory and inherited identity.

As a scholar, Dubnow was less pugnacious than Graetz, because despite his Romantic tendencies, he saw himself as a true man of science. At the end of

---

44   See for example Simon Dubnow, *Letters on the Old and New Judaism*, Tel Aviv: Dvir, [1897–1906] 1937 (in Hebrew), 18.

45   Ibid., 29.

the nineteenth century, on the threshold of the twentieth, positivist science still held sway among European intellectuals, and so, in the transition from Graetz to Dubnow, the writing of history as a sequence of novels was abandoned, at least in appearance, and the age of professional historiography began. Graetz had had no real connection to the European tradition of meticulous investigation of the past, which had developed since von Ranke, but this tradition left a clearer imprint on Dubnow's work. Graetz had completely isolated the history of the Jews from their surroundings, while Dubnow sought to connect it to the societies in which they lived. His books made effective use of the methodological tools that had been developed in the course of the nineteenth century in the various fields of historiography: source references, supporting evidence, and cross-references had become standard elements of historical narrative.

Dubnow's *World History of the Jewish People*—the wide-ranging book that he began to write early in the new century—begins not with the ancient Hebrews but with a broad survey of the Near East based on recent archaeological discoveries.[46] The findings at Tell el-Amarna, the Elephantine papyri, Hammurabi's code of laws, the Mesha Stela—all are cited to show that this was a scientific, or, as Dubnow called it, "sociological," work. He used the word "sociological" to indicate a study of the history of the Jews based not on their ideas, namely their religion, but on their existence as "a living national body."[47] The present living body was the totality of autonomous Jewish communities. Because of their common origin, together they constituted a single nation, rather than a scattering of religious communities, as Jost and his colleagues had thought. "The national type had reached its finished form at the time of the first political downfall," Dubnow asserted, and this would be his guiding motif throughout the work.[48]

The "national body" is present in Dubnow's work from a very early stage. A secular rationalist, he could hardly adopt the whole of the Book of Genesis as historical testimony, and he was aware that it had been written long after the events described therein. He therefore proposed to select those stories that seemed to conform more or less with reality, and to treat the others as metaphors, depicting the past in symbolic terms. For example, the story about Abraham the Hebrew symbolized the historical separation of the Hebrews

---

46   Dubnow published the first parts of the first edition in Russian between 1901 and 1906. He completed the work in 1914–21, and in 1925–29 it appeared in German as well as in Hebrew, supervised by Dubnow himself. I use the edition *History of the World-People*, 10 vols. Tel Aviv: Dvir, 1962 (in Hebrew).

47   Ibid., vol. 1, 10.

48   Ibid., 3.

from the nomadic Semites, and Isaac and Jacob represented the branching-off of the "people of Israel" from the other Hebrew peoples. The biblical characters were collective prototypes; the events described, even if not exactly true, reflected real, large-scale processes.

Dubnow's narrative strategy would be adopted by all the Zionist historians who followed him—namely, that the Bible is indeed full of imaginary tales, but its historical core is trustworthy. Why? Because the legendary quality was added by later popular tradition and literary modification, which adapted the living "people's memory" that had been preserved, and which testified to a long and natural historical sequence. This embodiment of the people's memory constituted an authentic, indisputable testimony to the actual experiences of the nation. But when was the Old Testament actually written? "It is most probable that the early events in the book were written in the time of David and Solomon, and their literary adaptation was done at the end of the two kingdoms, in about the eighth century," according to Dubnow.[49] The contradictions in the biblical text were entirely due to the fact that some parts were written by Judeans and others by "Ephraimites." Dubnow argued that Julius Wellhausen and other Bible critics were correct in their specific philological-scientific analysis, and that some of the books of the Bible were indeed written in later periods, but that these extremist scholars overindulged in superfluous details, especially in their conclusions. Specifically, one ought to reject their basic premise that

> prohibits discussing an ancient Israelite culture predating the period of monarchy ... The source of the general Oriental elements in Judaism is ancient Babylonia in the time of Hammurabi and the kings who succeeded him who also ruled over Canaan—not the new Babylonia of Nebuchadnezzar and the Persian kings who succeeded him and likewise captured Judea. It is not possible to ignore the effect of the cultural environment of the Israeli tribes in the second millennium BCE, as do the school of Wellhausen and the proponents of the extreme "Ezraite" approach.[50]

Dubnow, like Graetz and like all the prenationalist and nationalist historians in modern times, wanted to push the birth of the "people" as far back in time as possible, and insisted that the "history of Israel" began in the twentieth century BCE![51] The similarity between the ancient Babylonian myths and laws and main elements in the Old Testament indicated the early chronology of the appearance of "the Children of Israel." Therefore the Exodus from Egypt

---

49   Ibid., 8.
50   Ibid., 271–72.
51   Ibid., 21.

must have taken place in the fifteenth or fourteenth century BCE, because the "defeat of Israel" mentioned in an inscription on a stela ordered by the Pharaoh Merneptah (discovered in 1896) proved that Israel was already present in Canaan at the end of the thirteenth century.

This last finding was problematic for Dubnow, and it illustrates the production process in his particular historiographic laboratory. He was well aware that at the assumed time of the Exodus and the subsequent conquest of Canaan, the pharaohs ruled over the entire region. How, then, could the enslaved Children of Israel rise up against the Egyptian kingdom, abandon it by force, and conquer Canaan—which was part of the Egyptian domain—without Egypt intervening? Moreover, the Merneptah stela clearly states that, at that time, Israel was destroyed by Egypt "and had no more seed"—although there is no mention of this defeat in the Bible. Here is how Dubnow resolves this conundrum:

> We must therefore assume that the hymn to the victorious pharaoh was inaccurate, and very likely the ruler of Egypt had to resist the rebellious peoples in Africa, or else this "victory" over Israel was in the desert, during the Exodus from Egypt, when there was no trace left there of the "seed of Israel." In any case, it is not possible that directly after the Children of Israel settled in Canaan, they were attacked by the king of Egypt.[52]

To ascribe such a distant time to the Old Testament narrative required support from the new archaeological discoveries. It was necessary only to know how to interpret them so as to provide a scientific basis for the stories of the early Jewish people. Here Dubnow initiated a lasting tradition in Jewish nationalism, which in later years would deploy digging implements to substantiate biblical stories—and with them, of course, the proprietary claim of the "People of Israel" to the "Land of Israel." At that time, archaeology, like historiography, was not yet Zionist, but already the Christian excavators took pains not to contradict the Old Testament, which might undermine the New Testament. What was a prenationalist or nationalist historian to do if a contradiction nevertheless emerged? In the creation of the national narrative, he would always prefer the "truth" of the theological text over the archaeological finding.

Except for the scientific garb in which Dubnow clothed his work, it remained wholly faithful to the Old Testament and, as in Graetz's work, simply eliminated the supernatural descriptions and the deity's direct interventions. The conquest of Canaan, the distribution of tribal lands, the period of the judges and that of the unified kingdom were given a detailed chronology and

---

52 Ibid., 34.

turned into modern "history" and "sociology." The Jewish historian devoted separate, detailed chapters to David's "great" and Solomon's "mighty" kingdoms, because "writing and literature were especially developed in the reigns of the two great monarchs, David and Solomon. They both had 'scribes' and 'clerks' who recorded everything that needed writing down in the administration of government, and certainly also wrote down all the events of their time."[53] As for David's son and royal successor, Dubnow had no doubt that the entire ancient world was aware of "the personality of Solomon, who did the same as the kings of Egypt and Babylon, and built magnificent buildings and perpetuated his name in stone edifices."[54] Dubnow had not seen this magnificent architecture but was apparently convinced that it would soon be discovered. However, at this stage of his work he was more concerned about the national predicament in which the ancient unified kingdom found itself following the traumatic split after the demise of Solomon.

Dubnow preferred to call the kingdom of Israel "Ephraim" to avoid confusion, because the biblical authors gave the name "Israel" to the entire people that came out of Egypt. He fully adopted the position of the ancient authors who demonized the secessionist northern kingdom, and even expressed some anger with it for building temples in addition to the ones in Judea. Despite this persistent sacrilege, he naturally preferred the kingdom of Ephraim, which was "almost Jewish," over Edom, Ammon and Moab, the other Canaanite powers in the region (though he quotes almost in full the stela inscription of Mesha, king of Moab).[55] Summing up Ephraim's sad plight when it was destroyed and the Assyrian rulers settled it with foreign deportees, Dubnow writes:

> And the Israelites who remained in their land mingled with the new settlers who had been exiled there, and lost their pure national type. Nevertheless, many of the Israelites retained their religion and nationality, moved to the southern kingdom of Judah and joined the salvaged core of the nation ... Following the great destruction, the forces began to concentrate in Judah, and this assured, amid the political upheavals in the east, the continued survival of the kingdom of Judah for nearly 150 years, and, later, of the Jewish nation.[56]

The later fall of Judah is painted in vivid, tragic colors, and the Russian-Jewish historian's optimism is restored only by the "Return to Zion," although many of the exiles refused to return to their homeland from Babylonia. The building

53   Ibid., 148.
54   Ibid., 85.
55   Ibid., 109.
56   Ibid., 127.

of the new temple in 516 BCE strengthened the nation, though it still had to contend with a painful spiritual threat. Those who had remained in Judah after the fall had begun to mingle with their neighbors, and there was a growing number of mixed marriages. The Jewish scholar of the early twentieth century was not a racist, but being concerned about continued national survival, he justified the biblical expulsion of the foreign wives as well as the outright prohibition on marrying them:

> These mixed marriages, customary alike among the humble and the great, jeopardized the purity of the race and the religion. The national culture of the Judahite people was not yet strong enough to absorb alien elements without their leaving a trace. During this period when it was constructing its habitation, it needed national isolation so as not to disappear among the nations, and so that Judaism would not become one of the numerous religious cults in the East, which lacked all universal value and were ultimately washed away in the deluge of history.[57]

Significantly, unlike Ezra and Nehemiah, Dubnow's justification of procreative isolation was not religious but secular and modern. Treitschke's and Graetz's old *völkisch* anxiety filtered fairly easily into the early Jewish historiography pursued in Eastern Europe. The clear ethnocentric identity that underlay Dubnow's historical discourse resembled other kinds of prenationalism and nationalism in contemporary Eastern Europe (Polish, Ukrainian, Latvian, and so on), but had a decisive advantage over them: it could go back to the sixth century BCE for criteria to define the living national body. Like Graetz's first historiographic project, it, too, faced with anti-Semitism and rejection of the Jew, could lean on "trustworthy" biblical sources to explain and to justify an opposite and complementary reaction: a modern, secular Jewish national self-isolation.

AN ETHNICIST STAGE IN THE WEST

Other than Dubnow, and just before the advent of professionalization and specialization in the discipline of history, there were two final attempts to produce a total history of the Jews: Ze'ev Yavetz's *Book of the History of Israel*,[58] which is of relatively minor historiographic value, and the more important book by Salo Wittmayer Baron, *A Social and Religious History of the Jews*.[59] It is

---

57 Ibid., 223.
58 Ze'ev Yavetz, *The Book of the History of Israel After the Primary Sources*, Tel Aviv: Ahiavar, 1932 (in Hebrew).
59 Salo Wittmayer Baron, *A Social and Religious History of the Jews*, New York: Columbia University Press, 1952.

not surprising that Yavetz stuck closely to the biblical narrative, as he was one of the new breed of Zionist rabbis who turned the Old Testament from a holy book into a national one while at the same time inveighing against a secular or reformist reading of it. More intriguing is the outlook of the holder of the first chair in Jewish history in the United States, who published the pioneering version of his work in 1937, reworked it and began to republish it in 1952, although he never completed the project.

Like his well-known predecessors Graetz and Dubnow, Baron was not an avowed Zionist, though he, too, was no stranger to the idea of a modern sovereignty for some of the Jews. And whereas Graetz looked at the history from the vantage point of unifying Germany, and Dubnow from the crumbling Tsarist empire, Baron observed the Jews from New York, the greatest refuge of Jews from Eastern Europe, to which he himself had migrated in 1926. This point of view contributed to a freer, less linear discourse than the one being developed at this time in the so-called Jerusalem school and its later successors in the State of Israel.[60] Baron was free from the "rejection of the diaspora" syndrome that lay at the heart of Zionist historiography, and this accounted for the different compass of his research.

Baron's description of the life of Jewish communities in the world is colorful, original, at times unusual—he disliked what he called the "whining" tone in depictions of the condition of Jews—but in anything connected with the birth of the "Jewish people," he could not avoid the prenationalist structures laid down by Graetz and Dubnow along biblical lines. Thus, in the very opening of his expansive work, he states confidently:

> The tendency now prevailing among Old Testament critics is to give ever greater credence to biblical records, including those of the early period. Partly as a result of a general reaction against the extremely radical, almost antibiblical, higher criticism of a few decades ago, and partly because of our increased knowledge of the ancient Near East, the present generation, on the whole, accepts the historicity of the fundamental facts underlying early biblical narratives.[61]

Henceforth, it would therefore be possible to ignore the philological research of Wellhausen and his successors, as Baron claimed American scholars were beginning to do, and instead to rely on the wealth of new archaeological

---

60   For the introduction of historiography at the Hebrew University in Jerusalem, see David N. Myers, *Re-Inventing the Jewish Past: European Jewish Intellectuals and the Zionist Return to History*, New York: Oxford University Press, 1995.

61   Baron, *A Social and Religious History*, 32.

discoveries, because, ever since Dubnow, the name of the historiographic game was science. Thus,

> The biblical tradition, though overlaid with legendary motifs, preserved the distinct recollection that Israel's patriarchs had stemmed from Chaldaea and more particularly from the cities of Ur and Haran. Ur, as we know from British excavations during the last two decades, had been an ancient center of Sumero-Accadian civilization. Whether or not Abraham's father, Terah, and his brother, Nahor, had any connection with like-sounding raiders in Syria and Palestine allegedly mentioned in two Ugaritic poems, their names have been plausibly deduced from Mesopotamian localities ... Certainly the invention of such coincidental names by a later Palestinian poet or historian, an hypothesis long accepted by biblical critics, would require much more arduous explanations than the now prevalent assumption of a solid kernel of authentic historic tradition in the biblical narratives.[62]

From now on, it would be possible to relate the history of the Jews almost exactly as it was told in the Old Testament, minus the wonders and miracles (supposedly these were volcanic natural phenomena) and the heavy religious sermonizing. History now appeared clothed in a more secular garb, freed from divine metaphysics but wholly subordinate to a specific, well-defined protonationalist discourse. Jewish history was the story of a nomadic people born in great antiquity, which had mysteriously and marvelously continued to exist throughout history. Graetz and Dubnow's great enterprise received, with some adjustments, the honored imprimatur of academe, and biblical truth became an unquestioned discourse—an integral part of twentieth-century historical research.

Baron also resorted to the biblical outlook in dealing with the history of Jews in later periods, not as the story of religious communities existing in symbiosis or conflict amid various religious and popular cultures, but as the narrative of a mobile, exceptional people. The American Jewish scholar was well aware of the epistemological dissonance caused by the depiction of the Jewish past in a nationalistic way, and admitted:

> To insist that "peculiar" destinies of individuals and nations "happen" precisely to those individuals and nations with an innate disposition for them may seem to be reaching out too perilously into the realm of metaphysics. Under the same circumstances, however, many other peoples would certainly have perished and disappeared from history. That the Jews survived is largely

---

62   Ibid., 34.

due to the fact that they were prepared for their subsequent destinies by their early history.[63]

To Baron, the Eastern European immigrant in New York, the land was much less significant as the starting point of the unique, dispersed nation, and this ideological aspect is prominent throughout the first volume of his work. As he saw it, Judaism did not spring from nature but in fact represented history's revolt against it. Therefore, the decisive quality of the identity of the eternal people, whose everyday cultural elements varied so much from place to place, was mainly its "ethnic" origin and its love of the past: "the common descent from Abraham, Isaac and Jacob is the main element that secures Israel's exalted position within the family of nations, wherever and under whatever conditions it may happen to live."[64]

According to Baron, ethnicity is a kind of nationality, in no way inferior to the sovereign nationality that lasted only a short time in the history of the Jewish people. Indeed, it is even superior to it in many major qualities, and in those qualities lies the secret of the Jews' persistent strength throughout history. And the birth date of this unique and unifying "ethnic" nationality, argued Baron, was the exodus of the Hebrews from Egypt.

Responding to the arguments of Wellhausen and his colleagues, who contended that Jewish monotheism could not have been born in a nomadic society with an underveloped culture, the New York scholar stated that the ancient Hebrews already had a complex culture while in bondage in Egypt. To imagine the descendants of Abraham as resembling today's Bedouin, he argued, was a romantic mistake. They must have retained a vivid memory of Akhenaton's quasi-monotheistic reform, and Moses must surely have been familiar with the philosophy of the pharaoh who first proposed the idea of a single deity. Moses's achievement was of course much finer and more original than that of his predecessors. The Ten Commandments was a unique document that enables us to comprehend the situation of the Hebrews of the time; even more important, the fact that it makes no mention of the Temple proves beyond doubt that this codex was composed in the desert and designed to serve a nomadic people.[65] For Baron, the wisdom of Moses lay in his having founded a religion for which neither country nor sovereignty was an essential condition.

He therefore devoted relatively little space to the period of the conquest of Canaan and the rise of the unified kingdom. How could the Hebrews have

63   Ibid., 17.
64   Ibid., 97.
65   Ibid., 46–53.

left Egypt and conquered a country that was under Egyptian power? It must have taken place at a time when Egyptian control had weakened. Why did the mighty kingdom of Saul and David arise and unite the tribes? Because of the pressure of outside enemies. Why did the great kingdom split? Because of divergences and political conflicts, but also Egyptian interference. Concerned with the social and religious history of the Jews, Baron was much less interested in the politics of the kingdom. Instead, the reader is regaled with colorful sociological analyses, which, unfortunately, lacked reliable sources.

Baron's rooted antipolitical outlook leads him to favor the ancient biblical historians. Despite his reservations concerning Wellhausen's school, he follows Dubnow in accepting that one ancient biblical historian generally rendered God's name as "YHWH" while another referred to the deity as "Elohim." He opined that the Yahwist came from the tribe of Judah, and the Elohist from Israel. Yet neither of them, Baron stated admiringly, was dismayed by the division of the kingdom, and both saw "Israel and Judah as an inseparable unity," a significant fusion that continued throughout the history of the Jews. In their disdain for their respective sovereignties and their preference for the united people, they differed from other kingdoms in antiquity and presaged the future. The respected academic historian evidently did not consider the possibility that later editors might have been responsible for this image of a theological-literary unity.

Baron describes the fall of the Temple and the deportation in a neutral, even a slightly approving, manner: "No longer would it be necessary to reside on the soil of Palestine or live under a Jewish government to be considered a Jew. Even in the dispersion, far from their own country and under a foreign king, Jews continued ethnically to be Jews."[66] The percentage of deportees was, he suggested, rather higher than had been assumed by other scholars, and the majority lived well in exile. There were some signs of assimilation, but fortunately the precious ethnicity continued to preserve the people's national identity. The universalism that filtered into Judaism during the Persian period was balanced by extreme isolationism. After the return to Zion, Ezra and Nehemiah did the people a great service—indeed, saved it—by their act of ethnic separation, indirectly making an immense contribution to benefit all humanity.[67]

---

66 Ibid., 96.

67 On the isolationist politics of Ezra and Nehemiah, Baron wrote, "Ideal holiness of the people through segregation found its counterpart in both Ezra's and Nehemiah's insistence upon ethnic purity and their prohibition of intermarriage. This principle of ethnic exclusiveness was for centuries to come a necessity for the preservation of the Jewish people even in Palestine. But in its essence it is the main safeguard of a people in dispersion against national extinction." Ibid., 163.

Throughout his book, Baron sought to maintain a balance between ethno-centricity, the consciousness of a common origin and unique spirituality that lay at the heart of Judaism, and the humanist universality that he believed the Jewish people carried into exile and made the essence of their being. It must not be forgotten that, to him, ethnicity was not merely a religious culture nor was it a truly secular one—indeed, he maintained that Jewish ethnicity was some kind of "way of life" that persisted beyond the set of beliefs and religious doctrines.[68] The meaning he gave to the term remained always ambiguous enough to avoid provoking much criticism from fellow historians and English readers who did not belong to the Jewish people. In this way, he reinforced the ideological basis for defining the Jews as a generous and valuable *ethnos* that could exist alongside the other racial groups within the great American nation, without blending too much with them. Like Dubnow, Baron held that the study of history could become part of the sacred duty of preserving the Jewish identity, and could even replace the religious study that had hitherto fulfilled this vital function.

This lack of aspiration in Baron's oeuvre for political sovereignty and for a return to the ancient homeland—that is, the absence of a well-defined nationalist teleology—dismayed another important historian, who responded publicly.

THE FIRST STEPS OF HISTORIOGRAPHY IN ZION

When Baron's book appeared in the 1930s, Yitzhak Baer was asked to review it in the periodical *Zion*, which was launched in late 1935 in Jerusalem. Baer had come to Palestine from Germany in 1929, and whereas Baron was the first occu-pant of an American chair in Jewish history, Baer possessed a similar position at the young Hebrew University in Jerusalem.[69] This may have accounted for the restrained and respectful tone with which the new "Palestinian" academic referred to his distinguished and influential colleague in New York. It did not, however, camouflage the hard core of his criticism. "The Jewish histo-rian," he wrote, "must discover in the biblical period the inner forces destined to continue to operate in the different and changing conditions of the later periods. Baron has located in the early chapter of Jewish history the same fixed

---

68   See Salo Wittmayer Baron, "Jewish Ethnicism," *Modern Nationalism and Religion*, New York: Meridian Books, 1960, 248.

69   For more information about this historian, see Israel Jacob Yuval, "Yitzhak Baer and the Search for Authentic Judaism," in *The Jewish Past Revisited: Reflections on Modern Jewish Historians*, D. N. Myers and D. B. Ruderman (eds.), New Haven: Yale University Press, 1998, 77–87.

pattern under which he proceeds to follow the history of the exile up to the present. By doing this, he has barred its organic understanding."[70]

Baron had read the biblical history through the lens of an exile, Baer is saying, when he should have done the opposite. The key to understanding the history of the Jews must be found in the concept that he, Baer, following his German teachers, dubbed "organic." This meant a homogeneous approach with a biological tinge, which declared that it was necessary, first of all, to determine the origin of the human subjects in order to find the thread of their progress through history. The history of the Jews had an organic sequence, which bound all its stages, from inception to the present, into a single entity.[71] Despite Baron's considerable scholarship and vivid style, he had sinned by failing to understand those inner forces of the Jewish nation that had arisen in ancient times and continued to animate it till the present. Baron had detached Jewish monotheism from its homeland in the first stage of its appearance, and then erroneously depicted an idealized and fairly comfortable exile. There was no description in his work of the longing for a natural existence in the homeland, or the aspiration for sovereignty that had accompanied and defined the Jews throughout their wanderings in history.

In 1936, two years before writing this review, Baer had published in Berlin his book *Galut* (meaning "exile" in Hebrew), a kind of theoretical précis of all his future historiographical work. The book opened with the assertion that "the Bible had told of the slow process of selection and ripening that took place among God's people; it confirmed their claim to the promised land of Palestine and showed them their special place in the history of the nations."[72] *Galut* concludes with a credo so formative in the shaping of future Jewish-Israeli historical consciousness that it merits being quoted at length:

> God gave to every nation its place, and to the Jews he gave Palestine. The *Galut* means that the Jews have left their natural place. But everything that leaves its natural place loses thereby its natural support until it returns. The dispersion of Israel among the nations is unnatural. Since the Jews manifest a national unity, even in a higher sense than other nations, it is necessary that they return to a state of actual unity ... The Jewish revival of the present day is in its essence not determined by the national movements of Europe: it harks back to the ancient national consciousness of the Jews, which existed before the history of Europe and is the original sacred model for all the national ideas

70   Yitzhak Baer, "A Social and Religious History of the Jews," *Zion*, vol. 3, 1938, 280.
71   Yitzhak Baer, *Studies in the History of the Jewish People*, Jerusalem: The Historical Society of Israel, 1985 (in Hebrew), 27–32.
72   Yitzhak Baer, *Galut*, New York: Schoken Books, 1947, 11.

of Europe … If we today can read each coming day's events in ancient and dusty chronological tables, as though history were the ceaseless unrolling of a process proclaimed once and for all in the Bible, then every Jew in every part of the Diaspora may recognize that there is a power that lifts the Jewish people out of the realm of all causal history.[73]

This was not written by an eloquent Zionist leader or activist, or a hyperbolic Romantic poet. This was written by the first professional scholar of Jewish history in Jerusalem, who taught and mentored many students. The fact that it was published in Nazi Germany is also significant in analyzing the character and components of the special national identity that bursts from it.

If Graetz in his writing opposed Treitschke, Baer in his writing opposed the German historians who had formed him, and who by and large greeted the new Nazi regime with understanding, if not enthusiasm. In 1936 the expulsion of Jews from the feverish body of the German nation was at one of its high points, and the Zionist historian, harshly rejected by his native Germany, completed the process by developing a painful counterconsciousness. Ironically, this self-consciousness drew on the same imaginary idea of nationhood that had nurtured his mentors for several generations: that the source determines the substance, and the goal is a return to the roots, the primeval habitat, be it Teutonic or Hebrew. For Baer, the biblical myth that indicated the origin embraced a distinct national telos that had previously seemed sheepish and timid—leaving the places of alienated exile and returning to the warm womb of the land that had given birth to the chosen people, whose proprietary claim to it was ultimately borne out by the Bible.

The year *Galut* was published, there occurred an academic event that would determine the character of all future historiography in Israel. While it generally followed the European model of academe, the Hebrew University decided to create not one but two history departments: one named Department of Jewish History and Sociology; the other, Department of History.[74] All the history departments of all the other universities in Israel followed suit— Jewish history was to be studied in isolation from the history of the gentiles, because the principles, tools, concepts and time frame of these studies were completely different.

---

73   Ibid., 118–20.
74   See Ariel Rein, "History and Jewish History: Together or Separate? The Definition of Historical Studies at the Hebrew University, 1925–1935," in *The History of the Hebrew University of Jerusalem: Origins and Beginnings*, S. Katz and M. Heyd (eds), Jerusalem: Magnes, 1997 (in Hebrew), 516–40. "Jewish Sociology" was added to Jewish History to create a teaching post for Arthur Ruppin, the first Zionist sociologist in Palestine.

Baer at first objected to this strange academic division but soon became its devoted supporter, as it actually suited his approach to history. The year before this fateful decision was taken, he had launched—together with Ben-Zion Dinur (Dinaburg), the other historian who obtained a position in the Jewish history department in Jerusalem—the magazine *Zion*, which came to be the leading venue for discussions of Jewish history in Mandatory Palestine, and later in independent Israel.[75] *Zmanim* ("Times"), the first periodical in Hebrew to deal with "general" history, was founded in Israel only in the late 1970s.

As the above quotations show, Baer saw the Bible as the decisive starting point of the organic development of the entire Jewish past. Yet he did not specialize in ancient history but in the Middle Ages. Only later, in the 1960s, did he turn to the Hasmonean kingdom. The age of grand syntheses had passed, and no individual professional historians in the Hebrew academic world would undertake on their own to repeat the pioneering projects of Graetz, Dubnow and Baron.[76] The requirements of the international academic world, especially in the latter half of the twentieth century, forced on the young Hebrew scholars certain norms that could not be easily circumvented. Baer, a cautious pedant in his empirical work (he was a typical product of German academia and a diligent explorer of archives), always asserted that he was professionally committed to the facts. He therefore admitted that Julius Wellhausen and his colleagues had eroded the biblical historical discourse, which may have caused his hesitation about dealing directly with the biblical period. At the same time, his duty as a national historian prevented him from undermining the founding myth, and prompted him to write the following:

> Graetz was the only Jew who wrote out of an original and independent understanding of Israelite history up to the fall of the First Temple, and but for the revolutionary conclusions that were reached in his final years in Bible criticism and the history of the period, the first two volumes of his work would have been rightly regarded as among the finest books about that time,

---

75   The guideline of the periodical was "Jewish history is the history of the Israelite nation ... Jewish history is united by a homogeneous unity through all the periods and in all places, each of which reflects the others. Our history in the Middle Ages, like our modern history, can shed light on the period of the Second Temple, and without the Bible, it is not possible to understand the struggles of the following generations, and the problems of our own time." Yitzhak Baer, *Zion*, vol. 1, 1.

76   There were occasional attempts at a general history, but these were always collective efforts of several scholars. See for example Benjamin Mazar (ed.), *History of the People of Israel*, Tel Aviv: Masada, 1967 (in Hebrew); or H. H. Ben-Sasson (ed.), *History of the Jewish People*, Tel Aviv: Dvir, 1969 (in Hebrew). Here, as elsewhere, transliterated English titles are used for books available only in Hebrew.

and from the viewpoint of the profession's development, will always remain interesting.[77]

The contradiction contained in this statement clearly expressed the dilemmas and tensions experienced by one of the founders of national historiography in Israel. He constantly swung between the mythological and the scientific, with the former remaining predominant, though periodically defeated by naughty little facts. Thus, in the 1950s, when the cult of Israel's past turned the nationalized Bible into a tribal campfire story, and fostered imaginings of reliving that past anew, Baer, the first "Zionist Palestinian" historian, joined the general exultation and endowed it with precious scientific reinforcement:

Without the biblical period we cannot understand the history of the Jewish people. The biblical period serves as a model and pattern for the following periods ... We know that the last two generations have seen a great development in the study of the biblical period. In the view that was widely accepted fifty years ago, the Israelites began as a nation like any other, and the theocratic tendency in its character appeared—according to that view—as the product of a late development, from shortly before and after the fall of the First Temple ... The biblical tradition that depicted the early stage of the nation—the time of the Patriarchs and the Wilderness Generation—as a primeval ideal was a construction unfounded in historical reality. This school of thought in Jewish history had been rejected by modern research. The accepted positions in Bible research today regard the patriarch Abraham as a historical figure who led a religious community, and was the archetype and first spiritual teacher of the reforming movement of the classical prophets; the ideal depiction of the Israelites in the desert, encamped around the Tabernacle with the cloud of God leading them, cannot be entirely a product of the late imagination.[78]

This resounding historical assertion was shared by Baer's colleague and close friend, the historian Dinur. But the latter, who was the more dominant personality, was far less inhibited by the shackles imposed by the invention of the nation—indeed, he was instrumental in forging them.

If Graetz was responsible for the foundation and scaffolding of the retroactive construction of the Jewish nation, Dinur laid the bricks, hung the beams, and fitted the windows and doors. He did this in two ways: as a teacher of Jewish history, he took part with Baer in shaping the power relations in this field of research; as a party cultural activist in the Zionist left, a member of the first Knesset, and from 1951 the minister of education for the State of Israel,

77   Baer, *Studies in the History of the Jewish People*, 33.
78   Yitzhak Baer, *Israel Among Nations*, Jerusalem: Bialik, 1955 (in Hewbrew), 14.

he was the chief architect of all history studies in the Hebrew educational systems.[79]

Dinur, who was born in the Ukraine, attended a yeshivah in Vilnius, and studied history in Germany, began his distinctive historiographic project before his appointment as a lecturer at the Hebrew University in the 1930s. Already in 1918, three years before his emigration to British-ruled Palestine, he had published in Kiev the book *Toldot Yisrael* (History of Israel), the first volume of his life's work as a scholar: a compilation of sources and documents through which could be delineated a continuous, organic narrative of the history of the Jews.[80] This project would culminate later in *Yisrael BaGolah* (Israel in Exile), the instructive series of volumes intended to cover the totality of Jewish history.[81] The many varied documents were organized and presented in a chronological and thematic order. Most were accompanied by succinct interpretations, guiding the Hebrew readers in the organic reading of history.

This compilation could in some ways be regarded as the culmination of Graetz's pioneering enterprise. Whereas the work of the German-Jewish historian was a nonconformist challenge to the predominant views held by educated people of Jewish background in Germany, and even throughout Europe, Dinur's compilation—like Salo Baron's, which appeared at almost the same time—was quickly accepted as the proper, standard historiography of the Jewish past. For Hebrew readers in Palestine, it became the dominant narrative, and any deviation from it, insofar as any appeared, would be viewed as peculiar or even hostile. From then on, the national-historical truth would be presented not only in the writings of a handful of subjective historians, but in scientific, objective, and systematic documentation.

As noted, Dinur devoted the first volume of the *History of Israel* to the biblical period. After joining the Hebrew University he revised it, expanded it, and began to publish it under the title *The History of Israel: Israel in Its Land*.[82] For all the differences between the 1918 edition and the first volume of the expanded edition of 1938, their method of creating positivist credibility for the history was identical. Dinur divided the Old Testament into sections and organized his book as a system of quotations from the biblical stories,

79   See the above-mentioned article by Uri Ram, "Zionist Historiography and the Invention of Modern Jewish Nationhood: The Case of Ben-Zion Dinur." Dinur also instituted the national award known as the Israel Prize, and was awarded it twice.

80   Ben-Zion Dinur (Dinaburg), *History of Israel*, Kiev: Society of Distributors of Education in Israel (in Hebrew).

81   Ben-Zion Dinur (Dinaburg), *Israel in Exile*, Tel Aviv: Dvir, 1926 (in Hebrew).

82   Ben-Zion Dinur (Dinaburg), *The History of Israel: Israel in Its Land*, Tel Aviv: Dvir, 1938 (in Hebrew).

interspersed with additional materials—a handful of epigraphic documents discovered in archaeological excavations in the Near East, a few quotes from Greek and Roman historians, brief commentaries from the Talmud.

It opens, naturally, with a discussion of the name "The Land of Israel" and the promised broad expanse,[83] then proceeds to describe the arrival of the Hebrews, their migration to Egypt, their return, their conquest of the inheritance promised to them, the founding of the united kingdom, and so forth. Every biblical verse is quoted as reliable evidence about the period it describes. The theology is almost eliminated, and the word of God, which appears on almost every page in the Bible, is replaced in part by one or another of the few extrabiblical sources mentioned. Dinur discarded the religious metaphysics of the holy book and turned it into a straightforward national-historical credo. Henceforth, impatient readers could skim the Old Testament, skipping the divine precepts and following the national truth alone.

In fact, this compilation reveals that although Dinur had begun his professional career as a teacher of the Bible,[84] he did not trust it as a pedagogical tool. Hence his decision to "rewrite" it, adapting it to the science of the time. This does not mean he doubted the historicity of the ancient texts—he accepted every detail and event, from Abraham the Hebrew to the Return to Zion. He totally rejected the Wellhausen school of Bible criticism, being convinced that the "stories of the patriarchs were not projections from the time of the prophets, but residues from generations and periods preceding the patriarchs."[85] He even believed, in contrast to current opinion, that the earliest historians were not the Greeks but the ancient biblical authors, and as a professional scholar felt able to assert without hesitation:

> Biblical historiography introduced an important theoretical innovation into general historiography by combining three elements: a) factual accuracy; the events are "God's secret" and may not be used imprecisely; b) the use of archival and official sources; c) a pragmatic method in perceiving and explaining things. That is why we may regard the biblical historiography of the period of monarchy, more than any other, as the beginning of modern historiography.[86]

---

83   On the use of the term "Eretz Israel," see my *Les Mots et la terre*, 193–208. The term began to appear in the writings of the Sages from the second century CE, as one of the country's names. In the Bible the common name is Canaan, and in the time of the Second Temple, Judea. The great Greek geographer Strabo called the country Judea. See *The Geography of Strabo*, 6.2. 21, Cambridge, MA: Harvard University Press, 1989, 756.

84   See Yitzhak Avishur's introduction to Ben-Zion Dinur's *Historical Writings*, vol.3, Jerusalem: Bialik, 1977 (in Hebrew), 7–12.

85   Ibid., 51.

86   Ibid., 167.

That ancient and "almost scientific" historiography, which as noted was slighty corrected by the national historian in Jerusalem, was meant to reveal the unique ethnic, religious, social, geographic, linguistic and political origin of the Jewish nation.[87] For Dinur, historical writing was primarily a national autobiography—enlisted history. That was why he maintained that Zionist scholars should reject the division into "Hebrew" and "Jewish" histories, a division employed by non-Jewish scholars, and indeed should emphasize the homogeneous continuity in the emergence and development of the "People of Israel" from its inception to the present.[88]

The most important contribution of "biblical historiography" to the creation of a national consciousness was, of course, its affirmation of the connection to the "Land of Israel." This spacious land, which naturally included the Bashan and Gilead, east of the Jordan river, was exclusively the land of the People of Israel, and what better testimony than the Bible to prove the Jews' historical claim to this land, which was promised to them alone? Like Baer, but even more passionately, Dinur had recourse to the Scriptures to prove the centrality of the Land of Israel in the life of the nation, which had longed to return to it throughout its long "exile."[89]

The nationalization of the Bible and its transformation into a reliable history book began with Heinrich Graetz's romantic impetus, developed with diasporic cautiousness by Dubnow and Baron, and completed and perfected by the founders of Zionist historiography who played a significant role in the ideological appropriation of the ancient territory. The first historians who wrote in modern Hebrew, which they erroneously believed to have evolved directly from biblical language,[90] were now regarded as the custodians and excavators of the Jewish nation's "long" memory.

POLITICS AND ARCHAEOLOGY

One of Dinur's many activities was participating in the regular Bible circle that in the 1950s met at the house of Israel's first prime minister, David Ben-Gurion. The charismatic leader was not only a keen reader of the ancient Hebrew book;

87   Ben-Zion Dinur, *Historical Writings*, vol. 4, Jerusalem: Bialik, 1978 (in Hebrew), 3. On the Bible's role in highlighting the "uniqueness of the Jewish experience and the spiritual unity of the people," see *Values and Roads*, Tel Aviv: Urim, 1958 (in Hebrew), 101–8.

88   Ben-Zion Dinur, *Historical Writings*, vol. 4, 30.

89   On Dinur's contribution to the centrality of "Eretz Israel" in Jewish history, see Jacob Barnai, *Historiography and Nationalism*, Jerusalem: Magnes, 1996 (in Hebrew), 120–1.

90   On the difference between ancient Hebrew and the language spoken in Israel today, see Ghil'ad Zuckermann, *Language Contact and Lexical Enrichment in Israeli Hebrew*, Hampshire: Palgrave Macmillan, 2004.

he also made cunning political use of it. Quite early he realized that the holy book could be made into a secular national text, serve as a central repository of ancient collective imagery, help forge the hundreds of thousands of new immigrants into a unified people, and tie the younger generation to the land. The biblical stories served him as a basis for everyday political rhetoric, and seemingly he genuinely identified with Moses and Joshua. Much as the leaders of the French Revolution felt they were assuming the roles of ancient Roman senators, so Ben-Gurion and other leaders of the Zionist revolution, senior military figures, and national intellectuals felt they were recapitulating the biblical conquest of Canaan and the construction of a state along the lines of David's kingdom. Current action became significant in the context of paradigmatic events of the past. In both cases the revolutionaries dreamed of creating a completely new man, but the materials they used in his construction were taken from a mythical past. In Ben-Gurion's imagination the new Israel was the kingdom of the Third Temple, and when the Israeli armed forces captured the entire Sinai peninsula in the 1956 war and reached Sharm el-Sheikh, he addressed the victorious troops with messianic passion:

> We can once more sing the song of Moses and the Children of Ancient Israel … With the mighty impetus of all the IDF divisions you have extended a hand to King Solomon, who developed Eilat as the first Israelite port three thousand years ago … And Yotvata, called Tiran, which until fourteen hundred years ago was an independent Hebrew state, will become a part of the third kingdom of Israel.[91]

The exclusive circle that met fortnightly at Ben-Gurion's house, whose discussions were sometimes reported in the daily press, included professional historians, qualified Bible interpreters and political figures who were amateur scholars in their free time. Besides Dinur, the regular participants included the professors Yehezkel Kaufmann, the well-known fundamentalist Bible interpreter, and Binyamin Mazar, the leading biblical archaeologist; the then and future presidents of Israel, Yitzhak Ben-Zvi and Shneur Zalman Shazar (Rubashov); and many other scholars and senior public figures. It was a junction of intellectual and political exchange, and it not only directed academic research but shaped public opinion and spread its values and findings throughout the educational system. The issues discussed by the learned participants included such questions as the number of Israelites in the Exodus from Egypt, their way of life during the

---

91   Ben-Gurion's telegram appeared in daily newspaper *Davar* on 7 September 1956 and was quoted in A. Israeli (A. Or and M. Machover), *Peace, Peace, When There is No Peace*, Jerusalem: Bokhan, 1961 (in Hebrew), 216–17.

conquest of Canaan, the number of kings they defeated in the process, and the like. Not surprisingly, the Book of Joshua was the most popular in these lively debates, and Joshua son of Nun was the star of the show.[92] Ben-Gurion also took part in public Bible conferences; promoted the Bible Quiz, which became a national media festival; and encouraged a fever of archaeological activity, though he did not necessarily adopt its unforeseen discoveries.

That a national leader should spend so much time being actively involved in historiographic issues is certainly unusual, and it may indicate the centrality of biblical mythistory in the construction of Zionist ideology. Reading Ben-Gurion's collection of articles, *Bibical Reflections*, one is struck by the easy swings between manipulative political pragmatism and a special and sincere belief in the ancient "truth."[93] He keeps repeating that the Bible is the identity card of the Jewish people, as well as the proof of its claim to the Land of Israel. His concept of history is clear and straightforward:

> When we went into exile, our nation was uprooted from the soil in which the Bible had grown, and torn from the political and spiritual reality in which it had formed … In exile, our nation was disfigured and the image of the Bible likewise deformed. Christian Bible researchers, with their Christian and anti-Semitic aims, turned the Bible into a plinth for Christianity, and even Jewish commentators, who had been removed from the environment of the Bible, its spiritual and material climate, could no longer understand the Holy Book properly. Only now, when we are again a free nation in our country, breathing once more the air which enveloped the Bible as it took shape, has the time come, I believe, in which we can perceive the nature and truth of the Bible, historical, geographical, as well as religious and cultural.[94]

His favorite Bible scholar was Yehezkel Kaufmann, who believed almost all the biblical assertions and regarded the rise of Jewish monotheism as a singular and extremely ancient phenomenon. Methodologically, the prime minister relied mainly on Dinur, the leading designer of the national historiography. After all, these two scholars breathed the same air as did the patriarch Abraham and Joshua son of Nun—as opposed to Jost or Wellhausen.[95]

92 On this circle, see Michael Keren, *Ben Gurion and the Intellectuals: Power, Knowledge and Charisma*, Dekalb: Northern Illinois University Press, 100–17.

93 David Ben Gurion, *Biblical Reflections*, Tel Aviv: Am Oved, 1969 (in Hebrew).

94 Ibid., 87.

95 For a comparison between Kaufmann, "who made a Copernican revolution in Bible research," and Wellhausen, "who shattered the Bible," see ibid., 95–6. On this scholar's passionate defense of the historical truth of the Bible, while forgoing its chronology, see Yehezkel Kaufmann, *The Biblical Story About the Conquest of the Land*, Jerusalem: Bialik, 1955 (in Hebrew).

Ben-Gurion, always a frustrated intellectual, also developed his own Bible theory. For example, he believed that monotheistic Hebrews had lived in Canaan for a long time before the arrival of Abraham, and it was their presence that attracted "the father of the nation" to their land.[96] The national history was therefore much longer than proposed by the professional Zionist historians. Ben-Gurion even speculated that the patriotic Hebrews did not migrate en masse to Egypt but remained in the country, and that only a single family emigrated. Thus, while the exodus from Egypt was an undoubted historical fact, the people's presence in the homeland was unbroken, and it is inaccurate to assume that the nation had taken shape, heaven forbid, on alien soil. He also asked some deep questions: How did the Hebrews preserve the Hebrew language during the 430 years of exile in the land of the pharaohs? Why, after they had been a single nation under a single leader in the time of Moses and Joshua, did they suddenly break up into separate tribes? The answers he proposed were invariably nationalistic. Indeed, his position corresponded to the official historiography and was formulated accordingly:

> When I find a contradiction between the Bible and external sources [archaeological or epigraphic findings], I am not obliged to accept the alien source. Could they not have mistaken or distorted the facts? From a purely scientific standpoint I'm free to accept the testimony of the Bible, even if challenged by an external source, provided the testimony contains no inner contradictions and is not obviously flawed.[97]

Despite this "scientific," secular approach, Ben-Gurion resorted when necessary to divine precepts. For example, he wrote that "the great event with a decisive significance in Jewish history was the promise of the Land of Canaan to the seed of Abraham and Sarah."[98] Certainly no external source could possibly challenge the biblical author's clear and incontrovertible testimony about the divine promise. Guided by historians, the national leader with his intellectual and messianic temperament led an entire national culture.

During the early years of the State of Israel, all the intellectual elites helped cultivate the sacred trinity of Bible–Nation–Land of Israel, and the Bible became a key factor in the formation of the "reborn" state. Civil servants were pressured to change their names to Hebrew ones, usually chosen from the

---

96   Ben Gurion, *Biblical Reflections*, 60–1.
97   Ibid., 87.
98   Ibid., 98. It has to be noted that the first prime minister of Israel included Sarah among the seed of Abraham, probably to prevent hereditary confusion with the "Ishmaelites."

Bible, and the rest of the population, seeking to emulate the established elites, did so willingly, even enthusiastically. The old "diasporic" family names were eliminated, and the children were given the names of mysterious, enchanted biblical figures. The process was applied not only to people; almost every new settlement was given an ancient Hebrew name. This served a dual purpose: erasing the local Arab name and leapfrogging over the long "exile," which had ended with the rise of the State of Israel.

But it was not the bureaucracy of the new state that imposed the worship of the Bible on the educational institutions. Long beforehand, both the pre-state institutions and the emerging Hebrew literature had made the Bible the locus for consciousness of the past.

The broad intelligentsia, including teachers, writers, essayists and poets, had anticipated high academe in the "correct" interpretation of Jewish history, and thus had helped shape the ideological present. With the expanding settlement movement in the early twentieth century and the opening of the first Hebrew schools, the Bible became the national textbook, taught in separate lessons rather than as an integral part of the language and literature studies. (This efficient system persists to the present day and is taken for granted in Israel's political culture.) Immigrant teachers, and people who became teachers after arriving in Palestine, did not have to wait for the academic and establishment elites to understand the value of using the Bible as a standard text for teaching the collective past.[99] They read Heinrich Graetz, Simon Dubnow and Ze'ev Yavetz, and understood the dual function of the Scriptures in shaping the national identity—the creation of a common "ethnic" origin for the religious communities scattered throughout the world, and self-persuasion in the claiming of proprietary rights over the country.[100]

The Hebraization that was consolidated in the educational systems developed around an ancient model of popular heroism and proud nationalism. The immense popularity of the monarchies of David and Solomon was matched only by that of the Hasmoneans, viewed as no less important. The teachers wanted their pupils to grow up to resemble not their weak parents and grandparents, but the ancient Hebrew peasants or warriors, whom the teachers' imagination depicted as following the conqueror Joshua, the warrior judges, or

99   On immigrant teachers and the technique of shaping Bible awareness in the school system, see S. D. Goitein, *Teaching the Bible: Problems and Methods of Modern Bible Teaching*, Tel Aviv: Yavneh, 1957 (in Hebrew), particularly 240–53.

100   On history and Bible history in the early Zionist colonization, see the doctoral dissertation of David Shahar, *The Teaching of National History in Zionist-Oriented Education on Eretz-Israel, 1882–1918: Trends and Roles*, Hebrew University in Jerusalem, 2001 (in Hebrew), 131, 140–1, 143–6, 259–67.

kings Saul and David, likewise military commanders. A sense of indigenous-ness was inculcated by several linked means: new history textbooks, homeland studies, arduous hikes to landscapes that made ideas concrete—all this, in addition to the separate, secular Bible lessons. After the establishment of the State of Israel, these pedagogical practices became standard in all branches of the state educational system.

It is possible to obtain an idea of how ancient history was used in the ideo-logical formation of the first native-born generation—the first sabras—from Moshe Dayan's book *Living with the Bible*. Written by one of the prominent heroes of the new society, it illustrates the absorption of the invented imaginary nationalism in close conjunction with the political aims of a settler society. The book opens with the following statements:

> I came to know the Bible stories in my early childhood. My teacher, Meshulam Halevy, not only taught and explained the book which describes the birth of our nation, but also concretized it for us. Things that had existed three and four thousand years ago seemed to be in us and before us. The surrounding reality helped our imagination to vault over the past and return to antiquity, to our forefathers and the heroes of our nation. The only language we knew and spoke was Hebrew, the language of the Bible. The Jezreel Valley in which we lived, the mountains and rivers around us, the Carmel and the Gilboa, the Kishon and the Jordan, were all there in the Bible.[101]

From here the former IDF chief of staff and minister of defense proceeds to describe the journeys of Abraham, Isaac and Jacob, interspersed with personal stories of his childhood and youth. The two narratives, despite their widely sepa-rated periods, seem to be intimately associated, as though they existed in a single eternity that canceled the historical dimension. The description of the Exodus and the march through the Sinai Desert are interwoven with the modern war of 1956. The conquest of Canaan is thrillingly described and is naturally associated with the conflict in 1948, even more so with the conquest of the West Bank in 1967. The victory of little David over gigantic Goliath symbolizes all the wars of Israel against the Arabs.[102] The Bible is the supreme justification for the presence and the colonization in modern times; every battle echoes an ancient act. The book concludes with an undisguised aspiration to see the modern state resemble the mighty kingdom of David, and a clear declaration of the desire to live in "a single Land of Israel" that spreads from the Mediterranean Sea to the Jordan River, from the desert to Mount Hermon.

---

101   Moshe Dayan, *Living with the Bible*, Jerusalem: Idanim, 1978 (in Hebrew), 15.
102   Ibid., 163.

The text is accompanied by beautiful photographs of the ancient "Jewish" land, interleaved with biblical scenes borrowed from Christian imagery. There are also photographs of ancient finds, many of them held by the proud author. Dayan did not hide his lifelong acquisitive desire for ancient artifacts; pictures of the Jewish commander's private garden show it to be full of various antiquities. Over the years, his house became a kind of miniature Land of Israel, and his possession of this precious collection, some of which he had simply stolen, testified to the domination of the Promised Land by this bold settlers' son. Dayan was known to be an uninhibited collector: while Ben-Gurion held a Bible circle in his modest residence, Dayan turned his spacious house into a private biblical museum. The ageing founder of the state gathered intellectuals around him, while his young disciple preferred to gather chiseled stones, pottery jars, and figurines. But both men wore a mantle of biblical mythology that elevated and justified their principal historical actions.[103]

Dayan was never more than an amateur archaeologist, but for another military chief of staff and Ben-Gurion protégé, excavating the Promised Land was a vocation and profession. Yigael Yadin had great influence over the direction of archaeology in Israel, and led the work at the most important sites such as Hazor, Megiddo and Masada. As an archaeologist, he was the direct heir of all those Christian excavators who came to the Holy Land beginning in the late nineteenth century to reaffirm the Old Testament and thereby the New. From the start, their religious motivation made local archaeology an adjunct to Bible research.[104] The greatest of these was William F. Albright, the son of an American Methodist missionary, who began to dig in the country in the 1920s and never ceased to defend the truth of the biblical story. His approach was adopted by the majority of Israeli archaeologists who came after him.

Albright's best-known, summarizing work, *The Archaeology of Palestine and the Bible*, suggests a possible date for Abraham's migration from Mesopotamia—the twentieth or nineteenth century BCE. Likewise, the migration of Jacob's family to Egypt is readily assigned to the eighteenth or seventeenth century BCE.[105] Albright asserted confidently that the ancient arch and "stables" found

---

103   Dayan's famous love of archaeology was limited to biblical findings. Ancient mosques, even from the eleventh century, were systematically destroyed by him. See the article by Meron Rapoport, "The operation to blow up the mosques," *Haaretz*, 6 July 2007.

104   For a popular example of the symbiosis between Christianity, archaeology and the Bible, see Werner Keller, *The Bible as History*, New York: Bantam Books, 1982. The book appeared in Hebrew back in 1958, but without the chapter on Jesus included in the German original.

105   William F. Albright, *The Archaeology of Palestine and the Bible*, London: Penguin, [1949] 1960, 83.

at Hazor dated from the reign of Solomon, which led him to the reasonable conclusion that "the age of Solomon was certainly one of the most flourishing periods of material civilization in the history of Palestine. Archaeology, after a long silence, has finally corroborated biblical tradition in no uncertain way."[106]

While preparing the second edition of this basic text on the biblical world, Albright asked Yigael Yadin, to add chapters of his own, and the Israeli archaeologist willingly complied. Yadin's appendix described his discoveries at the Hazor site, which, he maintained, proved that "only during Solomon's reign did Hazor rise as a great city."[107] Its previous dormant state was due, said the diligent digger, to having been destroyed by Joshua son of Nun.

Like Albright's discoveries, Yadin's excavations during the 1950s and 1960s exposed only findings that matched the biblical text. The pottery, weapons, structures, works of art and tombs were all presented as unmistakable evidence about the "time of the Patriarchs," the "Exodus," the "conquest of Canaan," the "boundaries of the Israelite tribal territories," and so on. Yadin's colleague, the professor Binyamin Mazar, who later became president of the Hebrew University and recipient of the Israel Prize, and his colleague and rival Professor Yohanan Aharoni, of Tel Aviv University, filled in the rich mosaic with plentiful additional evidence. The public was given a harmonious picture of the past that accorded with the dominant historiographic discourse. The material science of the past provided definitive support for the written science, and various sites became venues of pilgrimage for the reborn nation. Occasionally there were inconsistencies: some of the discovered material rudely contradicted the sacred text. But the archaeologists would resolve such problems with cunning arguments, speaking for the mute findings and making them fit the harmonious voices arising from the Bible.[108] Generally speaking, the last word was that of the written text, because it was the point of departure and the raison d'être in every excavation. Needless to say, the long "non-Jewish" periods in the history of "Canaan," "Judea" and "Palestine" hardly interested the archaeologists.[109]

106   Ibid., 123–124.
107   William F. Albright, *The Archaeology of Eretz-Israel*, Tel Aviv: Am Oved, 1965 (in Hebrew), 239.
108   See for example the article "The Exodus from Egypt and the Conquest of Canaan" in *Canaan and Israel: Historical Essays*, Benjamin Mazar, Jerusalem: Bialik, 1974 (in Hebrew), 93–120, or the chapter on "The Unified Kingdom" in Yohanan Aharoni's last book, *Archaeology of Eretz-Israel*, Jerusalem: Shikmona, 1978 (in Hebrew), mainly 169–170. On Israeli archaeology, see the intriguing work by Nadia Abu El-Haj, *Facts on the Ground: Archaeological Practice and Territorial Self-Fashioning in Israeli Society*, Chicago: The University of Chicago Press, 2002.
109   See about this subject Keith W. Whitelam, *The Invention of Ancient Israel*, London: Routledge, 1996, 1–10.

In 1964 Professor Aharoni, one of Israel's leading archaeologists, published a popular work, *Atlas of the Bible*, which informed a whole generation about ancient geography and the movements in it of all the principal biblical figures.[110] The wanderings of Abraham and Jacob, the Exodus from Egypt, the entry of the Israelite spies into Canaan, the transporting of the ark, Saul's search for the she-asses, the movements of David's troops, and the trade routes of Solomon's kingdom—all were neatly fitted with the extrabiblical archaeological discoveries, producing an impressive visual sequence. It was the geographic, and hence a more effective, equivalent of Dinur's old book: nothing looks more positive and reassuring than a detailed piece of cartography. The maps' seeming reality was highly convincing, and rounded off the verbal abstractions of the historians and Bible scholars. Needless to say, the atlas did not depict the narrow boundaries of the State of Israel at the time of publication, but only those of the powerful kingdoms of David and Solomon, as well as the battle moves of the various Israelite heroes. Not surprisingly, Aharoni was one of the first signatories of "The Whole Eretz Israel," a petition drafted following the Six-Day War in 1967, which called on all future governments of Israel never to cede an inch of the ancient homeland.

THE EARTH REBELS AGAINST MYTHISTORY

The 1967 war opened fresh perspectives for Israeli archaeological research. It had hitherto been confined to digging within the Green Line boundaries, but now the conquest of the West Bank opened wide spaces with numerous sites waiting to be explored in the heart of biblical Judea and, of course, around Jerusalem. International law prohibited Israeli archaeologists from excavating in the occupied territories and carrying away the ancient findings, but this was the ancient homeland—and who would presume to object?

At first, the euphoria of the victors in the war for the land blended with the jubilation of those digging under it. A large part of the Israeli intelligentsia had become addicted to the sweet dream of the great Land of Israel. Among them were many archaeologists who thought that their finest hour had come. Once and for all, they would fuse the ancient nation with its historical homeland, thereby proving the truth of the text. But as their investigations progressed, the elation that had filled Aharoni and his colleagues began to wane. Excavations in the central highlands, Mount Manasseh and Mount Ephraim, around Jerusalem and Mount Judah, uncovered more and more finds that heightened concerns and questions that had arisen earlier in sites within the borders of the State of Israel. Biblical

---

110   Yohanan Aharoni, *Carta's Atlas of the Bible*, Jerusalem: Carta, 1964 (in Hebrew).

archaeology, which had been an enlisted instrument of the nationalist ideology from 1948 to 1967, began to show symptoms of unease. More than twenty years would pass before the first discoveries were placed before the general public and the first cracks appeared in the consensus of the dominant scholarly culture. For this to happen, several developments had to take place both in the methods of exploring the past and in the national mood within Israel.

Significant changes occurred in the profession of history during the 1960s and especially in the 1970s, which affected the work of archaeologists the world over and eventually also in Israel. The decline of classical political historiography and the rise of social, and later anthropological, historical research led a good many archaeologists to consider other strata of ancient civilizations. Everyday material existence, the ancient world of labor, nutrition and burial, basic cultural practices, became increasingly the main objects of international research. The concept of *longue durée*, product of the French Annales historiography, especially suited the excavators, who happily adopted this approach, which tracks long processes.[111]

Echoes of this historical transition eventually reached the Israeli academic world, which, since biblical archaeology was essentially event-oriented and political, found its predominance gradually slipping. Young archaeologists began to have misgivings and escaped to earlier eras. More researchers encountered unresolved contradictions. But it was only after the outbreak of the First Intifada in 1987, and the advent of greater critical openness in the Israeli public arena, that the excavators began to speak up, their voices hoarse from having so long been muffled by sacred soil.

The first to feel the tremor was the "time of the Patriarchs." The period that had been so dear to the hearts of Dubnow, Baron and all the Zionist historians bristled with unanswered questions. Did Abraham migrate to Canaan in the twenty-first or the twentieth century BCE? The nationalist historians had of course assumed that the Bible exaggerated the astonishing longevity of Abraham, Isaac and Jacob. But the crucial migration from Mesopotamia led by the "father of the Jewish people" was associated with the promise that his offspring would inherit the land of Canaan, hence the obvious desire to preserve the historical heart of the first immigration to the Land of Israel.

Already toward the end of the 1960s, Mazar, one of the fathers of nationalist archaeology, encountered a difficulty that left him troubled. The stories of the patriarchs mention Philistines, Aramaeans, and a great many camels.

---

111   On this concept see Fernand Braudel, "History and Social Sciences: The Long Durée," in *Histories: French Constructions of the Past*, J. Revel and L. Hunt (eds.), New York: The New Press, 1995, 115–45.

Yet all the archaeological and epigraphic evidence indicated that the Philistines appeared in the region no earlier than the twelfth century BCE. The Aramaeans, who play a significant role in the Book of Genesis, first appeared in Near Eastern inscriptions from the eleventh century and become a notable presence from the ninth onward. The camels, too, gave no end of trouble. They were first domesticated at the start of the first millennium BCE, and as beasts of burden in commercial activity from the eighth century BCE. To preserve the historicity of the Bible, Mazar was obliged to sacrifice his original chronology and push the stories of the patriarchs to a later period, concluding that they "generally fitted the closing of the time of Judges or the early monarchy."[112]

Other, non-Israeli scholars, notably the bold American Thomas L. Thompson, had realized some time before that the old dating was illogical, as was the shaky chronology proposed earlier by Albright and his followers.[113] Instead, they suggested treating the story cycle of the patriarchs as a collection of late literary creations composed by gifted theologians. This meant that the detailed plots, the references to locations and the names of nearby tribes and peoples did not indicate a misty popular myth that had multiplied and improved over time, but rather a conscious ideological composition made hundreds of years later. Many of the names mentioned in the Book of Genesis appeared in the seventh or even the sixth century BCE. The authors of this book were undoubtedly familiar with the kingdoms of Assyria and Babylonia, which of course arose long after the hypothetical first migration in the twentieth century BCE.

The late authors of the Pentateuch wanted to emphasize the different, nonlocal origin of their imaginary forefathers. They were not like modern patriots, rooted in the national land and confident that they had sprung from its soil. They were more concerned to claim a higher cultural lineage than national proprietary rights over the country. That was why the exalted forefather of the "nation" originated in Ur of the Chaldees in Mesopotamia, and when his circumcised son Isaac came of age Abraham would not consider marrying him to a local pagan Canaanite girl. Hence a special messenger was dispatched to bring him a kosher bride from Nahor, a city that was not more monotheistic than Hebron but was, in the Babylonian world of the sixth or fifth century BCE, regarded as more illustrious than the little city of the patriarchs in Canaan. Ur, by contrast, was the center of a well-known, respected culture—if not the New York, at any rate the Paris of the ancient Near East. The Chaldeans began to settle there in the ninth century, and the Chaldean king Nabonidus developed it as a

---

112   Mazar, *Canaan and Israel*, 136.
113   Thomas L. Thompson, *The Historicity of the Patriarchal Narratives: The Quest for the Historical Abraham*, Berlin: Walter de Gruyter, 1974, 4–9.

major religious center only in the sixth century BCE. Was it fortuitous that the anonymous, and probably quite late, authors originated from the same place?

A similar search for a lineage from a great cultural center animated the story of the emergence from Egypt, the second significant myth to be shaken. The fragility of this story had been known for some time, but the centrality of the Exodus in the very definition of Jewish identity, not to mention the role of the Passover festival in its culture, made for a stubborn refusal to examine it. We have seen that Dubnow was uneasy about the Merneptah stela of the late thirteenth century BCE. Its pharaonic inscription declares that, among the various cities and tribes that had been subdued, Israel was destroyed "and has no more seed." This could have been pharaonic hyperbole, but it certainly suggests that there was some small cultural entity named Israel, among other small groups, in Egyptian-ruled Canaan.[114]

In the thirteenth century BCE, the purported time of the Exodus, Canaan was ruled by the still-powerful pharaohs. This means that Moses led the freed slaves out of Egypt ... to Egypt? According to the biblical narrative, the people he led through the wilderness for forty years included six hundred thousand warriors; they would have been traveling with their wives and children, implying a party of around three million in total. Aside from the fact that it was utterly impossible for a population of such size to wander through the desert for so long, an event of such magnitude should have left some epigraphic or archaeological traces. The ancient Egyptians kept meticulous records of every event, and there is a great deal of documentation about the kingdom's political and military life. There are even documents about incursions of nomadic groups into the realm. Yet there is not a single mention of any "Children of Israel" who lived in Egypt, or rebelled against it, or emigrated from it at any time. Pithom, mentioned in the biblical story, does in fact appear in an early external source, but it was built as an important city only at the end of the sixth century BCE. No traces have been found in the Sinai desert of any significant movement of population through it during the said period, and the location of the famous biblical Mount Sinai has yet to be discovered. Etzion-Gever and Arad, mentioned in the story of the wanderings, did not exist in that period, and appear much later as permanent, flourishing settlements.

After forty years of wandering, the Children of Israel arrived in Canaan and took it by storm. Following the divine command, they annihilated most of the local population and forced the remainder to serve them as hewers of

---

114   Niels Peter Lemche, "The So-called 'Israel-Stele' of Merneptah," in *The Israelites in History and Tradition*, London: SPCK, 1998, 35–8.

wood and drawers of water. After the conquest, the people that had been united under Moses split up into separate tribes (like the late Greek settlement in twelve city-states) and divided the territorial booty among them. This ruthless myth of settlement, described in the Book of Joshua in colorful detail as one of the earliest genocides, never actually happened. The famous conquest of Canaan was the next myth to fall apart in the skirmishes of the new archaeology.

For a long time the Zionist historians, followed by the Israeli archaeologists, ignored well-known findings. If at the time of the supposed Israelite conquest the country was ruled by Egypt, how was it that not a single Egyptian document mentioned this? Moreover, why does the Bible make no mention of the Egyptian presence in the country? Archaeological excavations in Gaza and Beth Shean had long revealed the Egyptian presence at the time of the supposed conquest and after, but the ancient national text was too precious to forswear, and so the scholars learned to muffle these feisty little facts with evasive and vague explanations.

New excavations at Jericho, Ai, and Heshbon, those powerful walled cities which the Children of Israel supposedly captured with fanfare, confirmed the old findings: in the late thirteenth century BCE Jericho was an insignificant little town, certainly unwalled, and neither Ai nor Heshbon had yet been settled at all. The same holds for most of the other cities mentioned in the story of the conquest. Traces of destruction and fire have been found in Hazor, Lachish and Megiddo, but the collapse of these old Canaanite cities was a slow process that took about a century and was very likely caused by the arrival of the "Sea Peoples," such as the Philistines, who at that time invaded the entire eastern littoral of the Mediterranean, as attested by a wealth of Egyptian and other documentation.[115]

The new Israeli archaeologists and scholars concerned themselves less with event-oriented political exploration and more with social-anthropological investigation—conducting regional surveys and exploring ancient living conditions, means of production, and cult practices over large areas—and they made a number of discoveries and new working hypotheses regarding colonization in the highlands of Canaan. In the lowlands, after the decline of the Canaanite cities, the settlement on land was probably carried out by local nomads who gradually, and with many interim phases, formed sedentary agricultural communities. The starting population from which the king-

---

115 The narrative of the conquest of Canaan was already being questioned in the twenties and thirties of the last century by German scholars of the Bible, including Albrecht Alt and Martin North. In the sixties and seventies, George Mendenhall and Norman Gottwald added new sociohistorical hypotheses concerning the appearance of the Hebrews.

doms of Israel and Judah would gradually arise was probably autochthonous Canaanite, which slowly emerged from under the Egyptian overlords as they withdrew from the country between the twelfth and tenth centuries BCE. The pottery and working tools of these new peasants did not differ from those of other Canaanites except for one cultural feature: the absence of pig bones from their settlements.[116] This is a significant fact, but it indicates neither the conquest of Canaan by an alien *ethnos* nor that these farmers were monotheists. The development from scattered communities of cultivators to the rise of cities based on their produce was a long and extremely gradual process that culminated in the emergence of two small local kingdoms.

The next biblical story to lose its scientific historicity as a result of new archaeological discoveries was the jewel in the crown of the long national memory. Ever since Graetz, through Dinur and the Israeli historians who followed, the united national kingdom of David and Solomon was the glorious golden age in Jewish history. All the future political models fed on this paragon of the biblical past and drew from it imagery, thinking and intellectual exhilaration. New novels embedded it in their plots; poems and plays were composed about the towering Saul, the fearless David and the wise Solomon. Excavators discovered the remains of their palaces, and detailed maps completed the historical picture and outlined the boundaries of the united empire that spread from the Euphrates to the border of Egypt.

Then came the post-1967 archaeologists and Bible scholars, who began to cast doubt on the very existence of this mighty kingdom, which, according to the Bible, grew rapidly after the period of the Judges. Excavations in Jerusalem in the 1970s—that is, after the city had been "reunified forever" by the Israeli government—undermined the fantasies about the glorious past. It was not possible to dig under the Haram al-Sharif, but explorations at all the other sites that were opened up around it failed to find any traces of an important tenth-century kingdom, the presumed time of David and Solomon. No vestige was ever found of monumental structures, walls or grand palaces, and the pottery found there was scanty and quite simple. At first it was argued that the unbroken occupation of the city and the massive construction in the reign of Herod had destroyed the remains, but this reasoning fell flat when impressive traces were uncovered from earlier periods in Jerusalem's history.

Other supposed remains from the united kingdom also came to be questioned. The Bible describes Solomon's rebuilding of the northern cities of Hazor, Megiddo

---

116   The theory about these shepherd-peasants is presented in Israel Finkelstein and Neil Silberman, *The Bible Unearthed*, New York: Free Press, 2001, 105–13.

and Gezer, and Yigael Yadin located in the grand structures of Hazor the city of Solomon the Wise. He also found palaces from the time of the united kingdom in Megiddo, and discovered the famous Solomonic gates in all three ancient cities. Unfortunately, the building style of these gates was found to be later than the tenth century BCE—they greatly resembled vestiges of a palace built in Samaria in the ninth. The technological development of the carbon-14 test confirmed that the colossal structures in the area dated not from Solomon's reign but from the time of the northern kingdom of Israel. Indeed, no trace has been found of the existence of that legendary king, whose wealth is described in the Bible as almost matching that of the mighty imperial rulers of Babylonia or Persia.

The inescapable and troublesome conclusion was that if there was a political entity in tenth-century Judea, it was a small tribal kingdom, and that Jerusalem was a fortified stronghold. It is possible that the tiny kingdom was ruled by a dynasty known as the House of David. An inscription discovered in Tell Dan in 1993 supports this assumption, but this kingdom of Judah was greatly inferior to the kingdom of Israel to its north, and apparently far less developed.

The documents from el-Amarna, dating from the fourteenth century BCE, indicate that already there were two small city-states in the highlands of Canaan—Shechem and Jerusalem—and the Merneptah stela shows that an entity named Israel existed in northern Canaan at the end of the thirteenth century BCE. The plentiful archaeological finds unearthed in the West Bank during the 1980s reveal the material and social difference between the two mountain regions. Agriculture thrived in the fertile north, supporting dozens of settlements, whereas in the south there were only some twenty small villages in the tenth and ninth centuries BCE. The kingdom of Israel was already a stable and strong state in the ninth century, while the kingdom of Judah consolidated and grew strong only by the late eighth. There were always in Canaan two distinct, rival political entities, though they were culturally and linguistically related—variants of ancient Hebrew were spoken by the inhabitants of both.

The kingdom of Israel under the Omride dynasty was clearly greater than the kingdom of Judah under the House of David. It is about the former that we have the oldest extrabiblical evidence: the inscription on the so-called Black Obelisk of Shalmaneser III of Assyria, the famous Mesha stela, and the inscription found at Tell Dan. All the grand structures previously attributed to Solomon were in fact later projects of the kingdom of Israel. At its zenith, it was one of the most populated and prosperous kingdoms in the territory between Damascus in the north, Moab in the east, the Mediterranean Sea in the west, and the kingdom of Judah in the south.

Archaeological excavations in various locations have also shown that the inhabitants of the mountainous northern region were, like the peasants in Judah, devout polytheists. They worshipped the popular Yahweh, who gradually became, like the Greek Zeus and the Roman Jupiter, the central deity, but they did not forsake the cults of other deities, such as Baal, Shemesh and the beautiful Asherah.[117] The authors of the Pentateuch, who were late Judean monotheists, detested the rulers of Israel but were no less envious of their legendary power and glory. They expropriated their prestigious name— "Israel," which was probably well established—while never desisting from the denunciation of their moral and religious transgressions.

The great sin of the people and rulers of Israel was, of course, the fact that their kingdom was defeated by the Assyrian empire in the second half of the eighth century BCE—that is, a good while before the fall of Judah in the sixth. Moreover, they left no agents of divine remembrance to clothe their ardent religion in attractive pseudohistorical garments.

The conclusion accepted by a majority of the new archaeologists and Bible scholars was that there never was a great united monarchy and that King Solomon never had grand palaces in which he housed his 700 wives and 300 concubines. The fact that the Bible does not name this large empire strengthens this conclusion. It was late writers who invented and glorified a mighty united kingdom, established by the grace of the single deity. Their rich and distinctive imagination also produced the famous stories about the creation of the world and the terrible flood, the wanderings of the forefathers and Jacob's struggle with the angel, the exodus from Egypt and the parting of the Red Sea, the conquest of Canaan and the miraculous stopping of the sun in Gibeon.

The central myths about the primeval origin of a marvelous nation that emerged from the desert, conquered a spacious land and built a glorious kingdom were a boon for rising Jewish nationalism and Zionist colonization. For a century they provided textual fuel of canonical quality that energized a complex politics of identity and territorial expansion demanding self-justification and considerable sacrifice.

Troublesome archaeologists and Bible scholars, in Israel and abroad, undermined these myths, which by the end of the twentieth century seemed about to be relegated to the status of fiction, with an unbridgeable gulf gaping

---

117 On the development of belief systems in Israel and Judea, and the lingering appearance of monotheism in the area, see the challenging collection of essays edited by Diana V. Edelman, *The Triumph of Elohim: From Yahwisms to Judaisms*, Michigan: Eerdmans, 1996.

between them and real history. But although Israeli society was no longer so engaged, and no longer so in need of the historical legitimation that had supported its creation and its very existence, it still had difficulty accepting the new findings, and the public obstinately resisted the change in the direction of research.

THE BIBLE AS METAPHOR

Ever since Benedict Spinoza and Thomas Hobbes in the seventeenth century—in other words, since the beginning of modern philosophy—there has been a continuing debate about the Bible authors' identity. Knowing their identity would place them in specific eras and would shed light on the diverse motives that would have driven this magnificent text. From the traditional assumption that Moses, inspired by God, wrote the Pentateuch, through the Bible criticism of the nineteenth century that dissected the text and assigned the sections to different times and places, to current interpretations that attribute the greater part of the work to the Persian or even the Hellenistic period, there have been numerous and conflicting hypotheses. But while there has been considerable progress in the field, resulting directly from the achievements of philology and archaeology, it is doubtful that we shall ever know with certainty when the Bible was written and who its authors were.

The position of the Israeli pioneers of the Tel Aviv school—Nadav Na'aman, Israel Finkelstein, Ze'ev Herzog and others—who argue that the historical core of the Bible was composed in the reign of Josiah, toward the end of the kingdom of Judah, offers attractive conclusions, but much of its interpretation and reasoning is less than solid. Their analyses, showing that the Bible could not have been written before the end of the eighth century BCE and that most of the stories it contains lack all factual substance, are fairly persuasive.[118] But their basic assumption—that the invented past was an obvious product of a manipulative ruler, Josiah—inadvertently leads to a problematic anachronism.

For example, *The Bible Unearthed*, a rich and stimulating book by Israel Finkelstein and Neil Asher Silberman, depicts a fairly modern national society whose sovereign, the king of Judah, seeks to unify his people and the refugees from the defeated kingdom of Israel by inventing the Torah. The desire to annex the territory of the northern kingdom prompts the writing of a rallying history in order to unite the two parts of the new nation. Yet these two able

---

118   Nadav Na'aman, *Ancient Israel's History and Historiography: The First Temple Period*, Winona Lake: Eisenbrauns, 2006; also see the article of Zeev Herzog, "Deconstructing the Walls of Jericho: Biblical Myth and Archaeological Reality," *Prometheus* 4 (2001), 72–03.

archaeologists, and others who follow in their footsteps, have no extrabiblical evidence about a monotheistic cult reform in Josiah's little kingdom in the seventh century BCE. They are content to rely on this text as long as there are no findings to contradict it, and they load it repeatedly with elements typical of political modernity. On encountering their work, the reader is likely to imagine that although the inhabitants of Judah and the refugees from Israel did not have television or wireless sets in every rural hut, they could at least read and write, and eagerly circulated the newly printed Torahs.

In an illiterate peasant society without an educational system or a standard common language, and with limited means of communication—only a few percent could read and write—a copy or two of the Torah might have been a fetish but could not have served as an ideological campfire. Similarly, a sovereign's dependence on his subjects' goodwill is also a modern phenomenon, which archaeologists and Bible scholars, with little historical awareness, keep grafting onto ancient history. Kings did not need to rally the masses around a national politics. They generally contented themselves with a loose ideological-dynastic consensus among the administrative class and a narrow stratum of landed aristocracy. They did not need the commitment of the people, nor did they have the means of yoking its consciousness, such as it was, to their monarchy.

Explaining the origin of the first monotheism in the context of widespread propaganda conducted by a small, marginal kingdom seeking to annex the land to the north is a very unconvincing historiographic argument. However, it might be indicative of an anti-annexationist mood in early twenty-first-century Israel. It is a strange theory that the bureaucratic and centralistic needs of the government of little Jerusalem before its fall gave birth to the monotheistic cult of "YHWH-alone" and the composition of a retrospective theological work in the form of the historical parts of the Bible.[119] Surely Josiah's contemporaries, reading the narratives describing Solomon's mighty palaces, would have expected to witness remnants of past grandeur in their city streets. But since those vast ancient palaces had never existed, as archaeology has shown, how could they have been described prior to their imaginary destruction?

It is more probable that the ancient kingdoms of Israel and Judah left detailed administrative chronicles and vainglorious victory inscriptions, composed by obedient court scribes—such as the biblical Shaphan, son of Azaliah[120]—as was the case in other kingdoms in the region. We don't know,

---

119   Finkelstein and Silberman, *The Bible Unearthed*, 248–9.
120   In the Bible, it was Shaphan the scribe that brought the Torah to Josiah (2 Kings. 22:1–13).

and never will know, what those chronicles contained, but in all probability some were preserved in the surviving archives of the kingdoms, and after the fall of the kingdom of Judah the authors of the books of the Bible used them, with amazing creativity, as raw material from which to compose the most influential texts in the birth of monotheism in the Near East. To these chronicles they added some parables, legends and myths that circulated among the intellectual elites throughout the region, producing a fascinating critical discourse about the status of the earthly ruler from the viewpoint of a divine sovereign.[121]

The upheaval of the exile and "return" in the sixth century BCE could have allowed the literate Judean elite—former court scribes, priests and their offspring—greater autonomy than they might have enjoyed under a direct dynastic monarchy. A historical contingency of political breakdown and the resulting absence of an exigent authority gave them a new and exceptional opportunity for action. Thus was born a new field of unique literary creativity whose great reward lay not in power but in religion. Only such a situation could explain, for example, how it was possible both to sing the praises of the dynastic founder (David) and at the same time depict him as a sinner punished by a superior divine being. Only thus could the freedom of expression, so rare in premodern societies, produce a theological masterpiece.

We may therefore propose the following hypothesis: the exclusive mono-theism that stands out on almost every page in the Bible was the result not of politics—the politics of a minor local king seeking to expand his realm—but of culture: the remarkable encounter between Judean intellectual elites, in exile or returning from exile, with the abstract Persian religions. This monotheism prob-ably found its source in an advanced intellectual system but was extruded from it and, like many revolutionary ideologies throughout history, seeped into the margins under political pressure from the conservative center. It is no accident that the Hebrew word *dat* ("religion") is of Persian origin. This early monotheism would become fully developed in its late encounter with Hellenistic polytheism.

The theory of the Copenhagen-Sheffield school—Thomas L. Thompson, Niels Peter Lemche, Philip Davies and others[122]—is more convincing, even if

121   See for example the affinity between the epigrams of Ahiqar the Assyrian and the parables in the Bible. Avinoam Yalin (ed.), *The Book of Ahiqar the Wise*, Jerusalem: Hamarav, 1937 (in Hebrew); and also James M. Lindenberger, *The Aramaic Proverbs of Ahiqar*, Baltimore: Johns Hopkins, 1983.

122   See the book by Niels Peter Lemche, *Ancient Israel: A New History of Israelite Society*, Sheffield: Sheffield University Press, 1988; Philip R. Davies, *In Search of "Ancient Israel,"* Sheffield: Sheffield University Press, 1992; Thomas L. Thompson, *The Mythic Past: Biblical Archaeology and the Myth of Israel*, London: Basic Books, 1999.

we do not adopt every one of its assumptions and conclusions. It says, in effect, that the Bible is not a book but a grand library that was written, revised and adapted in the course of three centuries, from the late sixth to the early second BCE. It should be read as a multilayered literary construction of a religious and philosophical nature or as theological parables that sometimes employ quasi-historical descriptions for educational purposes, aimed especially at future generations (as the system of divine punishment often punishes the descendants for their forebears' transgressions).[123]

The various ancient authors and editors sought to create a coherent religious community, and drew lavishly on the glorious politics of the past to prepare a stable, durable future for a cult center in Jerusalem. Concerned to isolate it from the idolatrous population, they invented the category of Israel as a sacred, chosen people whose origins lay elsewhere, in contrast to Canaan, a local anti-people of hewers of wood and drawers of water. This text-group's appropriation of the name Israel was perhaps due to its rivalry with the Samaritans, who saw themselves as heirs to the kingdom of Israel.[124] This self-isolating literary politics, which began to develop between the little "province of Yahud" and the centers of high culture in Babylonia, accorded well with the global identity policies of the Persian empire, whose rulers took pains to separate communities, classes and linguistic groups in order to retain control over their vast possessions.

Some of the leaders, judges, heroes, kings, priests and prophets (mainly the later ones) who populate the Bible may have been historical figures. But their time, their relationships, their motives, their real power, the boundaries of their rule, their influence and manner of worship—that is to say, what really matters in history—were the product of a later imagination. Likewise, the intellectual and religious consumers of the biblical story cycles—namely, the early Jewish faith communities—took shape much later.

Knowing that Shakespeare's play *Julius Caesar* tells us little about ancient Rome but a good deal about England in the late sixteenth century does not detract from its power and helps us to view its historical testimony in a different light. Sergei Eisenstein's film *The Battleship Potemkin*, which is set during the revolution of 1905, tells us little about that uprising but much about

---

123   "For I the LORD thy God am a jealous God, visiting the iniquity of the fathers upon the children unto the third and fourth generation of them that hate me." Ex. 20:5. See also Deut. 5:9.

124   On Jewish tradition's later attempts to deny the Samaritans their Israelite origin, see Gedaliah Alon, *Studies in Jewish History*, vol. 2, Tel Aviv: Hakibutz Hameuhad, 1958 (in Hebrew), 1–14.

the ideology of the Bolshevik regime in 1925, when the film was made. Our attitude to the Bible should be the same. It is not a narrative that can instruct us about the time it describes but is instead an impressive didactic theological discourse, as well as a possible testimony about the time it was composed. It would have been a more reliable historical document if we knew with greater certainty when each of its parts was written.

For many centuries the Bible has been regarded by the three monotheistic cultures—Judaism, Christianity and Islam—as a divinely inspired work, evidence of God's manifestation and preeminence. With the rise of nationalism in modern times, it began to be seen increasingly as a work composed by human beings as a reconstruction of their past. Even in prenationalistic Protestant England, and even more so among the Puritan settlers in North America and South Africa, the book became, through anachronism and fervent imagination, a kind of ideal model for the formation of a modern religious-political collectivity.[125] In the past, Jewish believers tended not to delve into it. But with the rise of the Jewish enlightenment, growing numbers of cultivated individuals began to read the Bible in a secular light.

Yet, as this chapter has tried to show, it was only the appearance of prenationalist Jewish historiography in the latter half of the nineteenth century that gave the Bible a leading role in the drama of the rise of the modern Jewish nation. The book was transferred from the shelf of theological tracts to the history section, and adherents of Jewish nationalism began to read it as if it were reliable testimony to processes and events. Indeed, it was elevated to the status of mythistory, representing an incontrovertible truth. It became the locus of secular sanctity that was not to be touched, and from which all consideration of people and nation must begin.

Above all, the Bible became an ethnic marker, indicating a common origin for individuals of very different backgrounds and secular cultures yet all still hated for their religion, which they barely observed. That was the meaning that underlay this image of an ancient nation, dating back almost to the Creation, that came to be imprinted in the minds of people who felt themselves dislocated in the rough-and-tumble of modernity. It became imprinted in their consciousness of the past. The welcoming bosom of the Bible, despite

---

125 During the early North American colonial era, many Puritans considered themselves to be the children of Israel to whom the new land of milk and honey was promised. These early colonists set out west holding the Old Testament in their hands, imagining themselves as the true descendants of Joshua the Conquerer. A similar biblical imaginary directed the Afrikaners. See Bruce Cauthen, "The Myth of Divine Election and Afrikaner Ethnogenesis," in *Myths and Nationhood*, 107–131.

(or perhaps because of) its miraculous and legendary character, could provide a long, almost an eternal, sense of belonging—something that the fast-moving, freighted present could not give them.

In this way, the Bible became a secular book that schoolchildren read to learn about their ancient forefathers—children who would later march proudly as soldiers fighting wars of colonization and independence.

CHAPTER THREE

The Invention of the Exile: Proselytism and Conversion

After being forcibly exiled from their land, the people kept faith with it throughout their Dispersion and never ceased to pray and hope for their return to it and for the restoration in it of their political freedom.
—The Declaration of the Establishment of the State of Israel, 1948

As a result of the historic catastrophe in which Titus of Rome destroyed Jerusalem and Israel was exiled from its land, I was born in one of the cities of the Exile. But always I regarded myself as one who was born in Jerusalem.
—S. I. Agnon, accepting the Nobel Prize for Literature, 1966

Even Israelis who are not familiar with the historic opening passage of their Proclamation of Independence must have held a fifty-shekel note that bears the moving words spoken by S. I. Agnon when he received the Nobel Prize. Just like the authors of the proclamation, and like most of Israel's citizens, the eminent author knew that the "Jewish nation" was exiled after the fall of the Second Temple in 70 CE, then wandered about the world, inspired by the "two-thousand-year-long hope ... of being a free people" (in the words of the Israeli national anthem) in its ancient homeland.

Uprooting and deportation are concepts deeply embedded in Jewish tradition in all its forms. But their significance has changed over the history of the religion; they did not always bear the secular meaning with which they came to be imbued in modern times. Jewish monotheism began to take shape among the cultural elites who were forcibly deported after the fall of the kingdom of Judah in the sixth century BCE, and the imagery of exile and wandering already reverberates, directly or metaphorically, in a major part of the Torah, the Prophets, and the Writings (the final section of the Old Testament). From the expulsion from Eden, through Abraham's migration to Canaan and Jacob's descent into Egypt, to the prophesies of Zachariah and Daniel, Jewish religion gazed back through a perspective of wanderings, uprootings, and returns. The Torah already stated: "And the Lord shall scatter thee among all people, from one end of the earth even unto the other, and there thou shalt serve other gods, which neither thou nor thy fathers have known" (Deut. 28:64). The fall of the First Temple was associated with expulsion, and this literary-theological memory helped shape subsequent Jewish religious sensibilities.[1]

However, a close examination of the historical event that apparently engendered the "second exile" in the year 70 CE, and an analysis of the Hebrew term *golah* (exile) and its connotation in late Hebrew, indicate that the national historical consciousness was a patchwork of disparate events and traditional elements. Only in this way could it function as an effective myth that provided modern Jews with a pathway to ethnic identity. The ultra-paradigm of deportation was essential for the construction of a long-term memory wherein an imaginary, exiled people-race could be described as the direct descendants of the former "people of the Bible." As we shall see, the myth of uprooting and exile was fostered by the Christian tradition, from which it flowed into Jewish tradition and grew to be the truth engraved in history, both the general and the national.

THE "PEOPLE" EXILED IN 70 CE

It must first of all be emphasized that the Romans never deported entire peoples. We might add that neither did the Assyrians and Babylonians move entire populations from the countries they conquered. It did not pay to uproot the people of the land, the cultivators of produce, the taxpayers. But even the efficient policy of deportation practiced by the Assyrian, and later the Babylonian, empire—in which whole sections of local administrative and cultural elites were deported—was not followed by the Roman Empire. Here and there in the western Mediterranean countries, local farming communities were displaced to make room for the settling of Roman soldiers, but this exceptional policy was not applied in the Near East. Roman rulers could be utterly ruthless in suppressing rebellious subject populations: they executed fighters, took captives and sold them into slavery, and sometimes exiled kings and princes. But they definitely did not deport whole populations in the countries they conquered in the East, nor did they have the means to do so—none of the trucks, trains or great ships available in the modern world.[2]

Flavius Josephus, the historian of the Zealot revolt in the year 66 CE, is

---

1 On the concept of exile see Arnold M. Eisen, "Exile," in *Contemporary Jewish Religious Thought: Original Essays on Critical Concepts, Movements, and Beliefs*, A. A. Cohen and P. Mendes-Flohr (eds.), New York: Free Press, 1988, 219–25; and also the book by A. M. Eisen, *Galut: Modern Jewish Reflection on Homelessness and Homecoming*, Bloomington: Indiana University Press, 1986.

2 Exiling was generally from the center outwards. See Gordon P. Kelly, *A History of Exile in the Roman Republic*, Cambridge: Cambridge University Press, 2006.

almost the only source for this exile, aside from archaeological findings dating to that time. His book *Wars of the Jews* describes the tragic outcome of that period's conflict. The devastation did not spread throughout the kingdom of Judea, but affected mainly Jerusalem and a number of other fortified cities. Josephus estimated that 1.1 million people died in the siege of Jerusalem and the great massacre that followed, that 97,000 were taken captive, and that a few thousand more were killed in other cities.[3]

Like all ancient historians, Josephus tended to exaggerate his numbers. Today most scholars believe that virtually all demographic figures from antiquity are overstated, and that a good many have numerological significance. Josephus does state that a large number of pilgrims had gathered in Jerusalem before the uprising, but the assumption that more than a million people were killed there is not credible. The population of the city of Rome at the height of the empire in the second century CE might have approached the size of a medium modern conurbation,[4] but there was no such metropolis in the little kingdom of Judea. A cautious estimate suggests that Jerusalem at that time could have had a population of sixty thousand to seventy thousand inhabitants.

Even if we accept the unrealistic figure of seventy thousand captives, it still does not mean that the evil Titus, who destroyed the Temple, expelled "the Jewish people." Rome's great Arch of Titus shows Roman soldiers carrying the plundered Temple candelabra—not, as taught in Israeli schools, Judean captives carrying it on their way to exile. Nowhere in the abundant Roman documentation is there any mention of a deportation from Judea. Nor have any traces been found of large refugee populations around the borders of Judea after the uprising, as there would have been if a mass flight had taken place.

We do not know exactly how large the population of Judea was prior to the revolt of the Zealots and the war against Rome. Here, too, Josephus's figures are useless; he states, for example, that there were three million inhabitants in the Galilee. Archaeological surveys conducted in recent decades suggest that in the eighth century BCE, in the whole land of Canaan—that is, the strong kingdom of Israel and the small kingdom of Judah—there were some 460,000 inhabitants.[5] Magen Broshi, an Israeli archaeologist, calculated—on the basis of the wheat-growing capacity of the country between the sea and the Jordan

---

3 Flavius Josephus, *Wars of the Jews* 6. 9. According to Tacitus, 600,000 were besieged. See Tacitus *History* 5. 13.

4 On Rome's population and the debate about it, see Jérôme Carcopino, *Daily Life in Ancient Rome*, New Haven: Yale University Press, [1940] 1968, 16–21.

5 Magen Broshi and Israel Finkelstein, "The size of the population in Eretz Israel in 734 BCE," *Cathedra* 58, 1991 (in Hebrew), 3–24.

river—that at its most flourishing, during the Byzantine period in the sixth century CE, it could have sustained no more than one million inhabitants.[6] Hence it is reasonable to assume that on the eve of the Zealot uprising, the population of the extended kingdom of Judea was between half a million and one million people. Wars, epidemics, droughts, or onerous taxation could reduce the population, but before the botanical and agro-industrial revolutions of modern times, the number of inhabitants could not increase to any great extent.

The Zealots' internecine wars and their uprising against the Romans dealt the country massive blows, and the demoralization of the cultural elites after the destruction of the Temple must have been profound. It's quite likely that the population in and around Jerusalem remained diminished for some time. But, as already stated, it was not expelled and, before long, recovered economically. Archaeological discoveries have shown that Josephus exaggerated the devastation, and that several cities had recovered their populations by the end of the first century CE. Moreover, the Jewish religious culture was about to enter one of its most impressive and fruitful periods.[7] Unfortunately, there is little information about the systems of political relations during this period.

We also have little information about the second monotheistic revolt, which shook Judean history in the second century CE. The uprising that broke out in 132 CE, in the reign of the Emperor Hadrian, popularly known as the Bar Kokhba revolt, is mentioned briefly by the Roman historian Cassius Dio, and by Eusebius, the bishop of Caesarea and author of *Ecclesiastical History*. Echoes of the events appear in the Jewish religious texts as well as in archaeological findings. Regrettably, there was no historian of the stature of Josephus at that time, so any reconstruction of events can only be fragmentary. The question arises, was the traditional story of the expulsion due to the traumatic consequences of that revolt? Describing the conclusion of the revolt, Cassius Dio wrote:

---

6   Magen Broshi, "The population in Eretz Israel in the Roman-Byzantine period," in *Eretz Israel From the Destruction of the Second Temple to the Muslim Conquest*, Zvi Baras, et al. (eds.), Jerusalem: Ben Zvi, 1982 (in Hebrew), 442–55; and "Demographic changes in ancient Eretz Israel: Methodology and estimation," in *Man and Land in Eretz Israel in Antiquity*, A. Kasher, A, Oppenheimer, and U. Rapaport (eds.), Jerusalem: Ben Zvi, 1986 (in Hebrew), 49–55. Significantly, back in the 1930s, Arthur Ruppin, the first demographer at the Hebrew University, estimated the size of the population of Judea at about one million. See *The War of the Jews for Their Existence*, Tel Aviv: Dvir, 1940 (in Hebrew), 27.

7   Shmuel Safrai, "The Recovery of the Jewish Population in the Yavneh Period," in *Eretz Israel From the Destruction of the Second Temple to the Muslim Conquest*, 18–39.

Fifty of their most important outposts and nine hundred and eighty-five of their most famous villages were razed to the ground. Five hundred and eighty thousand men were slain in the various raids and battles, and the number of those that perished by famine, disease and fire was past finding out. Thus nearly the whole of Judaea was made desolate.[8]

The characteristic exaggeration is plain to see (the figures used by ancient historians always seem to call for the subtraction of a zero), but even this grim report says nothing about deportations. Jerusalem was to be renamed Aelia Capitolina, and circumcised men were for some time barred from entering it. For three years, harsh restrictions were imposed on the local populace, especially around the capital, and religious persecution was intensified. Captive fighters were probably taken away, and others must have fled from the area. But the Judean masses were not exiled in 135 CE.[9]

The name Provincia Judea was changed to Provincia Syria Palaestina (later Palestine), but its population in the second century CE remained predominantly Judeans and Samaritans, and it started to flourish again for one or two generations after the end of the revolt. By the end of the second century and beginning of the third, not only had most of the farming population recovered and agricultural production stabilized, but the country's culture attained what came to be thought of as its golden age in the time of Rabbi Judah ha-Nasi.[10] The year 220 CE saw the completion and final arrangement of the six parts of the Mishnah—a far more decisive historical event than the Bar Kokhba revolt in the development of Jewish identity and religion. So what was the origin of the great myth about the exiling of the Jewish people following the destruction of the Temple?

Chaim Milikowsky, a scholar at Bar-Ilan University, has found evidence in numerous contemporary rabbinical sources that in the second and third centuries CE the term *galut* (exile) was used in the sense of political subjugation rather than deportation, and the two meanings were not necessarily connected. Other rabbinical sources refer to the Babylonian exile as the only *galut*, which they regarded as ongoing, even after the fall of the Second

---

8   Cassius Dio *Roman History* 69. 14.

9   Nor does Eusebius make any mention of a mass exile. See Eusebius Pamphilius *Ecclesiastical History* 4. 6. See also two interesting articles on the subject: Ze'ev Safrai, "The condition of the Jewish population in Eretz Israel after the Bar Kokhba Revolt," and Joshua Schwartz, "Eretz Yehudah following the oppression of Bar Kokhba Revolt," in A. Oppenheimer and U. Rapaport (eds.), *The Revolt of Bar Kokhba: New Researches*, Jerusalem: Ben Zvi, 1984 (in Hebrew), 182–223.

10   See Lee Israel Levine, "The Age of Rabbi Yehudah Hanassi," in *Eretz Israel From the Destruction of the Second Temple to the Muslim Conquest*, 93–118.

Temple.[11] Israel Jacob Yuval, a historian at the Hebrew University in Jerusalem, went further. He proposed to show that the renewed Jewish myth about the exile in fact arose fairly late, and was due mainly to the rise of Christian mythology about the Jews being exiled in punishment for their rejection and crucifixion of Jesus.[12] It seems that the source of the discourse regarding the anti-Jewish exile lies in the writings of Justin Martyr, who in the mid-second century linked the expulsion of circumcised men from Jerusalem after the Bar Kokhba revolt with divine collective punishment.[13] He was followed by other Christian authors who regarded the presence of Jews outside their sacred land as the punishment and proof of their sins. The myth of exile began to be slowly appropriated and integrated into Jewish tradition.

It was in the Babylonian Talmud, however, that the first statements appear linking the exile with the fall of the Second Temple. A Jewish community had existed in Babylonia continuously since the sixth century BCE, and not even during the powerful Hasmonean kingdom did it ever seek to "return" to Zion. Perhaps, following the destruction of the Second Temple, this gave rise to the narrative linking the fall with renewed exile as an echo of an ancient event, a catastrophe that provided a religious rationale for "weeping by the rivers"—rivers that flowed not very far from Jerusalem.

With the triumph of Christianity in the early fourth century CE, when it became the religion of the empire, Jewish believers in other parts of the world also began to adopt the notion of exile as divine punishment. The connection between uprooting and sin, destruction and exile, became embedded in the various definitions of the Jewish presence around the world. The myth of the Wandering Jew, punished for his transgressions, was rooted in the dialectic of Christian-Jewish hatred that would mark the boundaries of both religions through the following centuries. What is more significant, however, is that henceforth the concept of exile took on

---

11   Chaim Milikowsky, "Notions of Exile, Subjugation and Return in Rabbinic Literature," in *Exile: Old Testament, Jewish and Christian Conceptions*, James M. Scott (ed.), Leiden: Brill, 1997, 265–96.

12   Israel Jacob Yuval, "The myth of the exile from the land: Jewish time and Christian time," *Alpayim* 29, 2005 (in Hebrew), 9–25. In fact, Adiyah Horon, the intellectual father of the "Canaanite" movement, said as much long ago: "There is no truth in the claim that the 'exile' occurred mainly after the destruction, when Titus and Hadrian supposedly expelled the 'Jews' from Palestine. This idea, based on historical ignorance, derives from a hostile fabrication by the fathers of the Christian church, who wanted to show that God punished the Jews for the crucifixion of Jesus." A. G. Horon, *East and West: A History of Canaan and the Land of the Hebrews*, Tel Aviv: Dvir, 2000 (in Hebrew), 344.

13   On Justin, see David Rokéah, *Justin Martyr and the Jews*, Leiden: Brill, 2002; and also, Justin Martyr *Dialogue with Trypho* 2. 92, 2.

an outright metaphysical connotation within Jewish traditions, going far beyond simply being away from one's homeland.

Claiming descent from the original Jerusalem deportees was essential, like belonging to the seed of Abraham, Isaac and Jacob; otherwise the standing of the Jewish believer as a member of the chosen people was not assured. Moreover, being in "exile" became an existential situation of diminishing territorial significance. Exile, in fact, was anywhere, even in the Holy Land. Later the Kabbalah made it a central attribute of the divinity, for the Shekhinah (the divine spirit) is always in exile.

The concept of exile came to shape the definitions of rabbinical Judaism vis-à-vis Christianity's growing might.[14] The devotees of the Old Testament's Judaic faith rejected the salvation of the world that Jesus brought with his sacrifice. Continuing to identify themselves as Jews, they did not accept the Christian concept of grace created by the resurrection of the crucified savior. To them, the existing world was still suffering, and would continue to suffer until the coming of the true messiah. Thus the exile was a form of religious catharsis, which also served to wash away sins. The longed-for salvation, the antithesis of exile, could come only with the End of Days. Exile, therefore, was not a location away from the homeland, but a condition that is not salvation. The anticipated salvation would come when the messiah king of the seed of David arrived, and with this, a mass return to Jerusalem. Salvation would include the resurrection of the dead, who would also congregate en masse in Jerusalem.

For an oppressed religious minority living in the midst of a hegemonic religious culture, the exile connoted a temporal defeat—the fall of the Temple—but the future that would annul it was wholly messianic and totally outside the power of the humbled Jews. Only that future, whether immediate or distant, but certainly lying outside of human time, guaranteed the salvation and perhaps the coming of universal power. That was the reason Jews did not "always seek to return to their ancient homeland," and the few who did so were denounced as false messiahs. There were, of course, some devout pilgrims who were permitted to make an individual act of "going up to" Jerusalem, and many went in order to be buried there. But a collective migration for the purpose of living a full Jewish life in the holy city was not part of the religious imagination, and the few who proposed it were exceptional or eccentric.[15]

---

14 An analysis of the concept of exile is also found in Amnon Raz-Krakotzkin, *Exil et souveraineté: Judaïsme, sionisme et pensée binationale*, Paris: La Fabrique, 2007.

15 There were some group migrations, such as that of Rabbi Moshe ben Nahman (Nahmanides) in the thirteenth century, or Judah Ha-Hassid in 1700, but these and a few others were exceptional. On the life of Jews in the Holy Land a short time before the

Curiously, it was the Karaites' relationship with Jerusalem that led a good many of them to migrate there, and even to call on their fellow believers to do so. These "protestant Jews," who stuck to the Old Testament and refused to accept the Oral Law (the Mishnah and Talmud), were unaffected by rabbinical Judaism's rigid and confining conception of exile. They could ignore its prohibitions relating to the holy city and settle there in large numbers. With their distinctive mourning over the destruction—they were known as the "mourners of Zion"—they apparently constituted the majority of Jerusalem's population in the ninth and tenth centuries.

A number of rabbinical prohibitions forbade hastening the salvation, and therefore migrating to the source from which it would arise. The most prominent prohibitions were the famous three vows in the Babylonian Talmud: "That Israel must not [seek to] rise up over the wall; that the Holy One Blessed Be He adjured Israel not to rise up against the nations of the world; that Holy One Blessed Be He adjured the idolaters not to enslave Israel overmuch" (*Tractate Ketubot* 110: 72).

"Rise up over the wall" meant mass migration to the Holy Land, and this clear-cut prohibition affected Jews throughout the ages, instilling an acceptance of exile as a divine ordinance not to be broken. It was forbidden to hasten the end and rebel against God's spirit. To the believers, the exile was not a temporary concrete condition that could be altered by migration across the world, but a situation that defined the entire existing physical world.[16]

Therefore, when the Jewish cultural centers in Babylonia declined, the Jews migrated to Baghdad, not to Jerusalem, although both cities were ruled by the same caliphate. The Jewish deportees from Spain migrated to cities all around the Mediterranean, but only a few chose to go to Zion. In the modern age, with its ferocious pogroms and the rise of aggressive nationalism in Eastern Europe, masses of the Yiddish people migrated westward, mainly to the United States.

Only when the American borders closed in the 1920s, and again after the horrendous Nazi massacres, did significant numbers migrate to Mandatory Palestine, part of which became the State of Israel. The Jews were not forcibly deported from their "homeland," and there was no voluntarily "return" to it.

EXILE WITHOUT EXPULSION—HISTORY IN THE TWILIGHT ZONE

When Heinrich Graetz came to describe the fall of the Second Temple in his book *History of the Jews*, he began by comparing it with the destruction of the First Temple:

construction of the Jewish nation, see Israel Bartal, *Exile in the Homeland: Essays*, Jerusalem: Hassifria Hazionit, 1994 (in Hebrew).

16   On the significance of the three vows, see Aviezer Ravitzky, *Messianism, Zionism and Jewish Religious Radicalism*, Tel Aviv: Am Oved, 1993 (in Hebrew), 277–305.

Once more did Zion sit weeping amid the ruins, weeping over her sons fallen in battle, over her daughters sold into slavery or abandoned to the savage soldiery of Rome; but she was more desolate now than in the days of her first captivity, for hushed was the voice of the prophet, who once foretold the end of her widowhood and her mourning.[17]

The historical story was thus fashioned on the biblical model of the destruction, as was the deportation that followed. This first proto-Zionist historian proceeded to narrate the tragedy in an agonized tone:

It would indeed be difficult to describe the suffering of those who were taken captive in the war, estimated to number nine hundred thousand ... Youths under the age of sixteen and most of the female captives were sold into slavery at an incredibly low price, for the market was glutted.[18]

Graetz naturally borrowed the narrative about the end of the Zealot revolt from Josephus, and further inflated his numbers. He even added information lacking in the original, highlighting the sacred pairing of destruction and exile:

[A]ll these calamities came with such crushing force on the remaining Jews that they felt utterly at a loss as to what they should do. Judea was depopulated ... The third banishment—the Roman Exile [Galut Edom], under Vespasian and Titus—had commenced amid greater terror and cruelty than the Babylonian Exile under Nebuchadnezzar. Only a few were spared ... What was to be the future of the Jewish nation, of Judaism?[19]

He answers these menacing rhetorical questions in the negative: the "nation of Judah" would survive, and so would its religion, else Graetz would not have been able to write his fine book. Moreover, unlike the fall of the First Temple, this one left "a remnant of the people clinging to its homeland." This enables the historian to continue the pathos-filled narrative about the Jewish people in its land. But already at this stage he creates an indirect ultra-image of uprooting and wandering. This is reinforced in his description of the consequences of the Bar Kokhba revolt that broke out sixty-five years later:

Thus all the warriors were destroyed, all the towns and villages laid waste, and the land literally converted into a desert. The prisoners, mostly women and children, were dragged by the thousands to the slave markets of Hebron

17   Graetz, *History of the Jews*, vol. 2, 309–310.
18   Ibid., 311.
19   Ibid., 321–2.

and Gaza, where they were sold ... Many fugitives, however, fled to Arabia, whence that country obtained its Jewish population, which afterward played so important a part in its history.[20]

Note that nowhere does Graetz speak of the whole people being exiled. He stresses the captivity and the flight of many from Judea. Very skillfully, in the literary genre of tragedy, he interweaves and links the two historical uprisings into a single "national" sequence. The repeated comparison with the fall of the First Temple, with consequences familiar to most of his readers, rounds off the picture.

Simon Dubnow also makes no mention of deportation. Moreover, unlike Graetz, the Russian-Jewish historian avoids associating the destruction of Jerusalem with a forced exile. He follows the literary examples of Josephus and Graetz in describing the fall in dramatic and shocking terms. Thousands of captives are carried away to the ends of the empire, leaving Judea thinly populated. A similar description follows the end of the Bar Kokhba revolt: a great number of captives are sold into slavery, and an equal number of rebels become fugitives. But Dubnow does not create a meta-image of the Jewish people going into exile after the destruction of the Temple, and it is clear to readers that the people was not forcibly uprooted from its country.[21]

Salo Baron employs a similar rhetoric. The New York historian does not link the destruction with a deportation, but, as we shall see, tends rather to highlight other reasons for the presence of Jews outside Judea. He lingers on the tragic consequences of the two uprisings, but is more meticulous in stressing the end of Judean statehood. This is not depicted as a drama but rather as a lengthy, logical historical process.

To Baron, the most significant issue (and one related to the subject of the previous chapter) is to avoid a connection between the end of Judea as a political entity and the disappearance of the Jewish "ethnic nation." He confronts the historical analyses of Theodor Mommsen, Julius Wellhausen and other gentile historians who described Jewish communities after the fall of Jerusalem as religious groups rather than as one people, by asserting that from the time of Nebuchadnezzar to modern times, there has been a distinctive Jewish *ethnos*, which "never completely fitted into the general patterns of national divisions."[22] The Jews, then, are a people with an extraordinary past unlike any other people.

---

20 Ibid., 419.
21 Dubnow, *History of the World-People*, vol. 3, 28–29.
22 Baron, *A Social and Religious History*, vol. 2, 104.

We find, as we proceed to typical Zionist historiography, that the essence of the discourse does not change. Neither, surprisingly, did the Zionist historians describe an expulsion following the destruction of the Temple. But here we find a different chronological surprise. The historian Yitzhak Baer's well-known book *Galut* begins by describing the meaning of the long exile:

> The destruction of the Second Temple widened the breach in the nation's historical continuity and augments the treasury of national-religious jewels whose loss is to be mourned: the Temple and its cult, the mutilated theocracy, the national autonomy, the holy soil ever further from reclamation.[23]

For Baer, the ground is slowly slipping from under the people's feet, but the Jewish nation is not torn from it in a single violent act, even though its kingdom has been lost for a long time. Life on the national soil goes on, despite the massive destruction, and so does the heroic struggle:

> The struggles of the Zealots for political freedom and the firm establishment of God's supremacy continued from the time of Bar Kokhba's revolt up to the conquest of Palestine by the Arabs. Only after stubborn resistance was the lesson learned: that love cannot be prematurely aroused, that the kingdom of God cannot be set up by force, that one cannot rise in rebellion against overlordship of the nations.[24]

Baer was a painstaking and thoughtful historian. He not only knew the mass of sources about the fall of the Second Temple but was also familiar with the abundant materials of medieval Judaism. But if there was no expulsion, it was still necessary to have a forced exile; otherwise it would be impossible to understand the "organic" history of the "wandering" Jewish people, which for some reason never hastened to return to its homeland. The start of the "exile-without-expulsion" was different from the exile that Jewish tradition mistakenly dated to the fall of the Temple in the first century CE—the long exile was in fact considerably shorter, because it began only with the Arab conquest.

This exile-without-expulsion, which began in the seventh century CE—that is, some six centuries after the fall of the Second Temple—was not Yitzhak Baer's invention alone. This astonishing discovery was made by other Zionist scholars as well, notably Baer's friend and historiographical comrade-in-arms, Ben-Zion Dinur. The first volume of his famous collection of sources, *Israel in Exile*, first published in the 1920s, later acquired a subtitle: *From the Conquest*

---

23   Baer, *Galut*, 10.
24   Ibid., 13.

of the Land of Israel by the Arabs to the Crusades. Aware that he had to prepare his readers for a new national historical sequence, Dinur prefaced the sources with a long exposition on his novel chronology:

> I begin the period of "Israel in Exile" with the conquest of the Land of Israel by the Arabs. Until that time, the history of Israel was mainly that of the Jewish nation in its homeland ... It is not necessary to explain that the true "exile" (in relation to the nation, as a mass-historical entity, not its individual members) began only when the Land of Israel ceased to be a land of Jews, because others arrived, settled in it permanently and claimed it for generations ... True, tradition and popular perception do not distinguish between our people's loss of power over the country, and the loss of the land from under its feet. But from the historical viewpoint it is necessary to distinguish between these two situations. They were not contemporaneous, and are historically distinctive.[25]

The chronological revision is significant and decisive, and may well be seen as undermining Jewish tradition. It seems to have originated from two linked causes:

1. The basic requirements of professional historiography prevented the first two Zionist historians from asserting that the Jewish people had been expelled after the fall of the Second Temple.
2. The urge to reduce the time in exile to a minimum so as to maximize the national proprietary claim over the country. This consideration also prompted Dinur to date the beginning of the rebellion against exile and the "early zephyrs of modern aliyah" to the immigration of Judah he-Hasid and his companions in 1700.[26]

The way the Roman Empire gradually reduced the political power of the kingdom of Judea was important, but not as important as the historical development that actually led to the exile. The invasion of the country by desert dwellers in the seventh century, and their seizure of Jewish-owned lands, changed the country's demographic character. Emperor Hadrian's decrees had, of course, expropriated lands in the second century, but the arrival of the Muslims greatly accelerated the process and eventually led to the emigration of the Jews and "the creation of a new national majority in the country."[27] Until that time, the Jews had constituted the majority of the population, and Hebrew

---

25   Dinur, *Israel in Exile*, vol. 1, 1, 5–6.
26   Dinur, *Historical Writings*, vol. 1, Jerusalem: Bialik, 1955 (in Hebrew), 26.
27   Dinur, *Israel in Exile*, vol. 1, 1, 6.

was still the dominant language.[28] The arrival of the new settler-conquerors altered the country's cultural morphology and put an end to the presence of the Jewish people in its land.

It is true that there was no deliberate policy of expulsion, but that does not mean that exile was undertaken voluntarily—God forbid. Dinur was worried that if it were accepted that the Jews left their country of their own volition, it would undermine their renewed claim to it in modern times. He struggled with this grave issue for years, and ultimately reached a more satisfactory historical summary:

> Every Jewish habitation in the diaspora began with exile—that is, as an outcome of compulsion and force ... This does not mean that the Jews came to most of these countries after the fall of Jerusalem as prisoners of war, fugitives or deportees. The road from the devastated Jerusalem to their final settlement in any given generation was extended and protracted, with numerous sojourns along the way lasting a long time. But because they arrived as fugitives seeking shelter, and as the fall of their country was famous and its circumstances were known to all, it was natural that people in the countries to which these fugitives came were satisfied with knowing the original circumstances which had led them thither. Sometimes the Jews themselves sought to stress the Jewish aspect of their exile, by playing down their connection with their previous place of exile and stressing the first, or primary, cause.[29]

Thus, even if the exile following the destruction of the Second Temple was a vague myth, it was justified, because it was followed by other expulsions and wanderings. The long exile is like a shadow cast by the destruction, hence its chief significance: to encompass all future exiles. Dinur willingly accepted the Christian, and subsequently anti-Semitic, myth about the Wandering Jew who finds no rest. He therefore defined the Jewish identity not as belonging to a religious minority that lived for centuries among other, dominant religious cultures, sometimes repressive and at other times protective, but as the identifying profile of an alien ethnic-national body that has always been on the move and is destined to keep wandering. Only this conception of exile gave an organic sequence to the history of Jewish dispersal, and only in this way could it clarify and justify "the return of the nation to its birthplace."

Dinur gave the secularization of the Jewish exile its strongest and clearest historical expression. It was essentially revolutionary, and altered not only the Jewish time-structure of the exile but also the underlying significance of

28 Dinur, *Historical Writings*, vol. 4, 14. This assumption about the language has little ground to stand on.

29 Ibid., 182.

this religious time. The historian felt its national power vis-à-vis the declining tradition, and although he repeatedly resorted to it, he also turned it inside out. As a historian and public intellectual, he replaced thousands of rabbis, those "organic" intellectuals of the Jewish past, who defined Judaism itself through the concept of exile. He therefore did not scruple to issue a new halakhic decision: "The three vows of Rabbi Yossi ben Hanina were vows to preserve the exile. They were revoked by the end of the exile, and the vow 'not to rise up over the wall' is likewise null and void. This generation's only answer must be indeed 'to rise up over the wall.' " [30]

This bold historian, who became Israel's minister of education in 1951, assumed that the power relations between Judaism and Zionism in the state permitted him to pronounce the end of the exile. And he was right—the nationalization of religion in Israel was advancing rapidly, and he could claim ideological victory.

To round off the description of how the concepts of expulsion and exile were transformed in Zionist historiography in the new homeland, we might consider briefly two more scholars who dealt directly with this issue and contributed much to the development of national consciousness and collective memory in the flourishing Israeli society: Joseph Klausner of the Hebrew University in Jerusalem, who was in effect the first important historian of the period of the Second Temple, and his colleague Yehezkel Kaufmann, author of the important work *Golah Venekhar* ("Exile and Estrangement"). Both received the Israel Prize.

It was Klausner who wrote *The History of the Second Temple*, a work in five volumes that was reprinted many times and read by countless readers. The final volume concludes with the events of the great revolt, and the renowned scholar lavishes praise on the fighters and their national courage. Having described the tragic end of the siege of Masada, he closes with the following words:

> Thus ended the great uprising and the most glorious war for liberty in antiquity. The fall of the Second Temple was complete. No self-rule, not even internal autonomy worthy of the name, remained in Judea. Enslavement, corpses, ruins—such were the sights wherein the second destruction was revealed in all its horror.[31]

That is the historical summary, and nothing further is said. Even this very nationalistic historian, with his right-wing orientation, did not dare to add expulsion to the

---

30   Ibid., 192.
31   Joseph Klausner, *The History of the Second Temple*, Jerusalem: Ahiassaf, 1952 (in Hebrew), 290.

destruction of the Second Temple, and thus to his book's highly dramatic ending. He knew perfectly well that such a description clashed with the fact that sixty years later another mass uprising broke out within the extensive Judean population that had not been exiled and that, moreover, was led by "a hero like Bar Kokhba and the heroic warriors of Betar."[32] Therefore he, too, like other Zionist historians, preferred to keep the beginning of the exile in the historiographic twilight zone.

Similarly, Kaufmann's *Exile and Estrangement* contains a great deal on "exile" and "nation" but nothing about expulsion. This book is one of the most intriguing attempts to ascribe the Jews' long exile to their being a stubborn, resistant nation rather than simply religious communities. But his meticulous analysis of the Jewish exile avoids touching on the historical circumstances that gave rise to this "weird, strange and scattered community" that remained, as he saw it, "a people," through all the circumstances and adversities. Now and then he speaks of "Israel, that was exiled from its country and scattered,"[33] but the text does not spell out when this happened, how, why, and to where Israel scattered. The origin of the exile is taken as known, requiring no detailed explication, despite the book's subtitle: *A Socio-Historical Study on the Issue of the Fate of the Nation of Israel from Ancient Times until the Present*. The action of expulsion, such a central and fundamental event in the history of the Jewish people, should have been studied in scores of investigations, yet, amazingly, it has not resulted in a single such work.

The historical reality of the expulsion was thus accepted as self-evident—not discussed and never doubted. Every historian knew that the myth combining destruction and expulsion was very much alive in the mind of the public, having derived from religious tradition and become firmly rooted in secular consciousness. In the popular discourse, as in the political statements and the educational system, the expulsion of the people of Israel after the fall of the kingdom was carved in stone. Most intelligent scholars evaded this dubious area with professional elegance; here and there, as though unwittingly, they supplemented their writings with alternative explanations of the prolonged exile.

AGAINST ITS WILL, THE PEOPLE EMIGRATE FROM THE HOMELAND

One of the main problems bedeviling the myth of destruction-expulsion was the fact that long before 70 CE there were large Jewish communities outside Judea.

---

32   Joseph Klauzner, *In the Time of the Second Temple*, Jerusalem: Mada, 1954 (in Hebrew), 80.

33   Yehezkel Kaufmann, *Exile and Estrangement*, Tel Aviv: Dvir, 1929 (in Hebrew), 176.

It was widely known that after Cyrus's declaration ending the so-called Babylonian exile, only some of the exiles and their offspring returned to Jerusalem. The rest, possibly the majority, chose to remain and prosper in the cultural centers of the flourishing East, where the elites nurtured rich religious traditions that would spread around the ancient world. It is not too fanciful to state that the first monotheism was, to a considerable extent, formulated in those regions of exile where these founders of Judaism made their permanent home. The fact that they continued to regard Jerusalem as a sacred center did not contradict their religious thinking. Later forms of monotheism, such as Christianity and Islam, also had sacred centers that, rather than being magnets for migration, were sites of religious longing and pilgrimage (perhaps, too, the presence of a permanent mass population in a sacred locale would, in the long run, undermine the beliefs associated with it). For years after Cyrus's decree, the settled rabbinical schools in Sura, Nehardea and Pumbedita were the principal laboratories in which the Jewish religion and its cult practices were refined. It seems that the synagogue was born there, and the Babylonian Talmud created there was esteemed more highly than the Jerusalem Talmud, because it had emerged from a more elevated cultural context.

Josephus had already noted that there were countless thousands of Jews living in the country of the Parthians. He described two adventurous brothers, Hasinai and Hanilai, who in the first century CE established near Nehardea a Jewish principality that aimed to rob its neighbors. They ran it for some fifteen years until they fell out, predictably, when Hanilai married a beautiful foreign woman.

But if the Jewish center in Babylonia was born of an ancient act of expulsion, what was the origin of all the other Jewish communities that kept springing up in the nearby regions of Asia and North Africa, and later spread all around the Mediterranean basin, long before the destruction? Did they, too, result from expulsion?

It begins with the Jewish communities in neighboring Egypt. According to the author of the Book of Jeremiah, Judeans settled there when the First Temple fell, but they soon became idolatrous, and were punished by God (Jer. 44). The earliest Jewish settlement in Egypt attested by archaeology was on Elephantine Island (Yeb, in Hebrew), near today's Aswan Dam. It was a military colony of Persian Jews who in the sixth century BCE built a temple to Yahweh (apparently not as the sole deity). A correspondence in Aramaic from the fifth century BCE has been found—an exchange of letters between the Yeb garrison and the governor of Yehud province, near Jerusalem, and also with Samaria to its north. It is not known where these soldiers came from or who they were, only that their Jewish temple was destroyed late in the fifth century BCE.

The big bang in the birth of Jewish communities in Egypt and the entire eastern end of the Mediterranean occurred when the Persian empire was brought down by Alexander the Great, and the great Hellenistic world took shape. As the empire's rigid boundaries disintegrated, a tremendous wave of trade and ideas washed over the region, producing a new and open culture. Hellenism spread everywhere, stimulating and giving rise to novel intellectual and religious symbioses, as well as safer communication.

Josephus tells us that, following the conquest of Judea and Samaria by Ptolemy I, one of Alexander's successors, many captives were taken to Egypt, where they became settled as respected citizens with equal rights. He then adds, "there were not a few other Jews who, of their own accord, went into Egypt, as invited by the goodness of the soil, and by the liberality of Ptolemy."[34] Relations between the two regions grew closer, with merchants, mercenaries and Judean scholars settling mainly in the new metropolis, Alexandria. Over the next two hundred years, the number of Jews in Egypt kept growing, causing the Alexandrian philosopher Philo Judaeus to state early in the first century CE, with the exaggeration characteristic of the age, that they numbered one million.[35] His estimate was of course too high, but it is safe to assume that in his lifetime there were as many Jews in Egypt as there were in the kingdom of Judea.

There were as well quite a few Jewish believers in Cyrenaica, west of Egypt, also ruled by the Ptolemies, and a good many in Asia Minor, ruled by the Seleucids. Josephus mentions in his *Antiquities of the Jews* that the Seleucid king Antiochus III settled, in the provinces of Lydia and Phrygia, two thousand families of Jewish mercenaries from Babylonia. But how did large communities spring up also in Antioch and Damascus, and later in Ephesus, Salamis, Athens, Thessaloniki and Corinth in Europe? Here again there are no sources to enlighten us.

With the growth of the Roman Empire, the epigraphic record reveals the presence of many Jews in Rome, too. Already in 59 BCE the famous Roman orator Cicero complained about their numbers: "You know how numerous that crowd is, how great is its unanimity, and of what weight it is in the popular assemblies."[36] Later inscriptions found in the Roman catacombs testify to the rich religious life of these Jews and to their economic prosperity. The community in Rome was large, and there were also communities in other Italian cities. In short, before and after the fall of the Second Temple, there were Jewish believers all over the

---

34 Flavius Josephus *Antiquities of the Jews* 12. 1.
35 Philo, *Flaccus*, 43.
36 Marcus Tullius Cicero *Oration For Flaccus* 38.

Roman Empire, as well as in the Parthian territory in the east, in numbers vastly exceeding those of the inhabitants of Judea. From North Africa to Armenia, from Persia to Rome, there were thriving Jewish communities, primarily in large cities but also in towns and even villages. Josephus, quoting Strabo, the Greek historian and geographer, wrote: "Now these Jews are already gotten into all cities; and it is hard to find a place in the habitable earth that hath not admitted this tribe [*phylon*] of men, and is not possessed by them."[37]

Salo Baron suggested that there were eight million Jews in the first century CE.[38] This is obviously a highly exaggerated estimate, which the Jewish-American historian too readily adopted from the even larger figures given by the ancient historians. Half that number—four million, as suggested by Arthur Ruppin and Adolf von Harnack[39]—seems more reasonable in light of the wealth of evidence about the huge numbers of Jewish believers throughout the ancient world.

Historians from Heinrich Graetz to present-day Israelis have always proposed an alternative to the highly unsatisfactory theory of expulsion (which, as we have seen, was chronologically problematic): Jewry's amazing expansion between 150 BCE and 70 CE was the result of an extensive migration of Judeans to all parts of the world. Following the upheaval of the wars of Alexander the Great, the restless inhabitants of Judea began to emigrate en masse, to wander from country to country, while producing numerous offspring. Moreover, this migration was not wholly voluntary, but impelled by hardship. Numerous captives were taken, but many people of Judea rose up and left their beloved homeland because they had no other choice. It stands to reason, because ordinary people do not leave their homes voluntarily. And it was this dynamic, if painful, process that produced the thriving Israelite diaspora.

The model of emigration and dispersal was copied directly from the histories of the Phoenicians and the Greeks. Those cultural-linguistic entities also began at a particular moment to move and spread, as other tribes and peoples had done earlier. Graetz, for example, before proposing his implied connection between the destruction and the exile in 70 CE, wrote as follows:

---

37   Josephus, *Antiquities of the Jews* 14. 7. The Greek term *phylon* is not the same as the modern term "people." It suggests a tribe or small group of people, almost always congruent with a cultic community. For Josephus (or whoever added this statement to the text), the Christians were also a *phylon* (Josephus, *Antiquities* 18. 64). At that time the concept was already changing its meaning. Similarly, the Latin term *tribus* originally denoted a community of shared origin, but later referred to any community regardless of origin living in a particular area.

38   Baron, *A Social and Religious History*, vol. 1, 170.

39   See Ruppin, *The War of the Jews*, 27; and Adolf Harnack, *The Mission and Expansion of Christianity in the First Three Centuries*, Gloucester, MA: P. Smith, 1972, 8.

A cruel destiny seemed to be ever thrusting them away from their central home. Yet this dispersion was the work of Providence and was to prove a blessing. The continuance of the Judaean race was thus assured ... Just as the Greek colonies kindled in various nations the love of art and culture, and the Roman settlements gave rise in many lands to communities governed by law, so had the far wider dispersion of the oldest civilized people contributed to overthrow the errors and combat the sensual vices of the heathen world. In spite of being thus scattered, the members of the Judaean people were not completely divided from one another.[40]

Although Dubnow did not employ the mobilized-mobilizing pathos, the national pride and the assertion of unbroken ethnic continuity remained largely the same. The Judeans were uprooted from their homeland as captives or forced to leave it as fugitives.[41] The Russian-Jewish historian also quoted the Alexandrian Philo, who stated that the Jewish communities had come from Judea,[42] and his broad outline presented a dramatic saga of a people constantly on the move.

Baron's comprehensive work depicts the "diaspora" somewhat differently, though emigration is still the favorite cause of the dispersal: "The vital energies of the Jewish people were revealed by their continued expansion throughout the eastern Mediterranean basin," he writes. "Other Jews continued to penetrate east into Persia, south into Arabia and Abyssinia, west to Mauritania-Morocco, Spain, and possibly France," he says elsewhere. And still elsewhere: "Migratory movements from one Diaspora country to another likewise assumed ever vaster proportions."[43] These and similar statements occur in the long, intricate narrative about Jewish expansion, even though the author is well aware, given his supposedly sociological approach, that this description is inaccurate.

Once we come to the Zionist historians, from Yitzhak Baer and Ben-Zion Dinur on, the traditional migration discourse plods on to complement, not always comfortably, the problematic theory of expulsion. True, say these historians, Judeans were already living outside their "homeland" long before the fall of the Second Temple, but they had been forced to do so and had the status of refugees. Menahem Stern, a respected historian of the second generation of Israeli scholars of the Second Temple, summarizes a long historiographic tradition:

---

40 Graetz, *History of the Jews*, vol. 2, 200–1.
41 Dubnow, *History of the World-People*, vol. 2, 112.
42 Ibid., 255.
43 Baron, *A Social and Religious History*, vol. 1, 167, 169, 172.

Various factors caused the geographic spread and numerical increase of the Jewish dispersal: deportations from the country; political and religious pressures in Judea; economic opportunities discovered in prosperous countries, such as Egypt in the third century BCE; and a proselytizing movement that began in the early days of the Second Temple and reached its climax in the first century CE.[44]

Note the descending order of factors—deportations naturally first, followed by displacement caused by hardship, then voluntary emigration, and finally proselytizing. This is the clearest example of how information is disseminated in the study of national history, and it is replicated repeatedly in the narratives of other Israeli historians, as well as all the textbooks of the state educational system.

Nevertheless, all these dispersal stories contained an unresolved conundrum. How could a farming people that had turned its back to the sea and had never established a far-ranging empire produce so many emigrants? The Greeks and Phoenicians were seafaring people with a large proportion of traders, so that their expansion was a logical outcome of their occupations and general way of life. They emigrated and started new colonies and cities all around the Mediterranean Sea. They spread and clustered around it like "frogs round a puddle," in Plato's vivid phrase. Their commerce brought them into many existing societies whose cultures they affected. Later the Romans did much the same. But two facts should be kept in mind:

1. For all their expansion, the homelands of the Greeks, Phoenicians and Romans were not suddenly emptied and left desolate.
2. They generally continued to use their own languages in their diasporas.

By contrast, most of the Judeans in their own country, as Josephus reiterated, were not merchants but tillers of the sacred soil: "As for ourselves, therefore, we neither inhabit a maritime country, nor do we delight in merchandise, nor in such a mixture with other men as arises from it; but the cities we dwell in are remote from the sea."[45] Although merchants, mercenaries and political and cultural elites did exist in Judean society, they never amounted to more than a tenth of the population. If at the height of the Second Temple period there were a total of some eight hundred thousand inhabitants in the kingdom of Judea, how many of them would emigrate? At most a few tens of thousands.

44   Menahem Stern, "The Time of the Second Temple," in *History of the People of Israel*, Haim Ben Sasson (ed.), Tel Aviv: Dvir, 1969 (in Hebrew), 268.
45   Flavius Josephus, *Against Apion* 1. 12.

And why didn't the Judean communities speak their own languages, Hebrew or Aramaic, in their emigrant communities? Why were their names, generally speaking, not Hebrew names in the first generation? And if they were cultivators, why did they not found even one Judean-Hebrew farming community in their diaspora?

A few thousand or even a few tens of thousands of Judean emigrants could not, in two hundred years, have grown into a population of several million Jewish believers spread around the cultural universe of the Mediterranean. As noted above, in that era there were no significant demographic increases, as the population, urban and rural alike, was limited by its capacity for agricultural production. The general population did not really increase much in the Hellenistic and Roman world—it grew only with the colonization and cultivation of virgin lands—and remained stable, with minor increases, for a very long time. The emigrant Judeans were not a "highly prolific race" with greater "vital energies" than any other people, as Baron, for example, following the anti-Jewish Roman historian Tacitus, suggested. They did not conquer new lands and make them fertile; nor presumably were they the only people who did not murder their children, as a senior Israeli historian has recently suggested.[46]

Enslaved Judean captives were certainly transported, but it is doubtful that they were congenitally more fertile, or more nurturing parents, than were their wealthy pagan masters. The migration of Jewish merchants, mercenaries and scholars out of Judea is an attested fact, but such a trickle, however significant, could not have grown into hundreds of thousands, let alone millions, no matter how great their vitality or fertility.

Unfortunately, monotheism did not make for greater biological fecundity, and the spiritual sustenance it gave its believers could not feed their hungry infants. It did, however, beget and nurture numerous offspring of another kind.

---

46 Baron, *A Social and Religious History*, vol. 1, 167, 172. Baron also wrote: "The steady influx from Palestine, combined with the extraordinary fecundity of the earlier Jewish settlers, helped overcome all racial admixtures and preserve a measure of ethnic unity" (Ibid., 183). In an interview with Moshe Gil, a well-known historian and expert in the history of Jews in the Muslim countries, Gil makes the following statements: "Birth-rate among the Jews was usually high. Moreover, unlike other nations, the Jews did not practice the custom of exposing or even killing some of the children … Among Jews, exposing or killing a child was as serious a crime as any other murder. That is why the population increased so greatly, as the sources reveal." *Zmanim* 95, 2006 (in Hebrew), 97. The "sources" in question are the comment of Tacitus, who, in his hostile description of the Jews, wrote following the Pseudo-Hecataeus: "It is a crime among them to kill any newly-born infant." Tacitus *History* 5. 5.

"ALL NATIONS SHALL FLOW UNTO IT"

In almost all the narratives produced by the proto-Zionist and even Zionist historians, conversion is mentioned as one reason for the vast presence of Jewish believers throughout the ancient world before the fall of the Second Temple.[47] But this decisive factor was sidelined, as we have seen, while the more dramatic players of Jewish history dominated the field: expulsion, displacement, emigration and natural increase. These gave a more appropriate ethnic quality to the "dispersion of the Jewish people." Dubnow and Baron did make greater allowance for conversion, but the stronger Zionist writings played it down, and in the popular historical works—above all in the textbooks, which shape public consciousness—it all but vanished from the picture.

It is generally assumed that Judaism has never been a missionizing religion, and if some proselytes joined it, they were accepted by the Jewish people with extreme reluctance.[48] "Proselytes are an affliction to Israel," the famous pronouncement in the Talmud, is invoked to halt any attempted discussion of the subject. When was this statement written? Did it in any way reflect the principles of the faith and the forms of Jewish experience in the long period between the Maccabee revolt in the second century BCE and the Bar Kokhba uprising in the second century CE? That was the historical period in which the number of Jewish believers in the Mediterranean cultural world reached a level that would again be matched only in the early modern age.

The period between Ezra in the fifth century BCE and the revolt of the Maccabees in the second was a kind of dark age in the history of the Jews. Zionist historians rely on the biblical narrative for the time leading up to that period, and on the Books of the Maccabees and the final part of Josephus's *Antiquities of the Jews* for the end of it. Information about that obscure period is very sparse: there are the few archaeological finds; the abstract biblical texts, which may reflect the time at which they were written; and Josephus's short

---

47   Graetz devoted a special essay to this issue, in which he even accepted that the Jews conducted a campaign of proselytizing. See "Die jüdischen Proselyten im Römerreiche unter den Kaisern Domitian, Nerva, Trajan und Hadrian," in *Jahres-Bericht des jüdisch-theologischen Seminars Fraenkel'scher Stiftung*, Breslau: 1884.

48   In the late twentieth century, as the Jewish "ethnic" identity grew stronger in the Western world, there were again attempts to play down the history of proselytizing and to deny entirely the missionary aspect of Judaism. See Martin Goodman, *Mission and Conversion: Proselytizing in the Religious History of the Roman Empire*, Oxford: Clarendon Press, 1994. Not surprisingly, this book, the final version of which was composed in "unified" Jerusalem, was highly regarded by Israeli scholars. A similar outlook was expressed in the book by two French scholars, Edouard Will and Claude Orrieux, *Prosélytisme juif? Histoire d'une erreur*, Paris: Les Belles Lettres, 1992.

narrative. The Judean population must have been quite small then, and when the inquisitive Herodotus passed through the country in the 440s BCE he missed it altogether.

What we do know is that, while the abundant biblical texts during this Persian period promoted the tribal principle of an exclusive "sacred seed," other authors wrote works that ran counter to the hegemonic discourse, and some of those works entered the canon. The Second Isaiah, the Book of Ruth, the Book of Jonah and the apocryphal Book of Judith all call for Judaism to accept gentiles, and even for the whole world to adopt the "religion of Moses." Some of the authors of the Book of Isaiah proposed a universalist telos for Judaic monotheism:

> And it shall come to pass in the last days *that* the mountain of the Lord's house shall be established in the top of the mountains, and shall be exalted above the hills; and all nations shall flow unto it. And many people shall go and say, Come ye, and let us go up to the mountain of the Lord, to the house of the God of Jacob; and he will teach us of his ways, and we will walk in his paths (Isa. 2:2–3).

Ruth the Moabite, great-grandmother of King David, follows Boaz and marries him without any problem.[49] Similarly, in the Book of Judith, Achior the Ammonite, influenced by Judith, converts to Judaism.[50] Yet both of them belonged to peoples that Deuteronomy strictly prohibited: "An Ammonite or Moabite shall not enter into the congregation of the Lord; even to their tenth generation shall they not enter into the congregation of the Lord for ever" (Deut. 23:3). The creators of these proselytized characters depicted them to protest against the overweening isolationism of Ezra and Nehemiah's priests, those authorized agents of the Persian kingdom.

Every monotheism contains a potential element of mission. Unlike the tolerant polytheisms, which accept the existence of other deities, the very belief in the existence of a single god and the negation of plurality impels the believers to spread the idea of divine singularity that they have adopted. The acceptance by others of the worship of the single god proves his might and his unlimited power over the world. Despite the isolationist caste tendency

---

49 "So Boaz took Ruth, and she was his wife: and when he went in unto her, the Lord gave her conception, and she bore a son ... and they called his name Obed: he *is* the father of Jesse, the father of David." Ruth. 4:13, 17.

50 Jdt. 14:6. Curiously, even the isolationist authors of the Book of Joshua acknowledge the services of Rahab, the Canaanite harlot of Jericho, by permitting her to remain among the special people that conquered the country by force: "And Joshua saved Rahab the harlot alive, and her father's household, and all that she had; and she dwelleth in Israel *even* unto this day." Jo. 6:25.

implanted in the Jewish religion in the time of Ezra and Nehemiah, which would return in response to the harsh strictures of the triumphant Christian church, it was not as exceptional in propagating monotheism as many think. Heterodox voices in the Old Testament calling on the gentiles to acknowledge Yahweh are found not only in Isaiah but also in Jeremiah, Ezekiel, Zephaniah, Zechariah and the Book of Psalms.

Jeremiah advises the Babylonian exiles in Aramaic, "Thus shall ye say unto them, The gods that have not made the heavens and the earth, *even* they shall perish from the earth, and from under these heavens" (Jer. 10:11). "Them" presumably refers to the gentiles, and the message is given in their language. In Ezekiel, God says: "Thus will I magnify myself, and sanctify myself; and I will be known in the eyes of many nations, and they shall know that I *am* the Lord" (Ezek. 38:23). The last days are described thus in Zephaniah: "For then will I turn to the people a pure language, that they may all call upon the name of the Lord, to serve him with one consent" (Zeph. 3:9). Zechariah says, "Yea, many people and strong nations shall come to seek the Lord of hosts in Jerusalem, and to pray before the Lord. Thus saith the Lord of hosts; In those days *it shall come to pass,* that ten men shall take hold out of all languages of the nations, even shall take hold of the skirt of him that is a Jew, saying, We will go with you: for we have heard *that* God *is* with you" (Zech. 8:22–3). The author of the Book of Psalms sings ecstatically, "O clap your hands, all ye people; shout unto God with the voice of triumph. For the Lord most high *is* terrible; *he is* a great King over all the earth" (Ps. 47:1–2), and "O bless our God, ye people, and make the voice of his praise to be heard" (Ps. 66:8), and "Declare his glory among the heathen, his wonders among all people" (Ps. 96:3).

Numerous other verses express the preaching, exhortatory side of the first Jewish monotheism that addressed the gentiles. The Old Testament, having been written by many authors and then edited and reedited by others over many years, is full of contradictions. For every expression of contempt, rejection or superiority over the gentiles, there is also sermonizing, sometimes subtle and sometimes explicit. The severe Book of Deuteronomy, for instance, instructs very firmly, "Neither shalt thou make marriages with them; thy daughter thou shalt not give unto his son, nor his daughter shalt thou take unto your son ... For thou *art* a holy people unto the Lord thy God: the Lord thy God hath chosen thee to be a special people unto himself, above all people that *are* upon the face of the earth" (Deut. 7:3, 6). Yet the heroes of biblical mythology ignored these divine prohibitions—Abraham, Isaac, Joseph, Moses, David and Solomon are all shown as lovers of gentile women who never bothered to convert their chosen spouses. Abraham lived happily with Hagar until forced by Sarah to send her away; Joseph took the Egyptian Aseneth to wife; David married a princess of Geshur; and Solomon, the great lover, had no qualms about taking Edomite, Sidonite, Ammonite and Moabite women, among others. When these stories were written, whether during the Persian or Hellenistic period, a child's religious and communal identity was not determined by the mother, and evidently the anonymous authors were unperturbed by this issue.

The oldest extrabiblical evidence of people having adopted the Jewish religion, or aspects of it, is found in documents from the Sumerian city of Nippur, dating from the Persian period. In these documents, quite a few of the paternal names are typically Babylonian, whereas their children's names are typically Hebrew. While it is true that many Jews had non-Hebrew names—Zerubbabel son of Shaltiel and Mordecai the Jew are among the best known—the tendency to give Hebrew names to the children of Judaized converts was not a passing fad, and could be an indication of conversion at a fairly early stage. There are similar examples in the Elephantine papyri, where the parents bear Egyptian names and the children's names are frequently Hebrew. Here the conversion hypothesis looks stronger, but Judean emigrants did not have Egyptian names. In those documents there are also cases of adults taking Hebrew names, and of marriage with gentile men and women, who join the expanding community. The religion practiced by the inhabitants of Elephantine was not purely monotheistic, and they did not know the Bible.[51] It is reasonable to assume that the community of Jewish believers in the province of Yehud, which included the region around Jerusalem, also increased in spite of Ezra and Nehemiah's strict isolationist policy.

It is not known when the biblical Book of Esther was composed. Some assume that it was first written in the late Persian period, and finally redacted in the Hellenistic. It is also possible that it was composed after the conquests of Alexander the Great. Toward the end of the story, after the triumph of Mordecai and Esther over Haman the Agagite in faraway Persia, it says, "And many of the people of the land became Jews; for the fear of the Jews fell upon them" (Esther 8:17). This is the only mention in the Bible of conversion to Judaism, and this statement about mass conversions—not at the End of Days but in the present—indicates the strengthening confidence of the young Jewish mono-

---

51 Not a single biblical text was found among the papyri of Elephantine. This is significant, since some of them were written in the late fifth century BCE. The only composition found at the site was the Aramaean-Assyrian *Ahiqar*. On the Judaizing in Nippur and Elephantine, see the doctoral dissertation of Uriel Rapaport, *Jewish Religious Propaganda and Proselytism in the Period of the Second Commonwealth*, Jerusalem: The Hebrew University, 1965 (in Hebrew), 14–15, 37–42.

theism. It may also hint at the source of the great increase in the number of Jewish believers in that period.

A 1965 doctoral thesis by Uriel Rapaport—unfortunately not published, though its author became a well-known historian of the Second Temple period—deviated from the usual historiographic discourse and sought, without success, to draw researchers' attention to the widespread wave of conversions. Unlike all the ethnonationalist historians, Rapaport did not hesitate to conclude his brilliant thesis with this statement: "Given its great scale, the expansion of Judaism in the ancient world cannot be accounted for by natural increase, by migration from the homeland, or any other explanation that does not include outsiders joining it."[52]

As he saw it, the reason for the great Jewish increase was mass conversion. This process was driven by a policy of proselytizing and dynamic religious propaganda, which achieved decisive results amid the weakening of the pagan worldview. In this, Rapaport joined a (non-Jewish) historiographic tradition that included the great scholars of ancient history—from Ernest Renan and Julius Wellhausen to Eduard Meyer and Emil Schürer—and asserted, to use the sharp words of Theodor Mommsen, that "ancient Judaism was not exclusive at all; it was, rather, as keen to propagate itself as Christianity and Islam would be in future."[53]

If propagating the faith began in the late Persian period, under the Hasmoneans it became the official policy. It was the Hasmoneans who truly produced a large number of Jews and a great "people."

THE HASMONEANS IMPOSE JUDAISM ON THEIR NEIGHBORS

There are some indications that Judaism attracted proselytes even before the upheavals of Alexander's wars, but the explosion of conversions that led to Judaism's sudden spread probably resulted from its historic encounter with Hellenism. Just as Hellenism itself had begun to shed the vestiges of the narrow identities associated with the old city-states, so too did Ezra's isolationist religion begin to lower its exclusionary barriers.

In antiquity, the rise of a new cultural space embracing the eastern Mediterranean, and the fall of old tribal-cultic boundaries, constituted a true revolution. The effects were weaker in the rural populations, but the local aris-

52   Ibid., 151. It may be no accident that the dissertation was written in the 1960s, and was well received at the Hebrew University. This was before the war of 1967, before the hardening of ethnocentrism in Israel, and then in Jewish communities in the Western world.

53   Mommsen, *Römische Geschichte*, vol. 6, 193. On the intensity of the proselytizing drive, see Louis H. Feldman, *Jew and Gentile in the Ancient World*, New Jersey: Princeton University Press, 1993, 288–341.

tocracies, the established towns and the new poleis felt the new winds bearing new communications, beliefs, governing technologies, and institutions. The Greek spirit manifested itself in architecture, burial customs, and linguistic change, blending with local practices to form combinations that marked a new cultural age. The fusions that took place in such centers as Alexandria and Antioch radiated outward and eventually reached Judea.

At this time, Judaism was already undergoing cautious expansion, and absorbed many new features from Hellenism. Rich and varied cultural elements, conceptual and material—from the rhetorical and philosophical ideas of Athens to the wine-jar forms of Rhodes—took root in Jerusalem. That city took on some quality of a cosmopolitan polis, but it was chiefly the Judean coastal cities that became Hellenized. The priestly and landed aristocracies became Hellenized and adopted prestigious Greek names. The temple that Herod was to build would be in a typical Greek architectural style; after its fall, even the Passover meal, the Seder, would take on the character of a symposium—i.e., a Greek feast.[54]

The Zionist tradition of professional historiography, especially its popular, pedagogical sector, presented Judaism as opposed to Hellenism, and described the Hellenization of the urban elites as treason against the national character of the Jewish people. At the same time, the religious festival of Hanukkah, originally a pagan event, was recast as a purely national holiday. The expulsion and elimination of Jerusalem's Hellenized priests were depicted as marking the rise of a national kingdom that proudly restored the ancient kingdom of David. But more substantial historical facts cheekily contradict these nationalized stories and present a completely different picture of the period.

The Maccabees and their followers did in fact rebel against "unclean" religious practices and were antagonistic toward idolatrous tendencies. Moreover, it is possible to assume, cautiously, that Mattathias's devout priestly family that left Jerusalem was still a Hebrew one, as the sons' names indicate. But the Hasmonean rule that followed the successful religious uprising was no more national than was that of Josiah, four hundred years earlier. A political structure in which the peasantry speaks a different language from that of city people, and in which these two populations do not use the same language in their dealings with government bureaucrats, cannot be described as a national entity. In the second century BCE the rural population still spoke either Hebrew or Aramaic, most merchants communicated in Greek, and the governing and intellec-

54   See Lee I. Levine, *Judaism and Hellenism in Antiquity: Conflict or Confluence?*, Peabody, MA: Hendrickson, 1998, 119–24.

tual elites in Jerusalem spoke and wrote mainly in Aramaic.[55] The quotidian, secular culture involving the subjects and their sovereign lacked consistency, and no sovereign was so nationalistic as to seek to create a consistent culture. But the political, cultural and economic elites already shared a certain religious common denominator, which was far more significant in antiquity than any imaginary nationalism projected onto the past by accredited historians.

We may question the degree of monotheism in the kingdom of Judah before it fell in the sixth century BCE, but the Hasmonean kingdom was the first Jewish kingdom that unquestionably deserved to be described as monotheistic, while also being a typical Hellenistic province. These two adjectives were not mutually contradictory, and indeed the political entity's distinctive Jewish character can be understood only in the context of the encompassing Hellenism. Of course, the kingdom had not yet been exposed to the precepts of the Talmud, the core of the later rabbinical Judaism. But the power structure of the Hasmonean kingdom was governed by the uncompromising, confident first monotheism, which gave it its cultural distinctiveness.

Zionist historians have sought to play down the uncomfortable fact that after Mattathias the priest expelled the Hellenized leadership from Jerusalem and "restored the ancient glory," his grandson, who because of his descent became the ruler, added to his Hebrew name Yohanan the typical Greek name Hyrcanus. The great-grandson of the rebel priest was called Judas Aristobulus, and his successor would be known as Alexander Jannaeus. The process of Greek acculturation did not stop in Judea. In fact, as the Hasmonean dynasty consolidated, it accelerated and triumphed. By the time of Aristobulus, the priestly ruler—though not of the House of David—had become a Hellenistic monarch; like the other regional kings, these new rulers had even earlier begun to mint coins. These coins bore Greek as well as Hebrew words, with such Hellenistic symbols as a wheel, a star and certain plants (though, notably, neither human profiles nor animals). As there were no nation-states at that time, the army was made up of mercenaries, not even of conscripts from among the peasantry.[56] The Hellenistic influence reached its height when Salome Alexandra (known as Shlomzion) was crowned queen—a gender innovation in the Judean monarchy, not rooted in the ancient biblical precepts.

It may seem odd and paradoxical, but what the Maccabees drove out of

---

55   On the various languages spoken in Judea, see Ibid., 72–84.

56   On the names, coins and army in the Hasmonean kingdom, see the article by Uriel Rapaport, "On the 'Hellenization' of the Hasmoneans," in *The Hasmonean State: The History of the Hasmoneans during the Hellenistic Period*, U. Rapport and I. Ronen (eds.), Jerusalem: Ben Zvi and The Open University, 1993 (in Hebrew), 75–101.

Judea was not Hellenism but polytheism. The rebels could not have had a firm concept of the people's "authentic" Hebrew culture, much less as a contrast to Hellenism. Such a description is an anachronistic fantasy of cultural sensitivity typical of modern times, but lacking all meaning in antiquity. The Hasmoneans and their power structures were both uncompromisingly monotheistic and typically Hellenistic. Archaeological findings from that period reveal both modest ritual baths and luxurious public baths. In their intrigues and rivalries, the royal courts of Judea closely resembled other Hellenistic courts in the region, as did the system of dynastic succession. The present work cannot go into extensive exploration of the Hasmonean kingdom and its fascinating dualistic development beyond its essential Judeo-Hellenistic aspects, which made it an important factor in the spread of Judaism in antiquity.

This was perhaps the first time in history that a clearly monotheistic religion combined with a political government: the sovereign became a priest. Like other single-deity religions that would hold power in the future, the Hasmonean theocracy used the sword to spread not only its territorial domain but also its religious following. And with the historical option of cultural Hellenization came the possibility of conversion to Judaism. The boundaries opened in both directions. Hellenism injected Judaism with the vital element of anti-tribal universalism, which in turn strengthened the rulers' appetite for propagating their religion, leading them to abandon the exclusive commandments of Deuteronomy and Joshua. The Hasmoneans did not claim descent from the House of David, and they saw no reason to emulate the story of Joshua, the mythological conqueror of Canaan.[57]

In 125 BCE Yohanan Hyrcanus conquered Edom, the country that spread south of Beth-zur and Ein Gedi as far as Beersheba, and Judaized its inhabitants by force. Josephus described it in *Antiquities of the Jews*:

> Hyrcanus took also Dora and Marissa, cities of Idumea, and subdued all the Idumeans; and permitted them to stay in that country, if they would circumcise their genitals, and make use of the laws of the Jews; and they were so desirous of living in the country of their forefathers, that they submitted to the use of circumcision, and of the rest of the Jewish ways of living, at which time therefore this befell them, that they were hereafter no other than Jews.[58]

---

57 On the Maccabees and the biblical myth, see Katell Berthelot, "The Biblical Conquest of the Promised Land and the Hasmonaean Wars According to 1 and 2 Maccabees," in *The Books of the Maccabees: History, Theology, Ideology*, G. G. Xeravits and J. Zsengellér (eds.), Leiden: Brill, 2007, 45–60.

58 Josephus *Antiquities of the Jews* 13. 9. Josephus later refers to the event in other words: "Hyrcaus had made a change in their political government, and made them receive the Jewish customs and law" (Ibid., 15. 7). See also the article of Steven Weitzman, "Forced

Thus did the ruling Hasmonean high priest annex an entire people not only to his kingdom but also to his Jewish religion. Henceforth, the Edomite people would be seen as an integral part of the Jewish people. At that time, joining the religion of another group was regarded as joining its people—its cult community. But it was only the progress of monotheism that made attachment to the faith as important as the traditional association with origin. This was the beginning of the slide from what we might call Judeanity—a cultural-linguistic-geographic entity—toward Judaism, a term denoting a broader kind of religion-civilization. This process would evolve till it reached its height in the second century CE.[59]

Who were the Edomites? There are several sources. The important Greek geographer Strabo, who lived at the time of Augustus, erroneously stated, "The Idumaeans are Nabataeans. When driven from their country by sedition, they passed over to the Jews, and adopted their customs."[60] Ptolemaeus, an obscure historian from Ascalon, was probably more accurate when he stated, "The Idumaeans, on the other hand, were not originally Jews, but Phoenicians and Syrians; having been subjugated by the Jews and having been forced to undergo circumcision, so as to be counted among the Jewish nation, and to keep the same customs, they were called Jews."[61] Their number is not known, but it could not have been insignificant, since their territory was about half the size of the kingdom of Judea. Needless to say, the Edomite peasants and shepherds probably did not all become good monotheists overnight. Nor, presumably, did all the Judean farmers. But it is almost certain that the higher and middle strata adopted the Mosaic religion and became an organic part of Judea. The converted Jews of Edomite origin intermarried with the Judeans and gave Hebrew names to their children, some of whom would play important roles in the history of the Judean kingdom. Not only Herod came from among them; some of the disciples of the strict Rabbi Shammai and the most extreme Zealots in the great revolt were also of Edomite descent.

Jewish historiography has always been ill at ease about the forced conversion and assimilation practiced by the Hasmoneans. Graetz condemned the acts of Hyrcanus, asserting that they were catastrophic for the Jewish people. Dubnow, in his gentle way, sought to soften the history and depicted

---

Circumcision and the Shifting Role of Gentiles in Hasmonean Ideology," *Harvard Theological Review* 92:1 (1999), 37–59.

59   On this subject see Cohen, *The Beginnings of Jewishness*, 104–6.
60   Strabo, *Geography* 16. 2. 34.
61   Quoted in Menahem Stern (ed.), *Greek and Latin Authors on Jews and Judaism*, vol. 1, Jerusalem: The Israel Academy of Sciences and Humanities, 1976, 356.

the Edomites as "tending to cultural assimilation with the Jews," and Baron remained laconic in his treatment of the "problematic" issue.[62] Zionist and Israeli historiography was divided. Klausner, the proud nationalist, saw the conquest of Edom and the conversion of its inhabitants as righting an old injustice, since the Negev had been part of the kingdom of Judah during the First Temple period.[63] One of the later historians of the Hasmonean kingdom, Aryeh Kasher, went out of his way to show that the mass conversion of the Edomites was voluntary, not imposed by force. He argued that the Edomites had been circumcised before the conversion—and that everyone knows Jewish tradition has always opposed forced conversion.[64]

Urban Edomites had long been under Hellenistic influence and were probably uncircumcised. Moreover, though the rabbinical tradition did in fact renounce any attempt to force people to change religion, it only did so much later—after the Zealot uprising in the first century CE, when forced conversions to Judaism were no longer feasible. Under the Hasmonean rulers of the late first century BCE, it was a regular feature of Jewish policy, and Hyrcanus was not the only one who implemented it. In 104–103 BCE his son Judas Aristobulus annexed the Galilee to Judea and forced its Iturean inhabitants, who populated the northern region, to convert to Judaism. According to Josephus, "He was called a lover of the Grecians; and had conferred many benefits on his own country, and made war against Iturea, and added a great part of it to Judea, and compelled the inhabitants, if they would continue in that country, to be circumcised, and to live according to the Jewish laws." In support, he quotes Strabo, who wrote, "This man was a person of candor, and very serviceable to the Jews, for he added a country to them, and obtained a part of the nation of the Itureans for them, and bound them to them by the bond of the circumcision of their genitals."[65]

Judeans probably lived in the Galilee earlier, but it was populated and governed predominantly by the Itureans, the center of whose kingdom was in Chalcis in Lebanon. Their origin is obscure—probably Phoenician and possibly tribal Arab. The territory annexed by Aristobulus stretched from Bet She'an (Scythopolis) in the south to beyond Giscala in the north—that is, most of today's Galilee minus the coast. Masses of Itureans, the original inhabitants of the Galilee, assimilated into the expanding Judean population, and many

---

62 Graetz, *History of the Jews*, vol. 2, 8–9; Dubnow, *History of the World-People*, vol. 2, 73; and Baron, *A Social and Religious History*, vol. 1, 167.
63 Klauzner, *History of the Second Temple*, vol. 3, 87.
64 Aryeh Kasher, *Jews, Idumaens, and Ancient Arabs*, Tübingen: Mohr, 1988, 44–78.
65 Josephus, *Antiquities of the Jews* 13. 11.

became devout Jews. One of Herod's associates was Sohemus the Iturean.[66] It is not known if John (Yohanan) of Giscala, a Zealot leader in the great revolt, was of convert origin like his comrade and rival, Simon Bar Giora.

Aristobulus's brother and successor, Alexander Jannaeus, also sought to convert the people he conquered, but he conducted wars mainly against the Hellenistic trading coastal cities along the borders of Judea, and was less successful in converting their inhabitants. The Hellenists, who were proud of their culture, might have been willing to convert to Judaism of their own free will, as indeed some of them did in the countries around the Mediterranean. But it appears that they were not willing to accept the forced Hasmonean conversion, which would have meant losing the political and economic privileges granted to them by the poleis—the city-states. According to Josephus, Alexander destroyed the city of Pella in Transjordan "because its inhabitants would not bear to change their religious rites for those peculiar to the Jews."[67] We know that he totally destroyed other Hellenistic cities: Samaria, Gaza, Gederah and many more.

Judas Aristobulus's father, Hyrcanus, had to deal with a complicated problem of conversion. When he conquered the region of Samaria in 111 (or 108) BCE, he could not forcibly convert the Samaritans, who were in part descendants of the ancient Israelites. They were already monotheists—they avoided pagan customs, observed the Sabbath and practiced circumcision. Unfortunately, it was forbidden to marry them, their liturgy was slightly different, and, moreover, they insisted on holding their ceremonies in their own temple. Hyrcanus therefore destroyed Shechem (Nablus), the main Samaritan city, and obliterated the temple on Mount Gerizim.[68]

A long Jewish tradition marks the twenty-first day of the month of Kislev, the day when the Samaritan temple was destroyed, as a propitious day in the Hebrew calendar, on which it is forbidden to fast or mourn the dead (see the *Tractate Ta'anith*). The national memory, too, honors the figure of Yohanan Hyrcanus, the Jewish Titus, destroyer of the Samaritan temple. Today in Israel, many streets proudly bear the name of this victorious Hasmonean priest.

---

66 Ibid., 15.6.
67 Ibid., 13.15. The widespread practice of compulsory Judaization is illustrated by Josephus's story about the two strangers who sought shelter in the Galilee, and but for his intervention, "the Jews would force them to be circumcised, if they would stay among them" (Josephus, *The Life of Flavius Josephus,* 23). See also how the Roman commander Metilius, captured by the rebels, saved his own life: "for when he entreated for mercy, and promised that he would turn Jew, and be circumcised, they saved him alive" (Josephus, *The War of the Jews* 2. 17).
68 Josephus wrote: "After this he [Hyrcanus] took Samega, and the neighboring places; and besides these, Shechem and Gerizim, and the nation of the Cutheans [Samaritans], who dwelt at the temple which resembled that temple which was at Jerusalem, and ... was now deserted two hundred years after it was built" (Josephus, *Antiquities of the Jews* 13. 9).

FROM THE HELLENISTIC SPHERE TO MESOPOTAMIAN TERRITORY

It would not be an exaggeration to say that, but for the symbiosis between Judaism and Hellenism, which, more than anything, turned the former into a dynamic, propagative religion for more than three hundred years, the number of Jews in today's world would be roughly the same as the number of Samaritans. Hellenism altered and invigorated the high culture of the kingdom of Judea. This historical development enabled the Jewish religion to mount the Greek eagle and traverse the Mediterranean world.

The conversions carried out by the Hasmonean kingdom were only a small part of a far more significant phenomenon that began in the early second century BCE. The pagan world was already beginning to rethink its beliefs and values when Judaism launched its campaign of proselytization and became one of the factors that prepared the ground for the great Christian revolution. Judaism did not yet produce professional missionaries, as its younger sibling would do before long, but its encounter with the philosophies of the Stoic and Epicurean schools gave birth to a new literature that demonstrated a strong desire to win souls.

At this time Alexandria was, if not the most important, one of the leading cultural centers of the Hellenistic world. It was there that the initiative was born, as early as the third century BCE, to translate the Bible into the widespread, common Greek dialect Koine. The Babylonian Talmud and the work known as the Letter of Aristeas would attribute the initiative to King Ptolemy II Philadelphus. It is doubtful if the Septuagint was in fact carried out at the behest of the Egyptian king, and it was certainly not a singular, brief act. It is more likely that the entire Old Testament was translated over many years by a large number of Jewish scholars, but the enterprise testified to the important symbiosis taking place between Judaism and Hellenism, through which the former was turning into a multilingual religion.

Was the purpose of the translation to spread monotheism among the gentiles? Israeli historians reject this supposition, arguing that many Jews knew no Hebrew and that the translation was intended for them. But why did the Jewish believers not know their national language at such an early stage of what was supposedly their exile? Was it because they no longer spoke it in their homeland? Or was it because most of them were Hellenistic converts who did not know even Aramaic, the language spoken by many Judean inhabitants?

We don't know the answers to these questions, but we can be certain that this translation, in its numerous copies, even in the absence of printing, was an essential vehicle for the dissemination of the Jewish religion among the cultural elites all around the Mediterranean. The impact of the translation is best attested by Philo Judaeus, the philosopher who was probably the first to merge skillfully the Stoic-Platonic logos with Judaism, and who wrote the following in the early decades of the Common Era:

> [E]ven to this very day, there is every year a solemn assembly held and a festival celebrated in the island of Pharos [where the translation was believed to have been made], to which not only the Jews but a great number of persons of other nations sail across, reverencing the place in which the first light of interpretation shone forth, and thanking God for that ancient piece of beneficence which was always young and fresh ... In this way those admirable, and incomparable, and most desirable laws were made known to all people, whether private individuals or kings, and this too at a period when the nation had not been prosperous for a long time ... I think that in that case every nation, abandoning all their own individual customs, and utterly disregarding their national laws, would change and come over to the honour of such a people only; for their laws shining in connection with, and simultaneously with, the prosperity of the nation [*ethnos*], will obscure all others, just as the rising sun obscures the stars.[69]

Philo's use of the word *ethnos*—like Josephus's use of *phylon* or *phyle*—already designated a growing cult community rather than an isolationist community of origin, and it certainly does not correspond to the modern term "nation." The Alexandrian philosopher viewed conversion to Judaism as a reasonable and positive phenomenon that demographically enlarged his *ethnos*.

This was a historical phase in which the distinctive nature of the spreading monotheism began, under the influence of Hellenism, to undermine earlier identities. In the traditional identities, the pagan cults corresponded more or less to the cultural-linguistic communities—the "peoples," the "commonalties," the cities or tribes. From this time on, the ancient association between religious boundaries and everyday cultural and language characteristics began to fail.[70] For example, Philo himself, for all his extensive knowledge, knew neither Hebrew nor Aramaic, yet this did not diminish his devout attachment to the Mosaic religion, which he, like many of his fellow believers, knew in its famous translation. Some of his writing was probably also intended to persuade gentiles to change their ways and abandon "their own individual customs."

The Septuagint was the hesitant start of Jewish religious missionizing also realized in the form of the works known as the books of the Apocrypha. The *Letter of Aristeas* that mentions the translation was written in Greek before 200 BCE by a Jewish

---

69   Philo, *On the Life of Moses* 2. 41–44.
70   On this process, as analyzed by a different conceptual method from the present work, see Cohen, "From Ethnos to Ethno-religion," in *The Beginnings of Jewishness*, 109–139.

believer in Alexandria. Aristeas may have been the author's real name, though perhaps he took the typical Greek name—that of a bodyguard of Ptolemy II Philadelphus—to appeal to Hellenistic readers. As well as relating the legendary history of the translation, the letter attacks idolatry and praises the Jewish faith, though it does so in an allegorical manner. For example, it says nothing about circumcision, to avoid discouraging the gentiles, but launches into an idyllic, even utopian, description of Jerusalem and its temple. It describes Jewish scholars as wiser than the pagan Greek philosophers, though paradoxically their superiority is demonstrated via the principles of Greek philosophy, giving the impression that the anonymous author was more familiar with the latter than with the Torah.

Similar rhetoric is found in the third book of an ancient collection known as the *Sibylline Oracles*, a book that most scholars date to the second century BCE, namely, the Hasmonean period. It too was translated in Alexandria and, like the *Letter of Aristeas*, denounces the Egyptian animal cults. Jewish sermonizing in the form of verses supposedly uttered by a Greek-style female prophet was a bold move in Hellenistic assimilation. The author is a missionary who addresses all the children of man who were created in God's image, and prophesies that in future the people of the great God will again serve all mortals as brave teachers.[71] Idolatry was low and debased, it is declared, whereas the Jewish faith was a religion of justice, fraternity and charity. The idolatrous were infected with homosexuality, whereas the Jews were far from committing any abomination. Therefore the worshippers of wood and stone should convert to the true faith or be chastised by a wrathful God.

The obvious Jewish confidence of this work paralleled the success and rising power of the Hasmonean kingdom. The *Wisdom of Solomon*, written probably in the early first century BCE, also links the proselytizing impulse in the Jewish communities in Egypt with the Judean rulers' drive for converts. The first, visionary part of the work is in Hebrew and comes from Judea; the second, more philosophical part is in Greek and is Alexandrian in character. This work also derides the cult of animals and revolves around the disdain for the worship of images. Like the third Sibylline oracle, the *Wisdom of Solomon* associates the worship of many gods with licentiousness and immorality, dooming one to punishment. Here, too, the objects of persuasion are gentiles, chiefly rulers and kings, and the rhetoric is entirely derived from Greek heritage. The Stoic logos is put into the mouth of King Solomon, who utters well-known Platonic statements.[72]

---

71   See Valentin Nikiprowetzky, *La Troisième Sibylle*, Paris: Mouton, 1970.
72   The second Book of the Maccabees, written in the late first century BCE, quotes the marvelous tale of the "evil" Antiochus, who in his old age was persuaded by the Jewish

Other works, too, propagated Judaism or a universalist view of the deity: *Joseph and Aseneth, Additions to the Book of Daniel, Pseudo-Phocylides* and others contained commentaries that sought to convince the reader of the superiority of abstract monotheism centered on an omnipotent deity.[73] Much of the propaganda was carried out in the proliferating synagogues—attractive houses of prayer that appealed to many gentiles—and it was clearly successful. We have seen that Philo took pride in the growing number of Jews. Josephus, the historian who lived a generation after the Alexandrian philosopher, summarized the situation in his own way:

> We have already demonstrated that our laws have been such as have always inspired admiration and imitation into all other men; nay, the earliest Grecian philosophers, though in appearance they observed the laws of their own countries, yet did they, in their actions and their philosophic doctrines, follow our legislator [Moses], and instructed men to live sparingly, and to have friendly communication one with another. Nay, farther, the multitude of mankind itself have had a great inclination of a long time to follow our religious observances; for there is not any city of the Grecians, nor any of the barbarians, nor any nation whatsoever, whither our custom of resting on the seventh day hath not come, and by which our fasts and lighting up lamps, and many of our prohibitions as to our food, are not observed; they also endeavour to imitate our mutual concord with one another, and the charitable distribution of our goods, and our diligence in our trades, and our fortitude in undergoing the distresses we are in, on account of our laws; and, what is here matter of the greatest admiration, our law hath no bait of pleasure to allure men to it, but it prevails by its own force; and as God himself pervades all the world, so hath our law passed through all the world also.[74]

Josephus's writings are not mere apologetics for Judaism, but rather are explicitly missionizing. In *Against Apion*, from which the above quote is taken, he states proudly that "many of them [the Greeks] have come over to our laws, and some of them have continued in their observation, although others of them had not courage enough to persevere, and so departed from them again." He cautions that "it will be also worth our while to see what equity our legislator would have us exercise in our intercourse with strangers."[75] He goes so far

---

religion, converted to it and set out to propagate it: "Yea also, that he would become a Jew himself, and would go through every place of the earth, and declare the power of God" (2 *Macc.* 9:17).

73   See Walter T. Wilson, *The Sentences of Pseudo-Phocylides*, New York: Walter de Gruyter, 2005.

74   Josephus *Against Apion* 2. 40.

75   Ibid., 1. 29.

as to boast that the Bible is the source of Greek wisdom, and that Pythagoras and Plato, for example, had learned about God from Moses. Hostility to Jews, he states, was the result, among other reasons, of the fact that "when they saw our institutions approved of by many others, they could not but envy us on that account."[76]

But though the whole world did not convert to Judaism, as the Jewish historian might have hoped, the large numbers of gentiles who were drawn to Judaism, and the full conversion of many of them, added up to the presence of hundreds of thousands, perhaps millions, of Jews around the southeastern Mediterranean.

Damascus was a flourishing Hellenistic center second only to Alexandria, and conversion to Judaism there was even greater than in Egypt. Josephus relates in *Wars of the Jews* that when the people of Damascus wanted to massacre the local Jews, they hesitated to do so because "they distrust their own wives, which were almost all of them addicted to the Jewish religion; on which account it was that their greatest concern was, how they might conceal these things from them."[77] He adds that in Antioch, the favor shown to the Jews by the rulers gave rise to the following situation: "they both multiplied to a great number and adorned their temple gloriously by fine ornaments, and with great magnificence, in the use of what had been given them. They also made proselytes of a great many of the Greeks perpetually, and thereby, after a sort, brought them to be a portion of their own body."[78]

The popularity of Judaism before and after the Common Era spread beyond the Mediterranean region. In *Antiquities of the Jews*, Josephus tells the fabulous story of the conversion to Judaism in the first century CE of the rulers of Adiabene (Hadyab).[79] As this conversion is described in other sources, there is no reason to doubt its broad outline.

The kingdom of Adiabene was in the north of the Fertile Crescent, roughly corresponding to today's Kurdistan and Armenia. Jewish proselytizing led to the conversion of the kingdom's much-loved heir to the throne, Izates, as well as his mother Helena, herself an important personage in the kingdom. They were persuaded to convert by a merchant named Hananiah, who assured the prince that it was enough to observe the precepts without being circumcised. However, when the prince ascended the throne, a stricter Jewish preacher,

---

76 Ibid., 1. 25.
77 Josephus, *Wars of the Jews* 2. 20.
78 Ibid., 7. 3.
79 Josephus, *Antiquities of the Jews* 20. 2–4. There was also a Jewish royal dynasty in Armenia in the first century CE.

a Galilean named Eleazar, demanded that he circumcise himself in order to complete his conversion, and Izates complied. Josephus reports that the ruling dynasty's conversion annoyed Adiabene's nobility, some of whom tried to rebel. But Izates succeeded in suppressing and eliminating his pagan enemies, and when his brother Monobazus II (Monobaz) succeeded him, he too converted to Judaism, along with the rest of the royal family. Queen Helena, accompanied by her son, went on a pilgrimage to Jerusalem, where she helped the Judeans to survive a severe drought, and she was buried in the holy city in a grand "royal tomb" built for her. The sons of Izates also went to the holy city in the center of Judea to be educated in the faith.

The Judaizing kings of Adiabene impressed not only Josephus; their memory is deeply engraved in Jewish tradition. Monobazus II is mentioned in a number of Talmudic tractates (including *Bereshit Rabba*, *Yoma* and *Baba Bathra*) and elsewhere. Yet it is difficult to ascertain how far the new religion spread through Adiabene society. Josephus states in the introduction to his *Wars of the Jews* that the people of Adiabene learned about the Zealots' revolt from his writings,[80] meaning that there were a number of converted readers in the kingdom who took an interest in the Judean uprising. If the nobles were disturbed by the royal dynasty's conversion, it was probably because of fears about the normative changes in the administration of the realm. It is also possible that the rulers of Adiabene converted in order to win the support of the Jews and the many converts in Mesopotamia, in hopes of leading a broad empire.[81] It was no accident that representatives of Adiabene took part in the Zealots' revolt against Rome, and that some of the kingdom's princes were captured and taken to Rome.

The kingdom of Adiabene was the first political entity outside Judea to convert to Judaism, but it was not the last. Nor was it the only one to give rise to an important Jewish community that would survive until modern times.

JUDAIZING IN THE SHADOW OF ROME

If Alexander's conquests created an open Hellenistic sphere, Rome's expansion and her enormous empire completed the process. Henceforth, all the cultural centers around the Mediterranean basin would undergo the dynamism of blending and the forging of new phenomena. The littorals grew closer, and

---

80   "Those of our nation beyond Euphrates, with the Adiabeni, by my means, knew accurately both whence the war began, what miseries it brought upon us, and after what manner it ended." Josephus, *Wars of the Jews* 1. 2.

81   See the article of Jacob Neusner, "The Conversion of Adiabene to Judaism," *Journal of Biblical Literature* 83 (1964), 60–6.

the passage from the eastern to the western end became easier and faster. This emerging world opened a fresh perspective for the spread of Judaism; at its high point there, Judaism was professed by 7 to 8 percent of all the empire's inhabitants. The word "Jew" ceased to denote the people of Judea, and now included the masses of proselytes and their descendants.

At the height of Judaism's expansion, in the early third century CE, Cassius Dio described this significant historical development, asserting: "I do not know how this title [Jews] came to be given to them, but it applies also to all the rest of mankind, although of alien race, who affect their customs."[82] His near contemporary, the Christian theologian Origen, wrote: "The noun *Ioudaios* is not the name of an *ethnos*, but of a choice [in the manner of life]. For if there be someone not from the nation of the Jews, a gentile, who accepts the ways of the Jews and becomes a proselyte, this person would properly be called a *Ioudaios*."[83] To understand how these two scholars arrived at the same definitions, we need to follow the discourse from its beginnings in Rome.

The first mention of Judaism in Roman documents has to do with conversion, and some of the references in Roman writings to Jews who were not inhabitants of Judea address this key issue. If hostility to Jews occasionally broke out, it was due mainly to their religious preaching. The Romans were, by and large, typical polytheists, tolerant toward other beliefs, and Judaism was legal (*religio licita*). But the Romans did not understand the exclusivity of monotheism, and even less so the urge to convert other people and cause them to abandon their inherited beliefs and customs. For a long time, conversion to Judaism was not illegal, but it was plain to see that the converts rejected the gods of the empire, and this was perceived as a threat to the existing political order.

According to Valerius Maximus, a contemporary of Augustus, as early as 139 BCE Jews and astrologers were deported to their places of origin, because they tried "to infect the Roman customs with the cult of Jupiter Sabazius."[84] This was the time when the Hasmonean dynasty was consolidating its rule in Jerusalem, and in 142 BCE Simon, a son of Mattathias, sent a diplomatic mission to Rome, seeking to form an alliance. Jewish monotheism was starting its expansion and was acquiring confidence and a sense of superiority over paganism.

---

82 Cassius Dio, *Roman History* 37. 17.
83 Quoted in Cohen, *The Beginnings of Jewishness*, 134.
84 Elsewhere Valerius Maximus states, "The same Hispalus banished the Jews from Rome, because they attempted to transmit their sacred rites to the Romans, and he cast down their private altars from public places." Quoted in Stern (ed.), *Greek and Latin Authors*, vol. 1, 358.

It is not known where these Jewish preachers came from, and there are different opinions about the term "Jupiter Sabazius." Perhaps it was a syncretic Jewish-pagan cult, but more probably "Jupiter" meant God and "Sabazius" was a corruption of *sabaoth* or Sabbath. The great Roman scholar Varro identified Jupiter with the Jewish god and concluded, with incisive Latin logic, "It makes no difference by which name he is called, so long as the same thing is understood."[85]

This was not the only expulsion from Rome because of proselytization. In the year 19 CE, during the reign of Emperor Tiberius, Jews as well as the followers of certain other gods were exiled from the capital, this time in large numbers. Tacitus noted in his *Annals* that "four thousand of the freedmen class who were infected with those superstitions and were of military age should be transported to the island of Sardinia ... The rest were to quit Italy, unless before a certain day they repudiated their impious rites."[86] Similar descriptions are given by other historians. Suetonius noted that "those of the Jews who were of military age he assigned to provinces of less healthy climate, ostensibly to serve in the army; the others of that same race or of similar beliefs he banished from the city."[87] Cassius Dio reported later, "As the Jews flocked to Rome in great numbers and were converting many of the natives to their ways, he [Tiberius] banished most of them."[88] Josephus in *Antiquities of the Jews* enlivened the story with an anecdote about four Jews who persuaded a converted noblewoman, one Fulvia, to send gold to the Temple, but pocketed it themselves. Tiberius heard about it and decided to punish all Jewish believers in Rome.[89]

The third expulsion took place in the reign of Claudius in 49–50 CE. According to Suetonius, though this emperor was known to favor the Jews, he expelled them, as they "constantly made disturbances at the instigation of Chrestus."[90] At this stage, we must remember, there was not yet a clear distinction between Judaism and Christianity, and in all probability this was a still undifferentiated Judeo-Christian expansion. In addition, there were also Jewish Christian and Jewish pagan groups, and Roman law did not distinguish between them until the year 64 CE. About this particular event, Cassius Dio wrote that Claudius did not expel the Jews, "who had again increased so greatly that by reason of their multitude it would have been hard without raising a tumult to bar them from the City, he did not drive them out, but ordered them

85   Ibid., 210.
86   Tacitus, *Annals* 2. 85.
87   Suetonius, "Tiberius," *The Lives of the Caesars* 3. 36.
88   Cassius Dio, *Roman History* 57. 18.
89   Josephus, *Antiquities of the Jews* 18. 3.
90   Suetonius, "Claudius," *The Lives of the Caesars* 5. 25.

to follow that mode of life prescribed by their ancestral customs and not to assemble in numbers."[91]

We have seen that Cicero had already noted the large presence of Jewish believers in Rome in the first century BCE, and it is known that many followers of Yahweh took part in the funeral of Julius Caesar. So it is well to remember that this substantial presence existed for a long time before the war of 70 CE, and had nothing to do with any imaginary "mass expulsions" from Judea after the fall of the kingdom and the Bar Kokhba revolt. Most Roman sources indicate that this presence was due to the spread of the Jewish religion. As the rate of conversion to Judaism intensified, so did the government's disquiet and the resentment on the part of many Latin intellectuals.

The great Roman poet Horace made a humorous reference to the Jewish missionary drive in one of his poems: "like the Jews, we [the poets] will force you to come over to our numerous party."[92] The philosopher Seneca thought the Jews were a damned people, because "the customs of this accursed race have gained such influence that they are now received throughout all the world. The vanquished have given laws to their victors."[93] The historian Tacitus, no lover of Jews, was even more acerbic about the converts to Judaism:

> The most degraded out of other races, scorning their national beliefs, brought to them their contributions and presents. This augmented the wealth of the Jews … Circumcision was adopted by them as a mark of difference from other men. Those who come over to their religion adopt the practice, and have this lesson first instilled into them, to despise all gods, to disown their country, and set at nought parents, children, and brethren.[94]

Juvenal, the author of the *Satires*, written in the early second century CE, was especially sarcastic. He did not hide his disgust at the wave of Judaization sweeping over many good Romans, and ridiculed the process of conversion that had become popular in his time:

> Some who have had a father who reveres the Sabbath, worship nothing but the clouds, and the divinity of the heavens, and see no difference between eating swine's flesh, from which their father abstained, and that of man; and in time they take to circumcision. Having been wont to flout the laws of Rome, they learn and practise and revere the Jewish law, and all that Moses committed to

---

91   Cassius Dio, *Roman History* 60. 6.
92   Horace, *Satires* 1. 4.
93   Seneca, "De Superstitione," quoted in Stern (ed.), *Greek and Latin Authors*, vol. 1, 431.
94   Tacitus, *The Histories* 5. 5.

his secret tome, forbidding to point out the way to any not worshipping the same rites, and conducting none but the circumcised to the desired fountain. For all which the father was to blame, who gave up every seventh day to idleness, keeping it apart from all the concerns of life.[95]

At the end of the second century, Celsus, a philosopher known for his dislike of the Christians, was much less hostile to the Jews. But as the conversions grew apace, and the old religions were abandoned, he became openly antagonistic toward the proselytized masses, stating, "If, then, in these respects the Jews were carefully to preserve their own law, they are not to be blamed for so doing, but those persons rather who have forsaken their own usages, and adopted those of the Jews."[96]

This mass phenomenon annoyed the authorities in Rome and upset a good many of the capital's prominent literati. It upset them because Judaism became seductive to broad circles. All the conceptual and intellectual elements that would make for the future appeal of Christianity and its eventual triumph were present in this transient success of Judaism; traditional, conservative Romans felt the danger and voiced their concern in various ways.

The crisis of the hedonistic culture, the absence of an integrating belief in collective values, and the corruption infecting the administration of the imperial government appeared to call for tighter normative systems and a firmer ritual framework—and the Jewish religion met those needs. The Sabbath rest, the concept of reward and punishment, the belief in an afterlife, and above all the transcendent hope of resurrection were enticing features that persuaded many people to adopt the Jewish faith.

Furthermore, Judaism also offered a rare communal feeling that the spreading imperial world, with its corrosive effects on old identities and traditions, seemed to lack. It was not easy to follow the new set of commandments, but joining the chosen people, the holy nation, also conferred a precious sense of distinction, a fair compensation for the effort. The most intriguing element of this process was its gender aspect—it was the women who led the large-scale movement of Judaization.

Josephus's story about Damascus noted that Judaism was especially popular among the city's women, and as we have seen, Queen Helena of Adiabene had a decisive role in the conversion of the royal family. In the New Testament, we are told, Saul of Tarsus, known as Paul, had a disciple who was

95   Juvenal, *Satires* 14. The progress from the Sabbath-observant father to the circumcised son is a remarkable depiction of gradual Judaization.
96   Quoted in Origen, *Contra Celsus* 5. 41.

"the son of a certain woman which was a Jewess and believed, but his father *was* a Greek" (Acts 16:1). In Rome, too, the women were drawn more readily to Judaism. The poet Martial, who came from Iberia, made fun of the women who observed the Sabbath.[97] Epigraphic material from the Jewish catacombs names as many female converts as male. Especially notable is the inscription about Veturia Paulla, who was renamed Sarah after her conversion and became the "mother" of two synagogues.[98] Fulvia (wife of Saturninus)—on whose account, according to Josephus, Jews were expelled in the year 19 CE—was a full convert. Pomponia Graecina, the wife of the famous commander Aulus Plautius, who conquered Britain, was put on trial and divorced by her husband for her devotion to the Jewish (or possibly the Christian) faith. Poppaea Sabina, the emperor Nero's second wife, made no secret of her tendency to Judaism. These women and many other matrons spread the Jewish faith in Rome's upper classes. There is evidence that Judaism was also becoming popular among the lower urban classes, as well as among the soldiers and freed slaves.[99] From Rome, Judaism spilled over to parts of Europe annexed by the Roman Empire, such as the Slavic and Germanic lands, southern Gaul and Spain.

The pivotal role of women in proselytization might indicate a particular female interest in the religion's personal laws, such as the early rules of personal purification, which were preferred to the common pagan customs. Possibly it was also due to the fact that women did not have to undergo circumcision, which was a difficult requirement that deterred many would-be male converts. In the second century CE, after Hadrian prohibited all circumcision, the emperor Antoninus Pius permitted the Jews to circumcise their sons, but forbade males who were not children of Jews to do it. This was another reason that, parallel with the increase of converts, there was a growing category of "God-fearers"—probably an adaptation of the biblical term "fearers of Yahweh" (*sebomenoi* in Greek; *metuentes* in Latin).[100]

These were semi-converts—people who formed broad peripheries around the Jewish community, took part in its ceremonies, attended the synagogues,

---

97   Quoted in Stern (ed.), *Greek and Latin Authors*, vol. 1, 524.

98   See Nurit Meroz, *Proselytism in the Roman Empire in the First Centuries AD*, MA thesis, Tel Aviv University, 1992 (in Hebrew), 29–32. Of the several hundred Jewish tombstones, only a few bear Hebrew names, and the majority are Greek or Latin.

99   Ibid., 44. Many of the converts were slaves or freed slaves. Jewish and Judaized families were obliged to circumcise their male slaves and proselytize the females.

100   "Fearers of Yahweh" are mentioned in Malachi 3:16, and Psalms 115:11–13. "Fearers of Elohim" are mentioned in Exodus 18–21. On the semi-Judaized or Judaism-sympathizers, see Jean Juster, *Les Juifs dans l'Empire romain*, vol. 1, Paris: Geuthner, 1914, 274–90; and also the article by Louis H. Feldman, "Jewish 'Sympathizers' in Classical Literature and Inscriptions," *Transactions and Proceedings of the American Philological Association*, vol. 81, 1950, 200–8.

but did not keep all the commandments. Josephus mentions them several times, and describes Nero's wife as God-fearing. The term is also found in many extant synagogue inscriptions as well as Roman catacombs. The New Testament confirms their massive presence. For example: "And there were dwelling at Jerusalem Jews, devout men, out of every nation under heaven" (Acts 2:5). When Paul reached Antioch, he entered a synagogue on the Sabbath and began his sermon with the words, "Men of Israel, and ye that fear God, give audience" (Acts 13:16). In case some of his hearers were puzzled by this address, he said further: "Men *and* brethren, children of the stock of Abraham, and whosoever among you feareth God, to you is the word of this salvation sent" (13:26). The text goes on: "Now when the congregation was broken up, many of the Jews and religious proselytes followed Paul and Barnabas" (13:43). The next week, a row broke out between zealous Jews and the two successful preachers—"But the Jews stirred up the devout and honourable women, and the chief men of the city, and raised persecution against Paul and Barnabas, and expelled them out of their coasts" (13:50). The two missionaries went on their way and reached the city of Philippi in Macedonia. There, "we sat down, and spake unto the women which resorted *thither*. And a certain woman ... whose heart the Lord opened ... was baptized, and her household" (Acts 16:13–15).[101]

It was precisely in these gray areas, between troubled paganism and partial or full conversion to Judaism, that Christianity made headway. Carried by the momentum of proliferating Judaism and the flourishing varieties of religious syncretism, an open and more flexible belief system arose that skillfully adapted to those who accepted it. It is amazing to what extent the followers of Jesus, the authors of the New Testament, were conscious of the two competing marketing policies. The Gospel of Matthew offers additional testimony to outright Jewish missionizing as well as its limitation: "Woe unto you, scribes and Pharisees, hypocrites! for ye compass sea and land to make one proselyte; and when he is made, ye make him twofold more the child of hell than yourselves" (Matt. 23:15).[102]

---

101   See also the story about Cornelius in Acts 10:1–2.

102   See Martin Goodman's convoluted argument that this was not an attempt to Judaize in *Mission and Conversion*, 69–72. There is no documentation about rabbis traveling especially to convert, unless we include the journeys of such central rabbis as Gamaliel the Second, Yehoshua ben Hananiah, Elazar ben Azariah, and Rabbi Akiva's journey to Rome, as attempts to propagate Judaism. But such interpretation has been totally rejected by the Zionist ethnocentric historiography. See Shmuel Safrai, "The Visits of the Yavneh's Sages in Rome," in *The Book of Memory to Shlomo Umberto Nachon*, Reuven Bonfil (ed.), Jerusalem: Mossad Meir, 1978 (in Hebrew), 151–67. Yet the fact that the establishment of a Yeshivah in Rome after that six-month-long visit may indicate otherwise.

This was, of course, the criticism of experienced, professional preachers about the strict commandments from which they were distancing themselves. These new preachers were better at interpreting the sensitivities of the shaky polytheistic world, and knew how to offer it a more sophisticated, user-friendly approach to the monotheistic deity.

But what was the attitude of their rivals, the more traditional Jewish scholars, toward proselytization and the great spread of Judaism?

HOW RABBINICAL JUDAISM VIEWED PROSELYTIZING

As we have seen, from the time of the Hellenistic Jewish writers in the second century BCE to Philo Judaeus of Alexandria in the first century CE, not only was conversion favorably received, but some of the writings actually promoted it. These books may be seen as a direct outcome of attitudes expressed in certain biblical texts written at the end of the Persian period, just as we may regard the Christian literature as a direct continuation of the Jewish-Hellenistic literary endeavor. The intellectual cosmopolitanism born of the encounter between Judaism and Hellenism prepared the ground for the Pauline revolution, which would totally change the cultural morphology of the ancient world.

If the junction of Zion and Alexandria produced a universalist outlook, the junction of Judea and Babylonia gave rise to Pharisee Judaism, which would bequeath to future generations new principles of religion and worship. The scholars, who came to be known as the sages, and their successors the *tanaim* and *amoraim*, had already begun before and after the fall of the Temple to construct the anvil on which to harden the doctrinal steel of a stubborn minority so that it could survive all hardships in bigger and mightier religious civilizations. These groups were not genetically programmed to uphold isolation and to refuse to spread the Jewish religion. Later, in the European cultural centers, the painful dialectic between Pharisee Judaism and Pauline Christianity would intensify this tendency, especially in the Mediterranean, but the proselytizing urge did not fail for a long time.

Rabbi Chelbo's oft-quoted statement "Proselytes are as injurious to Israel as a scab" (*Tractate Yevamot*) certainly does not express the attitude of the Talmud toward proselytizing and proselytes. It is contradicted by the no less decisive assertion of Rabbi Eleazar, which probably preceded it, that "the Lord exiled Israel among the nations so that proselytes might swell their ranks" (*Tractate Pesachim*). So all the trials and tribulations of exile, and the separation from the Holy Land, were meant to increase and strengthen the congregation of Jewish believers. Between them, these two statements span a wide spectrum of attitudes, determined by the changes and upheavals that marked the early centuries of the Common Era as well as by the personalities of the individual rabbis.

It is impossible to date precisely all the relevant statements and commentaries included in the Halakhah. We may consider a hypothesis that the negative statements about proselytizing were made in times of stress, rebellion and persecution, whereas times of placid relations with the authorities allowed for greater openness and a desire for growth. Ultimately, though, it was not so much the pagan resistance as the rise of Christianity—seen as a grave heresy—that prompted stronger objections to proselytization. Christianity's final triumph in the early fourth century CE extinguished the passion for proselytizing in the main cultural centers, and perhaps also prompted the desire to erase it from Jewish history.

The Mishnah, Talmud and the many commentaries are full of statements and debates designed to persuade the Jewish public to accept the proselytes and treat them as equals. A series of halakhic responses sought to mitigate the impulse toward exclusion on the basis of class or identity that marks the dynamic of any social system receiving new members.

Evidence of widespread conversions to Judaism is found in *Shir ha-Shirim Rabbah* (the commentary on the Song of Solomon): "As the old man sat preaching, many proselytes were converting at that time." The commentary on Ecclesiastes reinforces it: "All the rivers run into the sea, yet the sea is not full. All the proselytes enter Israel, yet Israel is not diminished." There are other comments remarking on the many gentiles choosing Judaism.

Various rabbis reiterated that converts were to be accepted, and demanded their complete integration among the believers. The sages of the Mishnah stressed that a convert must not be reminded of his origin: "If he is the son of proselytes, do not say to him, Remember the acts of your forefathers" (*Baba Metzia*). The addition to this tractate states: "When a proselyte comes to learn the Torah, it must not be said, Look who is coming to study here, whose mouth consumed carrion and unclean beasts, insects and crawling creatures." Another statement says, "Whoever brings one living soul into the fold is to be lauded as though he has formed and bore him." And again, "Why do all men wish to marry the proselyte [woman], but not the freed [woman] slave?—Because the proselyte [woman] is preserved, while the freed [woman] slave is wanton" (*Horayot*).

Both the Jerusalem and Babylonian Talmud are rich in statements favoring the proselytes, but there are also passages that express suspicion and anxiety about gentiles drawing too close: "Rabbi Eliezer ben Yaakov says, A gentile whose nature is bad, the scripture repeatedly warns against him" (*Gerim*).

Another says, "Misfortune after misfortune befall those who accept the prose-lytes" (*Yevamot*). Another: "Proselytes and those who play with infants hinder the messiah" (*Niddah*). Here and there one sees attempts to establish a hier-archy between people who are Jewish by birth and converts. Nevertheless, most scholars maintain that the positive attitude toward, and the acceptance of, converts was always significantly more widespread than its opposite, and possibly the more open approach was stronger outside Judea.[103]

It must not be forgotten that some of the sages were converts or sons of converts, hence they themselves were affected by the rulings. During the reign of Queen Salome Alexandra (Shlomzion)—that is, after the great drive of Hasmonean forced conversion—two converts headed the religious hierarchy in the kingdom of Judea. Shemaiah and Abtalion were, respectively, the president of the Sanhedrin and the chief justice, and were also the spiritual mentors of the famous rabbis Hillel and Shammai who followed them. Ben Bag Bag, also known as Rabbi Yochanan the Convert, and Ben Haa-Haa were two well-known and popular proselytes. Some claimed that the great Rabbi Akiba ben Joseph was of gentile descent—the medieval Maimonides stated that his father was a proselyte. Most sources concur that Akiba's brilliant disciple Rabbi Meir was the son of converts. Even this brief list must include Achilles, the great translator of the Torah into Greek (not Aramaic), believed by some to have been known also as Onkelos, while others assume they were two different men who were prominent converts. This revered second-century figure was probably of Roman origin, and both Jewish and Chris-tian traditions suggest he was related to the emperor Hadrian.

There were other rabbis of proselyte origin, but there is little information about the ratio of converts in the general community. Historical evidence invari-ably concerns the elite. In addition to these rabbis and scholars, we know of kings and rebel leaders of convert descent—such as Herod and Simon Bar Giora—but have no way of guessing the percentage in the general population that followed the Jewish cult. Dislike of idolatry led people to try to erase the convert's shameful history and regard him or her as "newly born" (*Tractate Yevamot*), obliterating the former identity. By the third generation the descendants of proselytes were regarded as wholly Jewish, not as outsiders. (Later the proselytes were seen as Jewish souls who used conversion as a clever way of returning to this world.)[104]

---

103   See for example Bernard J. Bamberger, *Proselytism in the Talmudic Period*, New York: Ktav Publishing House, [1939] 1968; and William G. Braude, *Jewish Proselytizing in the First Centuries of the Common Era: The Age of the Tannaim and Amoraim*, Wisconsin: Brown University, 1940.

104   On Judaism's position on proselytizing, see Marcel Simon, *Versus Israel*, Paris: Boccard, 1964, 315–402.

The Talmud reports the debate about the proper way to convert a gentile to Judaism. Some argued that circumcision was sufficient; others insisted on the primacy of immersion. In the end, both acts were decreed essential to the admission of a male to Judaism; the third requirement, making a sacrifice, fell into disuse with the destruction of the Temple. Circumcision predated immersion as a requirement. Neither Josephus nor Philo mentions the latter, so it must have entered Jewish ritual relatively late. Curiously, rabbinical Judaism and Pauline Christianity adopted the act of immersion/baptism at almost the same time, and it remained a common ritual in the two diverging religions.

In this lively culture of God-fearers, partial converts, full converts, Christian Jews, and born Jews, canceling commandments while preserving the belief in the one god was a revolutionary move of liberation and alleviation. For the spreading monotheism to withstand persecution and external opposition, it had to loosen the exclusivist tendency that lingered in it from the time of Ezra and Nehemiah. In the rising Christian world, there was greater equality between new and established members, and there was even some preference for the "poor in spirit," namely the newcomers. The young religion discarded the element of privileged genealogy—now limited to Jesus as the son of God—and opted for a more sublime genealogy, that of the messianic-universal telos: "There is neither Jew nor Greek, there is neither bond nor free, there is neither male nor female: for ye are all one in Christ Jesus. And if ye *be* Christ's, then are ye Abraham's seed and heirs according to the promise" (Gal. 3: 28–9)

It was Paul who completed the transformation of "Israel in the flesh" into "Israel in the spirit," an idea that conformed with the open and flexible policy of identities that increasingly characterized the Roman Empire. It was not surprising that this dynamic monotheistic movement, which introduced the idea of charity and compassion for all (and the resurrection of at least one person), eventually triumphed over paganism, and cast it into the rubbish bin of history throughout Europe.

The crushing of the Zealot revolt in Judea in the years 66–70 CE did not stop the widespread wave of proselytizing that had begun with the Maccabees' uprising two centuries earlier. Nevertheless, the failure of two messianic challenges to Greco-Roman polytheism—the armed uprising of the Judaic communities in the southern littoral of the Mediterranean in 115–117 CE, and the Bar Kokhba revolt in Judea 132–135 CE—began to weaken the forces of Judaism, reduce the numbers of people wishing to join it, thin the ranks of its followers, and thus open the way to the more pacific conquest of the Christian "religion of love."

In the third century CE, throughout the Mediterranean region, the number of Jews began slowly to fall, though it remained fairly stable until the advent of

Islam in Judea. In Babylonia and possibly western North Africa, the diminishing number of Jews was the result not only of the mass casualties in the uprisings or of believers reverting to paganism; it was caused chiefly by people making the lateral move to Christianity. When Christianity became the state religion in the early fourth century, it halted the momentum of Judaism's expansion.

The edicts passed by the emperor Constantine I and his successors show that conversion to Judaism, though flagging, went on until the early fourth century. They also explain why Judaism began to isolate itself in the Mediterranean region. The Christianized emperor ratified the second-century edict of Antoninus Pius, forbidding the circumcision of males who were not born Jews. Jewish believers had always Judaized their slaves; this practice was now forbidden, and before long Jews were forbidden to own Christian slaves.[105] Constantine's son intensified the anti-Jewish campaign by forbidding the ritual immersion of proselytized women and forbade Jewish men to marry Christian women.

The legal status of Jews was not drastically altered, but a Jew who circumcised his slave was condemned to death; in addition, owning a Christian slave became punishable by the confiscation of property, and any harm done to a Christianized Jew was punished by burning at the stake. By contrast, new proselytes—if there still were any—risked losing all their property. In the pagan world, Judaism, though persecuted, was a respectable and legitimate religion. Under repressive Christianity, it gradually became a pernicious, contemptible sect. The new church did not seek to eradicate Judaism—it wanted to preserve Judaism as an aged, humbled creature that had long since lost its admirers, and whose insignificant existence vindicated the victors.

In these circumstances, the large number of Jews around the Mediterranean inevitably declined at an accelerating rate. Zionist historians, as we shall see in the next chapter, tend to suggest that those who left Judaism in times of isolation and stress were mainly the newly converted. The "ethnic" hard core of "birth Jews"—a term often found in Zionist historiography—kept the faith and remained unalterably Jewish. There is, of course, not a shred of evidence for this *völkisch* interpretation. It is equally likely that the numerous families that had taken to Judaism by choice, or even their descendants in the next few generations, would have clung to it more fervently than those born to it effortlessly. Converts and their offspring famously tend to be more devoted to their chosen religion than old believers. No wonder the tanna rabbi Simeon ben Yohai asserted in the commentary attributed to him that God loved the

---

105   See Amnon Linder, "The Roman power and the Jews in the time of Constantine," *Tarbiz* 44 (1975 [in Hebrew]), 95–143.

proselytes even more than the born Jews. We have to accept that we shall never know who remained attached to the stubborn minority religion at all costs, and who chose to join the triumphant new religion.

From the time of the late Amoraim, the rabbinical elite of the Jewish minority regarded proselytization as a dark cloud that menaced the community's very existence. Judaism's core identity policy changed direction: it expressed in the clearest ideological terms an inner censorship, accepted the decree of the Christian powers, and grew increasingly into a self-isolating group that treated seekers with suspicion and rejection. This identity policy became vital for its survival in the Christian world.

But the proselytizing Jewish monotheism did not quite give up. It retreated to the margins and continued actively to seek converts. It would do so on the borders of the Christian cultural world and, in some areas, even made significant progress.

But before we proceed to deal with this important issue, on which the number of Jewish believers in history depends, we might stop and consider the situation of the Jews in the region where the campaign of proselytizing began, and which invented the long, imaginary exile—Judea, renamed Palestine by the second-century Roman rulers and their successors. To that renaming, the Jewish sages responded defensively with "the Land of Israel."

THE SAD FATE OF THE JUDEANS

If the Judeans were not exiled from their country, and if there was never a large-scale emigration of its agrarian population, what was the historical fate of most of the inhabitants? The question did arise, as we shall see, in the early days of the Jewish national movement, but it vanished into the black hole of the national memory.

We have seen in the course of the present discussion that Yitzhak Baer and Ben-Zion Dinur, the first two professional historians at the Hebrew University in Jerusalem, knew perfectly well that there was no forced expulsion after the destruction of the Second Temple; they moved the exile up to the seventh century CE, to the Muslim conquest. As they described it, it was only the arrival of the Arabs that caused the demographic upheaval that uprooted masses of Judeans from their native land and made it the homeland of strangers.

Taking into account the mass uprising led by Bar Kokhba, as well as the thriving Judean culture and agriculture in the time of Judah ha-Nasi and even after, we may readily agree with the two pioneering historians that "the Children of Israel" were not exiled after the destruction of the Temple. Most scholars also agree that between the fall of the kingdom in the year 70 CE and the Muslim conquest six centuries later, there seemed to be a Judean majority between the Jordan River and the Mediterranean. However, the chronological postponement of the forced exile to the seventh century CE is less convincing. According to Dinur, it was only because of "the ceaseless penetration of the desert people into the country, their amalgamation with its alien (Syrio-Aramaean) elements, the capture of the agriculture by the new conquerors and their seizure of Jewish lands" that the country changed hands.[106]

Did the Arabs really implement a policy of land colonization? Where did the hundreds of thousands of dispossessed Judean peasants go? Did they obtain or capture land in other countries? Did they establish Hebrew agricultural settlements in some other place, near or far? Or did the "tillers of the soil" change their occupation in the seventh century and become transformed into a peripatetic people of merchants and money-changers wandering about the alien lands of "exile"? The Zionist historiographic discourse offers no rational answers to these questions.

In 324 CE the province of Palestine became a Christian protectorate, and a large part of its population became Christian. Jerusalem—home of the first Christian community, founded by local Judeans in the first century CE,[107] and from which circumcised men were expelled after the Bar Kokhba revolt—gradually became a predominantly Christian city. The list of participants in the first Christian council, in Nicaea in 325 CE, reveals that there were also Christian communities in Gaza, Jabneh, Ashqelon, Ashdod, Lod (Lydda), Beit She'an, Shechem, Gadara and elsewhere. It appears that the disappearance of Jews from the country coincided with the conversion of many of them to Christianity.

Yet the evidence shows that the spread of Christianity did not eliminate the Jewish presence in the country, and that the population was a diverse mosaic of many new Christians, a solid bloc of Jewish believers, a strong Samaritan minority, and of course the pagan peasantry, which would persist for a long time on the margins of the monotheistic religious cultures. The tradition of rabbinical Judaism in Judea, reinforced by its strong connections to Babylonia, limited the ability of dynamic Christianity to win souls all over the Holy Land. Nor did the Christian repressions of the Byzantine authorities succeed in extinguishing the Jewish faith and worship or in stopping new synagogues going up, as the last uprising in the Galilee in 614 CE, led by Benjamin of Tiberias, clearly proved.[108]

---

106   Dinur, *Israel in Exile*, vol. 1, 7, 30. There is an embarrassing lack of material cited by Dinur in his effort to substantiate his thesis on the uprooting and exile of the Jews. See ibid., 49–51.

107   Acts 4:4 and 21:20.

108   Scholarly literature in Israel has usually sought to minimize the scope of Jewish

Baer, Dinur and other Zionist historians were not mistaken in stating that this significant Jewish presence was drastically reduced following the Muslim conquest in the seventh century, but this was not due to the uprooting of Jews from the country, for which there is no shred of evidence in the historical record. Palestine, the former Judea, was not swept by masses of migrants from the Arabian Desert who dispossessed the indigenous inhabitants. The conquerors had no such policy, and neither exiled nor expelled the Judean agrarian population, whether they believed in Yahweh or in the Christian Trinity.

The Muslim army that swept like a typhoon out of Arabia and conquered the region between 638 and 643 CE was a relatively small force. The largest estimate of its strength is forty-six thousand troops, and the bulk of this army was later sent on to other fronts on the borders of the Byzantine Empire. While the troops stationed in the conquered country brought in their families, and probably seized land so as to settle them there, this could hardly have made for a serious change in the population. It might have reduced some of the residents to tenant farming. Moreover, the Arab conquest interrupted the thriving commerce around the Mediterranean, leading to a gradual demographic decline in the region, but there is no evidence that this decrease led to the replacement of a people.

One of the secrets of the Muslim army's power was its relatively liberal attitude toward the religions of the defeated people—provided they were monotheists, of course. Muhammad's commandment to treat Jews and Christians as "people of the Book" gave them legal protection. The Prophet stressed in a famous letter to the army commanders in southern Arabia: "Every person, whether a Jew or a Christian, who becomes a Muslim is one of the Believers, with the same rights and duties. Anyone who clings to his Judaism or Christianity is not to be converted and must [pay] the poll tax incumbent upon every adult, male or female, free or bond."[109] No wonder that the Jews, who had suffered harsh persecution under the Byzantine Empire, welcomed the new conquerors and even rejoiced at their success. Jewish and Muslim testimonies show that they helped the victorious Arab forces.

An irreparable split had occurred between Judaism and Christianity by the latter's division of the deity, which aggravated the rivalry between them. The gulf

---

conversion to Christianity. See for example Joseph Geiger, "The expansion of Christianity in Eretz Israel," in *Eretz Israel From the Destruction of the Second Temple*, 218–33. Rabbinical literature censored itself on the phenomenon, but occasionally it broke through in a metaphorical manner. See Binyamin Sofer, *The Jews' Civilization*, Jerusalem: Carmel, 2002 (in Hebrew), 240–1.

109   Quoted in Dinur, *Israel in Exile*, vol. 1, 1, 164.

was widened by the myth of the murder of the Son of God, which intensified the mutual hatred. Triumphant Christianity's attempts to suppress Judaism made things worse. By contrast, although Muhammad fought against the Jewish tribes in the Arabian Peninsula—one of them was exiled to Jericho—the advent of Islam was viewed by many as a liberation from persecution and even as a possible future fulfillment of the messianic promise. Rumors about the rise of a new prophet in the desert spread and heartened many Jewish believers, especially as Muhammad presented himself as a successor of earlier prophets, not as a divinity. The seventh-century Armenian bishop Sebeos described the Arab conquest of Palestine as the descendants of Ishmael coming to the aid of the descendants of Isaac against the Byzantine Empire, in fulfillment of God's promise to their common ancestor Abraham.[110] A contemporary Jew wrote in a letter:

> God it was who inspired the Ishmaelite kingdom to aid us. When they spread forth and captured the Land of the Hind from the hand of Edom, and reached Jerusalem, there were Israelites among them. They showed them the place of the Temple, and have dwelled with them to this day. They made it a condition that they preserve the place of the Temple from any abomination, and would pray at its gates, and none would gainsay them.[111]

This description of a joint conquest may have been an exaggeration, but other sources testify that some Judean fugitives who had escaped the oppressions of the Byzantine Empire returned with the victorious army. Under Islam, Jews were allowed to enter the holy city, which even awakened secret dreams of rebuilding the Temple: "The Ishmaelite kings treated them with kindness, allowing Israelites to come to the house and there build a prayer house and a study house. All the Israelite congregations near the house would go thither on holy days and festivals and pray therein."[112]

The new conquerors had an extraordinary system of taxation: Muslims did not have to pay any taxes; only the unbelievers did. Given the benefits of Islamization, it is not surprising that the new religion quickly attracted great numbers of converts. Exemption from taxation must have been seen as worth a change of deity, especially as he seemed so much like the former one. In fact, the caliphs' taxation policy had to be modified later, as the mass conversion to Islam by the conquered populations threatened to drain their treasury.

---

110   The testimony of Sebeos quoted in Dinur, ibid., 6–7.
111   Ibid., 32. There were probably some Yemeni Judaizers among the Muslim soldiers who captured Jerusalem. See Shlomo Dov Goitein, *Palestinian Jewry in Early Islamic and Crusader Times*, Jerusalem: Ben Zvi, 1980 (in Hebrew), 11.
112   Dinur, *Israel in Exile*, vol. 1, 1, 42.

Did the similarity between the religions, Islam's relative tolerance toward the other monotheisms, and the religious system of taxation induce Jewish, Christian and Samaritan believers to convert to Islam? Historical logic would say yes, though there are insufficient sources to provide a definitive answer. The traditional Jewish elites were pained by the apostasy, and tended to ignore and suppress it. Zionist historiography followed them, turning its back on any meaningful discussion of the issue. Abandoning the Jewish religion was generally interpreted by modern sensibilities as betraying the "nation," and was best forgotten.

During the Byzantine period, despite the persecutions, a good many synagogues were built. But after the Arab conquest, construction gradually came to an end, and Jewish prayer houses grew scarcer. It is reasonable to assume that a slow, moderate process of conversion took place in Palestine/Land of Israel, and accounted for the disappearance of the Jewish majority in the country.

REMEMBERING AND FORGETTING THE "PEOPLE OF THE LAND"

"He shall even return, and have intelligence with them that forsake the holy covenant" (Dan. 11: 30)—the consoling prophecy of the prophet from Babylon—was interpreted by Rabbi Saadia Gaon in the tenth century CE as follows: "They are the Ishmaelites in Jerusalem; and then they defiled the mighty temple." The great Jewish scholar, who translated the Bible into Arabic, continued his commentary: "[He] shall speak marvelous things against the God of gods" (Dan. 11: 36)—"outrageous words against the Lord of Eternity, till he discharge his anger with Israel, then the Creator will destroy the enemies of Israel." He went on to interpret the verse "And many of them that sleep in the dust of the earth shall awake, some to everlasting life and some to shame *and* everlasting contempt" (Dan. 12: 2), saying, "That is the resurrection of the Israelite dead, destined to eternal life. Those who will not awake are those who turned away from the Lord, who will descend to the lowermost level of hell, and will be the shame of all flesh."

In 1967 these comments from the works of Saadia Gaon, expressing his profound grief about Islamization, were presented and highlighted in a fascinating essay by the historian Abraham Polak, the founder of the Department of Middle Eastern and African History at Tel Aviv University.[113] Soon after Israel seized the West Bank and the Gaza Strip, this scholar thought that the

---

113   Abraham Polak, "The Origin of the Arabs of the Country," *Molad* 213 (1967 [in Hebrew)]), 297–303. See also a hostile response to the article, and Polak's sharp response in the following issue of *Molad* 214 (1968), 424–9.

conquered population would become an insoluble problem for the State, and cautiously brought up the vexed issue of "the origin of the Arabs of the Land of Israel." Polak, a confirmed Zionist, was a bold student of Islam, and he disliked unjustifiable suppressions of memory, as we shall see in the next chapter. Since no one was willing to talk about those who did "forsake the holy covenant," those "Ishmaelites in Jerusalem," or those "enemies of Israel" who "turned away from the Lord," he took the almost impossible mission upon himself.

His important essay did not argue that all Palestinians were the direct or exclusive descendants of the Judeans. As a serious historian, he knew that over thousands or even hundreds of years almost any population, especially in such geographic junctions as the land between the Jordan River and the Mediterranean, mingles with its neighbors, its captives or its conquerors. Greeks, Persians, Arabs, Egyptians and Crusaders had all come to the country and always mingled and integrated with the local population. Polak assumed that there was considerable likelihood that Judeans did convert to Islam, meaning that there was a demographic continuity in the agrarian "people of the land" from antiquity to our time, and that this should be the subject of a legitimate scientific study. But as we know, what history did not wish to relate, it omitted. No university or other research institution responded to Polak's challenge, and no funds or students were assigned to the problematic subject.

Bold as he was, Polak was not the first to raise the issue of mass Islamization, and he pointed this out in his introduction. In the early days of Zionist settlement, before the rise of Palestinian nationalism, the idea that the bulk of the local population descended from the Judeans was accepted by a good many.

Israel Belkind, for example, one of the first Zionists who settled in Palestine in 1882, and a leading figure in the small BILU movement, always believed in the close historical connection between the country's ancient inhabitants and the peasantry of his own day.[114] Before he died he summed up his thinking on the subject in a small book, which included all the controversial assumptions that would later be erased from national historiography: "The historians are accustomed to say that after the destruction of Jerusalem by Titus, the Jews were scattered all over the world and no longer inhabited their country. But this, too, is a historical error, which must be removed and the true facts discovered."[115]

Belkind argued that the subsequent uprisings, from the Bar Kokhba revolt to the insurgence in Galilee in the early seventh century, indicated that most

---

114   Regarding this unusual personality, see Israel Belkind, *In the Path of the Biluim*, Tel Aviv: Ministry of Defence, 1983 (in Hebrew). As well as founding the first Hebrew school, he also composed the final wording of the Hatikvah anthem.

115   Israel Belkind, *The Arabs in Eretz Israel*, Tel Aviv: Hameir, 1928 (in Hebrew), 8.

of the Judeans continued to live in the country for a long time. "The land was abandoned by the upper strata, the scholars, the Torah men, to whom the religion came before the country," he wrote. "Perhaps, too, so did many of the mobile urban people. But the tillers of the soil remained attached to their land."[116] Many findings reinforce this historical conclusion.

Many Hebrew place names have been preserved, unlike the Greek and Roman names that were meant to replace them. A good number of burial places, sacred to the local inhabitants, are joint Muslim and Jewish cemeteries. The local Arabic dialect is strewn with Hebrew and Aramaic words, distinguishing it from literary Arabic and other Arabic vernaculars. The local populace does not define itself as Arab—they see themselves as Muslims or fellahin (farmers), while they refer to the Bedouin as Arabs. The particular mentality of certain local communities recalls that of their Hebrew ancestors.

In other words, Belkind was convinced that he and his fellow pioneers were meeting "a good many of our people ... our own flesh and blood."[117] To him, the ethnic origin meant more than the religion and the daily culture derived from it. He argued that it was imperative to revive the spiritual connection with the lost limb of the Jewish people, to develop and improve its economic condition, and to unite with it for a common future. The Hebrew schools must open their doors to Muslim students, without offending their faith or their language, and, in addition to Arabic, must teach them both Hebrew and "world culture."

Belkind was not the only one to promote this historical outlook and this distinctive cultural strategy. Ber Borochov, the legendary theoretical leader of the Zionist left, thought the same. During the Uganda controversy that shook the Zionist movement, Borochov adopted a consistent anti-Herzl position. He was, in contemporary parlance, a sworn Palestinocentric, arguing that the only solution that would ensure the success of the Zionist enterprise was settlement in Palestine. One of the arguments cited by this Zionist Marxist seeking to convince his leftist readers was historical, flavored with ethnocentrism:

> The local population in Palestine is racially more closely related to the Jews than to any other people, even among the Semitic ones. It is quite probable that the fellahin in Palestine are direct descendants of the Jewish and Canaanite rural population, with a slight admixture of Arab blood. For it is known that the Arabs, being proud conquerors, mingled very little with the populations in the countries they conquered ... All the tourists and travelers confirm that, except for the Arabic language, it is impossible to distinguish between a Sephardic porter and an Arab laborer or fellah ... Hence, the racial difference

---

116   Ibid., 10–11.
117   Ibid., 19.

between the diaspora Jews and the Palestinian fellahin is no more marked than between Ashkenazi and Sephardic Jews.[118]

Borochov was convinced that this kinship would make the local population more receptive to the new settlers. As theirs was a lower culture, the fellahin around the Jewish colonies would soon adopt the ways of Hebrew culture, and would eventually merge with it entirely. The Zionist vision, based partly on "blood" and partly on history, determined that "a fellah who speaks Hebrew, dresses like a Jew and adopts the outlook and customs of Jewish common people would be in no way distinguished from the Jews."[119]

Among the Poale Zion membership, the political-ideological movement led and shaped by Borochov, were two gifted young men whose names would become famous. In 1918, when David Ben-Gurion and Itzhak Ben-Zvi were staying in New York, they wrote a sociohistorical book entitled *Eretz Israel in the Past and in the Present*. They wrote it first in Hebrew, then translated it into Yiddish in order to reach a wider Jewish-American public. This was the most important work about "Eretz Israel" (which, in the book, consisted of both sides of the Jordan River and stretched from El-Arish in the south to Tyre in the north), and it was very successful. It was well researched, and its statistical material and bibliographic sources were impressive. But for its passionate nationalistic tone, it might have been an ordinary academic work. Israel's future prime minister contributed two-thirds of the text, and the rest was written by the future president. The second chapter, which dealt with the history and present situation of the fellahin, was composed by Ben-Gurion in full agreement with his coauthor. They wrote, in complete confidence,

The fellahin are not descendants of the Arab conquerors, who captured Eretz Israel and Syria in the seventh century CE. The Arab victors did not destroy the agricultural population they found in the country. They expelled only the alien Byzantine rulers, and did not touch the local population. Nor did the Arabs go in for settlement. Even in their former habitations, the Arabians did not engage in farming ... They did not seek new lands on which to settle their peasantry, which hardly existed. Their whole interest in the new countries was political, religious and material: to rule, to propagate Islam and to collect taxes.[120]

---

118   Ber Borochov, "On the Issue of Zion and the Territory," in *Works*, vol. 1, Tel Aviv: Hakibbutz Hameuhad, 1955 (in Hebrew), 148. The Hebrew text always rendered "Palestine" as "Eretz Israel," though most early Zionist thinkers, before the First World War, used the former name.

119   Ibid., 149.

120   David Ben-Gurion and Yitzhak Ben-Zvi, *Eretz Israel in the Past and in the Present*, Jerusalem: Ben-Zvi, 1979 (in Hebrew), 196.

Historical reason indicates that the population that survived since the seventh century had originated from the Judean farming class that the Muslim conquerors had found when they reached the country.

> To argue that after the conquest of Jerusalem by Titus and the failure of the Bar Kokhba revolt Jews altogether ceased to cultivate the land of Eretz Israel is to demonstrate complete ignorance in the history and the contemporary literature of Israel ... The Jewish farmer, like any other farmer, was not easily torn from his soil, which had been watered with his sweat and the sweat of his forebears ... Despite the repression and suffering, the rural population remained unchanged.[121]

This was written thirty years before Israel's Proclamation of Independence, which asserts that the whole people was forcibly uprooted. The two committed Zionists wished to join the local "natives," believing wholeheartedly that this could be achieved thanks to their shared ethnic origin. Although the ancient Judean peasants converted to Islam, they had done so for material reasons—chiefly to avoid taxation—which were in no way treasonous. Indeed, by clinging to their soil they remained loyal to their homeland. Ben-Gurion and Ben-Zvi saw Islam, unlike Christianity, as a democratic religion that not only embraced all converts to Islam as brothers, but genuinely revoked the political and civil restrictions and sought to erase social distinctions.[122]

The authors underlined that the Jewish origin of the fellahin could be revealed by means of a philological study of the local Arabic language, as well as by linguistic geography. They went even further than Belkind in stressing that a study of ten thousand names of "all the villages, streams, springs, mountains, ruins, valleys and hills 'from Dan to Beersheba' ... confirm[s] that the entire biblical terminology of Eretz Israel remains alive, as it had been, in the speech of the fellah population."[123] Some 210 villages still bore clear Hebrew names, and in addition to the Muslim law there was, for a long time, a code of "fellahin laws, or unwritten customary judgments, known as Shariat al-Khalil—the laws of the patriarch Abraham."[124] Beside many village mosques there were local shrines (*maqam*) commemorating such sainted figures as the three patriarchs, certain kings, prophets and great sheikhs.

---

121   Ibid., 198.
122   Ibid., 200.
123   Ibid., 201.
124   Ibid., 205.

Ben-Zvi considered the chapter on the origin of the fellahin to be the fruit of his own independent research, and was apparently offended that Ben-Gurion appropriated his material. In 1929 he returned to this important theme in a special booklet in Hebrew that bore his name alone.[125] It does not differ significantly from the chapter on this subject in the book that the two Zionist leaders published together, but it does have some expanded material and new emphases. The future president of the state added a somewhat more extensive social analysis of the historical differences between the educated Judean elites and the agrarian society that clung to the soil through all the upheavals. The forced conversion to Christianity before the arrival of Islam is also stressed, providing added justification for the mass conversion to Islam that would follow. It was not only the system of taxation that led many Jews to adopt the conquerors' religion, but also the fear of being displaced from the soil.

In 1929 Ben-Zvi's position was more moderate: "Obviously it would be mistaken to say that all the fellahin are descendants of the ancient Jews, but it can be said of most of them, or their core."[126] He maintained that immigrants arrived from many places, and the local population was fairly heterogeneous, but the traces left in the language, place-names, legal customs, popular festivals such as that of Nebi Musa (the prophet Moses), and other cultural practices left almost no doubt that "the great majority of the fellahin do not descend from the Arab conquerors but before that, from the Jewish fellahin, who were the foundation of this country before its conquest by Islam."[127]

The Arab uprising and the massacre in Hebron, which happened the year Ben-Zvi published his booklet, and subsequently the widespread Palestinian revolt of 1936–39, took the remaining wind out of the sails of the integrationist Zionist thinkers. The rise of a local nationalism made it very clear to the educated settlers that their ethnocentric bear-hug had no future. The inclusive concept briefly adopted by Zionists was based on the assumption that it would be easy to assimilate a "low and primitive" Oriental culture, and so the first violent resistance from the objects of this Orientalist fantasy shook them awake. From that moment on, the descendants of the Judean peasantry vanished from the Jewish national consciousness and were cast into oblivion. Very soon

125 Itzhak Ben-Zvi, *Our Population in the Country*, Warsaw: The Executive Committee of the Youth Alliance and the JNF, 1929 (in Hebrew).
126 Ibid., 38.
127 Ibid., 39. On the Zionist position regarding the origin of the Palestinians, see also Shmuel Almog, " 'The Land for its Workers' and the Proselytizing of the Fellahin," in *Nation and History*, vol. 2, Shmuel Ettinger (ed.), Jerusalem: Zalman Shazar, 1984 (in Hebrew), 165–75.

the modern Palestinian fellahin became, in the eyes of the authorized agents of memory, Arabian immigrants who came in the nineteenth century to an almost empty country and continued to arrive in the twentieth century as the developing Zionist economy, according to the new myth, attracted many thousands of non-Jewish laborers.[128]

It is not impossible that Baer's and Dinur's postponement of the exile to the Muslim conquest of the seventh century was also an indirect response to the historical discourse proposed by such central figures as Belkind, Ben-Gurion and Ben-Zvi. To Zionist thinking, this pioneering discourse defined too loosely the parameters of the "ancient nation"—and worse, it might have granted too many historical rights to the "native populace." It was imperative to bury it as quickly as possible and erase it from the national agenda.

From now on, early Islam did not convert the Jews but simply dispossessed them. The imaginary exile in the seventh century CE came to replace the baseless religious narrative about a mass expulsion after the fall of the Second Temple, as well as the thesis that the Palestinian fellahin were descendants of the people of Judea. The time of the expulsion was unimportant—the main thing was the precious memory of a forced exile.

National mythology determined that the Jews—banished, deported or fugitive emigrants—were driven into a long and dolorous exile, causing them to wander over lands and seas to the far corners of the earth until the advent of Zionism prompted them to turn around and return en masse to their orphaned homeland. This homeland had never belonged to the Arab conquerors, hence the claim of the people without a land to the land without a people.

This national statement, which was simplified into a useful and popular slogan for the Zionist movement, was entirely the product of an imaginary history grown around the idea of the exile. Although most of the professional historians knew there had never been a forcible uprooting of the Jewish people, they permitted the Christian myth that had been taken up by Jewish tradition to be paraded freely in the public and educational venues of the national memory, making no attempt to rebut it. They even encouraged it indirectly, knowing that only this myth would provide moral legitimacy to the settlement of the "exiled nation" in a land inhabited by others.

On the other hand, the mass conversion to Judaism that produced great Jewish communities around the Mediterranean left almost no trace in the national historiography. Such vestiges as there had been in the past faded away

---

128   For a more balanced Israeli attitude towards Palestinian history in modern times, see B. Kimmerling and J. S. Migdal, *The Palestinian People: A History*, Cambridge, MA: Harvard University Press, 2003.

in the construction of the State's memory. The proselytes themselves, as we have seen, tended to cover up their gentile origins. Eager to be purified and integrated in the holy nation, all proselytes sought to erase their impure past—a past when they had consumed unclean animals and worshipped celestial bodies—and so become newborn in the eyes of their community and faith. Their children's children hardly knew, or wished to know, that their forefathers were unclean gentiles who had entered the special Jewish congregation from outside.

They also aspired to the prestige of belonging by birth to the chosen people. Despite Judaism's positive attitude toward proselytizing, and the praise and flattery directed at the proselytes, genealogical membership was still highly valued in the halakhic heart. The honor of belonging to the deportees from Jerusalem fortified the spirit of the believers and reinforced their identity in a menacing, and sometimes seductive, outside world. Asserting an origin from Zion also reinforced their claim to privileged status in the holy city upon which, according to tradition, the world was founded, and which both Christians and Muslims revered.

It was no accident that modern Jewish nationalism opted for the fictitious ethnic element of the long tradition. It fell upon that concept with glee, manipulated it thoroughly in its ideological laboratories, nurtured it with questionable secular historical data and made it the foundation of its view of the past. The national memory was implanted on a base of ritual oblivion, hence its amazing success.

Had the memory of the mass conversion to Judaism been preserved, it might have eroded the metanarrative about the biological unity of the Jewish people, whose genealogical roots were believed to trace back all the way to Abraham, Isaac and Jacob—not to a heterogeneous mosaic of human populations that lived in the Hasmonean kingdom, in the Persian domain and in the far-flung expanses of the Roman Empire.

Forgetting the forced Judaization and the great voluntary proselytization was essential for the preservation of a linear timeline, along which, back and forth, from past to present and back again, moved a unique nation—wandering, isolated, and, of course, quite imaginary.

CHAPTER FOUR

Realms of Silence:
In Search of Lost (Jewish) Time

Some of the Berbers followed the Jewish religion, which they received from their powerful Israelite neighbours of Syria. Among the Jewish Berbers were the Djeraoua, inhabitants of Aurès, the tribe of Kahina, who were killed by Arabs in their early conquests.
— Ibn Khaldun, *History of the Berbers*, 1396

It is even possible that my ancestry might not move in the direction of ancient Israel at all ... After 965, the Khazars were through as an organized power, but Judaism may have remained, and it may well be that many East European Jews are descended from Khazars and the people they ruled. I may be one of them. Who knows? And who cares?
— Isaac Asimov, *It's Been a Good Life*, 2002

Johann Wolfgang von Goethe compared architecture to music frozen in space. Can we compare historical Judaism since the fourth century CE to an immobile architectural structure whose sounds have meekly turned inward for hundreds of years?

The depiction of Judaism as a self-absorbed sect that turned its fervent faith into a Talmudic, casuistic colloquium suited the dominant Christian view that fixed the Jewish image in the Western world. While proto-Zionist and Zionist historiography disliked the demeaning element in this condescending view, it submitted to it unreservedly. The historiographers supported the imagery of the "ethnic" people as a drifting body that cannot live or function until it returns to its purported birthplace.

In reality, before Judaism turned inward—chiefly due to the exclusionary walls built around it by Christianity—it continued its efforts at proselytization in the still-virgin lands that had yet to experience the spread of monotheism. From the Arabian Peninsula to the lands of the Slavs, the Caucasus and the steppes between the Volga and the Don rivers, the areas around the destroyed and then rebuilt Carthage, the pre-Muslim Iberian Peninsula, Judaism continued to gain believers, thus securing its impressive presence in history. The cultures in the regions it reached were generally in a stage of transition from the phase of tribalism to that of organized state, and were all, of course, purely pagan.

Other than Syria and Egypt, Arabia was one of the regions nearest to Judea, and so the influence of the Jewish religion reached it fairly early. The Arab kingdom of the Nabataeans that bordered the kingdom of Judea disintegrated in 106 CE, not long after the fall of Jerusalem. Beyond it stretched the peninsula inhabited by nomadic Arab tribes and crossed by traders carrying goods from south to north. The oases on the main routes were also reached by Judean merchants, some of whom chose to settle in them. Along with their earthy goods, they brought the belief in a single god, and its spiritual offerings—an omnipotent universal creator and the resurrection of the dead—began to captivate followers of the various idolatrous sects. For example, a passage in the Mishnah states: "All [the converts] from Reqem are pure; Rabbi Yehudah sees them as unclean, because they are erring proselytes" (*Tractate Niddah*). Reqem was probably a settlement in southeastern Transjordan, whose conversion to Judaism did not seem convincing to Rabbi Yehuda Bar Ilai. Jewish or Judaizing burial inscriptions have also been found in various parts of the northern Hejaz.

Before the advent of Islam, in the era called in Arab historiography "the age of ignorance"—in the fourth or early fifth century CE—Jews settled in Taima, Khaybar and Yathrib (later named Medina), in the heart of the Hejaz. Not long before the rise of Islam, Judaism began to make its way into the powerful tribes that inhabited these centers. The best known of these, because Muhammad clashed with them early in his campaign, were the Qaynuqa, the Quraiza and the Nadhir in the region of Yathrib. But tribes in Taima and Khaybar—Arabic-speaking and bearing typical local names—had also converted to Judaism. The atmosphere among these Judaizers may be deduced from the late description by the Arab historian Abd Allah al-Bakri, who lived in the eleventh century and wrote, concerning a tribe in Taima, that the tribesmen "were prevented by the Jews from entering their fort as long as they professed another religion, and only when they embraced Judaism were they admitted."[1]

The spread of Jewish monotheism, which was not yet rabbinical, must have helped prepare the spiritual ground for the rise of Islam. Although the new religion clashed strongly with its precursor, the Qur'an testifies to the crucial role played by Judaism's ideological preparation. The Muslim holy book contains various phrases, stories and legends taken from the Old Testament and flavored with local imagination. From the Garden of Eden to the Shekhinah, through the tales of Abraham, Joseph and Moses, to the messages of David and Solomon, who are called prophets, echoes of the Old Testament are heard throughout the Qur'an (though it does not mention the great prophets like

---

1   Baron, *A Social and Religious History*, vol. 3, 65.

Jeremiah and Isaiah, and, of the later ones, only Zechariah and Jonah). Judaism was not the only religion that penetrated the Arabian Peninsula—Christianity also contended for believers, successfully in some places, though ultimately the Holy Trinity was not absorbed into the Muslim canon. Furthermore, in the territory between these two well-defined religions were some lively syncretic sects, such as the Hanifs, all of which contributed to the bubbling crucible from which the new monotheism sprang.

The triumph of Islam in the early seventh century CE curtailed the spread of Judaism and led to the gradual assimilation of the proselytized tribes. Moreover, the new religion forbade Muslims to convert to Judaism, and anyone who propagated such conversions was condemned to death. As noted in the previous chapter, the privileges granted to those who joined the religion of Muhammad were hard to resist.

Yet prior to the rise of Muhammad, in the center of the Arabian Peninsula, Jewish preaching had led to the astonishing conversion of an entire kingdom in the south. Unlike the developments that took place in Yathrib or Khaybar, this mass conversion gave rise to a stable religious community that withstood the temporary gains of Christianity as well as the later triumph of Islam, and survived until modern times.

In the early centuries of the Common Era, the population in the heart of the Hejaz was still tribal, but the region known today as the Yemen was developing a more coherent state organization, and it was searching for a centralizing religious belief.

ARABIA FELIX—THE PROSELYTIZED KINGDOM OF HIMYAR

This legendary region in the southern end of the peninsula intrigued the Romans, who called it "Happy Arabia." Under Augustus they dispatched a garrison there, to which Herod contributed a company from Judea. But the mission failed, and most of the soldiers were lost in the blazing desert. Himyar was the name of a large local tribe, which in the second century BCE began to subdue its neighbours and to consolidate into a tribal kingdom. Its capital was the city Zafar, and it came to be known also as "the kingdom of Saba, Dhu-Raydan, Hadhramaut and Yamnat," and of the Arabs of Taud and Tihamat. By such a resounding name it became known far and wide. Rome did form some ties with it, and much later so did the Sassanid kings of Persia. Around the Himyarite ruler, known in the Arabian traditions as *tubba*, corresponding to "king" or "emperor," and in Himyarite inscriptions as *malik*, were consolidated the kingdom's administration, the nobility and the tribal leadership.

Himyar's confirmed rival was the Ethiopian kingdom of Aksum across the Red Sea, which periodically sent forces across the strait to blockade its wealthy neighbor.

A possible visit by the Himyarites to the Holy Land was suggested by some tombs in Beit She'arim near Haifa, uncovered in 1936. A Greek inscription engraved over one of the niches describes the interred as "people of Himyar." We know they were Jews, because one of them was named "Menah[em], Elder of the Congregation," and two characteristic Jewish emblems, a candelabra and a ram's horn, were carved beside the inscription. No one knows how these Himyarite tombs, dated probably to the third century CE, came to be in Beit She'arim.[2]

The Arian Christian historian Philostorgius wrote that in the middle of the fourth century, Constantius II, emperor of the eastern Roman Empire, sent a mission to the Himyarites to convert them to Christianity. The mission was resisted by the local Jews, but in the end the Himyarite king accepted Christianity, says Philostorgius, and even built two churches in his kingdom. The story has not been verified. However, it was at about that time that the Ethiopian kingdom became Christian, and it is possible that there was a struggle between the contending religions in Himyar at that time. Possibly one of the kings converted to Christianity, but if so, the victory was short-lived.

There is much archaeological and epigraphic evidence, some of it newly discovered, that indicates with near certainty that toward the end of the fourth century CE the Himyar kingdom abandoned paganism and adopted monotheism, but it was not Christianity that it chose. In 378 CE, Malik Karib Yuhamin built structures on which were discovered such inscriptions as "By the might of their Lord, Lord of Heavens." There are also inscriptions reading "Lord of the Heavens and the Earth" and "Rahmanan" (the Merciful). The latter is a characteristic Jewish term; it appears in the Talmud in its Aramaic form, Rahmana, and was only later, in the early seventh century, adopted by the Muslims as one of the names of Allah. Christians in the Arab world also used the term, but they invariably added "the Son and the Holy Spirit."

If researchers disagreed about the character of this pioneering monotheism, the issue was more or less resolved when another inscription was discovered in the city of Beit al-Ashwal, dedicated to the son of Malik Karib Yuhamin. It says, in Hebrew, "written by Yehudah, the well-remembered, amen shalom, amen," and, in Himyari, "by the power and grace of his lord, who

---

2   On the discovery of the tombs in Bait-She'arim, see the extensive work of Haim Ze'ev Hirschberg, *Israel in Arabia: The History of the Jews In Hedjaz and Himyar*, Tel Aviv: Byalik, 1946 (in Hebrew), 53–7.

created his soul, lord of life and death, lord of heaven and earth, who created all things, and with the financial help of his people Israel and the empowerment of his lord."[3] Whether or not this inscription was ordered by the royal house itself, it praises the king on the terms of the Jewish religion, and its author clearly assumes that this religion is shared by the ruler.

Himyar was ruled from the last quarter of the fourth century CE to the first quarter of the sixth—that is, between 120 and 150 years, almost as long as the duration of the Hasmonean kingdom—by a strong, monotheistic Jewish monarchy. Muslim tradition associates the Judaization of the Himyarite kingdom to Abu Karib Assad, Malik Karib Yuhamin's second son, who apparently ruled between 390 and 420 CE. Legend has it that this king went to war in the north of the peninsula but, instead of fighting, returned with two Jewish sages and began to convert all his subjects to Judaism.[4] At first the subjects rejected the new religion, but were eventually persuaded and entered the covenant of Abraham.

There is also evidence from 440 CE that confirms the Jewish faith of Surahbi'il Yaffur, Assad's son. The great dam of Ma'rib, repaired and rebuilt by this king, bears an inscription with his name and titles, and the help given him by the "lord of heaven and earth." Another epigraph dating from the same time includes the expression "Rahmanan," the divine title that recurs in inscriptions of successive kings.

The story of the execution of Azqir, a Christian missionary from the city of Najran in northern Himyar, indicates that "Rahman Judaism" had become the hegemonic religion. There are many Arabic legends about the killing of this preacher, described in Christian hagiography as a martyr at Jewish hands. This occurred in the reign of the Himyarite king Surahbi'il Yakkaf. After Azqir built a chapel with a cross on top, he was arrested by agents of the kingdom and the chapel was destroyed. The king tried to persuade him to abandon his belief in the redeemer, but Azqir refused and was sentenced to death. At the advice of a rabbi close to the king, it was decided to carry out the sentence in Najran, as an example to others. Christianity had made some headway in the city, and it was felt necessary to deter the local populace. Before he was put to death, the martyr Azqir performed some miracles that impressed the public and were recorded in the tradition of the church.[5]

---

3   The word "people" here denotes a religious community, not a national one. See the article by Shlomo Dov Goitein, "A Himyarite-Hebrew 'bilingual' inscription," *Tarbiz* 41 (1972 [in Hebrew]), 151–6.

4   See the article by Michael Lecker, "The Conversion of Himyar to Judaism and the Jewish Banū Hadl of Medina," in *Jews and Arabs in Pre- and Early Islamic Arabia*, Aldershot: Ashgate, 1998, 129–36; see also in this volume "Judaism among Kinda and the *Ridda* of Kinda," 635–50.

5   A Christian document telling this story was translated by Ze'ev Rubin in his excellent

The kingdom went into decline after Surahbi'il Yakkaf's death, and his two sons were unable to fight off the Ethiopians, who penetrated Himyar and for a time succeeded in reinforcing their remaining Christian supporters. The struggle between Himyar and the Ethiopian kingdom of Aksum was not only a religious one, but also a conflict of political and commercial interests. Aksum was influenced by the Byzantine Empire, which sought to control the Red Sea strait in order to secure its trade with India. Himyar opposed Byzantium and firmly resisted the Christian domination of the region.[6] The prolonged devotion to Judaism among large elements in the kingdom might have been due to strong conflicts of interest. The nobility and the merchants supported the Jewish monarchy, because it safeguarded their economic independence. But Judaism was not confined to the nobility—there is much evidence that it struck root in various tribes, and even crossed the strait and penetrated the rival realm of Ethiopia.[7]

After several years of Christian hegemony, Judaism returned to power in the figure of Dhu Nuwas, the last Jewish Himyarite ruler. There is abundant material about this *malik*, mainly because of his intense struggle against Christianity and his bitter war against Ethiopia. Procopius's book *On the Wars*; the testimony of the itinerant merchant Cosmas, known as *Christian Topography*; a hymn composed by the Abbot John Psaltes; the fragmented *Book of the Himyarites*; a letter of the Syrian bishop of Beit-Arsham;[8] and many other Christian documents all offer evidence about the power of the Jewish king as well as his cruelty and persecution of the followers of Jesus. A good many Arabic sources confirm these stories, if with less anti-Jewish intensity.[9]

article, "The Martyrdom of Azqir and the Struggle Between Judaism and Christianity in Southern Arabia in the 5th century CE," in *Dor Le-Dor: From the End of Biblical Times to the Redaction of the Talmud*, A. Oppenheimer and A. Kasher (eds.), Jerusalem, Bialik, 1995 (in Hebrew), 251–85.

6   On the interests of the Eastern Roman Empire in the region, see the article by Ze'ev Rubin, "Byzantium and Southern Arabia: The Policy of Anastasius," in *The Eastern Frontier of the Roman Empire*, D. H. French and C. S. Lightfoot (eds.), *British Archaeological Reports* 553, 1989, 383–420.

7   It is quite possible that Judaism trickled from Himyar to Axum, leading to mass Judaization and the rise of the Falasha Beta Israel. It is known that the Bible was translated into Ge'ez between the fourth and sixth centuries CE. Did the Judaized tribe, led by its queen Yudit or Judit, capture the kingdom in the tenth century? This "history" is thickly shrouded in legends and lacks sufficient documentation to make a scholarly assessment. See Steven Kaplan, *The Beta Israel (Falasha) in Ethiopia*, New York: New York University Press, 1992, 44–7.

8   A section of this letter was translated by H. Z. Hirschberg in his article "Jews in the Islamic Countries," in Hava Lazarus-Yafeh (ed.), *Chapters in the History of the Arabs and Islam*, Tel Aviv: Reshafim, 1970 (in Hebrew), 264.

9   On these sources, as well as testimonies from Arabic literature, see Israel Ben Ze'ev, *The Jews in Arabia*, Jerusalem: Ahiassaf, 1957 (in Hebrew), 47–72.

Dhu Nuwas's official name was Yusuf As'ar Yath'ar, and later Arabic traditions also call him by the epithet "Masruk," probably meaning "long-haired." He was famous for his flowing locks, and legends describe his heroic last battle and how, riding his great white horse, he sank in the Red Sea. There is no doubt about his Judaism, but it is not certain that he was of royal birth, nor exactly when he ascended the throne. It was probably not much later than 518 CE, as until that year the Himyarite capital was ruled by a viceroy, a protégé of the Ethiopians, against whom Dhu Nuwas led a widespread revolt in the mountains. He succeeded in capturing Zafar and consolidating his power over the whole kingdom. The nobility supported him, and those who had not converted to Judaism did so after his victory. One testimony states that Jewish sages came from Tiberias to fortify the Mosaic faith when Dhu Nuwas was established on the throne.[10]

With Judaism again in power, the city of Najran, with its Christian majority, rebelled again. The Himyarite king besieged it for a long time and finally captured it. Numerous Christians perished in the battle, which served Ela Asbeha, the king of Aksum, as a pretext to launch war against Jewish Himyar. With the support and logistical assistance of the Byzantine Empire, which provided the ships, Christian armies crossed the Red Sea, and in 525 Dhu Nuwas was defeated after a long, grim battle. The city of Zafar was destroyed, fifty members of the ruling family were taken captive, and this was the end of the Judaizing kingdom in the southern Arabian Peninsula. An attempted rebellion, led by Sayf ibn Dhu Yazan, a descendant of Dhu Nuwas, was crushed.

The Ethiopian-backed regime that succeeded the Jewish kingdom was of course Christian, but in the 570s the region was conquered by the Persians. This halted Himyar's complete Christianization, but the country did not become Zoroastrian (this religion won few followers outside Persia). We know that the Judaized community of Himyar persisted under the Ethiopian and the Persian powers, because when the forces of Muhammad arrived in 629, the prophet warned them in a letter not to force the local Christians and Jews to convert to Islam. The type of tax imposed on the Jews reveals that many of them subsisted on agriculture, but we have no way of estimating how many remained faithful to their religion, or how many converted to the victorious religion. In all probability, a good many of the Jews had earlier become Christian, and others converted to Islam afterward. But, as noted earlier, a good many continued

10   See Hirschberg's article, "The Jewish Kingdom of Himyar," in Y. Yeshaiahu and Y. Tobi (eds.), *The Jews of Yemen: Studies and Researches*, Jerusalem: Ben Zvi, 1975 (in Hebrew), xxv.

to believe in the old *rahman* god, and by maintaining theological ties to the centers in Babylonia, the Himyarite Jewish community survived until the twentieth century.

The existence of a Judaizing kingdom in the southern Arabian Peninsula was already known in the nineteenth century. Heinrich Graetz devoted several pages to it in his famous work, based on stories drawn from Arab historians as well as Christian sources. He wrote accounts of Abu Karib Assad and Dhu Nuwas laced with colorful anecdotes.[11] Simon Dubnow, too, wrote about this kingdom, not at such length as Graetz but with more accurate dates.[12] Salo Baron followed their example with several pages about "the ancestors of the Jewry of the Yemen," and sought in various ways to justify their harsh treatment of the Christians.[13]

Later Zionist historiography paid less attention to the Himyarite kingdom. Dinur's monumental compilation *Israel in Exile* opens with the "Jewish people going into exile" in the seventh century CE, and so the earlier Jewish kingdom in southern Arabia disappears. Some Israeli scholars questioned the Jewishness of the Himyarites, which was probably not entirely rabbinical; others simply passed over this troublesome historical chapter.[14] School textbooks issued after the 1950s made no mention of the proselytized southern kingdom that lay buried under the desert sand.

Only historians who specialized in the history of the Jews of the Arab countries sometimes referred to the many Himyarite proselytes. Notable among them was Israel Ben-Ze'ev, who first published his book *Jews in Arabia* in the late 1920s in Egypt, edited it and translated it into Hebrew in 1931, and expanded it considerably in 1957. The other scholar who discussed the Jewish kingdom in depth was Haim Ze'ev Hirschberg, whose book *Israel in Arabia* appeared in 1946. These two works provide a broad canvas depicting the history of the Jews in the south of the Arabian Peninsula, and despite their nationalist tone, their scholarship is of high quality. In recent years archaeology has uncovered additional epigraphic material, and Ze'ev Rubin, a prominent historian at Tel Aviv University, is one of the few who keep up the research about the lost time of the Himyarites.

At the end of his fascinating description of the Judaized kingdom, Hirschberg, perhaps the best-known historian of the Jews in the Arab world, asked the following questions: "How many Jews lived in the Yemen? What was their racial origin—

11   Graetz, *History of the Jews*, vol. 3, 61–7.
12   Dubnow, *History of the World-People*, vol. 3, 79–83.
13   Baron, *A Social and Religious History,* vol. 3, 66–70.
14   See for example Yosef Tobi, *The Jews of Yemen*, Leiden: Brill, 1999, 3–4.

were they of the seed of Abraham, or Judaized Yemenites?" Needless to say, he could not answer these questions but, unable to stop himself, continued:

> Nevertheless, the Jews who had come from the Land of Israel, perhaps also from Babylonia, were the living soul of the Jewish community in the Yemen. They were not too few, their importance was considerable, and they decided every issue; when the persecutions began, they remained faithful to their people and their faith. In fact, many of the proselytized Himyarites could not withstand the suffering and converted to Islam. The Christians vanished altogether from the Yemen, but the Jews remained as a distinct element, apart from the Arabs. They cleave to their faith to this day, despite the contempt and humiliation surrounding them ... Other proselytes, such as the Khazars, assimilated and integrated among the nations, because the Jewish element among them was scanty, but the Jews of the Yemen remained a living tribe of the Jewish nation.[15]

Compared with the meticulous description of Himyar's history, and the strict use of original sources at every stage of the work, this concluding paragraph seems out of place, even somewhat absurd. Yet it deserves to be quoted, because it demonstrates the nature and thinking of Zionist historiography on the subject of proselytizing. Hirschberg had not the slightest evidence concerning the number, if any, of "born Jews" in the different classes of Himyarite society, nor about the origins of those who clung to the Jewish faith. But the ethnocentric imperative was stronger than his historical training, and demanded that he conclude his work with the "call of the blood." Otherwise, the readers of this respected scholar's work might fall into the error of thinking that the Jews of the Yemen were descendants of Dhu Nuwas and his hardened nobles, and not of the peaceable Abraham, Isaac and Jacob, the purported patriarchs of all the Jews in the world.

Hirschberg's ethnobiological passion was by no means exceptional. Virtually everyone who wrote about the Jewish community of Yemen applied to it a politically correct genealogy reaching back to the ancient Judahites. Some scholars even argued that, following the destruction of the First Temple, many Judahites were exiled not to Babylonia but to southern Arabia. Others suggested that the first Yemenite Jews were of the dynasty of the Queen of Sheba. King Solomon's sexy guest must have returned to her country accompanied by "Jewish courtiers," who with great dedication obeyed the command to multiply and be fruitful. This queen must have produced numerous offspring, because the Ethiopians also believed that their kings were her descendants.

---

15 Hirschberg, *Israel in Arabia*, 111.

REALMS OF SILENCE 199

Thus the chapter about the Judaizing Himyarites was abandoned by the historiographical roadside in Israel's educational system, and secondary-school graduates know nothing about it. It is the sad fate of this mighty Jewish kingdom, which dominated its region, that its descendants are not proud of it and that many others fear to mention its very existence.[16]

PHOENICIANS AND BERBERS: THE MYSTERIOUS QUEEN KAHINA

The Himyarites are not the only ones who have vanished from the historical memory of Israel; the origin of their fellow Jews in North Africa has been similarly suppressed. If, according to national mythology, the Jews of Yemen are the descendants of King Solomon's courtiers, or at least of the Babylonian exiles, the Jews of the Maghreb are likewise supposed to be descendants of the First Temple exiles, or of the Jews of European Spain, a supposedly higher lineage. The latter are also described as having been "exiled" to the western end of the Mediterranean from the desolate kingdom of Judah after the fall.

The present chapter, above, referred to the spread of Judaism to North Africa, and the great uprising against Rome between 115 and 117 CE. A Jewish Hellenistic king named Lucas (some historians called him Andreas) arose in the course of this large-scale messianic, anti-pagan revolt, and temporarily seized the province of Cyrenaica, in the east of today's Libya. His ferociously swift conquests took him as far as Alexandria in Egypt. Evidence shows that this fiery religious revolt was especially vicious, like future monotheistic conflicts, and that it was put down with an iron hand by the Roman armies.[17] The propagation of Judaism slowed down in this province but was not entirely extinguished. There remained Jews and proselytes in Cyrenaica, and, following the upheavals, the Judaizing process advanced slowly westward.

The suspicious Rabbi Hosea, who lived in the Holy Land in the third century CE, was concerned about the proselytizing in North Africa, and the Jerusalem Talmud quotes him as asking, "The proselytes coming from Libya, should they have to wait three generations?" (*Tractate Kilayim*). The leading *amora* known as Rav declared: "From Tyre to Carthage people know the Israelites and their

---

16 Yemeni historians, on the other hand, insist that the Jews of Yemen are "an inseparable part of the Yemeni people. These people converted and adopted the Jewish religion in their homeland, which was then religiously tolerant." This was stated in a letter from el-Qodai Mohammed Hatem and Ben-Salem Mohammed, entitled "Zionism in Yemeni Eyes," which appeared in the Israeli daily *Haaretz*, but originally in the *Yemen Times*. Amazingly, a street in Israeli Jerusalem is named after the king Du Nuwas.

17 Cassius Dio, *Roman History* 68. 32. See also Eusebius, *Ecclesiastical History* 4. 2.

father in heaven, and westward from Tyre and eastward from Carthage people do not know the Israelites and their father in heaven" (*Tractate Menahot*).

The successful spread of Judaism in the Maghreb was probably due to the presence of a Phoenician population in the region. Although Carthage was destroyed back in the second century BCE, not all its inhabitants perished. The city was rebuilt, and was soon an important commercial port once more. Where, then, did all the Punics—the African Phoenicians—who populated the coastline go? Several historians, notably the French Marcel Simon, have suggested that a large number of them became Jews, accounting for the distinctive strength of Judaism throughout North Africa.[18]

It is not beyond reason to assume that the close resemblance of the language of the Old Testament to ancient Phoenician, as well as the fact that some of the Punics were circumcised, helped promote mass conversion to Judaism. The process may also have been stimulated by the arrival of captives from Judea after the fall of the kingdom. The old populace, originating from Tyre and Sidon, had been hostile to Rome for a very long time, and probably welcomed the exiled rebels and adopted their particular faith. Marcel Simon suggests that the philo-Jewish policy of most of the Severan emperors, a dynasty originating in North Africa, might also have contributed to the popularity of Judaization.

North Africa was one of the outstanding successes in the history of proselytization in the Mediterranean region. Although in the third and fourth centuries CE, as noted in the previous chapter, the rate of conversion to Judaism slowed down in Egypt, Asia Minor, Greece and Italy—the heart of the ancient Western civilization—along the coast of the Maghreb the communities of believers in Yahweh did quite well. Archaeological and epigraphic evidence depicts thriving Jewish religious life. Archaeological excavations near ancient Carthage uncovered a number of tombs from the third century CE inscribed in Latin characters, or even Hebrew or Phoenician, with images of candelabra engraved alongside. Also all over the region a large number of tombstones have been found at the graves of proselytes with Greek or Latin names, and their religion is always stated beside their non-Hebrew names. A synagogue from the same period, bearing inscriptions and designs of candles, candelabras and ram's horns, was discovered in Hammam-Lif (ancient Naro), near today's Tunis. On the floor is written, "Your maidservant Julia the young woman repaired with her fortune this mosaic for the sake of the holy synagogue of Naro." It is not surprising that the inscription goes on to name the head of the synagogue as Rusticus and his son as Asterius.

---

18   Marcel Simon, *Recherches d'Histoire Judéo-chrétienne*, Paris: Mouton, 1962, 44–52.

In North Africa, as elsewhere, many of the Judaizers remained in a state of semiconversion, or as they would later be known, "heaven worshippers" (*Coelicolae*). The New Testament mentions God-fearers, Jews and proselytes coming to Jerusalem from the "parts of Libya about Cyre'ne" (Acts 2: 10). Many syncretist sects flourished in various cities, and it was this heterogeneous throng that gave rise to Christianity, which grew powerful in this region as in other Mediterranean lands. Two of the leading thinkers of early Christianity, Tertullian and, later, Augustine, were born in Africa.

The former was especially concerned about the strength of Judaism in his native city of Carthage. His extensive knowledge of the Old Testament and Jewish tradition indicates the strength of the local Jewish religious culture. His sharp attacks against the proselytes also testify to the popular appeal of this movement. He sought to explain the success of Judaism, in contrast to that of the persecuted Christianity, by noting that it was a legal religion in Roman law, hence easier to adopt. He showed respect for the Jews, especially the Jewish women for their modesty, but fiercely attacked the Judaizers, arguing that they adopted the Jewish religion out of convenience, because on the holy Sabbath they could avoid all work.[19]

Evidence of Christianity's struggle against the strong Jewish presence is found in the writings of Augustine and in those of the Christian poet Commodianus. Augustine criticizes the "heaven worshippers," probably an intermediate Jewish-Christian sect, whom the church regarded as heretics or even unbelievers. In his work *Instructions*, Commodianus (whose exact dates are not known) attacked the numerous proselytes and mocked their switching and changing of religions and the blatant inconsistency of their worship.

The advance of the church was temporarily halted by the Vandal conquest. These Germanic tribes from Europe dominated North Africa between 430 and 533 CE, where they established an Arian Christian kingdom. There is next to no information about the situation of North Africa's Jews during the Vandal century, but it is known that relations between the Arians and the Jewish believers were much better than between the latter and the consolidating Orthodox Church. The return of the Byzantine Empire to the region restored the primacy of the church, and the suppression of heretics and unbelievers intensified. It is quite likely that, following this conquest, some of the coastal Jews—those former Punics—fled inland, and others moved further west. Here began the amazing story of a new wave of Judaization.

---

19 His opinion of Judaism was expressed in his "Aduersus Iudaeos," translated into English by Geoffrey D. Dunn, *Tertullian*, London: Routledge, 2004, 63–104. Information about the Jews of Carthage can be deduced from Claude Aziza, *Tertullien et le judaïsme*, Paris: Les Belles Lettres, 1977, 15–43.

As Ibn Khaldun, the great fourteenth-century Arab historian, wrote:

> [Possibly] some of the Berbers practiced Judaism, which they had received
> from their powerful Israelite neighbors in Syria. Among the Jewish Berbers
> were the Djeraoua, who inhabited Aurès, the tribe of Kahina, who was killed
> by the Arabs in their first conquests. Other Jewish tribes were the Nefouca,
> of the African Berbers, the Fendelaoua, the Medioun, Behloula, Giatha and
> the Berbers of the extreme Maghreb, the Fazaz. Idris the First of the Beni el-
> Hassan, son of El-Hassan who reached the Maghreb, wiped out all traces of
> the religions that persisted in his territory and crushed the independence of
> the tribes.[20]

Ibn Khaldun apparently assumed that at least some of the Berbers, North
Africa's longtime inhabitants, were descendants of the ancient Phoenicians or
some other Canaanite population that originated in the vicinity of Syria and
converted to Judaism (elsewhere he even speaks of the Himyarite origin of
some of the Berbers).[21] The Judaized tribes he lists were large and powerful, and
spread across North Africa. Other than the Djeraoua (Jerawa), who inhabited
the highlands of Aurès, the Nefouça lived near today's Tripoli, the Mediouna
tribes lived in today's western Algeria, and the Fendelaoua, Behloula and Fazaz
lived in the territory of Fès, in today's Morocco. Despite the mass conversion to
Islam that followed the Arab conquest, these tribal areas roughly correspond
to the sites where Jewish communities persisted until modern times.

Many cultural practices—not only the amulets—common among the
Berbers are also found in the religious rites of the Jews of North Africa. Some
of these Jews always spoke the Berber language in addition to Arabic. Were
the Judaized Berbers, as well as their proselytized Punic predecessors and a
handful of emigré Judeans, the ancestors of the Jews of North Africa? Moreover, to what extent did this great wave of Berber Judaization augment the
number of Jews in Spain during and after its conquest by the Arabs?

Ibn Khaldun returns elsewhere to the resistance to the Muslim conquest,
led by the queen of the Aurès mountains, Dihya al-Kahina. This leader of the
Judaized Berbers was believed to be a necromancer, hence her title *kahina*
(priestess), probably of Punic or Arabic origin. She was a strong ruler, and
in 689, when the Muslims launched their renewed effort to conquer North
Africa, she united several powerful tribes and succeeded in defeating the

---

20 Ibn Khaldun, *Histoire des Berbères et des dynasties musulmanes de l'Afrique
septentrionale*, Paris: Geuthner, 1968, 208–9. See also the great Arab historian's statement
about the war of the Berbers' ancestors in Syria against the Israelites, and their subsequent
migration to the Maghreb. Ibid., 198.
21 Ibid., 168, 176.

mighty forces of Hassan ibn al-Nu'man). Five years later, after the queen had implemented a scorched-earth policy and destroyed towns and villages along the coast, Arab reinforcements arrived and overwhelmed the forces of the bold Berber ruler, and she herself was killed in battle. Her sons converted to Islam and joined the conquerors, and this was the end of her long reign, which remains shrouded in myths and mystery.

Ibn Khaldun was not the only Arab historian to describe the fascinating deeds of Dihya al-Kahina. Earlier Arab writers, from the ninth century CE, described in detail her fight against the Muslim conquerors. The Baghdad-based writer al-Waqidi emphasized her cruel treatment of her own subjects; Khalifa ibn Khayyat al-Usfuri dated her defeat to 693 CE; the Persian historian Ahmad al-Baladhuri recounted the story in brief; and Ibn Abd al-Hakam, who lived in Egypt, expounded the story of the queen's son who also fought against the invaders.[22] Muslim historians who followed Ibn Khaldun continued to write about the Judaized queen, and her story was picked up by modern scholars.

Many legends formed around the acts and personality of the female Berber Jewish leader. During the colonial period, French writers revived the old myths in order to highlight the historical fact that the Arabs were invaders whom the local populace had fiercely resisted. Later, in the postcolonial period, Kahina became an Arab—sometimes a Berber—heroine, a forerunner of the French national heroine Joan of Arc. Since Arabic literature referred to her as a mysterious Jewess, some Zionist historians were intrigued, and a few took up the story as though Dihya was a late incarnation of the biblical prophetess Deborah.

Nahum Slouschz, a diligent Zionist historian of North Africa's Jews who completed his doctoral thesis in Paris, was the first to install Kahina in the modern Jewish memory.[23] As early as 1909 he published two essays about the Jewish Berbers, and an article entitled "The Kahina's Race."[24] He argued that North Africa was settled by large numbers of Jews who came from Jerusalem,

22 On these authors, see Abdelmajid Hannoum, *Colonial Histories, Post-Colonial Memories: The Legend of the Kahina, A North African Heroine*, Portsmouth: Heinemann, 2001, 2–15; also H. Z. Hirschberg, "The Berber Kahina," *Tarbiz* 27 (1957 [in Hebrew]), 371–6.

23 He was preceded by a French Jew named David Cazes, who argued that the great Queen Kahina was not Jewish, and indeed persecuted the Jews. For it is known that the "Children of Israel" have always been weak and persecuted, and could never be tyrannical rulers. See in this connection, Hannoum, *Colonial Histories*, 51–5

24 Nahum Slouschz, *Un voyage d'études juives en Afrique: Judéo-Hellènes et Judéo-Berbéris*, Paris: Imprimerie Nationale, 1909; and "La race de la Kahina," *Revue Indigène: Organe des Intérêts des Indigènes aux Colonies* 44 (1909), 573–83.

and was ruled by them for a long time before the arrival of the Muslims. To his mind, Kahina the warrior queen could not have been a mere proselytized Berber—she had to have been a Jew "by race."

In 1933 Slouschz expanded his publications and reissued them as a book in Hebrew. *Dihya al-Kahina* ("Judith the Priestess") contains fascinating historical material tinged with romanticism and seasoned with folklore and picturesque tales that Slouschz had borrowed from Arabic and French historiography.[25] He argues that Kahina's noble tribe, the powerful Djeraoua tribe of the Aurès—whom he calls the Gera—was "a nation of the race of Israel."[26] These "Geras" had come to the region from Libya and had previously lived in Egypt. The priests, who led the tribe, had come to the land of the Nile in the reign of Judah's king Josiah, in the exile of the Pharaoh Necho. Dihya was an affectionate Jewish nickname for a woman named Judith, and she was certainly of a priestly family. Jewish tradition does not permit women to be priests, but as the Canaanite influence was still strong among them, the Geras dubbed her a *kahina*.

Slouschz could tell that Kahina was good-looking and strong; she was said to be "handsome as a horse and powerful as a wrestler."[27] French scholars compared her to Joan of Arc, but Slouschz, drawing on Arab sources, stated that Kahina "indulged in carnal love with all the passion of her fiery youth," and was married three times. The problem was that these husbands were not Jews of her tribe, and it is known that one of them was a Berber and the other a Greek—namely, a Byzantine. Would a kosher Jewess have married uncircumcised gentiles? Slouschz explained that the Judaism of the Berber tribes was not of the severe, rabbinical form known to us; hence their customs were of a different sort:

> [Kahina] remained faithful to her ancestral faith in its ancient, "pre-Ezra" form, which was common among the faraway Jews in Africa, a Judaism that did not yet distinguish between peoples and continued to marry its neighbors, and would never keep up with the special isolation of the "Pharisees" that was predominant in the Roman and Arab cities.[28]

In this way Slouschz could remain an "ethnocentric Zionist"—asserting that the legendary amazon and her priests were of the right race, while admitting

---

25 Nahum Slouschz, *Dihya al-Kahina (Judith the Priestess): A Heroic Chapter from the History of the Faraway Jews in the Wilderness of the "Dark Continent,"* Tel Aviv: Omanut, 1933 (in Hebrew).

26 Ibid., 31.

27 Ibid., 62.

28 Ibid., 68–9. The image of Dihya al Kahina intrigued many people, and she was the subject of several historical romances. See, for example, Gisele Halimi, *La Kahina*, Paris: Plon, 2006.

that the other Berber tribes were generally proselytes. He was convinced that syncretism and a flexible religious policy had helped propagate Judaism and make it a popular religion before the arrival of Islam. Nevertheless, despite the unorthodox ways of the Jewish Berbers and their religious oddities, they and their descendants definitely belong to the "Jewish people." He asserted that he had gone to Africa to seek his "national brothers" and was convinced that "Israel was one nation in the world."[29]

Hirschberg, a far more cautious and reliable historian than Slouschz, was the second scholar to deal with the Judaized Berbers and their queen Kahina. The foreword to his book *History of the Jews in North Africa* includes the following passage:

> the obscurity of the history of most of the communities of the interior in the first half of the second millennium CE [provides] a certain background for the thesis that the great majority of Maghreb Jews are of Berber stock. This thesis was enunciated in various travel books and adopted in modern historical writings, without anybody giving it a thorough scrutiny ... The position with regard to sources is different here than in the case of the Himyar Judaizer in South Arabia or the Khazars on the banks of the Volga. We know that the great majority of the former adopted Islam in the days of Mohammed and that only Jews of Jewish stock were left in South Arabia, and it is also well known that the Khazar Judaizers have completely disappeared. Now is it to be supposed that precisely the Berbers in North Africa remained loyal to Judaism, especially as the evidence of their Judaization is extremely flimsy?[30]

Having demolished the possibility of a historical connection between the Jews of Yemen and the Himyarite kingdom, and declared its absence to be an established fact, Hirschberg felt obliged to clarify the origins of the Jews of North Africa. A thorough, pedantic scholar, he did not want to overlook uncomfortable historical passages that most of his colleagues dismissed out of hand. Certain older Arab historians had described the Berber tribes' conversion to Judaism, and their having neither approved nor disapproved made their descriptions more trustworthy. And since, as he knew, Jews never sought to convert others, it must have been the presence of Jewish communities in the Berber lands that led some of the inhabitants to adopt Judaism.

Hirschberg's readers were soon reassured—further along, he asserted that these proselytes were a tiny minority in the Jewish population. Moreover, he

---

29   See the second page in Nahum Slouschz, *Israel's Diasporas in North Africa from Ancient Times to Our Era*, Jerusalem: Kav LeKav, 1946 (in Hebrew).

30   Haim Ze'ev Hirschberg, *A History of the Jews in North Africa*, vol. 3, Leiden: Brill, 1974, 12–13.

noted, there is hardly any Jewish testimony on the subject of proselytes; the Berber language left little trace in written Judeo-Arabic culture; and the Old Testament was never translated into Berber. The fact that the Jews adopted Arabic very quickly after the Muslim conquest, whereas the Berbers put up stronger resistance to the linguistic acculturation, proves that the former were not of Berber origin. As for the story about the Judaized queen, it was not very meaningful, since she did not act in the spirit of Judaism and ultimately contributed nothing to it. In fact, her name was Kahya, and the Arab writers misread it as Kahina.[31]

Hirschberg knew, of course, that the Berbers' culture was largely an oral tradition, and consequently no traces of it are to be found in the Arabic literature and language of North Africa. He knew that there were many names, family appellations, superstitions and customs common to Jewish believers and Muslim Berbers. (For example, the custom of splashing passers-by with water at Pentecost was both Jewish and Berber; the relatively free status of the Jewish women also resembled Berber custom rather than Arabic; and so on.) In many Jewish communities the family name Cohen ("priest") did not appear at all, while in others almost all members of the congregation were called Cohen but had not a single Levy—which could have indicate collective conversions. Moreover, some Islamized Berber tribes had retained certain Jewish customs, such as not lighting fires on Sabbath eve and avoiding leavened bread during the spring festival. Yet this last fact only served to reinforce Hirschberg's conviction: "Ancient Christianity disappeared completely from North Africa, while Judaism persisted through the ages. Indeed, not only the Christian Berbers became Muslim—so did the proselytized Berbers. Only the Jews of the seed of Abraham remained."[32]

So firm was Hirschberg's conviction that he forgot his ethnoreligious belief that the Arabs, too, had descended from the great patriarch. But this typical slip is marginal. His constant effort to prove that the Jews were a nation-race that had been torn from its ancient homeland and gone into a wandering exile was far more significant, and, as we have seen thus far, it met the imperative of mainstream Zionist historiography. His inability to rise above the purifying essentialist ideology that guided all his research damaged his work, and it was

---

31   Ibid., 94–7.
32   H. Z. Hirschberg, "The Judaized Berbers in North Africa," *Zion*, vol. 22, 1957, 19. See also another careful article that seeks to adopt Hirschberg's "ethnic" outlook, J. Chetrit and D. Schroeter, "Les rapports entre Juifs et Berbères en Afrique du Nord," in P. Balta, C. Dana, and R. Dhoquois-Cohen (eds.), *La Méditerranée des Juifs*, Paris: L'Harmattan, 2003, 75–87.

this fault that constituted the "scientific source" in support of the common positions in the standard history textbooks of the Israeli educational system.

André Chouraqui, a French Israeli scholar and public figure who was born in Algeria, was less concerned about his pure descent; his book *Between East and West: A History of the Jews of North Africa* shows a significant historiographic shift: "But, while the last Christian communities of the Berbers survived only to the twelfth century, Judaism in North Africa retained the loyalty of its proselytes down to our own day. In the middle of the twentieth century, an estimated one half of the Jews of North Africa are descendants of Berber converts."[33]

Chouraqui had no more data for estimating the proportion of Berber descendants in the Maghreb's Jewish community than had Hirschberg—they could equally well have spoken of 9 percent as of 99 percent. His book was first published in French in the 1950s, and it clearly sought to align itself with French scholars of the Maghreb. At that time it was difficult to rebut the widespread view of ancient Judaism as a strongly proselytizing religion, and the book's later Hebrew readers were offered a version far less ethnocentric and more reasonable on the origins of the Jews of North Africa. The book highlights Jewish efforts to proselytize the Punics and does not hesitate to link this growing influence throughout the region with the mass Judaization of the Berbers. Chouraqui also wrote about the Jewish queen Kahina, arguing that although she also treated her Jewish subjects harshly, "the final battles of the Jewish people before modern times were not those against Rome in the Land of Israel in the first century CE, but rather in the seventh century against the Arabs in Africa."[34]

As we shall see further on, Chouraqui's national passion misled him a little: these were not the last battles of the Jewish people against the Arabs before the twentieth century. The Khazars, just before their mass conversion to Judaism, outdid Kahina and her Berber Jewish troops in halting the advance of Islam, and succeeded even after the battles in North Africa. But before we proceed to these eastern "faraway Jews" (the Volga and Don rivers being east of the Maghreb), it is necessary to mention the significant support for the view of the Maghreb Jews as descendants of Judaized Berbers and Judaized Arabs who accompanied the armies of Islam. It comes from the field of philology.

Professor Paul Wexler of Tel Aviv University was primarily interested in

---

33 André N. Chouraqui, *Between East and West: A History of the Jews of North Africa*, Philadelphia: The Jewish Publication Society of America, 1968, 37–8.

34 These sentences are missing from the English edition, but appear in the Hebrew one. See *A History of the Jews of North Africa*, Tel Aviv: Am Oved, 1975 (in Hebrew), 65.

Spanish Jewry, but since the history of this community became involved at an early stage with that of North Africa, he was able to shed new light on the issue. His book *The Non-Jewish Origins of the Sephardic Jews* argues, "the Sephardic Jews are primarily descendants of Arabs, Berbers and Europeans who converted to Judaism in the period between the rise of the first Jewish communities in western Asia, North Africa and southern Europe, and the 12th century."[35] There may, of course, have been some descendants of Judeans in these communities, but they must have been a tiny minority. How did Wexler reach such a heretical conclusion, counter to the hegemonic discourse in the academic world in which he worked?

The sad lack of historical testimony about the early formation of Jewish groups in the Iberian Peninsula, Wexler argued, forces us to rely on the evolution of their languages and their ethnographic data. As a "philological archaeologist," Wexler skillfully traced linguistic vestiges found in the texts and the languages that are still in use today, and concluded that the origins of the Sephardic Jews were extremely heterogeneous, and hardly Judean. Most came to Europe from North Africa with the Muslim conquest in the early eighth century CE, and traces of Judeo-Arabic from the Maghreb, as well as Berber customs, can be found in the Judeo-Iberian language and culture. And if the Arab language was the decisive factor from a linguistic viewpoint, in cultural-religious and demographic terms the Berber presence was the most significant.[36]

Furthermore—and this may be Wexler's most important discovery—Hebrew and Aramaic made their appearance in Jewish texts only in the tenth century CE, and were not a product of an earlier autochthonous linguistic development. This means that exiles or emigrés from Judea had not settled in Spain in the first century CE or introduced their original language. During the first millennium CE, Jewish believers in Europe knew no Hebrew or Aramaic. Only after the religious canonization of classical Arabic in the Muslim world, and of medieval Latin in Christendom, did Judaism adopt and propagate its own religious language as a high cultural code.[37]

Wexler's theory might explain the great conundrum in the history textbooks in Israel. The authorized scholars have failed to provide a reasonable explanation for the existence of such a large Jewish community in Spain—a lively and creative community that was considerably bigger, numerically, than

---

35   Paul Wexler, *The Non-Jewish Origins of the Sephardic Jews*, New York: SUNY, 1966, xv.

36   Ibid., 105–6.

37   Ibid., 118.

the groups of Jewish believers that had appeared in Italy, southern Gaul or the Germanic lands.

Judaism probably began to germinate in the Iberian Peninsula in the early centuries CE, mainly among proselytized Roman soldiers, slaves and merchants—much as it did in other imperial colonies in the northwestern Mediterranean. In the New Testament, Paul writes, "whensoever I take my journey into Spain, I will come to you" (Rom. 15:24); he probably intended to preach to the first Jewish Christian congregations that were beginning to be organized there. The decisions adopted by the council of bishops at Elvira bear evidence to the monotheistic syncretism that was still going strong in the south of Western Europe during the fourth century CE.[38] Later, the heavy-handed treatment of the Visigoth rulers toward Jewish believers and new proselytes, chiefly in the seventh century CE, drove many of them to flee to North Africa. Their historical revenge was not long in coming.

The Muslim conquest of Iberia, which began in 711 CE, was carried out mainly by Berber regiments that may well have included many proselytes, who enlarged the demographic size of the older Jewish communities. Contemporary Christian sources condemned the treasonable behavior of the Jews in various cities, who welcomed the invading forces and were even drafted by them as auxiliary troops. Indeed, as many Christians fled, the Jews, their rivals, were appointed acting governors of many cities.

In his compilation *Israel in Exile*, Ben-Zion Dinur had included many quotes from Arab sources that corroborate the Christian ones, such as the following:

> The third regiment, which had been sent against Elvira, besieged Granada, the capital of that state, and entrusted the blockade to a local force made up of Muslims and Jews, and that is what they did wherever Jews were found … Having captured Carmona, Musa attacked Sevilla … After a siege lasting many months, Musa captured the city, and the Christians fled to Baya. Leaving the Jews as the standing army in Sevilla, Musa advanced to Mérida. Moreover, when Tariq saw that Toledo was empty, he brought in the Jews and left some of his men with them, while he himself proceeded to Wadi al-Hajara [Guadalajara].[39]

Tariq ibn Ziyad, the supreme commander and first Muslim governor of the Iberian Peninsula (Gibraltar bears his name), was a Berber from the Judaized

---

38   See Alfredo M. Rabello, *The Jews in Spain before the Arab Conquest in the Mirror of Legislation*, Jerusalem: Zalman Shazar, 1983 (in Hebrew), 29–30. Regarding the Visigoths' attitude to conversion, see the chapter "Jewish Proselytism" in Solomon Katz, *The Jews in the Visigothic and Frankish Kingdoms of Spain and Gaul*, New York: Kraus Reprint, [1937] 1970, 42–56.

39   Dinur, *Israel in Exile*, vol. 1, 1, 116–17.

tribe of Nefouça. He reached Spain with seven thousand troops, which soon grew to twenty-five thousand, as many local men joined them. "Among them were many Jews," says Dinur. Drawing his information from Spanish scholars, the Zionist historian reluctantly admits that some of them "argue that all the Berbers who took part in the Arab conquests in Spain were Judaizers."[40]

It would be a wild exaggeration to argue that the conquest of Spain was a coordinated operation of Muslim and Jewish Berbers. But as we have seen, the fruitful cooperation between the two religions began in Iberia at the start of the invasion, so it is reasonable to assume that the Jews' favored status made for a meaningful expansion of their communities. However, the ability of established Jews to proselytize pagans and Christians was practicable only in the early stages of the Muslim presence, when Christian hegemony retreated and the massive conversion to Islam had not yet begun.[41] This option would begin to shrink in the ninth century, though it never quite ended.

The wave of Islamization did not stop the immigration of Jewish believers from all over southern Europe and even more from the coast of North Africa. In his important book on the Sephardic Jewry, Yitzhak Baer noted admiringly that Arabic Spain had become "a refuge for Jews."[42] The Jewish community thrived demographically, thanks to local proselytizing and to the waves of conquest and immigration. It also flourished culturally, thanks to the admirable symbiosis between it and the tolerant Arabism of the kingdom of Al-Andalus and the principalities that succeeded it. Jewish life in the Muslim regions proved the possibility of a multireligious society in a medieval world of hardening monotheism, which increasingly expressed itself in the abasement, and often the persecution, of the "infidel." At that same time, a kingdom at the other end of Europe was notable for its freedom from religious fanaticism.

JEWISH KAGANS? A STRANGE EMPIRE RISES IN THE EAST

In the middle of the tenth century, the Sephardic golden age, Hasdai Ibn Shaprut, a physician and important statesman in the court of the caliph of Cordoba, 'Abd ar-Rahman III, wrote a letter to the king of the Khazars, Joseph

---

40 Ibid., 24–5. Dinur refers readers to the book by Eduardo Saavedra, *Estudio sobre la invasión de los árabes en España*, Madrid: Progreso Editorial, 1892, 89.
41 Jane S. Gerber, *The Jews of Spain: A History of the Sephardic Experience*, New York: The Free Press, 1992, 19.
42 Yitzhak Baer, *A History of the Jews in Christian Spain*, vol. 1, Philadelphia: The Jewish Publication Society of America, 1971, 24. He follows this statement with the story of the priest Bodo, who went to Zaragoza in 839 CE, where he converted to Judaism and took the name Eleazar.

ben Aaron. Rumors about a great Jewish empire bordering on eastern Europe had reached the Jewish elites at the Continent's western end, and aroused intense curiosity: Was there, at long last, a Jewish kingdom that was not subordinate to Muslim or Christian powers?

The letter opens with a poem of praise for the king—with an acrostic composed by Menahem ben Saruq, Hasdai's secretary and the leading Hebrew poet in the Iberian Peninsula[43]—followed by the writer's introduction of himself (inter alia, of course, as a descendant of the exiles from Jerusalem) and a description of the kingdom in which he lives. Then he comes to the point:

> Merchants have told me that there is a kingdom of Jews called Alkhazar, and I did not believe it, because I thought they said this to please and approach me. I was puzzled about it, until emissaries arrived from Constantinople with a gift from their king to our king, and I asked them about it. They assured me that this was the truth, that the kingdom is called Alkhazar, and between al-Constantinople and their country there was a journey of fifteen days by sea, but on land there are many nations between us. And the name of its king is Joseph … And I, when I heard this, was filled with force and my hands grew strong and my hope intensified, and I bowed and made obeisance to the Lord of heaven. I searched for a faithful emissary to send to your land to find out the truth and to greet my lord the king and his servants our brothers, but it was difficult to do, for the distance is very great.[44]

Hasdai goes on to describe in detail all the difficulties entailed in dispatching the letter, and finally asks direct questions: Of what tribe is the king? What is the system of the monarchy? Is it passed from father to son, as was done by the ancestors in the Torah? How big is the kingdom? Who are its enemies, and over whom does it rule? Does war take precedence over the Sabbath? What is the country's climate? And so forth. Hasdai's curiosity was limitless, for which he apologized courteously.

It is not known how long it took before the Khazar king's reply arrived, but in the extant letter King Joseph answered Hasdai's questions as best he could. He described his origin and the boundaries of his kingdom:

> You have asked of what nation and family and tribe we are. Know you that we are of the sons of Japhet and of his son Togarmah … It is said that in his

---

43   On this poet, see Tova Rosen-Mokked, "Khazars, Mongols and pre-Messianic Sufferings," in *Between History and Literature*, Michal Oron (ed.), Tel Aviv: Dionon, 1983 (in Hebrew), 41–59.

44   The letter of Hasdai Ibn Shaprut and the answer of Joseph the king of the Khazars can be found in Abraham Kahana (ed.), *The Literature of History*, Warsaw, 1922 (in Hebrew), 38.

time my ancestors were but a few, and the Lord granted them strength and boldness, and they fought with many great nations mightier than they were, and with God's help drove them out and inherited their country ... Many generations passed until a king rose whose name was Bulan, a wise and God-fearing man, who put all his trust in the Lord, and removed all the sorcerers and idolaters from the country and lived under the Lord's wing ... This king summoned all his ministers and servants and told them all these things. They were content, and accepted the king's judgment and entered under the wing of the Shekhinah ... Then rose a king of his offspring, named Obadiah, a righteous and honest man, who reformed the kingdom and set the Law in the proper order, and built synagogues and seminaries and brought in many of the sages of Israel ...[45]

Writing in an epic and ornate style, the king describes the conversion to Judaism and lists the reasons that moved his ancestors to prefer the Jewish religion to the other two monotheistic faiths. In a tone suffused with fervent belief in the Torah and the commandments, he goes on to describe the location of his kingdom, its size, its population and the power of his enemies and rivals (the Russians and the Ishmaelites).

Various literary embellishments of and additions to the old texts led some scholars to conclude that these letters, especially the king's reply, were not written in the tenth century CE, and might be forgeries or emendations by Muslim authors. There are two versions of Joseph's letter, a long one and a short one, but certain terms in the short version do not belong in the Arabic lexicon, and its original author was not part of the Muslim cultural world. Moreover, the distinctive linguistic use of the biblical Hebrew "reversing connection" (*vav hahipukh*) indicates that Hasdai's letter and the king's reply were not written by one hand. The letter of the Khazar king was probably copied and embellished many times, but its core information seems fairly trustworthy, as it accords with contemporary Arab testimonies, and so cannot be dismissed as merely a literary creation.[46]

In any event, there is evidence from the late eleventh century that despite the difficulties of international communications, copies of both letters, in several versions, were found throughout the Jewish intellectual world. For example, Rabbi Yehudah al-Barzeloni, who questioned the accuracy of these copies, commented, "We have seen some versions of the letter written by Joseph the

---

45   Ibid., 42–3. The first printed version of the correspondence was published in or around 1577 by Isaac Abraham Akris.

46   On the letters' authenticity, see the excellent article by Menahem Landau, "The actual status of the problem of the Khazars," *Zion* 13 (1953), 94–6; and also D. M. Dunlop, *The History of the Jewish Khazars*, Princeton: Princeton University Press, 1954, 125–70.

king, son of Aaron the Khazar Priest, to Rabbi Hasdai son of Yitzhak, and did not know if it was true or not." Finally, though, this sharp scholar, who detested fables, became convinced, and he admitted as much: "That Khazars proselytized and had proselyte kings, I have heard that all this is written in the books of Ishmaelites who were living then and wrote about it in their books." He therefore copied the letter of King Joseph and quoted a part of it in his own work.[47]

It is almost certain that the twelfth-century Rabbi Yehudah Halevi was familiar with this correspondence. He ascribed the conversion to Judaism by the Khazar monarch to a three-sided monotheistic brainstorming session. Its depiction in the opening of his work *The Kuzari* is adapted from King Joseph's letter, with some changes in style and detail.[48] It should be noted that Rabad (Rabbi Abraham ben David), who was several decades younger than Yehudah Halevi and was one of the fathers of Kabbalah in Provence, wrote of Eastern Europe: "There were Khazar peoples who proselytized, and their king Joseph sent a letter to the president, Rabbi Hasdai son of Yitzhak, ben Shaprut, to tell him that he followed the rabbinate and so did all his people." He goes on to say that when in Tolitula [Toledo], he met Jewish students who told him that they were Khazars and faithful to rabbinical Judaism.[49]

Whereas the histories of the Judaized Himyarites and Berbers were all but erased from the general consciousness, it was more difficult to leave blank pages in the case of the Khazars. In the first place, the secular modern public knew about the *Kuzari*, the theological treatise completed in 1140 CE by Yehudah Halevi, a highly respected figure in Jewish tradition and a canonical one in Zionist culture because of his particular association with the Holy Land. Second, there was a mass of historical evidence about the Khazar kingdom from Arabic, Persian, Byzantine, Russian, Armenian, Hebrew and even Chinese sources. They all agreed that it was very powerful, and many of the sources also referred to its unexpected conversion to Judaism.

Furthermore, the historical standing of this kingdom and the events that followed its breakup had been echoed in the earliest Jewish historiography in Eastern Europe, which battled with this issue for decades. Even Zionist reconstructors

---

47   See the whole passage and commentary on it in Simcha Assaf, "Rabbi Yehudah al-Barceloni on the missive of Joseph the Khazar king," *Sources and Research on Israel's History*, Jerusalem: Harav Kook, 1946 (in Hebrew), 92–9.

48   At the beginning of Halevi's book he says, "[It] made me remember the arguments of the rabbi who studied with a Khazar king, who converted to Judaism some four hundred years ago. The king's story is well recorded in history books," *The Kuzari: In Defense of the Despised Faith*, Northvale: Jason Aronson, 1998, 1.

49   "The book of the Kabbalah of Abraham ben David" in *The Order of the Sages and the History*, copied from Clarendon at Oxford, 1967 (in Hebrew), 78–9.

of the past hesitated for a long time to tackle the subject, and few of them attempted to research it with appropriate thoroughness. But the widespread interest in the Khazar kingdom eventually began to shrink, and it all but evaporated with the rise of the memory establishment in Israel, after some ten years of its existence.

Although the medieval kingdom of the Khazars existed in distant obscurity, and no gifted theologians had praised and immortalized it as the biblical authors had done in their time and place, it is, however, attested by external sources far more varied and abundant than exist about the kingdom of David and Solomon. Jewish Khazaria was, of course, immeasurably bigger than any historical kingdom in the land of Judah. It was also more powerful than Himyar or the desert realm of Dihya al-Kahina.

The story of the Khazars is fascinating. It begins in the fourth century CE, when some nomadic tribes accompanied the Huns as they surged westward. It continues with the rise of a great empire in the steppes along the Volga River and the northern Caucasus, and ends with the Mongol invasion in the thirteenth century, which wiped out all traces of this extraordinary kingdom.

The Khazars were a coalition of strong Turkic or Hunnic-Bulgar clans who, as they began to settle down, mingled with the Scythians who had inhabited these mountains and steppes between the Black Sea and the Caspian Sea, which was known for a long time as the Khazar Sea.[50] At its peak, the kingdom encompassed an assortment of tribes and linguistic groups, Alans and Bulgars, Magyars and Slavs. The Khazars collected taxes from them all and ruled over a vast landmass, stretching from Kiev in the northwest to the Crimean Peninsula in the south, and from the upper Volga to present-day Georgia.

From the sixth century on, Persian testimonies followed by Muslim ones shed light on the early stages of the Khazar saga. They invaded the Sassanid kingdom and harassed its border inhabitants. They got as far as the area around Mosul in today's Iraq. In the early seventh century, during the reign of the Persian king Khosrau II, a marriage with the Khazar king's daughter sealed an alliance that enabled the Persians to build fortifications in the passes of the Caucasus Mountains. Remains of these fortifications against Khazar invasions can still be seen. Armenian and Byzantine sources reveal that in

---

50   There is even a description of their physical appearance in *Yaqut al-Hamawi, Kitab mu'jam al-buldan* (*Book of the Countries*), which quotes Ibn Fadlan: "The Khazars do not resemble the Turks. They are black-haired, and are of two kinds, one called the Kara-Khazars [black Khazars], who are swarthy verging on deep black as if they were a kind of Indian, and a white kind [Ak-Khazars], who are strikingly handsome." Quoted in Kahana (ed.) *Literature of History*, 50.

the following years the Khazar kingdom formed an alliance with the Eastern Roman Empire in its struggle against the Persians, and became a significant factor in the regional balance of power. The seventh-century Armenian bishop Sebeos wrote in his *History of Heraclius*: "They [Armenian nobles] went to serve the Great Kagan, king of the northern lands. At the command of their king, the Kagan ... they marched through the Jor pass to come to the aid of the king of Greece."[51]

The Kagan—this being the title of the ruler of Khazaria—maintained extensive relations with the Byzantine Empire. The future emperor Justinian II, who had been exiled to the Crimea, escaped at the end of the seventh century to the Khazar kingdom, where he married a Khazar princess. She was rebaptized as Theodora and would later be a powerful empress. Nor was this the only marital tie between the realms. In the tenth century, the ruler and author Constantine VII Porphyrogenitus wrote: "That Emperor Leo [III] ... allied himself by marriage with the Kagan of Khazaria, accepting his daughter as wife [for his son Constantine V], shaming the Byzantine Empire and himself, because he thereby abandoned the precepts of the forefathers and treated them with disdain."[52]

This nontraditional, interdynastic match took place in 732 CE, and the son born of it became the emperor who was known as Leo the Khazar. This was also the zenith of the diplomatic relations between the two mighty kingdoms. The Khazars succeeded in the course of many battles to halt the Muslims' northward sweep, and temporarily saved the Byzantine Empire from a menacing encirclement that would have precipitated its collapse.

The many battles between the Muslims and the Khazars were described by numerous Arab chroniclers, who had no qualms about copying each other's work. Ibn al-Athir wrote that "they fought very fiercely, and both sides held out. Then the Khazars and the Turks overcame the Muslims ... After al-Jarrah fell on the battlefield, the Khazars coveted [the country] and penetrated far into it, reaching Mosul."[53] This was in 730 CE, but the response was not long in coming. After a tremendous logistical effort and more battles, the Arab armies managed to repel the determined enemy. The commander, who would later be the Caliph Marwan II, even led strong forces into Khazaria itself, and his condition for withdrawal was the conversion of the Kagan to Islam. The Khazar sovereign accepted, and the Arab armies retreated to the Caucasus

---

51   Quoted in Dinur, *Israel in Exile*, vol. 1, 2, 47–8. (It is not certain that Sebeos wrote the book.)

52   Ibid., 51.

53   Ibid., 48.

Mountains, which was agreed as the final boundary between Khazaria and the Muslim world. As we shall see, the temporary conversion of the pagan Khazar kingdom was not very meaningful, though many of its subjects accepted the faith of Muhammad.

Most sources depict the Khazar kingdom as having a highly original dual government: a supreme holy leader as well as an active secular leader. Ahmad ibn Fadlan, a diplomat and author who was sent by the caliph al-Muqtadir in 921 CE to the Bulgar country by the Volga, crossed Khazaria, and described it in his rare travel notes. On the Khazars and their political system, he wrote:

> As for the king of the Khazars, known as Khakan [Kagan], he is seen only once in four months, and at a respectful distance. He is called the Great Khakan, and his deputy is called Khakan Bey. It is [the latter] who commands the armies, administers the kingdom and looks after it. He sallies and raids, and the kings of the vicinity surrender to him. He goes every day to see the Great Khakan, in a deferential manner, showing himself humble and modest.[54]

More information is found in the work of the geographer and chronicler Al-Istakhri, writing in about 932. His description is livelier and more picturesque:

> As for their regime and government, their master is called Khakan Khazar, who is more exalted than the king of the Khazars, though it is the king who empowers him. When they want to empower a Khakan they throttle him with a silk cord, and when he has almost suffocated they ask him, For how long do you wish to reign? And he replies, So many years. If he dies before that time [it is well], otherwise he is put to death at that time. Only the sons of well-known families may fill the post of Khakan, and he has no real power, but is worshipped and adored when people appear before him. Yet no one enters his presence except a small number, such as the king and those of his rank ... And no one is appointed Khakan except those who cleave to Judaism.[55]

Other Arabic sources corroborate the existence of a dual power system in Khazaria. This was an efficient regime—it maintained a mystique around the Great Kagan, and utilized the most gifted and competent prince as the Bey, who functioned as a military viceroy. The halo of sanctity that hung over the

---

54   Ibid., 24. The tenth-century chronicler Ahmad Ibn Rustah wrote that the deputy was also called "Aysha." See Abraham Polak, *Khazaria: History of a Jewish Kingdom in Europe*, Tel Aviv, Bialik, 1951 (in Hebrew), 286.

55   Dinur, *Israel in Exile*, vol. 1, 2, 42–3.

Kagan did not stop him from maintaining a harem of twenty-five women and sixty concubines, though this was not necessarily in devout emulation of the biblical King Solomon.

The seat of the rulers was the capital Itil, beside the Volga estuary on the Caspian Sea. Unfortunately, it appears that changes in the course of the great river's tributaries and the rise in sea level inundated the city, whose precise location remains unknown. If the kingdom maintained a documentary archive, it was lost, and scholars have had to rely mainly on external sources. Itil was largely a city of tents and wooden houses, and only the rulers' residences were built of bricks. Ibn Fadlan's description provides some details:

> Al-Khazar is the name of a region (and climate), and its capital is called Itil. Itil is the name of the river that runs into al-Khazar from the [land of] Russians and Bulgars. Itil is a city and al-Khazar is the name of the kingdom, not the city. Itil is in two parts ... The king resides in the western part, a parasang in length, surrounded by a wall, but it is built irregularly. Their houses are made of felt, except a few that are built of mud. And there are markets and public baths.[56]

The inhabitants were no longer nomadic herders like their forefathers, but the populace still migrated every spring to the rural areas to cultivate the soil and spent the harsh winter in the capital city, where the climate was more temperate because of its proximity to the sea. Al-Istakhri reported:

> In summer they go to the fields twenty leagues away, to sow and to gather. As some are close to the river and others to the prairie, they carry it [the produce] on carts and on the river. Their main nourishment is rice and fish. The honey and barley they send out of their country comes to them from the region of the Russians and Bulgars.[57]

Al-Istakhri also described another city: "The Khazars have a city named Samandar ... It has many gardens, and it is said to contain some four thousand vineyards, as far as the Serir boundary. Most of its produce is grapes."[58] It is known that this was the Khazar capital before the rulers moved to Itil, and that fishing was an important source of livelihood for the population.

So we know that the Khazars were typical rice-growers and regular consumers of fish and wine, though the bulk of the kingdom's income came from tolls. Khazaria straddled the Silk Road, and also dominated the Volga

---

56   Ibid., 23.
57   Ibid., 24.
58   Quoted in Polak, *Khazaria*, 282.

and the Don rivers, which were major transportation routes. A further source of income was the heavy tax imposed on the numerous tribes governed by the kingdom. The Khazars were known for their flourishing trade, especially in furs and slaves, and their growing wealth enabled them to maintain a strong and well-trained military force that dominated all of southern Russia and today's eastern Ukraine.

Thus far, the descriptions of the Arab chroniclers coincide and even accord with the testimony of King Joseph's letter. The question of the Khazar language, however, is obscure. No doubt the great mixture of tribes and populations spoke various languages and dialects, but what was the language of the Khazar power elite? Al-Istakhri, following al-Bakri, wrote: "The language of the Khazars differs from that of the Turks and the Persian language, and does not resemble the language of any other nation."[59] Nevertheless, most researchers assume that the spoken Khazar language consisted of Hunnic-Bulgarian dialects with others from the Turkic family.

There is no doubt, however, that the Khazars' sacred tongue and written communication was Hebrew. The few extant Khazar documents indicate as much, and the Arab writer al-Nadim, who lived in Baghdad in the tenth century, confirms it: "As for the Turks and the Khazars ... they have no script of their own, and the Khazars write in Hebrew."[60] Inscriptions have been found in Crimea that are in a non-Semitic language written in Hebrew characters; two of these characters (*shin* and *tzadik*), eventually entered the Cyrillic alphabet, presumably in the course of the Khazars' early rule over the Russians.

Why did the Khazar kingdom not adopt the Greek or Arabic language for religious usage and high-level communication? Why did the Khazars become Jews, when all their neighbors converted en masse either to Christianity or to Islam? And another question: When did the amazing collective proselytizing begin?

KHAZARS AND JUDAISM: A LONG LOVE AFFAIR?

One of the few surviving testimonies left by the Khazars themselves is the important document known to scholars as the Cambridge Document. Its originality is less disputed than that of King Joseph's letter. This Hebrew manuscript, written by a Jewish Khazar from the court of King Joseph, was found in the famous Cairo *genizah*, published in 1912, and has since been kept at

---

59   Ibid., 281. Some testimonies suggest that their language did resemble ancient Bulgarian.

60   Dinur, *Israel In Exile*, vol. 1, 2, 17.

the Cambridge University library.[61] Little is known about the writer or the addressee, but it appears to have been written in the tenth century CE and may have been another reply to Hasdai's request. The text is fragmented, and many words are missing, but it is still a rich source of information. After a few missing lines, the letter reads as follows:

> Armenia and our ancestors fled from them ... [for they could not] bear the yoke of the worshippers of idols. And [the princes of Khazaria] received them [for the men of] Khazaria were first without the Torah. And [they too] remained without Torah and Scriptures and made marriage with the inhabitants of the land [and mingled with them.] And they learned their deeds, and went out with them [to the war continually.] And they became [one] people. Only upon the covenant of circumcision they relied. And [some of them] observed the Sabbath. And there was no king in the land of Khazaria. Only him who won victories in the battle they would appoint over him them as general of the army. Now (it happened) at one time when the Jews went forth into the battle with them as was their wont that on that day a Jew proved mighty with his sword and put to flight the enemies who came against Khazaria. Then the people of Khazaria appointed him over them as general of the army in accordance with their ancient custom.[62]

The document also describes a tripartite brainstorming encounter between a Muslim, a Christian and a Jew—similar in essentials to the description in King Joseph's letter, and concluded, of course, with the appropriate decision in favor of Judaism.

It seems that this literary-historical model was very popular in that period, because early Russian chronicles describe the conversion of Vladimir I of Kiev to Christianity in almost the same manner, though naturally with a different outcome. A contemporary Arab writer also described the Judaization of the king of Khazaria following an intense theological debate, except that in his text the Jewish scholar hired an assassin to poison the Muslim scholar before the decisive confrontation, and in that way "the Jew turned the king to his religion and converted him."[63]

The rest of the so-called Cambridge Document, like its opening, suggests an interesting hypothesis concerning the Judaization of the Khazars:

---

61   Solomon Schechter, "An Unknown Khazar Document," *Jewish Quarterly Review* 3 (1912–13), 181–219. See also Vladimir A. Moin, "Les Khazars et les Byzantins d'après l'Anonyme de Cambridge," *Byzantion*, 6 (1931), 309–25.

62   The Cambridge Manuscript, in Schechter, "An Unknown Khazar Document," 213.

63   See the statement of the geographer al-Bakri quoted in Kahana, *The Literature of History*, 53.

Israel, together with the men of Khazaria, returned in perfect repentance. But also the Jews began to come from Baghdad, from Khorasan and from the land of Greece and strengthened the hands of the men of the land, and encouraged themselves in the covenant of the Father of the Multitude [Abraham]. And the men of the land appointed over them one of the wise men as judge. And they call his name in the tongue of Khazaria, Khagan. Therefore, the judges who arose after him are called by the name Kagan even unto this day. As to the great prince of Khazaria, they turned his name into Sabriel and thus made him king over them.[64]

It may be that this Sabriel was the postconversion name of King Bulan, mentioned in Joseph's letter, and this story may well be unreliable, and the dramatic descriptions of the Judaization merely fables and sermons. However, stories about migration as the catalyst in the process of proselytization seem much more relevant to understanding Khazar history. The arrival of Jewish believers from Armenia, from today's Iraq, from Khorasan (which covered parts of modern-day Iran, Turkmenistan, Uzbekistan, Tajikistan, Afghanistan and Pakistan) and from Byzantium may well have triggered the conversion of that strange kingdom to Judaism. Proselytizing Jews were driven from the arena of rival monotheisms, Christianity or Islam, to the lands of paganism. As in other regions that witnessed mass Judaization, so in Khazaria, it began with immigrants who convinced the pagans that their faith was preferable. The great mass proselytizing campaign that began in the second century BCE, with the rise of the Hasmonean kingdom, reached its climax in Khazaria in the eighth century CE.

The Khazar-Hebrew testimony about Jewish immigration finds support in Arabic literature. The Arab chronicler al-Mas'udi wrote:

As for the Jews, they are the king and his court and the Khazars his people. The Judaization of the king of the Khazars took place in the Caliphate of Harun al-Rashid. Many Jews who had heard of it joined him from all the Muslim cities and from Byzantium. The reason being that the Byzantine king in our time, the year 332 [944 CE], Armanus [Romanus] forcibly Christianized the Jews in his kingdom ... Upon which, many Jews fled from Byzantium to the land of the Khazars.[65]

The Abbasid Caliph Harun al-Rashid lived from 763 to 809 CE. The putative Byzantine emperor Romanus reigned in the first half of the tenth century. This passage suggests that the relation between the Khazar kingdom and Judaism developed in stages, the first of which was in the eighth century CE. We have seen that in that century the Khazar armies invaded Armenia, and even reached the city of Mosul in today's Kurdistan. In these regions there were still Jewish communities—people remaining from the ancient kingdom of Adiabene—who had spread deep into Armenia. Perhaps it was in this encounter that the Khazars were first exposed to the religion of Yahweh, and that some Jewish believers accompanied the army when it returned to Khazaria. It is also known that proselytized Jews bearing Greek names lived on the northern shores of the Black Sea, especially in the Crimea.[66] Later some of them fled from the vicious persecutions of the Byzantine emperors.

Yehudah Halevi noted in *The Kuzari* that the Khazars converted in 740 CE, but the date may not be correct. A Christian document written circa 864 CE in distant western France stated that "all the 'Gazari' obey the precepts of Judaism."[67] At some stage between the mid-eighth and mid-ninth centuries, the Khazars adopted Jewish monotheism as their particular faith and rite. It is also reasonable to assume that this was not a miraculous single act, but a long process. Even King Joseph's questionable letter describes the conversion as occurring in stages: King Bulan was persuaded by the logic of the Law of Moses and became a Jew, but only King Obadiah, his grandson or greatgrandson, "reformed the kingdom and set the law in the proper order," built synagogues and seminaries, and adopted the Mishnah and Talmud. It is also said that he invited Jewish sages from far away to bolster the true faith among his subjects.

If in the nineteenth century scholars were doubtful about the conversion of the Khazar kingdom, today it is not in dispute. The spreading monotheism reached the Caucasus and the steppes of the Volga and the Don—today's southern Russia—and convinced rulers and tribal elites to believe in the many advantages of a single deity. The question remains, Why did Khazaria opt for Judaism rather than the other monotheistic religions: with their less onerous requirements? If we set aside the magical sermon included in King Joseph's letter, the Cambridge Document, and Yehudah Halevi's book, we are left with the same explanation

---

66 Ibid., 107. Another theory suggests that the Jews reached Khazaria from Khorasan, east of the Caspian Sea. See Yitzhak Ben-Zvi, "Khorasan and the Khazars," *The Lost Communities of Israel*, Tel Aviv: The Ministry of Defense, 1963 (in Hebrew), 239–46.

67 See Peter B. Golden, "Khazaria and Judaism," in *Nomads and their Neighbors in the Russian Steppe*, Aldershot: Ashgate, 2003, 134. On dating the Judaization to 861 CE, see Constantine Zuckerman, "On the Date of the Khazars' Conversion to Judaism and the Chronology of the Kings of the Rus Oleg and Igor," *Revue des Études Byzantines* 53 (1995), 237–70.

that accounted for Himyar's conversion. The desire to remain independent in the face of mighty, grasping empires—in this case, the Orthodox Byzantine Empire and the Abbasid Muslim Caliphate—impelled the rulers of Khazaria to adopt Judaism as a defensive ideological weapon. Had the Khazars adopted Islam, for example, they would have become the subjects of the caliph. Had they remained pagan, they would have been marked for annihilation by the Muslims, who did not tolerate idolatry. Christianity, of course, would have subordinated them to the Eastern Empire for a long time. The slow and gradual transition from the ancient shamanism of the region to Jewish monotheism probably also contributed to the consolidation and centralization of the Khazar realm.

One of the leading collectors of material about the Khazars was a Karaite Russian named Abram Firkovich. This tireless researcher was also very devout; anxious to create the impression that Khazaria had converted not to rabbinical Judaism but to Karaism, he added and deleted material in various documents, sacred books and tomb inscriptions. Thus, despite his valuable work of preservation, he damaged many sources and created general distrust. Eventually his falsifications were discovered by other scholars (chiefly the important historian Abraham Eliyahu Harkavy), and closer investigation revealed that the Khazars' Judaism was not at all Karaite. It is quite possible that Karaism, no less than Talmud Judaism, spread through the expanses of Khazaria, especially to the Crimea, but the Jewish practice in the kingdom was, to a greater or lesser extent, rabbinical. The historical consolidation of Karaism came too late to have been the first catalyst that prompted the Judaization of the Khazars, and there is no reason to assume that it went on to capture all of them. Moreover, at the time of the Khazar conversion, copies of the Talmud were still a rarity, which enabled many proselytes to take up ancient rites, even priestly sacrifices. Remains of a body found in a burial cave in Phangoria in the Crimea were found clothed in leather garments in the style worn by servers in the Jerusalem Temple, as prescribed in detail in the Old Testament.

But one of the wonders of the eastern Jewish kingdom, for which it is still praised, was its religious pluralism, inherited from its early polytheistic shamanism, which was still popular in the region. As al-Mas'udi wrote: "The laws of the Khazar capital decree seven judges: two for the Muslims, two who judge in accordance with the Torah, for the Khazars, two who rule in accordance with the Gospels, for the Christians among them, and one for the Saqaliba (Bulgars) and Russians and other idolaters."[68]

---

68   Quoted in Polak, *Khazaria*, 288. Al-Istakhri has similar information; see Dinur, *Israel in Exile*, vol. 1, 2, 45.

It is almost certain that the Khazar power sheltered Jews, Muslims, Christians and pagans, and that synagogues, mosques and churches existed side by side in its cities. Ibn Hawqal, writing in 976–7CE, confirmed this in his description of Samandar: "There are Muslims living there, who have mosques in the place, and the Christians have churches and the Jews synagogues."[69] Yaqut al-Hamawi, drawing on ibn Fadlan, wrote:

> The Muslims have in this city [Itil] a big mosque where they pray, and which they visit on Fridays. It had a tall minaret for summoning to prayer and several criers. When the king of the Khazars heard in the year 310 [922 CE] that Muslims had destroyed a synagogue in Dal al-Babunaj, he ordered the minaret to be torn down, and this was done. And he put the criers to death. He said, If I did not fear that they would destroy all the synagogues in the Muslim lands, I would have destroyed this mosque.[70]

Jewish solidarity sometimes overcame the principle of religious tolerance, but did not do away with it—although when Jews were persecuted in the Byzantine Empire during the reign of the Emperor Romanus, King Joseph retaliated by persecuting Christian Khazars. Nevertheless, the Kagans implemented a policy similar to that of the Muslim kingdom of Al-Andalus, a mild monotheistic model, very different from the contemporary Christian civilization or from the "totalitarian" ethos of the Hasmonean kingdom. Muslims and Christians served in the Kagan's armies, and were even exempt from fighting when their fellow believers were on the other side.

The Cambridge Document supports the statement found in the letter of King Joseph, that the Kagans bore Hebrew names. King Joseph's letter mentions Hezekiah, Manasseh, Yitzhak, Zebulun, Menahem, Binyamin and Aharon. The manuscript mentions kings named Binyamin and Aharon, which reinforces the correctness of the king's letter, albeit partially.

The author of the manuscript also writes, "Now they say in our land that our ancestors came from the tribe of Simeon, but we are not able to prove the truth of the matter."[71] Proselytes have always striven to find some direct genealogical link to the patriarchs of biblical mythology, and this tendency

---

69 See Kahana, *Literature of History*, 5.

70 Quoted in Polak, *Khazaria*, 295.

71 Schechter, "An Unknown Khazar Document," 216. The legend of Eldad the Danite also describes the Khazars as descendants of the "ten tribes": "The tribe of Simeon and the half-tribe of Manasseh live in the Chaldees' land, six months' distant, and are more numerous than all the others and collect tribute from twenty-five kingdoms, and some from the marauding Ishmaelites." In Abraham Epstein (ed.), *Eldad the Danite*, Pressburg, AD: Alkalai, 1891 (in Hewbrew), 25.

affected many of the Khazars, who wanted to believe that they were descended from the Israelite tribes. The religious consciousness grew more decisive in the next generation, and in time it overcame the former tribal identities associated with idolatry. The pagan cults became abominable in the eyes of the proud new monotheists, and even more so for their offspring and their imagined identity. The kingdom therefore saw itself as more Jewish than Khazar, and so it was documented in the contemporary Russian epics: it was not the land of the Khazars, but the land of the Jews—*Zemlya Zhidovskaya*—that awed its Slav neighbors.

The desire for a sacred genealogy also gave rise to novel cultural markers. The list of kings in King Joseph's letter includes one named Hanukkah, and the Cambridge Document mentions an army commander named Pessah. This original practice of naming people after religious festivals was unknown in biblical times or in the Hasmonean kingdom, nor has it been found in the kingdom of Himyar and its descendants, or among the Jews of distant North Africa. In later times, these names migrated westward to Russia, Poland and even Germany.

Nevertheless, the question remains unanswered: Did Jews constitute the majority of the monotheistic believers in the whole of Khazaria? The sources are contradictory. Some of the Arab writers assert that the Jewish Khazars were an elite minority that held the power. For example, Al-Istakhri states that "the smallest community are the Jews, while most of the inhabitants are Muslims and Christians, but the king and his courtiers are Jews."[72] Others stated that all the Khazars were Jews. Yaqut, following ibn Fadlan, the most reliable source of the period, states: "The Khazars and their king are all Jews."[73] Al-Mas'udi likewise asserted: "As for Jews—they are the king and his courtiers and his subjects the Khazars."[74] It is quite possible that the bulk of the great Khazar tribe became Jews, while other tribes were only partly proselytized and that many became Muslims or Christians or remained pagan.

How big was the community of proselytized Khazars? The research has not come up with any figures. A major difficulty in history is that we never know much about the spiritual beliefs of the commonality. Most traditional Jewish historiography, as well as a major part of Soviet nationalist scholarship, emphasized that only the monarchy and the higher nobility became Jews, while the Khazar masses were pagan or adopted Islam. It must not be forgotten

---

72   See in Dinur, *Israel in Exile*, vol. 1, 2, 44; also Polak, *Khazaria*, 285.
73   Dinur, *Israel in Exile*, vol. 1, 2, 54.
74   Polak, *Khazaria*, 287.

that in the eighth, ninth and tenth centuries CE, not all European peasants had become Christian, and that the faith was quite tenuous in the lower echelons of the medieval social hierarchy. On the other hand, it is known that at the time of the early monotheistic religions, slaves were almost always forced to adopt their masters' faith. The wealthy Khazars, who owned many slaves, were no different (as the letter of King Joseph clearly states). Inscriptions engraved on many tombstones in the former Khazaria indicate widespread Judaism, though often with obvious syncretic deviations.[75]

The Khazar kingdom remained Jewish for too long—estimates range from two hundred to four hundred years—not to warrant the assumption that the practice and the faith trickled down to broader strata. Although it was probably not the pure and detailed Halakhic Judaism, at least some of the commandments and rituals must have reached extensive congregations; otherwise, the Jewish religion would not have attracted so much attention, as well as a good deal of emulation, throughout the region. It is known that proselytization also took place among the Alans, speakers of Iranian dialects who lived under the Khazar aegis in the mountains of the northern Caucasus. The Cambridge Document contains the statement that in one of the Khazars' many wars against their neighbors, "only the king of the Alani was in support of [Khazaria.] For some of them observed the Torah of the Jews."[76]

It was the same with the great Kabar tribe, which pulled away from Khazaria and joined the Magyars on their westward migration. Before their migration to Central Europe, the Magyars, who are among the forebears of today's Hungarian people, were subordinated to the Khazar kingdom. The Kabars, who had been part of the Khazar population, rebelled against the Kagan for some reason, joined the Magyars, and left Khazaria with them. It is known that among them were a good many proselytes, and their presence in the formation of the Hungarian kingdom and the rise of the Jewish community in it may not be void of significance.[77]

In addition to the letter of King Joseph and the long Cambridge Document, there is another Khazar document that was found in the Cairo *genizah* and

---

75 Ibid., 158–76.

76 Schechter, "An Unknown Khazar Document," 216. In the late twelfth century CE, the "constant voyager" Benjamin of Tudela, mentioned a Jewish community in the Alani country. See Mordechai Ben Nathan Adler (ed.), *The Travel Book of Rabbi Benjamin*, Jerusalem: The Publishing House of the Students Association of the Hebrew University, 1960 (in Hebrew), 31.

77 On the Kabars, see Arthur Koestler, *The Thirteenth Tribe: The Khazar Empire and Its Heritage*, London: Hutchinson, 1976, 99–105; also István Erdélyi, "Les relations hungaro-khazares," *Studia et Acta Orientalia* 4 (1962), 39–44.

brought to the same British university. Published only in 1962, it testifies to the spread of Judaism in the Slav regions of Khazaria.[78] A letter in Hebrew sent from Kiev about 930 CE asks for assistance for a local Jew named Yaakov ben Hanukkah, who has lost all his property. The signatories on the letter are typical Hebrew names as well as Khazar-Turkic ones, and together they claim to represent the "congregation of Kiyov." The letter also bears an endorsement in Turkish characters, saying, "I read it." This document almost certainly indicates the early presence of Khazar proselytes in the city that would soon become the Russian kingdom's first capital. It is even possible that the forebears of these Jews founded it, as the name Kiev derives from a Turkic dialect. There must have been a reason that a wide opening in the ancient city wall was known as the Jews' Gate, and that it led to a quarter known as Jewish and another called Khazar.[79]

Another early source attesting to the collective conversion of the Khazars is a Karaite one. In about 973 CE, one Yaakov Qirqisani, a scholarly traveler who was quite familiar with the regions around Khazaria, wrote a commentary in Aramaic on the verse "God shall enlarge Japheth" (Gen. 9:27): "This is what the words mean: he will dwell in the tents of Shem, which grant him a favor and advantage. And some commentators think that this refers to the Khazars, who became Jews."[80]

This Karaite testimony is not the only one confirming that the Judaization was not merely an "oriental" fantasy of Arab scholars. In addition to Hasdai ibn Shaprut's request and the statements of Rabad, the great Rabbi Saadia Gaon, who lived in Baghdad for several years in the tenth century, also wrote about the Khazars. We saw in the previous chapter that he lamented the Islamization of Jews in the Holy Land. Did he rejoice in the Judaization of a whole kingdom, by way of replacement? He may well have been dubious about these new Jews who showed up far north of Babylon, these believers in the law of Moses who were also tough warriors, riders of horses, periodic executioners of their own

---

78   On this and other Hebrew documents, see N. Golb and O. Pritsak, *Khazarian Hebrew Documents of the Tenth Century*, Ithaca: Cornell University Press, 1982.

79   On the Kiev letter and the start of the Jewish presence in the city, see also Joel Raba, "Conflict and Integration: Slavs, Khazars and Jews in the Beginning of Kievan Rus," in *The Contribution and the Recompense: The Land and the People of Israel in Medieval Russian Thought*, Tel Aviv: The Goldstein-Goren Diaspora Research Center, 2003 (in Hebrew), 46–61. See also the article by Julius Brutzkus, "The Khazar Origin of Ancient Kiev," *Slavonic and East European Review* 3:1 (1944), 108–24.

80   Quoted in the article of Menaham Landau, "The actual status of the problem of the Khazars," 96. The Karaite Yefet ben Ali, who lived in Basra in the late tenth century CE, also mentions the king of the Khazars. See Polak, *Khazaria*, 295.

kings, and very active slave traders. The worry that these wild Jews did not accept the full burden of the Torah and all the precepts of the Talmud may well have dismayed the Karaites' severest ideological opponent. In his writings, he referred to the Judaization of the Khazars in a matter-of-fact way, mentioned the Kagan once, and also described a Jew named Yitzhak bar Abraham who journeyed to the Khazars' land and settled there.[81]

Later, sometime in the early twelfth century, Rabbi Petahiah of Regensburg (Ratisbon) set out to journey from his city in Germany to Baghdad. On the way, he passed through Kiev, the Crimean Peninsula, and other regions that had been parts of Khazaria, which had already declined and diminished. His impressions of the journey, actually written by his disciple, were as follows:

> In the land of Kedar and the land of Khazaria it is customary that the women mourn and bewail their deceased parents all day and all night ... There are no Jews in Kedar, there are heretics, and R. Petahiah asked them, Why do you not believe in the words of the Sage[s]? They replied, Because our parents did not teach them. On the Sabbath eve they cut all the bread to be eaten on the Sabba[th], and eat in the dark, and spend all day sitting in one place, and do not pray but sing the Psalms. When Rabbi Petahiah taught them ou[r] prayer and the blessing of food, they liked it, and said, We have not heard of the Talmud.[82]

This description strengthens the supposition that Karaism was widespread in the region or, alternatively, that there was an undefined Jewish syncretism in the steppes. Later, however, when Petahiah reached Baghdad, he told a different story:

> The seven kings of Meshech were visited by an angel who told them in a dream to abandon their religions and laws and follow the law of Moses ben Amram, or their country would be destroyed. They tarried, until the angel began to devastate their land, and all the kings of Meshech and their people converted to Judaism, and asked the head of a seminary to send them Torah students, and poor students went there to teach them and their sons the Torah and the Babylonian Talmud. Students went from Egypt to teach them. He saw the emissaries and those who went to the tomb of Ezekiel, heard about the miracles and that the worshippers' petitions were answered.[83]

---

81 Abraham Harkavy (ed.), *Answers of the Geonim: For the Memory of the Rishonim*, Berlin: Itzkevsky, 1887 (in Hebrew), 278.

82 Petahiah ben Ya'acov, *The Travels of Rabbi Petahiah of Ratisbon*, Jerusalem: Greenhut, 1967 (in Hebrew), 3–4.

83 Ibid., 25.

Were these the last gasps of a dwindling Jewish kingdom? The desperate clinging to a faith that remained after the former royal glory? We know too little about the situation of Khazaria in the twelfth century CE to venture an opinion.

When did the great Khazar empire collapse? In the past it was assumed by many that it happened in the second half of the tenth century. The principality of Kiev, out of which grew the first Russian kingdom, was for many years a vassal of the rulers of Khazaria. The principality grew stronger in the tenth century, struck an alliance with the Eastern Roman Empire and attacked its powerful Khazar neighbors. In 965 (or 969), Sviatoslav I, the ruling prince of Kiev, attacked the Khazar city of Sarkel, which controlled the Don River, and captured it. Sarkel was a fortified city, originally built by Byzantine engineers, of important strategic value to the Jewish empire, and its loss marked the beginning of the empire's decline. Contrary to prevalent opinion, however, this was not the end of Khazaria.

Reports about the fate of the capital Itil in this war are contradictory. Some Arab sources state that it fell; others state that it survived the Russian victory. Since it consisted largely of huts and tents, it may well have been rebuilt. What is certain, though, is that in the second half of the tenth century Khazaria lost its hegemonic position in the region. Prince Vladimir I of Kiev, Sviatoslav's young son, expanded the boundaries of his principality as far as the Crimea, and, in a significant step for the future of Russia, converted to Christianity. His alliance with the Eastern Roman Empire undermined its long connection with Khazaria, and in 1016 CE a joint Byzantine-Russian force attacked and defeated the Jewish kingdom.[84]

Thereafter, the Russian church was headed by the patriarch of Contantinople, but this holy alliance did not last long. In 1071 the Seljuks, rising tribes of Turkic origin, defeated the empire's considerable forces, and eventually the Kievan Russian kingdom, too, fell apart. Little is known about the situation of Khazaria in the late eleventh century CE. There are some mentions of Khazar warriors fighting in the armies of other powers, but there is almost no information about the kingdom itself. Seljuk assaults on the Abbasid caliphate in Baghdad, beginning at about the same time, ended its flourishing intellectual renaissance, and most Arab chronicles fell silent for a long time.

Empires have risen and fallen throughout history, but the monotheistic religions, as noted in the first chapter, were far more durable and stable. From the decline of the tribal societies until modern times, religious identity meant

---

84   See Dunlop, *The History of the Jewish Khazars*, 251.

far more to people than did their superficial relationship to empires, kingdoms or principalities. In the course of its triumphant history, Christianity outlived many political regimes, and so did Islam. Why, then, not Judaism? It survived the fall of the Hasmonean kingdom, the collapse of Adiabene and Himyar and Dihya al-Kahina's heroic defeat. It also survived the last Jewish empire, which stretched from the Caspian to the Black Sea.

The decline of Khazaria's political power did not cause the collapse of Judaism in its main cities, or in extensions of it that reached deep into the Slav territories. The continued Jewish presence in them is documented. The fact that Jews held on to their faith in the mountains, in the steppes, in the river valleys and in the Crimean Peninsula is attested not only by Petahiah. Christian testimonies, too, reveal that followers of the law of Moses existed in various places.[85]

But if the internecine wars in the sprawling prairies between the Caspian Sea, the Black Sea and the Caucasus Mountains did not annihilate populations and religions, the torrential Mongolian invasion—led by Genghis Khan and his sons in the early thirteenth century—swept up everything in its path and wrecked the political, cultural and even economic morphologies of all of Western Asia and Eastern Europe. Some new kingdoms arose under the aegis of the "Golden Horde," apparently including a small Khazar kingdom, but the Mongols did not understand the needs of land cultivation in the vast territories they captured, and did not sufficiently care for the farming needs of the subjugated populations. During the conquest, the irrigation systems that branched from the wide rivers—systems that had sustained the cultivation of rice and vineyards—were demolished, causing the flight of masses of people and depopulating the prairies for hundreds of years. Among the emigrants were many Jewish Khazars who, together with their neighbors, advanced into the western Ukraine and hence to Polish and Lithuanian territories. Only the Khazars in the mountains of the Caucasus managed, to some extent, to hold on to their land, where agriculture was based mainly on precipitation. After the first half of the thirteenth century, there are no more mentions of Khazaria: the kingdom sank into historical oblivion.[86]

---

85 Baron, *A Social and Religious History*, vol. 3, 206–13; and also, Polak, *Khazaria*, 219–22.

86 On the end of the Khazar kingdom, see the article by Polak, "The last days of Khazaria," *Molad* 168 (1962 [in Hebrew]), 324–9.

MODERN RESEARCH EXPLORES THE KHAZAR PAST

Isaak Jost took an interest in the Khazars and wrote about them; later, so did Heinrich Graetz. The wisps of Khazar history available in the nineteenth century were the letters of Hasdai and Joseph. Despite the differences between these two notable historians, they shared the German condescension toward the culture of Eastern Europe, especially its Jews. Furthermore, in seeking to reconstruct the history of the Jews, they looked in particular for its spiritual expressions. The scanty Khazar output could make no impression on these hyper-Germanic intellectuals. Jost placed no credence at all in Joseph's letter, and Graetz, who indulged in descriptions, wrote that before their conversion to Judaism, the Khazars "professed a coarse religion, which was combined with sensuality and lewdness."[87] This was characteristic rhetoric—a systematic erasure of the past proselytes who had swelled the ranks of the "chosen people."

Graetz, with his basic positivist approach, gave credence to the Hebrew correspondence between Hasdai and the king, just as he believed all the biblical stories. It seems he was momentarily captivated by the image of the mighty kingdom of the Jewish Khazars, and was also convinced that Judaism had spread through much of its population. Yet in the final analysis, he viewed the Khazars' Judaization as a passing phenomenon, without significance, which had no effect on the history of the Jews.[88]

But if the historians of Ashkenaz did not attribute much importance to the Khazars, Eastern European scholars looked at it differently. In Russia, Ukraine and Poland there was lively interest in the lost Jewish kingdom, especially among the Jewish Russian scholars. In 1834, V. V. Grigoriev, an early scholar at the Saint Petersburg School of Eastern Studies, published a study about the Khazars, in which he stated: "An unusual phenomenon in the Middle Ages was the Khazar people. In the midst of wild nomadic tribes, it had all the qualities of a civilized nation: orderly administration, flourishing commerce and a standing army ... Khazaria was a bright meteor that shone in Europe's dark sky."[89] In the early nineteenth century, the idea that the Russian nation emerged in the light of a Jewish kingdom did not seem strange; interest in Khazaria spread following this pioneering study, and other historians began to research the subject from a sympathetic viewpoint that tended to glorify the

---

87 Graetz, *History of the Jews*, vol. 3, 139.
88 Ibid., 138–41.
89 Quoted in Yehoshua Lior's master's thesis, *The Khazars in the Light of the Soviet Historiography*, Ramat Gan: Bar Ilan University, 1973 (in Hebrew), 122.

Khazar past. At this time, Russian nationalism was in its infancy, and it was possible to show generosity to the exotic ancient Slavic peoples in the East.

Echoes of these works reached the Jewish communities as well. In 1838, Joseph Perl published his satiric book *Bohen Zaddik*, containing forty-one "letters" from imaginary rabbis concerning various aspects of Jewish life, including some mentions of the Khazars.[90] Letter 25 discussed past doubts about the Judaization of the eastern kingdom, contrary to the current scientific confirmation of the statements in Hasdai's letter (though not in Joseph's letter). Another supposed rabbi wrote in response that he was happy to learn about the historical existence of the Khazars.[91] Interest in Khazaria did not end there, and it grew stronger in the second half of the century. For example, in 1867 two books appeared that dealt directly and indirectly with Khazar history. One was a short work by Joseph Yehudah Lerner, entitled *The Khazars*; the other, Abraham A. Harkavy's *The Jews and the Language of the Slavs*.[92] Lerner trusted the Hebrew correspondence and relied on it rather uncritically. He already knew some of the Arab chronicles, and he used them to complete the historical reconstruction. But what is most interesting about his essay is his refusal to date the fall of the Khazar kingdom to 965 (or 969) CE. He argued that a Jewish kingdom persisted in the Crimean peninsula, ruled by a king named David, and that only in 1016, following the Byzantine conquest, did the independent Jewish monarchy fall apart and the large Jewish population turn to Karaism.[93] Lerner concludes with a defense of the findings of Abram Firkovich, who, as we have seen, was accused by other scholars of forging and distorting Jewish tombstone inscriptions—all of which suggests that Lerner himself came from a Karaite background.

One of the most trenchant critics of Firkovich and of the Karaite hypothesis was Abraham Harkavy, an early Jewish Russian historian. In 1877 Harkavy was appointed head of the department of Jewish literature and Oriental manuscripts in the Imperial Public Library in Saint Petersburg, a post he retained for the rest of his life. He was a cautious and pedantic researcher, and his works— *The Jews and the Language of the Slavs* and other works about the Khazars, notably *Stories by Jewish Writers on the Khazars and the Khazar Kingdom*—are regarded as reliable studies. He had no doubt that there were many Jews in

90   Joseph Perl, *Sefer Bohen Tzadic*, Prague: Landau, 1838 (in Hebrew).
91   Ibid., 89–91, 93.
92   The first was published in Hebrew, and the second in Russian, and translated into the biblical language two years later, despite the date of publication. See Joseph Yehuda Lerner, *The Khazars*, Odessa: Belinson, 1867 (in Hebrew), and Abraham Albert Harkavy, *The Jews and the Language of The Slavs*, Vilnius: Menahem Rem, 1867 (in Hebrew).
93   Lerner, *The Khazars*, 21.

Khazaria, and that they practiced rabbinical Judaism. It was he who in 1874 discovered in Firkovich's collection the longer version of King Joseph's letter, and his profound knowledge of Eastern tradition and literature made him a leading scholar on the subject of the Khazars. The Orientalist Daniel Abramovich Chwolson, a baptized Jew, was a colleague of his, with whom Harkavy argued intensely.[94]

By the time Dubnow consolidated his status in Jewish historiography, there was already a fair amount of material on Khazaria. The Cambridge Document was published in 1912, and in the first half of the twentieth century the Hasdai-Joseph correspondence began to be treated as a trustworthy source, even though it had been extensively redacted. In his comprehensive oeuvre *World History of the Jewish People*, Dubnow devoted more space to the Khazar kingdom than did his predecessors Jost and Graetz.[95] He outlined the development of the kingdom, described in vivid terms its voluntary Judaization on the basis of King Joseph's letter, and trusted the bulk of the Arab chronicles. Like Graetz, he was impressed by Khazaria's great power, but he did not fail to stress that only the higher strata converted, while the middle and lower classes remained pagan, Muslim, or Christian. He added a special appendix including a long bibliographic analysis, and stated that "the story of the Khazars is one of the most problematic issues in the history of the Jews."[96] But he did not explain why that was so. There seems to be some awkwardness in his writing on the subject, though the reason for it is unclear. Perhaps it was the fact that those tricky Khazars were not exactly the "ethno-biological descendants of Israel," and their history was alien to the Jewish metanarrative.

The Soviet government in its early days encouraged the study of Khazaria, and young historians enthusiastically began to research Russia's pre-imperial past. Between the early 1920s and the mid-1930s, this resulted in a wave of historiographical production whose findings were unhesitatingly idealized. The Soviet scholars' sympathy was due to the fact that the Khazar empire was not ruled by the Orthodox Church, and was tolerant of and open to all religions. The fact that it was a Jewish kingdom did not disturb the researchers, especially since many of them, for all their conspicuous Marxism, came from a Jewish background. Why not inject a little Jewish pride into the spirit of proletarian internationalism? But the most prominent of these scholars were not of Jewish origin.

---

94   The pre–First World War research should include Hugo Von Kutschera, *Die Chasaren: Historische Studie*, Vienna: A. Holzhausen, 1910.

95   Dubnow, *History of the World-People*, vol. 4, 140–7.

96   Ibid., 272.

In 1932, Pavel Kokovtsov published all the "Hebrew Khazar documents" in a systematic critical work, and although he expressed reservations about the authenticity of some of them, the publication itself encouraged further research as well as archaeological excavations in the region of the lower Don River. The archaeological mission was led by young Mikhail Artamonov, who published his summaries in *Studies on Khazaria's Ancient History*.[97] This work conformed to the Russian and Soviet tradition of being sympathetic to the Khazar narrative, and it lauded the ancient rulers who nurtured the embryonic Kievan Russia.

The great Soviet interest in Khazaria and its prominent place in the historiography of southeastern Europe influenced the work of Jewish scholars outside the USSR. For example, between the two world wars the important Polish-Jewish historian Yitzhak Schipper devoted several chapters in his books to Khazar history. Baron, too, in his comprehensive oeuvre, was determined to examine the Khazar phenomenon at length. Where Dubnow included Khazar history as a legitimate chapter in the history of the "Jewish people," Baron, writing in the late 1930s, treated it, surprisingly, as a major issue, as we shall see.

Despite Baron's essentially ethnocentric outlook, he did not hesitate to tackle the Khazar conundrum and install it in the history of the Jews. To integrate the Khazars into that sequence, he assumed that there had been a massive migration of Jews into the Khazarian territories, making its population mixed Khazar-Jewish, as he put it.[98] Other than that, Baron's Khazar narrative is solid, and based on most of the sources available to him at the time. In later editions, published in the late 1950s, he included new analyses and expanded on the subject with many updated clarifications.

Dinur did the same in his valuable collection of sources, *Israel in Exile*. As well as impressive quotes from the Hasdai-Joseph exchange, the Cambridge Document, and Arab and Byzantine chronicles, the 1961 edition included numerous scholarly comments and abundant new information. It devoted more than fifty pages to Khazar history, and Dinur adopted a straightforward position about it: "The 'Khazar kingdom,' 'the country of Jews' and 'the cities of Jews' within it were historical facts of great significance. They were transformed by the developments of Jewish history, and their impact was felt in the life of the Jewish people, despite their distance from its high road."[99]

For such a statement to be made, it was necessary to assume that there had been in Khazaria an early Jewish population, "a Jewish tribal community," and that

---

97   See Lior, *The Khazars in the Light of the Soviet Historiography*, 126.
98   Baron, *A Social and Religious History*, vol. 3, 196–7.
99   Dinur, *Israel in Exile*, vol. 1, 2, 3.

it was because of its presence that the kingdom converted to Judaism. Jewish migration to Khazaria was not merely a trickle of refugees and immigrants who made it to the strange country and proselytized with great skill—there had to have been "a continuing Jewish immigration to the country, and the Jews were a significant stratum of the population, bolstering its Jewish element."[100] Now that we are certain that many of the Khazars were "Jews by descent," we can take pride in their territorial and military might, and relish the memory of an ancient Jewish sovereignty, a kind of medieval Hasmonean kingdom, but much bigger.

Baron's and Dinur's updated Khazar history drew very largely on Abraham Polak's impressive research. Polak's book was published in Hebrew in 1944, with two further editions, the last one in 1951. *Khazaria: The History of a Jewish Kingdom in Europe* was the first comprehensive work on the subject, and although it won a prize from the city of Tel Aviv, it was received in some circles with reservations and mixed reactions. All the reviews praised its broad scope, energy and scholarly thoroughness. Polak, who was born in Kiev, knew Russian, Turkish, classical Arabic, ancient Persian, Latin and probably Greek, and his knowledge of the historical material was impressive. But some reviewers criticized his "vertiginous" treatment of history, a term used in the title of one of the most abrasive critiques of the book.[101] The author, it said, had overloaded the narrative with myriad details and had extracted more than was necessary from the sources. There is some truth to this argument: in cutting his path through the Khazar world, Polak followed the same positivist working principles that guided the local historians in reconstructing the history of the "First Temple period" and the "Second Temple period." But he did so with great skill, and his statements were hard to refute.

Polak's great sin, according to some of the reviews, lay in the assumption that concluded his work. This Israeli scholar asserted categorically that the great bulk of Eastern European Jewry originated in the territories of the Khazar empire. "I cannot imagine what greater joy and honor he grants us with this Turkish-Mongolian genealogy than our Jewish origin," complained the critic made dizzy by the book.[102]

But in spite of this and other criticisms, Baron and Dinur drew extensively on Polak's book and regarded it as the definitive work on the history of the

---

100   Ibid., 4.
101   Aharon Ze'ev Eshkoli, "The Vertigo of History," *Moznaim*, 18: 5 (1944 [in Hebrew]), 298–305, 375–83.
102   Ibid., 382. See also Polak's answer in *Moznaim* 19:1 (1945), 288–91, and the following issue 19:2, 348–52.

Khazars. Provided, of course, a Jewish ethnobiological seed was planted in the beginning of the history. Polak's publishers included on the back cover a prominent statement designed to reassure suspicious readers: "This empire [Khazaria] was Jewish not only by religion, but because it had a large Israelite population, and proselytized Khazars were only a minority in it." If the proselytes were but a small part of that vast Jewish kingdom, then the Khazar thesis conformed with the Zionist metanarrative and became more legitimate. The author himself, for all his supposed irresponsibility, was partly aware of the problem and sought to sugarcoat his bitter pill with a comforting ethnocentric palliative:

> There had been Jewish settlements in the country before the Khazars' conversion, even before the Khazar conquest. There had been a process of Judaization in the kingdom among other, non-Khazar people. There was Jewish immigration from other countries, mainly from Muslim Central Asia, eastern Iran and Byzantium. Thus a large Jewish community grew there, of which the proselyte Khazars were only a part, and whose cultural character was shaped mainly by the old population of the northern Caucasus and Crimea.[103]

In the late 1940s and early 1950s, such phrasing could still more or less meet the demands of Zionist historiography, and as we have seen, Dinur gave this "bold" move his stamp of approval. Moreover, Polak was a devout Zionist who gave generously of his intellectual and linguistic capabilities to Israeli military intelligence. At the end of the 1950s he was appointed chairman of Tel Aviv University's Department of Middle Eastern and African History, and in this setting managed to publish several works about the Arab world. But such an independent-minded scholar was not cut out for compromises, and as his historical approach grew increasingly out of step with the dominant reconstruction of Jewish historical memory, he continued to defend his pioneering work.

From 1951 to the present moment, not a single historical work about the Khazars has appeared in Hebrew. Nor was Polak's *Khazaria* ever reissued. It served till the end of the 1950s as a legitimate point of departure for Israeli researchers, but it lost this status over the years. Except for one modest MA thesis on this subject, and one (published) routine seminar paper, there has been nothing.[104] The Israeli academic world has been mute on this topic, and

---

103   Polak, *Khazaria*, 9–10.
104   Yehoshua Lior's abovementioned study on Soviet historiography was supervised by H. Z. Hirschberg. The seminar paper was by Menahem Zohori, *The Khazars: Their Conversion to Judaism and History in Hebrew Historiography*, Jerusalem: Carmel, 1976 (in Hebrew).

no significant research has taken place. Slowly and consistently, any mention of the Khazars in the public arena in Israel came to be tagged as eccentric, freakish and even menacing. In 1997, the prominent Israeli television commentator Ehud Ya'ari, who had for years been intrigued by the unique power of the Khazars, produced a short TV serial on the subject, cautious but full of fascinating information.[105]

What caused this silent lapse in the Jewish Israeli memory? Aside from the traditional ethnocentric conception that in some form dominates every aspect of Jewish nationalism, there are two possible hypotheses. One is that the wave of decolonization of the 1950s and 1960s drove the Israeli memory-merchants to avoid the very shadow of the Khazar past. There was anxiety about the legitimacy of the Zionist project, should it become widely known that the settling Jewish masses were not the direct descendants of the "Children of Israel"—such delegitimization might lead to a broad challenge against the State of Israel's right to exist. Another possibility, not necessary in conflict with the former, is that the occupation of large, densely populated Palestinian territories intensified the ethnic element in Israeli identity politics. The proximity of masses of Palestinians began to seem a threat to the imaginary "national" Israel, and called for stronger bonds of identity and definition. The effect was to put the kibosh on any remembrance of Khazaria. In the second half of the twentieth century, the connection with the orphaned Khazars was steadily weakened, as the "Jewish people" gathered again in its original "homeland" after two thousand years of wandering in the world.

The age of silence in Israel echoed in many ways the silencing in the USSR, though in the land of Russian socialism it took place in the previous generation. Between Artamonov's book in 1937 and the 1960s, hardly anything was published about the Khazars, and those few publications were mostly devoted to their repudiation and denigration. The existence of those strange Jews in the East became, not surprisingly, an aberration from the historical logic of Marxism-Leninism and the character of "Mother Russia" that was reborn under Stalin. The proletarian internationalism of the 1920s and the first half of the 1930s was replaced, even before the Second World War, by assertive Russian nationalism. After 1945, with the rise of the Cold War and the accelerated Russification of the non-Russian territories, this became an even harsher and more exclusive ethnocentrism.

All the Russian and, later, the Soviet historians who had written about

---

105   *The Kingdom of the Khazars with Ehud Ya'ari*, television serial, Naomi Kaplansky (producer), Ehud Ya'ari (narrator), Jerusalem: Israeli Television Channel 1, 1997. Quite a few novels have been written about the Khazars, among them, the Serb author Milorad Pavic's *Dictionary of the Khazars* (New York: Knopf, 1988), and Marc Alter's *The Wind Of The Khazars* (New Milford: The Toby Press, 2003).

Khazaria were denounced as bourgeois who had failed to comprehend the common Slav traits and so played down the importance of ancient Kievan Russia. In 1951 even the daily paper *Pravda* joined the call to excoriate the Khazar parasites and their old erring and misleading interpreters. P. Ivanov, an "establishment historian" (probably Stalin himself), published an important article exposing the poor research on the Khazars, and asserted that "our forefathers had to take up arms to protect our homeland against invasions from the steppes. Ancient Russia was the shield of the Slav tribes. It defeated Khazaria and liberated from its domination ... old Slav lands, and lifted the yoke of Khazaria from the backs of other tribes and nations."[106] The article made a point of attacking Artamonov, who had inappropriately shown sympathy for Khazar culture and had ascribed to it a positive historical role in the birth of Russia. The scientific council of the history institute at the USSR Academy of Sciences met after the *Pravda* article and concluded that the paper had been perfectly correct in its reasoning. Now all the stops were pulled out, and the Khazars became damned and tainted beings, who had by ill fortune stumbled into Russian history. Only in the 1960s, with the partial thaw of the Stalinist frost, did the study of the Khazars carefully begin anew—but from now on, it bore clear nationalist, and at times anti-Semitic, features.[107]

But whereas in Israel and the Soviet Union—the two states to which the Khazar past was most relevant—Khazaria research was treated for many years as taboo, fresh materials were emerging in the West. In 1954 a thorough and comprehensive study of Jewish Khazaria, by a British scholar named Douglas Dunlop, was published by Princeton University Press. Dunlop showed a thorough familiarity with the Arabic literature on the subject, and great caution on the fate of the Khazars after the fall of their empire.[108] In 1970 Peter Golden submitted a vast doctoral dissertation, entitled "The Q'azars: Their History and Language as Reflected in the Islamic, Byzantine, Caucasian, Hebrew and Old Russian Sources." Parts of this scholarly work were published in 1980.[109]

---

106   Quoted in Lior, *The Khazars in the Light of the Soviet Historiography*, 130.

107   In the 1950s Artamonov confessed that he had not been sufficiently nationalistic in the 1930s. In 1962 he published his second book on the Khazars, *History of the Khazars*, an appropriately patriotic work with some anti-Jewish tones. See the instructive review by Shmuel Ettinger in the periodical *Kiriat Sefer* 39 (1964 [in Hebrew]), 501–5, in which he also criticizes Artamonov for not having read the Israeli Abraham Polak.

108   An even more cautious summary of this work appeared as a short chapter in Bezalel Roth (ed.), *The Dark Ages: The Jews in Christian Europe*, Tel Aviv: Masada, 1973 (in Hebrew), 190–209. Dunlop also wrote the entry on the Khazars in the *Hebrew Encyclopedia*, vol. 20, 1971, 626–9.

109   Peter B. Golden, *The Q'azars: Their History and Language as Reflected in the Islamic, Byzantine, Caucasian, Hebrew and Old Russian Sources*, New York: Columbia

In 1976 Arthur Koestler dropped a literary bombshell entitled *The Thirteenth Tribe*, which was translated into many languages and provoked a variety of reactions. In 1982 the book by Norman Golb and Omeljan Pritsak, *Khazarian Hebrew Documents of the Tenth Century*, laid the critical foundations for the subject. The popular work by Kevin A. Brook, *The Jews of Khazaria*, appeared in 1999. This non-academic writer also started an extensive Web site dedicated to the subject of Khazaria.[110] Other works appeared in Spanish, French and German, and in recent years many of the books mentioned have been translated into Russian, Turkish and Persian.[111] None of them appeared in Hebrew, except Koestler's *Thirteenth Tribe*, which was issued in Jerusalem by a private publisher, who did not risk distributing it to the bookshops.[112]

Other than these, over the years there have been dozens of essays, articles and chapters in history books devoted to the history of the Khazars and its connection to Jewish history. There was even a scientific conference in Jerusalem in 1999, attended mainly by outside scholars. The event attracted little interest in local academic circles.[113] Although the ideological pressure of the late 1980s and 1990s has eased somewhat, Israeli historians have not taken up the subject of Khazaria, nor have they directed their students to these blocked historical paths.

But while the Khazars scared off the Israeli historians, not one of whom has published a single paper on the subject, Koestler's *Thirteenth Tribe* annoyed them and provoked angry responses. Hebrew readers had no access to the book itself for many years, learning about it only through the venomous denunciations.

THE ENIGMA: THE ORIGIN OF EASTERN EUROPE'S JEWS

Arthur Koestler was a Zionist pioneer in his youth, even a close supporter of the Zionist right-wing leader Vladimir Jabotinsky, but grew disillusioned with the settlement project and the Jewish national movement. (Later he was a

---

University, 1970; see also his book *Khazar Studies: An Historico-Philological Inquiry into the Origins of the Khazars*, Budapest: Akadémiai Kiadó, 1980.

110   Kevin A. Brook, *The Jews of Khazaria*, Northvale: Jason Aronson, 1999; also see www.khazaria.com.

111   Félix E. Kitroser, *Jazaria: El imperio olvidado por la historia*, Cordova: Lerner Ediciones, 2002; Jacques Sapir et Jacques Piatigorsky (eds.), *L'Empire khazar VIIe-XIe siècle: L'énigme d'un peuple cavalier*, Paris: Autrement, 2005; Andreas Roth, *Chasaren: Das Vergessene Großriech der Juden*, Stuttgart: Melzer, 2006.

112   In private conversation, the anonymous publisher told me that he hesitated to distribute the book because Israeli society was not yet ready for it.

113   The best lectures given at this conference were published in English (and it is no accident that they were not published in Hebrew). See P. B. Golden, H. Ben-Shammai and A. Rona-Tas (eds.), *The World of the Khazars*, Leiden: Brill, 2007.

Communist, but grew to detest Stalin and became bitterly anti-Soviet.) Nevertheless, he continued to support the existence of the State of Israel, and was concerned about the Jewish refugees who flocked to it. Throughout his life, he opposed all forms of racism in general, and anti-Semitism in particular, and fought against them with his considerable literary talent. Most of his books were translated into Hebrew and were quite successful. One of the impulses that prompted him to write *The Thirteenth Tribe* was his determination to defeat, while he still could, Hitler's heritage in the world. He wrote:

[T]he large majority of surviving Jews in the world is of Eastern European—and thus perhaps mainly of Khazar—origin. If so, this would mean that their ancestors came not from the Jordan but from the Volga, not from Canaan but from the Caucasus, once believed to be the cradle of the Aryan race; and that genetically they are more closely related to the Hun, Uigur and Magyar tribes than to the seed of Abraham, Isaac and Jacob. Should this turn out to be the case, then the term "anti-Semitism" would become void of meaning, based on a misapprehension shared by both the killers and their victims. The story of the Khazar Empire, as it slowly emerges from the past, begins to look like the most cruel hoax which history has ever perpetrated.[114]

Koestler was not certain, in the 1970s, whether the non-Ashkenazi Jews were descendants of the Judeans, and if the Khazar conversion was an exception in Jewish history. Nor did he understand that his battle against anti-Semitic racism might deal a mortal blow to Zionism's principal imaginary. Or rather, he did and did not understand, and naively assumed that if he declared an unambiguous political position at the end of the book, he would be exonerated:

I am aware of the danger that it may be maliciously misinterpreted as a denial of the State of Israel's right to exist. But that right is not based on the hypothetical origins of the Jewish people, nor on the mythological covenant of Abraham with God; it is based on international law—i.e., on the United Nations' decision in 1947 ... Whatever the Israeli citizens' racial origins, and whatever illusions they entertain about them, their State exists *de jure* and *de facto*, and cannot be undone, except by genocide.[115]

But it was no use. In the 1970s Israel was caught up in the momentum of territorial expansion, and without the Old Testament in its hand and the "exile of the Jewish people" in its memory, it would have had no justification for annexing Arab Jerusalem and establishing settlements in the West Bank,

114 Koestler, *The Thirteenth Tribe*, 17.
115 Ibid., 223.

the Gaza Strip, the Golan Heights, and even the Sinai Peninsula. The writer who was able, in his classic novel *Darkness at Noon*, to crack the Communist enigma, did not comprehend that the Zionist enigma was entirely caught up in the mythology of an eternal "ethnic" time. Nor did he foresee that the post-1967 Zionists would resemble the Stalinists in their ferocious response—both saw him as an irredeemable traitor.

When the book appeared, Israel's ambassador to Britain described it as "an antisemitic action financed by the Palestinians."[116] The organ of the World Zionist Organization, *In the Diasporas of the Exile*, suggested that "perhaps this cosmopolitan has begun, after all, to wonder about his own roots," but that most probably Koestler feared he was a forgotten writer, and "sensed that a Jewish theme, presented from a paradoxical and unusual perspective, and done skillfully, would restore public interest in him."[117] The Zionist publication expressed a deep concern that "thanks to its exotic elements and Koestler's prestige, the book would appeal to Jewish readers without either historical understanding or a critical faculty, who might accept its thesis and implications literally."[118]

Professor Zvi Ankori, of the Department of Jewish History at Tel Aviv University (among other institutions), compared Koestler to Jacob Fallmerayer, the German scholar who already in the nineteenth century had suggested that the modern Greeks were not descendants of the ancient Hellenes, as they imagined, but of a hotchpotch of Slavs, Bulgars, Albanians and others who had poured into the Peloponnese and gradually mixed with its original population. We might speculate, Ankori wrote, about Koestler's psychological reasons for borrowing from Abraham Polak's old thesis, which had been dismissed in the past and could harm Israel in the present.[119] Later Professor Shlomo Simonson, Ankori's respected colleague at Tel Aviv University, also wondered if the reasons for Koestler's writing about the Jewish Khazars might have to do with his conflicted identity as an Eastern European immigrant within British culture. "It is not surprising at all," added this senior Israeli historian, "that a recently published work on the history of Jewish self-hate devoted a substantial section to Koestler."[120] Simonson, like Ankori, noted that the source of this

---

116   Quoted in the article by Jacques Piatigorsky, "Arthur Koestler et les Khazars: L'histoire d'une obsession," in *L'Empire Khazar*, 99.

117   Israel Margalit, "Arthur Koestler Found the Thirteenth Tribe," *In the Diaspora of the Exile*, vol. 11, 83–4, 1978 (in Hebrew), 194.

118   Ibid.

119   Zvi Ankori, "Sources and History of Ashkenazi Judaism," *Kivunim: Periodical of Judaism and Zionism* 13 (1981, in Hebrew), 29–31.

120   Shlomo Simonsohn, "The Thirteenth Tribe," *Michael: On the History of the Jews in*

discredited story about the origin of Eastern European Jews was the work of their Tel Aviv colleague Professor Polak.

But neither Polak, a professional historian, nor Koestler, who did not claim to be one, invented the thesis that a large part of Eastern European Jewry originated in the territories of the Khazar empire. It should be stressed that this hypothesis—reviled since the 1970s as scandalous, disgraceful and anti-Semitic—had previously been accepted in various scholarly circles, both Zionist and non-Zionist, although it never became the consensus, because of the fears it aroused among the ethnocentric.

Already in 1867, for example, the great Jewish scholar Abraham Harkavy had written in the introduction to his book *The Jews and the Languages of the Slavs* that "the first Jews who came to the southern regions from Russia did not originate in Germany, as many writers tend to believe, but from the Greek cities on the shores of the Black Sea and from Asia, via the mountains of the Caucasus."[121] Harkavy stated that later waves of immigration brought Jews also from Germany, and since they were more numerous, the Yiddish language eventually became dominant among the Jews of Eastern Europe, but in the seventeenth century they still spoke Slavic. Dubnow, too, before he became a well-known and responsible historian, wondered in an early letter, "Whence did the first Jews who came to Poland and Russia originate—in the Western countries, or the lands of the Khazars and Crimea?"[122] He assumed that the answer would be found only as archaeology progressed, furnishing the historical narrative with further evidence.

Yitzhak Schipper, a senior socioeconomic historian and a prominent Zionist in Poland, believed for a long time that the "Khazar thesis" accounted well for the massive demographic presence of Jews in Eastern Europe. In this, he was following a series of Polish scholars, Jewish and non-Jewish, who had written about the first settlements of Jewish believers in Poland, Lithuania, Belorussia and Ukraine. Schipper also assumed that there had been "authentic" Jews in Judaizing Khazaria who contributed to the development of crafts and commerce in the powerful empire that stretched from the Volga to the Dnieper River. But he was also convinced that the influence of Judaism on the Khazars and the eastern Slavs gave rise to the large Jewish communities in Eastern Europe.[123]

the Diaspora, vol. 14, 1997 (in Hebrew), liv–lv.

121   Harkavy, *The Jews and the Languages of the Slavs*, 1.
122   Dubnow, *Discovery and Research*, Odessa: Abba Dochna, 1892 (in Hebrew), 10.
123   Since most of Schipper's work was written in Polish and Yiddish, we can get an idea of his outlook on the Khazars from Jacob Litman, *The Economic Role of Jews in Medieval*

We have seen that Salo Baron followed Polak and devoted a good many pages to the Khazar issue. Despite the built-in ethnicism of his work, he made an unusual digression from linear history when he stopped at the Khazar way station. Unable to overlook the views of most Polish historians between the world wars, let alone the comprehensive work of the Israeli historian Polak, Baron wrote:

> But before and after the Mongol upheaval the Khazars sent many offshoots into the unsubdued Slavonic lands, helping ultimately to build up the great Jewish centers of Eastern Europe . . . During the half millennium (740–1250) of its existence, however, and its aftermath in the Eastern European communities, this noteworthy experiment in Jewish statecraft doubtless exerted a greater influence on Jewish history than we are as yet able to envisage.
>
> From Khazaria Jews began drifting into the open steppes of Eastern Europe, during both the period of their country's affluence and that of its decline . . . After Sviatoslav's victories and the ensuing decline of the Khazar empire, on the other hand, refugees from the devastated districts, including Jews, sought shelter in the very lands of their conquerors. Here they met other Jewish groups and individuals migrating from the west and south. Together with these arrivals from Germany and the Balkans, they began laying the foundations for a Jewish community which, especially in sixteenth-century Poland, outstripped all the other contemporary areas of Jewish settlement in population density as well as in economic and cultural power.[124]

Baron was not a "self-hating Jew" and certainly not hostile to the Zionist enterprise, and neither was his Jerusalem colleague Ben-Zion Dinur. Nevertheless, the latter—Israel's minister of education in the 1950s—did not hesitate to join Baron and Polak and express an unambiguous position regarding the origins of the Eastern European Jews: "The Russian conquests did not destroy the Khazar kingdom entirely, but they broke it up and diminished it. And this kingdom, which had absorbed Jewish immigrants and refugees from many exiles, must itself have become a diaspora mother, the mother of one of the greatest of the diasporas—of Israel in Russia, Lithuania and Poland."[125]

Readers today might be astonished to hear that Israel's high priest of memory in the 1950s did not hesitate to describe Khazaria as the "diaspora mother" of Eastern European Jewry. It goes without saying that here, too, his rhetoric was suffused with characteristic ethnobiological thinking.

Poland: The Contribution of Yitzhak Schipper, Lanham: University Press of America, 1984, 117–16.

124   Baron, *A Social and Religious History*, vol. 3, 206.
125   Dinur, *Israel in Exile*, vol. 1, 2, 5.

Dinur, like Baron, needed the historical connection with the "born Jews" who were in Khazaria before it was Judaized. Nevertheless, the fact is that until the 1960s the assumption that the majority of the Yiddish people did not originate in Germany but in the Caucasus, the Volga steppes, the Black Sea and the Slav countries was an acceptable assumption, caused no shock, and was not considered anti-Semitic, as it was after the early 1970s.

The statement by the Italian philosopher Benedetto Croce that "any history is first of all a product of the time of its writing" has long been a common-place, but it still fits perfectly the Zionist historiography of the Jewish past. The conquest of the "City of David" in 1967 had to be achieved by the direct descendants of the House of David—not, perish the thought, by the offspring of tough horsemen from the Volga-Don steppes, the deserts of southern Arabia, or the coast of North Africa. In other words, the "whole, undivided Land of Israel" needed more than ever a "whole, undivided People of Israel."

Traditional Zionist historiography had always maintained that the Jews of Eastern Europe had come from Germany (before that, they had spent "some time" in Rome, to which they had been driven from "the Land of Israel"). The essentialist view of the exiled, wandering people, combined with the prestige of a "civilized" country such as Germany, overshadowed the lowly status of Europe's backward regions and created a winning product (just as the Jews from the Arab countries tend to describe themselves as Sephardic, so the Jews of Eastern Europe prefer to see themselves as Ashkenazi). Although there is no historical evidence showing that Jews migrated from western Germany to the Continent's east, the fact that Jews in Poland, Lithuania and Russia spoke Yiddish supposedly proved that the Eastern European Jews were originally German Jews—Ashkenazi Jews. As the vocabulary of the language spoken by these Jews was 80 percent Germanic, how did it happen that Khazars and all sorts of Slavs, who had previously spoken Turkic or Slavonic dialects, ended up speaking Yiddish?

Isaac Baer Levinsohn (also known as Rival), described as the father of Jewish enlightenment in Russia, stated in his book *Testimony in Israel*, published in 1828: "Our elders told us that some generations earlier the Jews in these parts spoke only this Russian language, and this Ashkenazi Jewish language we speak now had not yet spread among all the Jews living in these regions."[126] Harkavy, too, was convinced that before the seventeenth century most Eastern European Jews spoke Slavic dialects.

Polak, who gave much thought to this issue, proposed several hypotheses,

---

126   Isaac Baer Levinsohn, *Document in Israel*, Jerusalem: Zalman Shazar, 1977 (in Hebrew), 33n2.

some more persuasive than others. A less than convincing suggestion was that a large part of the Judaized Khazar population, especially those who lived in the Crimea, were still speaking an ancient Gothic language that had been common in the peninsula till the sixteenth century, and resembled Yiddish much more than the German that was current at that time in the German lands. A more plausible suggestion was that the Germanic colonization that spread eastward in the fourteenth and fifteenth centuries, bringing with it large German-speaking commercial and artisanal populations, led to the spreading of their language among those who acted as mediators between these economic powerhouses and the local nobility and peasantry, which continued to speak their Slavic dialects.[127] Some four million Germans had migrated from eastern Germany into Poland, where they created Eastern Europe's first bourgeoisie, and also brought the Roman Catholic clergy with them. The Jews, who came mainly from the east and the south—not only from the Khazar lands, but also from the Slavic regions under its influence—took on certain functions in the division of labor that formed with the first signs of modernization. Becoming tax collectors and prosperous minters of coins (silver coins bearing Polish words in Hebrew characters have been found), as well as humble carters, woodworkers and furriers, the Jews filled intermediate positions in production and mingled with the cultures and languages of the different classes (they might also have brought some of these skills from the Khazar empire). Koestler described this historical scene in vivid terms:

> One can visualize a *shtetl* craftsman, a cobbler perhaps, or a timber merchant, speaking broken German to his clients, broken Polish to the serfs on the estate next door; and at home mixing the most expressive bits of both with Hebrew into a kind of intimate private language. How this hotchpotch became communalized and standardized to the extent to which it did, is any linguist's guess.[128]

Later a limited immigration of Jewish elites from Germany—rabbis and Talmudic scholars, young and old—completed the process, further establishing the new language of the masses and apparently also modifying and consolidating their rituals. These religious elites, seemingly invited in from the west, enjoyed a prestige that many wanted to emulate and share, hence the expansion and consolidation of the German vocabulary. Yet such a pivotal word as "to pray"—a key concept in the ritual imaginary—was retained in its Turkish

---

127 Polak, *Khazaria*, 256–7.
128 Koestler, *The Thirteenth Tribe*, 176.

dialect form: *davenen*. Like many other words in Yiddish, it did not come from a German dialect.[129]

Although the immigrants from the west contributed significantly to it, Yiddish did not resemble the German Jewish dialect that developed in the ghettoes of western Germany. There the Jewish population was concentrated in the Rhine region, and its dialect incorporated many words and expressions from the local French and German dialects, of which there is not a trace in eastern Yiddish. Already in 1924 the philologist Mathias Mieses had argued that Yiddish could never have come from western Germany, although in that period the concentrations of Jews were in fact to be found there, not in the eastern part of the territory of German dialect speakers.[130]

More recently, the Tel Aviv linguist Paul Wexler published some thorough studies supporting the assumption that the spread of Yiddish was not due to migration of Jews from the west. Its basis is Slavic, and its vocabulary is predominantly southeastern German. In its origins, Yiddish resembles the Sorb language, which evolved in the boundary regions between speakers of Slavic and Germanic dialects; like Yiddish, it almost disappeared in the twentieth century.[131]

Demographically, too, the thesis that the Jews of Eastern Europe originated in western Germany is challenged by an inconvenient fact. The number of Jewish believers in the eleventh to thirteenth centuries in the territory between Mainz and Worms, Cologne and Strasbourg, was very small. There are no precise data, but estimates range from a few hundred to a few thousand, never more. It is possible that some wandered eastward during the Crusades—though there is no evidence to suggest this, and moreover it is known that the fugitives from the pogroms did not go far and usually returned to their homes—but in any case, such a trickle could not have given rise to the huge Jewish communities of Poland, Lithuania and Russia. If these communities originated in western Germany, as Israel's establishment historians argue today, why did they multiply so dramatically in the east while remaining demographically stable in the west, long before the use of birth control? Surely the quantities

---

129   Regarding "davenen," see Herbert Guy Zeiden, "Davenen: A Turkic Etymology," *Yiddish: A Quarterly Journal Devoted to Yiddish and Yiddish Literature* 10: 2–3, 96–9; "Khazar/Kipchak Turkisms in Yiddish: Words and Surnames," *Yiddish* 11: 1–2 (1998), 81–92; and also Paolo Agostini, "Once Again on the Etymology of Davenen," *Yiddish* 11: 1–2 (1998), 93–118.

130   Mathias Mieses, *Die jiddische Sprache*, Berlin: Benjamin Harz, 1924.

131   Paul Wexler, *The Ashkenazic Jews: A Slavo-Turkic People in Search of a Jewish Identity*, Columbus: Slavica Publishers, 1993; see also the chapter "The Khazar Component in the Language and Ethnogenesis of the Ashkenazic Jews," in *Two-tiered Relexification in Yiddish*, Berlin: Mouton de Gruyter, 2002, 513–41. Today the Sorbs are a small Slavic community in southern Germany.

of food and sanitary conditions in Eastern Europe were hardly superior to "depleted, hungry and unhygienic" Western Europe? In the final analysis, life in the poverty-stricken small towns in the east was no more conducive to propagation than life in the cities of Britain, France and Germany—yet it was in the east that the demographic "big bang" took place, with the result that speakers of Yiddish dialects constituted, on the eve of the twentieth century, 80 percent of all the Jews in the world.

Khazaria collapsed some time before the first indications of the presence of Jews in Eastern Europe, and it is difficult not to connect the two. Although Jewish believers in Russia, Ukraine, Poland, Lithuania and Hungary erased their Khazar or Slavic past from memory, and remembered instead, like the descendants of Himyar's and North Africa's Judaizers, how they "came out of Egypt's house of bondage," various vestiges of their true historical past did remain. In their migration westward, they left a few markers by the side of the road.

Back in the 1920s, Yitzhak Schipper discovered in the regions of the Ukraine, Transylvania, Istria, Poland and Lithuania a number of place names that contain some form of the terms "Khazar" or "Kagan."[132] There are also given and family names that hark back to the Khazar or Slavic east, rather than the Germanic west. Names for animals such as the hawk (*balaban*), deer, wolf and bear were not known in the kingdoms of Judea or Himyar, or among the Jews of Spain and North Africa, and they reached Western Europe quite late. Aside from these rather minor indications, there are some sociological and anthropological elements uniquely associated with eastern Jewry that cannot be found anywhere in the west.

The essential way of life of the typical Yiddish townlet, which must also have preserved the dialect, has never been found in the Rhine area or its vicinity. From the second century BCE, when Judaism began to spread in the world, it flourished in small faith communities mostly on the margins of cities and towns, and only rarely in villages. In Western and Southern Europe, Jews never created separate settlements. But the Jewish townlet, not always small (and not always exclusively Jewish), permitted its inhabitants to differ from its neighbors not only in religious practices and norms but also in more secular ways, such as language or the architectural style of prayer houses.

At the center of the Jewish townlet stood the synagogue, with a double

---

132   Tadeusz Lewicki, "Kabarowie (Kawarowie) na Rusi, na Węgrzech i w Polsce we wczesnym średniowieczu," in *Studia nad etnogenezą Słowian i kulturą Europy wczesno-średniowiecznej*, G. Labuda and S. Tabaczyński (eds), vol. 2, Wrocław: Zakład im. Ossolińskich, 1988, 77–87.

dome reminiscent of the Eastern pagoda. Jewish dress in Eastern Europe did not resemble that of the Jews of France or Germany. The yarmulke—also derived from a Turkic word—and the fur hat worn over it were more reminiscent of the people of the Caucasus and the horsemen of the steppes than of Talmudic scholars from Mainz or merchants from Worms. These garments, like the long silk caftan worn chiefly on the Sabbath, differed from the clothing worn by the Belorussian or Ukrainian peasants. But any mention of these features and others—from food to humor, from clothing to chants, all connected to the specific cultural morphology of their daily life and their history—scarcely interested the scholars who were occupied in inventing the eternal history of the "people of Israel." They could not come to terms with the troublesome fact that there had never been a Jewish people's culture, but only a popular Yiddish culture that resembled the cultures of their neighbors much more than it did those of the Jewish communities of Western Europe or North Africa.[133]

Today the descendants of the Jews of "Yiddishland" live mainly in the United States and Israel. The remains of millions of others are buried beneath the slaughterhouses constructed by Hitler in the twentieth century. When we consider the tremendous effort that the memory agents in Israel have invested in commemorating their dying moments, compared with the scanty effort made to discover the rich (or wretched, depending on one's viewpoint) life lived in Yiddishland before the vicious massacre, we can draw only sad conclusions about the political and ideological role of modern historiography.

Like the absence of costly archaeological exploration in southern Russia and the Ukraine to uncover the remains of Khazaria, the absence of sociological, linguistic and ethnographic studies about the long-standing ways of life in the townlets of Poland and Lithuania—work of innovative historical research, not mere folklore[134]—is no accident. No one wants to go looking under stones when venomous scorpions might be lurking beneath them, waiting to attack the self-image of the existing *ethnos* and its territorial ambitions. The

---

133   To illustrate, in the United States it is possible to speak of "Jewish humor" because almost all the Jews there originate from Eastern Europe. But the term is meaningless in Israel, because there is no Jewish humor any more than there is Christian humor. There may be Yiddish, or Maghrebi, humor, and so on. The height of absurdity was reached by an American historian, presumably a fan of Woody Allen and Jerry Seinfeld, who attempted to find the sources of the humor that accounts for the mentality of diaspora Jews in ancient texts. See Erich S. Gruen, *Diaspora: Jews amidst Greeks and Romans*, Cambridge, MA: Harvard University Press, 2002, 135–212.

134   Some hesitant steps in this direction may be found in Antony Polonsky (ed.), *The Shtetl: Myth and Reality*, Oxford: The Littman Library of Jewish Civilization, 2004.

writing of national history is not seriously meant to uncover past civilizations; its principal aim thus far has been the construction of a meta-identity and the political consolidation of the present.

History deals with books, not with things, a "patriotic" scholar might argue, having spent his or her entire life interpreting religious, governmental and ideological texts produced in the past by a paper-thin elite. This is true where the traditional study of the past is concerned. But the advent of anthropological history began, slowly but surely, to corrode the simplistic Zionist metahistories.

Sometimes it seems that most of the scholars who have specialized in the history of the People of Israel have yet to hear about this strange new form of historiography. A deeper exploration of the ways of life and communication in past Jewish communities might further expose a wicked little fact: that the further we move from religious norms and the more we focus our research on diverse daily practices, the more we discover that there never was a secular ethnographic common denominator between the Jewish believers in Asia, Africa and Europe. World Jewry had always been a major religious culture. Though consisting of various elements, it was not a strange, wandering nation.

There is a good deal of irony in the fact that people who adopted the religion of Moses had been living between the Volga and the Don rivers before the arrival there of Russians and Ukrainians, just as Judaizers had been living in Gaul before it was invaded by Frankish tribes. So, too, in North Africa, where Punics converted to Judaism before the arrival of the Arabs, and in the Iberian Peninsula, where a Judaic culture flourished and struck root before the Christian Reconquista. In contrast to the image of the past that Christian Judeophobes began to promote, and that modern anti-Semites echoed, there had never been in all history a cursed nation-race that was driven out of the Holy Land for killing the divine Messiah, and that settled uninvited among other "nations."

The offspring of the Judaizers around the Mediterranean, in Adiabene before and after the Common Era, the descendants of the Himyars, the Berbers and the Khazars, were linked by the Jewish monotheism that bridged the diverse linguistic-cultural groups that arose in far-flung lands and followed different historical paths. Many abandoned Judaism; others clung to it stubbornly and succeeded in carrying it to the threshold of the secular age.

Is Himyar, Berber and Khazar time lost beyond recovery? Is there no chance that a new historiography would invite those ancient Jews, who have been forgotten by their descendants, to reappear in the legitimate sphere of public memory?

The construction of a new body of knowledge always bears a direct connection with the national ideology in which it operates. Historical insights that diverge from the narrative laid down at the inception of the nation can be accepted only when consternation about their implications is abated. This can happen when the current collective identity begins to be taken for granted and ceases to be something that anxiously and nostalgically clings to a mythical past, when identity becomes the basis for living and not its purpose—that is when historiographic change can take place.

For now, it is difficult to predict whether the Israeli politics of identity will permit, in the early twenty-first century, the emergence of fresh paradigms for the investigation of the origins and history of Jewish faith communities.

CHAPTER FIVE

The Distinction: Identity Politics in Israel

The State of Israel … will foster the development of the country for the benefit of all its inhabitants; it will be based on freedom, justice and peace as envisaged by the prophets of Israel; it will ensure complete equality of social and political rights to all its inhabitants irrespective of religion, race or sex; it will guarantee freedom of religion, conscience, language, education and culture.
—The Declaration of the Establishment of the State of Israel, 1948

A candidates' list shall not participate in elections to the Knesset if its objects or actions, expressly or by implication, include one of the following: (1) negation of the existence of the State of Israel as the state of the Jewish people; (2) negation of the democratic character of the State; (3) incitement to racism.
—Basic Law: The Knesset, Clause 7A, 1985

Before the great secularization in Europe, Jewish believers clung to the religious axiom that sustained them through times of trouble: they were the "chosen people," God's sacred congregation, destined to "illuminate the nations." In reality, they knew that as minority groups existing in the shadow of other religions, they were subordinated to the stronger powers. The passion for proselytizing that had characterized these communities in the past had all but disappeared through the ages, largely from fear of the dominant religions. Over the centuries, thick layers of distrust and fear of propagating their faith padded the self-identification of the believers and bolstered the communal isolation that eventually became their distinguishing mark. In the Middle Ages, the exclusive belief in the "unique nation that dwells apart" also served to prevent large-scale desertion to the other monotheistic religions.

Like other minorities in periods of stress and hardship, the Jewish faith communities were knit together by group solidarity. In peaceful times, the rabbinical elites exchanged information about precepts and religious norms, and various aspects of their rites and ceremonies. For all the great differences between Marrakech and Kiev, Sanaa and London, differences not only in the secular sphere but even in the religious practices, there was always a common core of rabbinical attachment to the Talmudic law, a shared concept of deliverance from exile, and a profound religious devotion to the holy city Jerusalem, whence salvation would come.

The spread of secularization in Europe eroded the status of the religious frameworks and undermined the authority of the rabbis, their communities' traditional intellectuals. Like members of other religious, cultural and linguistic groups, those who discarded their Jewish religion were swept up in the momentum of modernization. The depiction in Zionist theoretical and historical writings notwithstanding, they were not the only ones struggling to assimilate into the national cultures that were rising at this time. Perhaps peasants in Saxony, Protestant shopkeepers in France and Welsh laborers in Britain were affected differently by the rapid changes in ways of life and the migratory upheavals, but they suffered no less than did the Jewish believers. Entire worlds disappeared, and assimilation into the general economic, political, linguistic and supracultural systems demanded a painful renunciation of long-standing customs and mores.

Despite the particular difficulties experienced by the Jews, in some countries—France, the Netherlands, Britain, Germany—most of them became "Israelites," meaning Frenchmen, Dutchmen, Britons or Germans of the Mosaic faith. They became eager supporters of the new states; some even stressed their national identity and took great pride in it. Rightly so, as they were among the pioneer speakers of the national languages and consolidators of the national cultures, largely because of their concentration in the cities. They were thus among the first Britons, Frenchmen and Germans (it would not be an exaggeration to say that the poet Heinrich Heine was a German before Adolf Hitler's grandfather became one, if indeed he ever did). During the First World War, which witnessed the peak of mass nationalism in Europe, they set out to defend these new homelands, and probably also killed, without notable qualms, Jewish soldiers fighting on the other side of the front line.[1] German Jewish reformists, French Jewish socialists and British Jewish liberals almost all volunteered to defend their newfound collective property: the national state and its territory.

Strangely enough, Zionists also became involved in the war culture that focused on Europe's national boundaries, despite their belief in a separate national entity. At that time they were still too weak to offer an alternative identity that could defuse the fighting spirit arising from the varied nationalist attachments of their supporters and activists. In fact, from 1897, the year of the first Zionist Congress, until the end of the First World War, Zionism was

---

1 Amos Elon, *The Pity of It All: A History of Jews in Germany, 1743–1933*, New York: Metropolitan Books, 305–37. The French and German Israelites did not demonstrate much sympathy. Their attitude toward the Jews of Eastern Europe, the "inferior" Ostjuden, was cold and disdainful. Much the same attitude was later shown by the same Eastern European Jews toward the new "Eastern Jews" they encountered in Israel.

a feeble and insignificant movement in the world's Jewish communities, and often yielded to the national demands of the gentiles (in Germany in 1914, Zionists accounted for less than 2 percent of Germans of Jewish origin, and in France even less).

The Zionist idea was born in the second half of the nineteenth century in Central and Eastern Europe, in the lands between Vienna and Odessa. It grew uneasily on the fringes of German nationalism and reached the lively cultural marketplaces of the Yiddish population. In fact, for all its marginality, Zionism was part of the last wave of nationalist awakening in Europe, and coincided with the rise of other identity-shaping ideologies on the Continent. It can be viewed as an attempt at collective assimilation into modernity, exactly like the surrounding national enterprises that were then starting to take shape.[2] While a significant number of its ideological progenitors belonged more or less to the Germanic culture—Moses Hess, Theodor Herzl, Max Nordau—those who developed, disseminated and implemented its theories came from the intelligentsia of the widespread Yiddish-speaking population, which was densely packed into the cities and towns of Poland, the Ukraine, Lithuania, Russia and Romania.

As noted in the second chapter, in these regions there was a secular, modern Yiddishist civilization such as did not exist in Jewish communities elsewhere, neither in London nor in Marrakech. It was this distinctive culture, rather than religion, that incubated the protonationalist and nationalist ferment. It was from this semi-autonomous world that young intellectuals arose. Finding their paths blocked to the centers of high culture—academic careers, free professions, civil service—many became socialist revolutionaries and democratic innovators, and a few became Zionists.

At the same time, the distinctive presence of the Yiddish communities fueled a revival of anti-Jewish feeling. The mosaic of nationalities emerging in Eastern Europe sought to eject the conspicuously different Yiddishist entity from its midst. Aside from the repression and traditional restrictions in the

---

2   Inevitably, the proponents of Jewish nationalism view it as unique and fundamentally different from other national movements. For example, the historian Jacob Katz wrote that "on the threshold of the modern age, the Jews were better prepared for a national movement than any other ethnic group in Europe"—this being a typical outlook among historians of other national groups. See his book, *Jewish Nationalism: Essays and Studies*, Jerusalem: The Zionist Library, 1983 (in Hebrew), 18. A historian of equal stature, Shmuel Ettinger, maintained that "the Jews may be the only known group in history that preserved its national consciousness for thousands of years." See *Studies in Modern Jewish History, I: History and Historians*, Jerusalem: Zalman Shazar, 1992 (in Hebrew), 174.

Tsarist regime and the Romanian kingdom, in the 1880s a wave of popular pogroms, with emergent nationalist features, shocked millions of Jews and accelerated their mass migration westward. Between 1880 and 1914 some two and a half million Yiddish-speaking Jews transited through Germany toward receptive countries in the West. Some of them ended up on the safe shores of the American continent; less than 3 percent of them chose to migrate to Ottoman-ruled Palestine, and few of them stayed there.

One of the by-products of this large population shift was that it indirectly exacerbated the traditional hostility that simmered beneath the surface in Germany, scene of the transit. This fierce hatred, much of which is still left unexplained, would play out in one of the most horrendous acts of genocide in the twentieth century. In the process, it showed that there is no direct correlation between technological progress or cultural refinement and morality.

Modern anti-Semitism flourished throughout the world of European modernity, but its manifestation in Western and Southern Europe, as well as on the American continent, was quite different from its features and expressions in Central and Eastern Europe. The uncertainties and inner struggles of the young national identity created anxiety and fear almost everywhere. The cultural problems involved in the construction of nationalities were precisely those that turned the long-standing "dislike of the unlike" into an integral part of the new democratic mass politics. Any form of difference—different skin pigmentation, distinctive dialects or unfamiliar religious customs—irritated the bearers of the new national consciousness who were struggling to define and demarcate themselves as unambiguous collectivities. The level of abstraction in constructing the imagery of the nation demanded a definitive and unequivocal characterization of those who would not be a part of it. The nation, therefore, was imagined as an ancient, extended "blood" family, and it was convenient that its nearest neighbor would also be its most threatening enemy. Since for hundreds of years Christian civilization had depicted the Jewish believer as the ultimate other, it was a simple matter for the new collective identities to pick this element out of the old tradition and install it as the border post that marked the new national community.

In territories where civil and political nationalism prevailed, it was possible to enclose and seal off the ancient hatreds that were part of the Christian heritage and to include the ostracized Jew in the new identity. The US Constitution, the French Revolution, the laws of Great Britain were sufficiently amenable, forming a stable foundation for the development of inclusive tendencies, which through gradual struggle achieved a hegemonic position in the public arena. In these and other countries, Jews became integral parts of the nation.

However, this successful process was not free from turmoil and regression. The highly dramatic Dreyfus Affair in France in 1894 was a good historical example of the nonlinear, uncertain evolution of modern nationalism. The outburst of intense anti-Semitism that extruded Dreyfus from the body of the "Gallo-Catholic" nation exposed the tensions between conflicting sensibilities. Did the Jewish officer belong to the French nation, or was he a representative of an alien people who had insinuated itself from the East? To preserve its greatness, should France not be fundamentally Christian? Might not the Italian origin of Émile Zola account for his antipatriotic support for the "traitorous" Jewish captain? These and similar questions roiled the national imaginary and set off vibrations that shook the country to its foundations.

The tide of anti-Semitism was ultimately turned by the political and intellectual circles that understood the value of the civil sphere, and the persecuted army officer was "reattached" to the French nation. Supporters of the ethnoreligious national identity did not disappear—they arose again during the Nazi occupation, and some persist to this day. But culturally inclusive nationalism was invigorated after the Dreyfus Affair, and despite the horrific relapse during the Second World War, it continued to entrench itself through the twentieth century.

Similar, though not identical, transitions occurred in a less dramatic and more nuanced way in the United States (during the McCarthy period, for instance), in Great Britain, and in most of the nation-states on both sides of the Atlantic. Anti-Semitism, like other forms of racism, did not become extinct in these countries, but it ceased to be a meaningful signifier in the trends that directed the continued development of the collective supra-identity.

On the other hand, as noted in the first chapter, ethnobiological and ethnoreligious ideologies triumphed in the regions between Germany and Russia, Austria-Hungary and Poland, where they continued to determine the nature of nationalism for many years. The dominance of this anxious and exclusionary mindset enabled the anti-Jewish code of hatred to continue as one of the main indications of the "true" supra-identity. Although anti-Semitism was not always publicly demonstrated, and the ink used in the printed media and textbooks was not always spiked with venom, Judeophobia continued to insinuate itself into the crucial nodes of identity.

One reason for this was that defining the national entity in those rambling, branching cultural spaces required a great many "past" indications of a common origin, and any element that might challenge the myth of a unifying source provoked revulsion and fear. Even nationalists who were confirmed atheists resorted to traditional religious symbols in their self-definition, while respected clergymen accepted the principle of "blood" as a boundary marker.

In other words, just as Germany at some stage needed abundant Aryanism to define itself, so Polishness needed Catholicism and Russianness needed Orthodox pan-Slavism to swaddle their national identities and imagery.

Unlike the Jewish religious reform movement, or the liberal and socialist intellectual groups that sought participation in the emergent national cultures, Zionism borrowed extensively from the dominant nationalist ideologies flourishing in the lands of its birth and infancy, and integrated them into its new platform. It included traces of German Volkism, while Polish romantic nationalist features characterized much of its rhetoric. But these were not mere imitations—it was not a case of an agonized victim taking on some features of his smiling executioner.

While the secular, seminationalistic outlook of the Bund, the widespread leftist Jewish movement, demanded cultural autonomy for the "people of Yiddishland," rather than a single independent polity for all the Jews of the world, educated Zionists emulated the other nationalists in Europe and assumed an ethnoreligious or ethnobiological identity to conceptualize their self-definition. Seeking to build a bridge that could connect Jewish believers—mainly former believers, whose languages and secular customs were polyphonous and diverse—they were unable to build on the lively popular mores and turn them into a homogeneous, domesticated modern culture, as the Bund tried to do. To achieve their aim, the Zionists needed to erase existing ethnographic textures, forget specific histories, and take a flying leap backward to an ancient, mythological and religious past.

As the previous chapters have shown, while the chosen "history" ostensibly matched the religious imaginary, it was not really religious, because Jewish monotheism was not grounded in historical evolutionary time. Nor was it wholly secular, since it ceaselessly utilized materials from the old eschatological faith in order to structure the new collective identity. We must remember that Jewish nationalism had undertaken an almost impossible mission—to forge a single *ethnos* from a great variety of cultural-linguistic groups, each with a distinctive origin. This accounts for the adoption of the Old Testament as the storehouse of national memory. In their urgent need to establish a common origin for the "people," the national historians embraced uncritically the old Christian idea of the Jew as the eternal exile. In the process, they erased and forgot the mass proselytization carried out by early Judaism, thanks to which the religion of Moses grew enormously, both demographically and intellectually.

For the Jewish nationalists, Judaism ceased to be a rich and varied religious culture, and turned into something hermetic, like the German *Volk* or the Polish and Russian *Narod*, though with the unique characteristic that it comprised an alien, wandering people, unrelated to the territories it inhabited. In this sense, Zionism became something of a negative reflection of the anti-Jewish image that accompanied the rise of collectivities in Eastern and Central Europe. This negative reflection correctly identified the national sensibilities in this region, and their physical proximity kept their menace in full view.

Zionism's basic assumptions were correct and, as noted before, it borrowed many elements from the nationalism in which it was embedded. At the same time, it adopted the most exclusionary and conceited aspect of the Jewish religious tradition, the divine commandment that "the people shall dwell alone, and shall not be reckoned among the nations" (Num. 23:9). The ancient ideal of an elect, holy, monotheistic congregation was reinterpreted in an isolationist, secular plan of action. Zionism from its inception was an ethnocentric nationalist movement that firmly enclosed the historical people of its own invention, and barred any voluntary civil entry into the nation its platform began to design. At the same time, any withdrawal from the "people" was depicted as an unforgivable offense, and "assimilation" as a catastrophe, an existential danger to be averted at all costs.

No wonder, then, that to bind together the frangible secular Jewish identity, it was not enough to write a history of the Jews, so culturally disparate, so chronologically fragmentary. Zionism had to resort to another scientific discipline, that of biology—which was conscripted to reinforce the foundation of the "ancient Jewish nation."

ZIONISM AND HEREDITY

The second chapter of this book depicted Heinrich Graetz as the father of ethnonationalist historiography. He adopted the assumptions of German historians about the nation being born in primeval time as a changeless entity that advances through history in a linear fashion. But his personal "spirituality" prevented him from adopting excessively materialistic interpretations of history. His friend Moses Hess, in some ways the first proponent of Jewish nationalism whose assumptions deviated from tradition, needed a good deal of racial theory to dream up the Jewish people. He absorbed the dubious scientific ideas of his time, especially in physical anthropology, and integrated them into a novel theory of identity. He was probably the first, but certainly not the last, to follow this ideological course in the formation of Jewish nationalism.

The thirty-five years that had passed since the publication of Hess's *Rome and Jerusalem* in 1862 had seen a substantial rise in the number of Zionists in Europe, and in the number of anti-Semites. The racist pseudoscience that flourished in all of Europe's laboratories of learning during the imperialist era of the late nineteenth century percolated through ethnocentric nationalism into the central public arenas and became part of the ideological texture of the new political parties. Among them was the young Zionist movement.

The concept of the nation as an ethnic entity was upheld, with varying intensity, by all the different Zionist camps, which was why the new biological science captivated so many. The idea of heredity helped justify the claim to Palestine—that ancient Judea that the Zionists ceased to view as a sacred center from which deliverance would come, and by a bold paradigmatic shift revamped as the destined national homeland of all the Jews in the world. The historical myth required the appropriate "scientific" ideology—for if the Jews of modern times were not the direct descendants of the first exiles, how would they legitimize their settlement in the Holy Land, which was the "exclusive homeland of Israel"? The divine promise would not have sufficed for nationalism's secular subjects, who had revolted against the passive tradition that left the conduct of history to the Almighty. If justice was not to be found in religious metaphysics, it had to be found, if only partially, in biology.

Nathan Birnbaum, perhaps the first Zionist intellectual—it was he who coined the term "Zionism" in 1890—picked up the argument where Hess left off:

> You cannot explain a people's particular mental and emotional distinction except by means of the natural studies. "Race is all," said our great fellow national Lord Beaconsfield [Benjamin Disraeli]. The distinction of the people stems from the distinction of the race. The variety of races accounts for the great diversity of nations. It is because of the differences between the races that the German or the Slav thinks differently from the Jew. It is this difference which explained why the German created the *Song of the Nibelungen* and the Jew, the Bible.[3]

As Birnbaum saw it, neither language nor culture, but only biology, could account for the rise of nations. Otherwise it was not possible to explain the existence of the Jewish nation, whose progeny were immersed in various national cultures and spoke different languages. Tribes and nations existed "because nature has produced, and keeps on producing, diverse races of men, just as it creates different seasons and climates."[4] When Houston Stewart Chamberlain published his famous racialist book *The Foundations of the Nineteenth Century* in 1899, Birnbaum viewed it with understanding, rejecting

---

3 From "Nationalism and Language," an article written in 1886, quoted by Joachim Doron in his *The Zionist Thinking of Nathan Birnbaum*, Jerusalem: The Zionist Library, 1988 (in Hebrew), 177.

4 Ibid., 63.

only the British thinker's erroneous anti-Semitic position. The Jews were not "a bastard race," as Chamberlain argued—they had actually preserved their lineage by marrying only among themselves, and they were, moreover, an integral part of the white race.

Although Birnbaum's part in the rise of the Zionist movement was not insignificant, it is not necessary to dwell on it too long when tracing the evolution of the Jewish nationalist idea. Though he coined the term "Zionist," he was not one of the leading thinkers of the new nationalism, and eventually he quit the movement and became Orthodox.

Theodor Herzl, the true founder of the Zionist movement, was less certain, and could not decide if the Jews arose from a homogeneous source. His writings include some comments that reflect a clearly ethnocentric outlook, and others that contradict it. The term "race" occurs several times in *The Jewish State*, but it is used in the manner of the period, as another word for "people," sans biological connotations.

One evening in London, Herzl dined with the Anglo-Jewish author Israel Zangwill, who would later join the Zionist movement. In his personal diary that day, the handsome leader expressed dismay that the writer, who was famously ugly, thought that they shared the same origin. "He obsesses about the racial aspect, which I cannot accept. It's enough for me to look at myself and at him. I say only this: We are a historical entity, a nation made up of different anthropological elements. That will suffice for the Jewish state. No nation has racial uniformity."[5] Herzl was not a theoretician, and scientific issues did not interest him beyond the demands of his immediate political work. He aspired to reach his goal without being overloaded with an excess of historical or biological arguments.

It was Max Nordau, Herzl's confidante and right hand, and the person who conducted all the early Zionist congresses, who gave a more meaningful ideological dimension to the rise of Jewish nationalism. This gifted journalist and essayist was better known than Herzl in the intellectual arena of fin de siècle Europe. As the author of the popular book *Entartung* ("Degeneration"), he was one of the best known among the conservatives seeking to warn the world against the dangers of modern art, homosexuality, and mental illness, all of which were associated with physical racial degeneracy.

His encounter with Herzl turned him into an enthusiastic Zionist, but earlier he had been concerned about the physical and mental condition of the

---

5   Noted by the Zionist leader on November 21, 1895. See Theodor Herzl, *Die Judensache* (The Jewish Cause: Diaries), vol. 1, Jerusalem: The Zionist Library, 1998 (in Hebrew), 258.

Jews. Born Simon Maximilian—Meir Simha—Südfeld (south field), he changed his "lowly Jewish" name for a proud European one, Nordau (north pasture). Like the Hungarian-born Herzl, he was from Budapest and, like him also, sought to identify himself as a German in every sense. The ugly anti-Semitism of the 1880s and 1890s halted the integration of this Eastern European Jew into the German nation. Like other Jews who found personal assimilation problematic, he opted for collective integration into the modern world—namely, Zionism. This was not, of course, the way Nordau himself thought of it. As he saw it, although anti-Jewish hate created nothing, it awakened the dormant consciousness of an existing race and revived its sense of its own distinction. The failure of "Germanization" led him to adopt a position of Jewish exclusivity, with the pessimistic conclusion that a race cannot be exchanged but only improved.

This Zionist leader, convinced that the Jews shared a homogeneous biological origin, wrote about the "blood ties that exist in the Israelite family."[6] But he wondered whether the Jews had always been physically small or had been made shorter by the conditions of their lives, which caused them to be weak and degenerate. Zionism opened exciting vistas for the improvement of the race by means of agricultural labor, accompanied by gymnastics and bodybuilding in the open air of the ancestral homeland. His famous speech at the second Zionist Congress, in which he first spoke of the lost "muscular Jewry," expressed a passionate longing for a brawny nation-race.[7] "In no other race or people can gymnastics fulfill such an important educational function, as it must do among us Jews," he wrote. "It is needed to straighten our backs, in body and character alike."[8] For the ancient blood to be revived, the Jews needed a soil, and only Zionism could give them that.

If Nordau failed to become an "authentic" German, he did succeed in becoming an original Zionist Volkist. The essentialist romanticism fostered in various channels of German culture was blended into the ideological project that began to guide the new national ideology.

Nordau was in some ways a hesitant Volkist. By contrast, Martin Buber, who was for several years the editor in chief of *Die Welt* ("The World"), the Zionist movement's main organ, was a bold and consistent Volkist. The philosopher of religious existentialism, who would later become a man of peace and strive to bring about a Jewish-Arab state in Palestine, began his nationalist career as one of the

---

6   Max Nordau, "History of Israel's Children," in *Zionist Writings*, vol. 2, Jerusalem: The Zionist Library, [1901] 1960 (in Hebrew), 47.

7   Max Nordau, "Address to the Second Congress," in *Zionist Writings*, vol. 2, 117. This speech was preceded by music from Richard Wagner's opera *Tannhäuser*.

8   Ibid., 187.

principal molders of the Jewish people as a "blood community" (*Blutsgemeinschaft*). Buber visualized the nation as a biological chain of generations from antiquity to the present, and felt the blood connection rising from an unfathomable past. There is a fair amount of Kabbalistic vagueness in the way he phrased it:

> [B]lood is a deep-rooted nurturing force within individual man ... the deepest layers of our being are determined by blood ... our innermost thinking and our will are colored by it. Now he finds that the world around him is the world of imprints and of influences, whereas blood is the realm of a substance capable of being imprinted and influenced, a substance absorbing and assimilating all into its own form ... The people are now for him a community of men who were, are, and will be—a community of the dead, the living, and the yet unborn—who, together, constitute a unity ...
>
> That his substance can, nevertheless, become a reality for the Jew is due to the fact that his origin means more than a mere connection with things past; it has planted something within us that does not leave us at any hour of our life, that determines every tone and every hue in our life, all that we do and all that befalls us: blood, the deepest, most potent stratum of our being.[9]

This neo-Romantic mysticism of heredity and soil underlay the spiritual nationalism of this charismatic thinker, who captivated young Jewish intellectuals in Eastern Europe. Among the Bar Kokhba circle of Buber's followers in Prague was Hans Kohn, mentioned in the first chapter. This future historian, the first to try to conceptualize critically the issue of "organic" nationalism, knew his subject well, and the search for hereditary nationalism was the first station in his intellectual biography.

Buber was always a moderate and cautious Zionist, and ultimately his religious humanism overcame the "ethnic call of the blood." By contrast, Vladimir (Ze'ev) Jabotinsky, the leader of Zionist revisionism, craved power and detested concession and compromise. Nevertheless, the two Zionist leaders, so unalike in their political perceptions, shared a basic ideological hypothesis: Jews have a distinctive blood that sets them apart from other people. The intellectual father of the Zionist right from the 1930s to the present had no doubt about it:

> It is quite clear that the source of the national sentiment cannot be found in education, but in something that precedes it. In what?—I thought about this question and answered myself: in the blood. And I persist in this view. The sense of national identity is inherent in man's "blood," in his physical-racial

---

9 Martin Buber, "Judaism and the Jews," in *On Judaism*, New York: Schocken Books, 1972, 15–16. Later Buber himself tried, not very successfully, to shake off the image of Volkism.

type, and only in that … The people's mental structure reflects their physical form even more perfectly and completely than does that of the individual … That is why we do not believe in mental assimilation. It is physically impossible for a Jew descended from several generations of pure, unmixed Jewish blood to adopt the mental state of a German or a Frenchman, just as it is impossible for a Negro to cease to be a Negro.[10]

For Jabotinsky, nations arise from racial groups ("ethnicities," in today's parlance), and their biological origin forms the psyche (today's "mentality") of peoples. Since Jews do not have a common history or a common language, nor a territory that they have inhabited for centuries, which might have given rise to a common ethnographic culture, one logically concludes as follows:

> Natural terrain, language, religion, shared history—all of these do not constitute the essence of a nation; they are merely descriptions of it … But the essence of a nation, the alpha and omega of its distinctive character is its special physical attribute, the formula of its racial composition … in the final analysis when all shells arising from history, the climate, natural surroundings, and outside influences, have been removed the "nation" is reduced to its racial kernel.[11]

"Race" was always a scientific concept for Jabotinsky. He believed that even if there were no truly pure races, there was a "racial formula," and he was also convinced that in the future it would be possible, by means of a blood test or a glandular secretion, to have a system of classification based on these formulae—the "Italian race," the "Polish race" and of course the "Jewish race." In order to understand the Jews and their conduct in history, it was necessary to discern their origin, and especially to preserve their distinctiveness. Without the protective armor of religion, prolonged residence among other nations might dissolve that distinctiveness and cause them to vanish. They should thus gather as soon as possible in a state of their own. Jabotinsky did have a liberal side, and even a surprisingly universalist worldview (or perhaps not surprising, as he had acquired his education in Italy rather than in Germany), but nevertheless he believed in the continued physical/biological existence of the Jewish people, which had sprung from a uniform ethnic and territorial source to which it must return as soon as possible. This was the focus of his entire historical thinking.

It should be pointed out that, despite the impression given by Israeli histo-

---

10 Ze'ev Jabotinsky, "Letter on Autonomism," in *Selected Writings: Exile and Assimilation*, Tel Aviv: Shlomo Zaltzman, 1936 (in Hebrew), 143–4.

11 From a Jabotinsky manuscript quoted by Gideon Shimoni, *The Zionist Ideology*, Hanover: Brandeis University Press, 1995, 240.

riography, the Zionist right did not have a monopoly on the essentialist concept of the nation. Even the well-known Marxist Ber Borochov was not free from "biology." Zionist socialism shared the same conceptual mechanisms, and it, too, padded them with universalist rhetoric, though of a different sort.

As we saw in the third chapter, Borochov regarded the Palestinian fellahin as an integral part of the Jewish race, a population that could easily be welded into the steel structure of socialist Zionism. So did his disciples and the future founders of the State of Israel, Ben-Gurion and Yitzhak Ben-Zvi—until the Arab uprising of 1929. Initially Borochov contended that, since the locals were as much descendants of the ancient people of Judea as were all the world's Jews, they should be taken back into the body of the nation, while becoming acculturated in a secular manner. The Zionist left would never have considered admitting into the warm bosom of the Jewish people Muslim peasants of a different biological origin. But after the 1929 "pogroms" these Muslim peasants became complete strangers with astonishing speed.

Arthur Ruppin was another leftist Zionist whose political outlook was profoundly shaken by the fateful events of 1929. That was when he began to distance himself from the pacifist Brith Shalom ("Peace Alliance") group, a movement of intellectuals who strove to reach an accommodation with the Arab population by renouncing the demand for a sovereign Jewish majority in Palestine. Ruppin became convinced—correctly, as it happens—that a national-colonialist clash was inescapable, and became a committed Zionist.

Ruppin is a unique and fascinating figure in the history of Zionism. His career in the Jewish national movement began, like Kohn's, in the new little "blood community" group of the Bar Kokhba circle in Prague. But earlier still, in 1900, he took part in an essay competition in Germany on the question, "What may be learned from the theory of evolution about internal political developments and political legislation?" The first prize went to Wilhelm Schallmayer, a pioneer of eugenics, whom the Nazis would greatly admire after his death. The second prize went to Ruppin for a paper that discussed Darwinism and the social sciences, and that two years later became his doctoral dissertation.

Ruppin was a confirmed Darwinist throughout his life. He believed that the Jewish nation was primarily a biological entity. He was aware that the Jews were not a "pure race," since in the course of their wanderings in the world they had absorbed alien elements. Nevertheless, they constituted a hereditary unit, which alone gave substance to their national demands.

[T]his very likeness to the Asiatic peoples, from whom they have been separated for 2,000 years, shows that the Jews have remained unchanged, and that in the Jews of to-day we may say we have the same people who fought victoriously under King David, who repented their misdeeds under Ezra and Nehemiah, died fighting for freedom under Bar-Kochba, were the great carriers of trade between Europe and the Orient in the early Middle Ages … Thus the Jews have not only preserved their great natural racial gifts, but through a long process of selection these gifts have become strengthened. The terrible conditions under which the Jews lived during the last 500 years necessitated a bitter struggle for life in which only the cleverest and strongest survived … The result is that in the Jew of to-day, we have what is in some respects a particularly valuable human type. Other nations may have other points of superiority, but in respect of intellectual gifts the Jews can scarcely be surpassed by any nation.[12]

Did all the Jews in the world possess such exceptional mental qualities? The young Ruppin thought they did not, and stressed in a footnote, "It is perhaps owing to this severe process of selection that the Ashkenazim are to-day superior in activity, intelligence and scientific capacity to the Sephardim and Arabian Jews, in spite of their common ancestry."[13] The Zionist leader was therefore undecided whether the influx of Jews from Yemen, Morocco and the Caucasus to the Land of Israel was a positive occurrence: "But the spiritual and intellectual status of these Jews is so low that an immigration *en masse* would lower the general cultural standard of the Jews in Palestine and would be bad from several points of view."[14]

The profoundly Eurocentric outlook was even stronger than the concept of the Jewish race, and this simplistic Orientalism was common in all the Zionist movements. But while there were doubts about the immigration of Jews from the Arab East, the Ashkenazi Jews were urged to hurry and return to their home-land so as to preserve and protect what was left of their racial distinction. For Ruppin as for other proponents of Zionism, assimilation of the Jews among the gentiles was an even greater threat to the existence of the people than was the gentiles' hatred: "It is certain, however, that by intermarriage the race-character is lost, and that descendants of a mixed marriage are not likely to have any remarkable gifts."[15] They might eventually eliminate the Jewish *ethnos*. It was Ruppin who expressed in 1923 an idea that was widespread, though not often proclaimed:

---

12 Arthur Ruppin, *The Jews of To-Day*, London: Bell and Sons, 1913, 216–17.
13 Ibid., 271.
14 Ibid., 294. Still, it would be good for small numbers of Jews from Arab countries to come, for they are satisfied with little and can replace the Arab laborers.
15 Ibid., 217.

I think that Zionism is less than ever justifiable now except by the fact that the Jews belong racially to the peoples of the Near East. I am now collecting material for a book on the Jews to be based on the problem of race. I want to include illustrations showing the ancient peoples of the Orient and the contemporary population and describe the types which used to and still predominate among the peoples living in Syria and Asia Minor. I want to demonstrate that these same types still exist among the Jews of today.[16]

The first edition of *The Sociology of the Jews*, in Hebrew and in German, appeared in 1930. The time—the beginning of the 1930s—and the places of publication—Berlin/Tel Aviv—were germane to the work's basic rhetoric. The first chapters are entitled "The Racial Composition of the Jews in Eretz Israel" and "The History of the Jewish Race outside Eretz Israel." The author states in the introduction that the subject of the origin of the Jews had preoccupied him for many years and remained unaltered. Alien blood had in fact seeped into the Jewish people, but the founder of the sociology department at the Hebrew University in Jerusalem continued to believe that "most Jews [continue to] resemble in their racial composition their ancient ancestors in Eretz Israel."[17]

At the end of Ruppin's first volume, there are many photographs of "typically Jewish" heads that provide visual support for the central theses about the distinctive variation and unity among Jews of different communities. The facial features and the shape of the skull supposedly proved that all the Jews had originated in ancient Asia. But the racial kinship with Asia did not need to cause anxiety—the cultural inferiority of the natives of Palestine ensured that the Jewish settlers would not intermarry with them.

Ruppin knew the "Orient" well. In 1908 he was appointed director of the Palestine Office of the central executive of the Zionist movement, with the specific task of buying land. He was the father of Jewish settlement, and it would not be an exaggeration to say that Ruppin was to Zionist colonization what Herzl was for the organized national movement. Although by 1948 only some 10 percent of the land of Palestine had been purchased, he could claim much of the credit for the agro-economic infrastructure on which Israel was established. He bought land all over the country, and also set up the central institutions that distributed it. He did much to ensure that the Zionist conquest of the soil would be totally separated from the Palestinian agricultural economy. The biological distinction had to be maintained by systematic "ethnic" separation.

---

16   Alex Bein (ed.), *Arthur Ruppin: Memoirs, Diaries, Letters*, London: Weidenfeld & Nicolson, 1971, 205.

17   Arthur Ruppin, "The Social Structure of the Jews," in vol. 1 of *The Sociology of the Jews*, 2nd edn., Berlin-Tel Aviv: Shtibel, [1930] 1934, 15.

Ruppin's practical activity did not entirely interrupt his theoretical work. In 1926 he was appointed lecturer in "the sociology of the Jews" at the Hebrew University in Jerusalem; thereafter, till his death in 1943, he continued to develop his demographic ideas about the Darwinist struggle of the "Jewish race." Right up until the outbreak of the Second World War, he even maintained academic ties with the eugenicist thinkers who were thriving in Germany. Amazingly, the victory of Nazism did not entirely curtail these contacts. After Hitler's rise to power, the Jerusalem lecturer traveled to Germany to visit Hans Günther, the "pope" of racial theory, who joined the Nazi party in 1932, was the architect of the extermination of the Gypsies, and remained a Holocaust denier to his dying day.[18]

This bizarre association with the National Socialists must not be misunderstood. The juxtaposition of ethnocentric nationalism and biology would give rise to a monstrous perversion in the first half of the twentieth century, but most Zionists did not think in terms of blood purity nor did they seek such purification. The project of systematically expelling "aliens" from their midst never came up, because it was hardly needed, especially since the traditional Jewish religion, though no longer a hegemonic religious belief, was still useful in part as the confirmation of a Jewish identity. The secular Zionists continued to recognize, though not to celebrate, religious conversion. It should be remembered that some of the race proponents— from Hess through Nordau to Buber—were married to gentile women of "alien blood."[19]

The purpose of Jewish biology was to promote separation from others, not actually to be purified of them. It sought to serve the project of ethnic nationalist consolidation in the taking over of an imaginary ancient homeland.

---

18   Ruppin noted in his diary in August 1933: "At Dr Landauer's suggestion, on 11 August I went to Jena to see Professor Gunther, the founder of the National-Socialist racial theory. We talked for two hours. Gunther was very affable. He argued that he had no copyright on the concept of Aryanism, and agreed with me that the Jews are not inferior, only different, and that the problem must be resolved fairly." Arthur Ruppin, *Chapters of My Life*, Tel Aviv: Am Oved, 1968 (in Hebrew), 223; see also ibid., 181–2.

19   Nordau wrote to Herzl on January 22, 1898: "My wife is a Christian Protestant. Of course, my upbringing makes me oppose any compulsion in matters of sentiment, and to prefer the human over the national. But today I think that it is necessary to place greater stress on the national element, and I regard mixed marriages as quite undesirable. Had I met my wife today, or had I met her in the past eighteen months, I would have resisted mightily my growing feeling for her, and would have told myself that as a Jew I have no right to allow my feelings to dominate me … I loved my wife before I became a Zionist, and I have no right to penalize her for the persecution of our race by her race." Shalom Schwartz, *Max Nordau in His Letters*, Jerusalem: Schwartz, 1944 (in Hebrew), 70.

Moreover, most if not all of the Zionist supporters of the blood theory rejected the explicit and deterministic hierarchy of "racial groups." In their outlook, the theory about superior and inferior races was marginal. To be sure, there was no shortage of praise and adulation for Jewish genius, no shortage of swaggering about its extraordinary qualities (at times, this resembled anti-Semitic stereotypes). But uttered by a helpless, persecuted minority, this was perceived as more ridiculous than threatening, pathetic but not dangerous.

It should be noted, however, that the Jewish blood theory was not held exclusively by the handful of leading thinkers quoted above. It was popular in all currents of the Zionist movement, and its imprint can be found in almost all its publications, congresses and conferences. Young intellectuals of the movement's second rank copied and distributed it among the activists and supporters, and it became a kind of axiom that inspired dreams and imaginings of the ancient Jewish people.[20]

The concept of Jewish heredity, and even the theory of eugenics associated with it, was especially prominent among the scientists and physicians who joined Zionism. Raphael Falk's bold book *Zionism and the Biology of the Jews* recapitulated their story in detail.[21] Dr. Aaron Sandler, a leading Zionist in Germany who emigrated to Mandatory Palestine in 1934 and became the physician of the Hebrew University in Jerusalem, knew that there were no pure races but argued that the Jews had, in effect, become a racial entity. On the other hand, Dr. Elias Auerbach, who settled in Haifa back in 1905, was convinced that the Jewish people had always been a pure race, and that Jews had not intermarried with gentiles since the time of Titus. Dr. Aaron Binyamini, who became, after his arrival in Palestine, the physician of the famous Gymnasia Herzliya, continued to measure and weigh his students to prove the principles of natural selection. Dr. Mordechai Boruchov, who also lived in Mandatory Palestine, argued in 1922 that "in the struggle between the nations, in the secret, 'cultural' war between one nation and another, the winner is the one who ensures the improvement of the race and the biological enhancement of his offspring."[22]

---

20   On the presence of Jewish racial theory in Zionist circles, see the excellent article by Rina Rekem-Peled, "Zionism: A Reflection of Anti-Semitism: On the Relationship Between Zionism and Anti-Semitism in Germany of the Second Reich," in J. Borut and O. Heilbronner (eds.), *German Anti-Semitism*, Tel Aviv: Am Oved, 2000 (in Hebrew), 133–56.

21   See Raphael Falk, *Zionism and the Biology of the Jews*, Tel Aviv: Resling, 2006 (in Hebrew), 97–109. This book is a treasure trove of information about Zionist and Israeli scientists' views on race and heredity, despite some conceptual weakness, especially in the summary. Regarding British and German scientists who searched eagerly for a Jewish race, see also John M. Efron, *Defenders of the Race: Jewish Doctors and Race Science in Fin-de-Siècle Europe*, New Haven: Yale University Press, 1994.

22   Quoted in Falk, *Zionism and the Biology of the Jews*, 147.

During the violent Arab uprising in 1929, Dr. Yaacov Zess, another physician, published an essay entitled "The Hygiene of the Body and the Spirit," in which he emphasized that "we, more than other nations, need racial hygiene." Dr. Yosef Meir, head of the Labor Federation's Sick Fund, who would later become the first director-general of the Israeli ministry of health, agreed with Zess, and stated in the 1934 guide to members of the fund, "For us, eugenics in general, and preventing the transmission of hereditary diseases in particular, is of even greater value than for other nations!"[23]

The greatest of them all was the well-known physician and biologist Redcliffe Nathan Salaman. This British Zionist, who contributed a great deal to the Faculty of Life Sciences at the Hebrew University in Jerusalem and was a member of its board of trustees, was also the first to try to transpose assumptions from physical anthropology to genetics, which was then a young science with a brilliant future. An article of his entitled "The Heredity of the Jews" appeared in the first issue of the pioneering *Journal of Genetics* in 1911. Thereafter, Salaman insisted that even if the Jews were not a pure race, it posed no problem—they were still a solid biological entity. Aside from the fact that the Jew was identifiable by the shape of his skull, his features and his bodily measurements, there was also a Jewish allele that was responsible for this distinctive physical appearance.[24] There were of course differences between the fair Ashkenazi and the swarthy Sephardi, but the reasons for them were straightforward: the latter had mixed more with their neighbors. The noticeable Ashkenazi fairness sprang from the ancient Philistines, who were absorbed by the Jewish nation in antiquity. Long-skulled European invaders became part of the Hebrew people, hence their whitish appearance. The reason the Yemenite Jews were of smaller stature and submissive character was that "they are not Jews. They are black, with an elongated skull, Arab half-castes ... The true Jew is the European Ashkenazi, and I support him against all the others."[25]

Salaman was more of a eugenicist than a geneticist; to him, Zionism was a eugenic project designed to improve the Jewish race. The young people in Palestine seemed to him bigger and stronger: "Some force has acted on them to produce anew the Philistine type in Philistia." The mysterious force was the natural selection that reinvigorated the Philistine genes in the genetic stock of the Jews. A similar process was taking place in Britain, where the Anglo-Jews,

23   Ibid., 150.
24   Ibid., 106–9. An allele is one of several alternative versions of a gene that is responsible for hereditary variation.
25   Ibid., 129.

especially those who donated money to the Zionist enterprise, were acquiring an unmistakable Hittite expression.[26]

Were it not for the tragic consequences of twentieth-century eugenics, and had Salaman been a marginal figure in the early days of Jewish science in the land of Israel, this text would merely make us smile. But eugenics contributed to grave ideological perversions, and as we shall see, Salaman had too many successors in the departments of life sciences in the State of the Jewish people.

The broad Israeli historiography contains a good deal of apologetics excusing the presence of "biology" in the Zionist discourse, noting that this was a common fashion at the end of the nineteenth and first half of the twentieth century. True, many scientific publications, as much as daily newspapers and popular weeklies, carried articles that confounded heredity and culture, blood and national identity. The term "race" was frequently used by anti-Semites, but it was also used by the respectable press and in liberal and socialist circles. The Zionist thinkers and promoters who discussed theories of blood and race, the argument goes, did not really take them seriously, and certainly they could not have anticipated the horrific developments that these ideas would help bring about. But this contextual historical argument, though convenient, is far from accurate.

It is true that borrowing from biology to describe historical developments was a widespread practice before the Second World War, but it must not be forgotten that the physical anthropology that classified races, and the science of blood that complemented it, was contested by scholars. The simplistic transposition of natural laws into human society and culture rang a warning bell among thinkers and scientists in various disciplines. Some of the critics even challenged directly the idea of a Jewish race, the very idea that anti-Semites and Zionists were beginning to acclaim. Two prominent illustrations, taken from two ends of the ideological spectrum of the late nineteenth and early twentieth centuries, can illustrate the argument.

In 1883 the well-known French scholar Ernest Renan was invited to address the Saint-Simon circle in Paris, which had a good number of French Israelites as members. In the 1850s and 1860s, Renan's early philological writings had contributed to the consolidation of Orientalism and "scientific" racialism throughout Europe. Racists of all sorts derived much encouragement from his classification of the Aryan and Semitic languages, which he padded with a fair amount of prejudice. Yet apparently the rise of racist anti-Semitism in the early 1880s worried him, leading him to entitle a lecture "Judaism as Race and as Religion."[27]

---

26   Ibid., 180.
27   Ernest Renan, *Le Judaïsme comme race et religion*, Paris: Calmann Lévy, 1883. This lecture continued the tendency expressed in his lecture the previous year, in which Renan

Renan's rhetoric was still replete with such terms as "race" and even "blood," but his historical erudition resisted the dominant verbal conventions. By dint of a short, sharp empirical analysis, he joined the outlook of the German historian Theodor Mommsen and attacked the popular views ascribing to the Jews qualities of an ancient, closed race of uniform origin.

Christianity, Renan stated, was not the first religion that called on all humanity to believe in a single deity; it was Judaism that began the great campaign of religious conversion. To demonstrate his thesis, he began by surveying the wave of Judaization during the Hellenistic and Roman period, until Cassius Dio's famous assertion in the third century CE that the term "Jew" no longer applied to people of Judean descent (see Chapter 3, above). The Jews used to convert their slaves, and their synagogues were effective venues that attracted their neighbors to join them. The masses of Jewish believers in Italy, Gaul and elsewhere were mostly local people who had converted to Judaism.[28] Renan went on to talk about the Adiabene kingdom, the Falashas, and the vast conversion under the Khazars.

In conclusion, Renan repeated, there is no Jewish race, nor one typical Jewish appearance. At most, self-isolation, endogenous marriage and the long periods in the ghettoes had produced certain Jewish types. The Jews' secluded social life had affected their behavior and even their physiognomy. Heredity and blood had nothing to do with it. This social existence and even the typical occupations had not been freely chosen by the Jews, but imposed on them in the Middle Ages. In many ways the Jews of France did not differ from the Protestants. The Jews, mainly Gauls who had been Judaized in antiquity and become an oppressed religious minority, were liberated by the French Revolution, which ended the ghettoes. Thereafter, the Jews were part and parcel of the national culture of France, and the question of race had no significance whatsoever.

This contribution by the leading French intellectual of his day, the Jean-Paul Sartre of the period, undoubtedly lent significant support to the liberal-democratic camp, which would ultimately roll back the ethnocentric and anti-Semitic nationalist wave of the Dreyfus Affair. A similar role, in another political, national and cultural arena, was played by Karl Kautsky.

This "pope" of the Marxism of the Second International, a methodical thinker of Czech origin, succeeded Marx and Engels at the head of Europe's socialist camp at the end of the nineteenth and beginning of the twentieth

---

sought to define the nation on a voluntarist basis (see the Chapter 1). The lecture on Judaism was translated into English and published by the American Jewish Committee as a response to German racism in *Contemporary Jewish Record* 6: 4 (1943), 436–48.

28 Ibid., 444.

century. Though there were anti-Semitic elements in the organized workers' parties, the movement itself opposed racism, and Kautsky was one of its leading guides in the labyrinth of ideological modernization. In 1914, on the eve of the war, he set out to tackle one of the most pressing questions on the German cultural scene. His book *Judaism and Race*—which appeared in English in 1926 under the title *Are the Jews a Race?*—sought to clarify the issue, which was becoming toxic and troubling.[29]

Unlike Marx, Kautsky was free of prejudice concerning Jews and Judaism, but he followed the great German thinker in his materialist view of history. Hence, though he accepted the Darwinist theories of evolution, he refused to apply them to the human sphere. All living beings adapt themselves to their environment in order to survive, he contended, but humanity also adapts its environment to suit its needs. Thus human labor creates a different kind of evolution, in which man's consciousness changes as he works—in other words, in the process of altering his environment.

As Kautsky saw it, many of the scientific theories in the capitalist era were used to justify the ruling classes' domination and exploitation of society. The new ideas about the human races went hand in hand with colonialist expansion, and were promoted mainly to legitimize the brutal might of the great powers: Why complain if nature, rather than social history, created masters and slaves? In Germany the racist ideology was also applied to the power relations in Europe: the descendants of the blond Teutons were gifted, while the Latins, heirs of the dark Celts who rose up in the French Revolution, lacked productive strength. These two races were locked in permanent struggle. But the worst and most dangerous race, according to the new racist scientists, were the Jews, a strange and alien element.

Jews were easily distinguished by their appearance: the shape of the skull, the nose, the hair, the eyes. All these were distinctive features of the dangerous wandering race. But Kautsky argued that significant statistics showed that there were variations in these physical features, which made it impossible to use them to identify supporters of the Mosaic religion. For example, Jews from the Caucasus were short-skulled (brachycephalic), and the Jews of North Africa and the Arab countries were long-skulled (dolichocephalic), while among European Jews the shape was average and varied. The Jews resembled in appearance the populations among whom they lived, far more than they

---

29   Karl Kautsky, *Are the Jews a Race?*, New York: Jonathan Cape, 1926. The quotes are taken from an online version available at www.marxists.org, where the entire text can be found. It is noteworthy that while several of Kautsky's works have been translated into Hebrew, this one has not.

resembled their coreligionists elsewhere. The same might be said of their physical conduct, their gestures and their mental qualities.

If certain Jewish communities had distinctive qualities, they were due to history, not biology. The economic functions to which they were diverted gave rise to a specific subculture and concomitant linguistic markers. But modernization was slowly eroding the traditional Jewish separation and was integrating Jewish believers into the new national cultures. Thus, if the arguments of anti-Semitism were scientifically worthless, so, too, were those of the Zionist ideology that complemented them with similar reasoning. Kautsky had witnessed the suffering of the Jews of Eastern Europe, especially the persecutions instigated by the Tsarist regime, but as a socialist he could propose only one solution to the problem of anti-Semitism— the struggle for a new and egalitarian world, in which national problems would be resolved and the issue of race would disappear from the political agenda.

In his lecture against the concept of a Jewish race, Kautsky referred, inter alia, to two anthropologists, both of them Americans of Jewish background, who contested both the popular biological interpretation of human history and the racialization of the Jews. Both Franz Boas, often described as the father of American anthropology, and Maurice Fishberg, who was also a demographer, published important books in 1911. Boas's book, *The Mind of Primitive Man*, sought to demolish the speculative connections between racial origin and culture, and Fishberg's *The Jews: A Study of Race and Environment* used an empirical approach to show that the physical form and the origin of the Jews were not uniform on any level.[30] Boas's decisive influence on freeing American anthropology from nineteenth-century biological Darwinism has been much written about. No wonder that in Germany, in 1933, excited Nazi students burned copies of the German edition of his book.[31]

Fishberg's book received less notice, but it helped discredit the views of anti-Jewish racists. His research was based on a morphological examination of three thousand immigrants in New York, accompanied by original observations that drew attention to the broad range of characteristics, linked to the history of the Jews. His comprehensive work ended with the conclusion that there was no basis for assuming an ethnic unity among modern Jews, nor a Jewish race, any more than one could speak of the ethnic unity of Christians or Muslims, or of a Unitarian, Presbyterian or Methodist race.

---

30   Franz Boas, *The Mind of Primitive Man*, New York: The Free Press, 1965. First published in 1911, it is considered a classic. See also Maurice Fishberg, *The Jews: A Study of Race and Environment*, Whitefish: Kessinger Publishing, 2007.

31   On Boas's theories, see Vernon Williams Jr., *Rethinking Race: Franz Boas and His Contemporaries*, Lexington: University Press of Kentucky, 1996.

THE SCIENTIFIC PUPPET AND THE RACIST HUNCHBACK

Fishberg's book was never translated into Hebrew, nor did three other books that continued his scientific legacy attract any attention in Israel: Harry L. Shapiro's antiracist *The Jewish People: A Biological History*, published in 1960; *The Myth of the Jewish Race*, a massive tome by Raphael Patai and his daughter Jennifer Patai; and *The Myth of the Jewish Race: A Biologist's Point of View*, by Alain Corcos. None of them was translated into Hebrew, and their theses were never discussed in Israeli arenas of culture and research.[32] It would seem that the "scientific" structure that Ruppin and Salaman installed in Jerusalem in the 1930s and 1940s effectively blocked the importation into Israel of anthropological and genetic literature that cast doubt on the very existence of a Jewish race-nation, and might have impeded the ideological production line of the Zionist enterprise.

After the Second World War, of course, the use of the terms "race" and "blood" became awkward. In 1950, a much-publicized declaration by a number of senior scientists, under the aegis of UNESCO, completely rejected any connection between biology and national cultures, stating that the concept of race was a social myth rather than a scientific fact, after which serious researchers avoided the term.[33] But this general acceptance did not deter the workers in the life sciences in Israel, nor did it undermine the profound Zionist belief in the common origin of the wandering people. "The Jewish race" disappeared from the vocabulary of conventional research, but it was replaced by a scientific field with a respectable title: "the study of the origin of the Jewish communities." Popular journalism dubbed it simply "the search for the Jewish gene."

The State of Israel, which had begun to import people from the Jewish communities of Europe and later imported many Jews from the Muslim world, was now confronted with the urgency of creating a new nation. As noted in previous chapters, the principal function in this cultural production was undertaken by the Hebrew intellectuals who had immigrated to Mandatory Palestine and whose early educational endeavor preceded the establishment of the State. The "organic history of the Jewish people," stretching from the Bible to the Palmah (a combat force of the pre-State Jewish community), was taught throughout the State educational system.

---

32   Respectively, Harry L. Shapiro, *The Jewish People: A Biological History*, Paris: UNESCO, 1960; Raphael Patai and Jennifer Patai, *The Myth of the Jewish Race*, Detroit: Wayne State University Press, 1989; and Alain F. Corcos, *The Myth of the Jewish Race: A Biologist's Point of View*, Bethlehem: Lehigh University Press, 2005.

33   *The Race Concept: Results of an Inquiry*, Paris: UNESCO, 1952.

Zionist pedagogy produced generations of students who believed whole-heartedly in the ethnic uniqueness of their nation. But in the age of scientific positivism, nationalist ideology needed more substantial reification than the "soft" materials produced in the humanities. The biological laboratories were called upon to provide it, and at first they did so in fairly subdued manner.

Nurit Kirsh, who in recent years completed her doctoral dissertation at Tel Aviv University, has investigated the early stages of genetics research in Israel.[34] Her conclusion is unambiguous: genetics, just like archaeology at the time, was a tendentious science subordinated to the national historical concept, which sought at all costs to discover a biological homogeneity among the Jews in the world. The geneticists internalized the Zionist myth and, consciously or not, attempted to adapt their findings to it. As she sees it, the main difference between the Zionist anthropologists in the pre-State period and the new scientists in Israel was that genetics became less prominent in the public arena in Israel. Research findings that, despite their ideological bias, were published in international scientific journals were hardly noticed in the Hebrew-language media. This meant that their pedagogical function in the general education system was marginal.

It is possible that in the 1950s and early 1960s the new and hesitant Israeli genetics served only the professional elite. But the attempt to detect a Jewish particularity in fingerprints, for example, or the search for diseases that only Jews were subject to, did not succeed. It transpired that Jews did not have fingerprints specific to ancient deicides, and that diseases found among Eastern European Jews (e.g., Tay-Sachs) did not resemble diseases found among Iraqi or Yemenite Jews (e.g., favism). But the valuable biomedical and genetic information accumulated in Israeli laboratories would later achieve a more respectable status.

In 1978 Oxford University Press published *The Genetics of the Jews*, by a team of researchers headed by Arthur E. Mourant.[35] This British scholar was influenced by a much-loved mentor who belonged to a sect that believed the British people were descendants of the "Ten Lost Tribes," hence his interest in the Jews. For much of his life, the enthusiastic Mourant believed that he and all

---

34 Nurit Kirsh, *The Teaching and Research of Genetics at the Hebrew University (1935–1961)*, unpublished, Tel Aviv University, 2003 (in Hebrew); also, see her article "Population Genetics in Israel in the 1950s: The Unconscious Internalization of Ideology," *ISIS, Journal of the History of Science* 94 (2003), 631–55.

35 Arthur E. Mourant et al., *The Genetics of the Jews*, Oxford: Oxford University Press, 1978.

274 THE INVENTION OF THE JEWISH PEOPLE

the people around him were authentic Jews. When the British forces captured Palestine, he was convinced that this signaled the beginning of salvation. Years later, he set out to discover the common biological origin of the "real" Jews, and adapted his genetic anthropology to the biblical story. As the Israeli geneticist Raphael Falk described it, the British scientist "first fired his arrows, then drew the target around them."[36] To Mourant and his colleagues, the marked differences between Ashkenazi and Sephardic Jews notwithstanding, they all had to have a single common origin. By examining the frequency of *A* and *B* alleles in separate communities, he strove to show that the genes of Jews from different regions displayed a higher degree of uniformity than could be found when those same subjects' genes were compared to those of their non-Jewish neighbors. But if the genetic findings did not exactly support the ideological purpose, it would be necessary to search for other results.

Although Mourant's theory was weak and unfounded—the application of genetics to such diffuse categories as "Ashkenazi" and "Sephardic" was senseless, as they represent varieties of religious rituals—it legitimized and invigorated the search for the Jewish gene in the life sciences at Israeli universities. The passage of time since the Second World War removed the remaining inhibitions. Israel's rule since 1967 over a growing non-Jewish population intensified the urge to find an enclosing ethnobiological boundary. In 1980 an article by Bat Sheva Bonné-Tamir of Tel Aviv University's School of Medicine, entitled "A New Look at the Genetics of the Jews," appeared in the Israeli science monthly *Mada* ("Science"). The writer proudly described the originality of the fresh search for the Jewish genes, and opened the article with the statement "In the 1970s many new studies were published in the field of the genetic anthropology of the Jews, studies dealing with such subjects as 'What is the origin of the Jewish people?' and 'Is there a Jewish race?' "[37]

Before the 1970s, she asserted, the studies were biased because of the antiracist motivations that lay behind them; they set out to emphasize the genetic differences between Jewish communities. The new studies, however, based on tremendous developments in the field, highlighted the basic genetic similarities among the various communities, and the small proportion of "alien" genes in the genetic stock characteristic of Jews: "One of the prominent findings shows the genetic kinship between the Jews of North Africa, Iraq and

36 Falk, *Zionism and the Biology of the Jews*, 175.
37 Bat Sheva Bonne-Tamir, "A New Look at the Genetics of the Jews," *Mada* 44: 4–5, 1980 (in Hebrew), 181–6. See also her much more cautious article, Bonne-Tamir et al., "Analysis of Genetic Data on Jewish Populations. I. Historical Background, Demographic Features, Genetic Markers," *American Journal of Human Genetics* 31: 3 (1979), 324–40.

the Ashkenazis. In most cases they form a single block, whereas the non-Jews (Arabs, Armenians, Samaritans and Europeans) were significantly remote from them."[38] The scientist hastened to point out that she had not set out to isolate a Jewish race—on the contrary, she had intended to use blood groups to reveal the heterogeneity of Jewish characteristics—but was quite astonished by the new findings. These corroborated the literature about the dispersal and wanderings of the Jews from ancient times to the present. At last, biology confirmed history.

The Zionist idea of the Jewish nation-race materialized as a solid life science, and a new discipline was born: "Jewish genetics." What could be more convincing than publication in respected journals in the Anglo-Saxon world? The gates of Western canonical science—mainly in the United States—opened to the industrious Israeli researchers, who regularly blended historical mythologies and sociological assumptions with dubious and scanty genetic findings. Despite the limited resources available in Israel for academic research, it became a world leader in the "investigation of the origins of populations." In 1981 Israel hosted the sixth international conference on human heredity, with Professor Bonne-Tamir acting as its secretary. From that time on, Israeli researchers received generous funds from government and private foundations, and the scientific results soon followed. Over the next twenty years, interest in Jewish genetics spread to the Hebrew University in Jerusalem, the Weizmann Institute in Rehovot, and the Technion in Haifa. No less significant was that, in contrast to the cautious 1950s, the findings were now trumpeted in the public arena. Toward the end of the twentieth century, the average Israeli knew that he or she belonged to a definite genetic group of fairly homogeneous ancient origin.

In November 2000 the Israeli daily *Haaretz* published an illuminating report about the research of Professor Ariela Oppenheim and her colleagues at the Hebrew University in Jerusalem. The actual findings were published that month in *Human Genetics*, a scientific periodical published by Springer Verlag in Germany.[39] The reason for the media interest was the discovery made by the team of a remarkable closeness between certain mutations in the Y-chromosome of Jews, both "Ashkenazi" and "Sephardic," and those of the "Israeli Arabs" and the

---

38   Bonne-Tamir, "A new look at the genetics of the Jews," 185.
39   Tamara Traubman, "The Jews and the Palestinians in Israel and the Territories Have Common Ancestors," *Haaretz*, November 12, 2000; and A. Oppenheim et al., "High-Resolution Y Chromosome Haplotypes of Israeli and Palestinian Arabs Reveal Geographic Substructure and Substantial Overlap with Haplotypes of Jews," *Human Genetics* 107 (2000), 630–41.

Palestinians. The conclusion reached was that two-thirds of the Palestinians and roughly the same proportion of Jews shared three male ancestors eight thousand years ago. In actual fact, the expanded scientific paper showed a somewhat more complex, and much more confusing, picture: those mutations in the Y-chromosome also indicated that the "Jews" resembled the "Lebanese Arabs" more than the Czechs, but the "Ashkenazis," as opposed to the "Sephardics," were relatively closer to the "Welsh" than to the "Arabs."

The study had been written and edited during the period of the Oslo Accords, before the outbreak of the Second Intifada. Unfortunately, by the time it appeared in print the uprising had already broken out. The genetic data showing that Jews and Palestinians had some ancient ancestors in common did not cause the conflict to be described as an internecine war, but it did indirectly reinforce the assumption, which had struck root some time earlier, that the origin of all the Jews lay unquestionably in the Near East.

The rigor of those investigating Jewish DNA in Israel was demonstrated by the sequel to the team's biological adventure. A little over a year after the first important discovery, the inside pages of *Haaretz* carried a sensational new scoop. It transpired that the genetic resemblance between the Jews and the Palestinians, discovered by the previous research, did not exist. The scientists admitted that their earlier experiment had not been sufficiently grounded and detailed, and that its conclusions had been hasty. In fact, the Jews—or, at any rate, the male ones—were related not to the neighboring Palestinians but rather to the distant Kurds. The new paper, published first by the *American Society of Human Genetics*, showed that the sly Y-chromosome had fooled its inexperienced investigators.[40] But never fear, the updated genetic picture still indicated that the Ashkenazi and Sephardic Jews were related, only now they did not resemble the local Arabs, but rather the Armenians, Turks, and chiefly, as noted, the Kurds. Needless to say, it is not suggested that the raging intifada had indirectly advanced the science of genetics in Israel, yet from then on the blood brothers were once more apart and alien.

The scientific correspondent of *Haaretz*, who was positive that the Jews were the descendants of the ancient Hebrews, at once approached historians of antiquity to explain this disturbing discovery of a strange origin. Several respected professors were unable to help—they had no information about an

---

40   Tamara Traubman, "A Great Genetic Resemblance Between the Jews and the Kurds," *Haaretz*, December 21, 2001; and Oppenheim et al., "The Y Chromosome Pool of Jews as Part of the Genetic Landscape of the Middle East," *American Society of Human Genetics* 69 (2001), 1,095–112. It should be noted that mutations on the Y-chromosome can point to a single patrilineal inheritance, not the entire descent on the father's side.

ancient migration from the northern Fertile Crescent to the area of Canaan (the patriarch Abraham famously "made aliyah" from southern Iraq). Was it possible that the finding corroborated the thesis that the Jews descended from the Khazars, rather than from the seed of the venerable Abraham? Speaking by telephone from Stanford University in the United States, the respected scientist Professor Marc Feldman assured the correspondent that there was no need to reach such an extreme conclusion—the particular mutation in the Y chromosome of the Kurds, Armenians and Jews was also found in other peoples in the region of the Fertile Crescent, not necessarily in the Khazars, people forgotten by God and history.

Barely a year later, *Haaretz* came up with a new report. It was now quite certain that the Jewish males originated in the Near East, but with respect to Jewish women the investigation had run into an awkward difficulty.[41] A new scientific study that investigated the mitochondrial DNA (which is inherited only from the mother) in nine Jewish communities discovered that the origin of the supposedly kosher Jewish women did not lie in the Near East at all. This worrisome finding showed that "each community had a small number of founding mothers," but they were not interconnected at all. The uncomfortable explanation was that Jewish men had come from the Near East unattached and were forced to take local wives, whom they undoubtedly converted to Judaism in the proper manner.

This last dubious revelation worried those rooting for the Jewish gene, and a doctoral dissertation apparently began to be written at the Haifa Technion, concluding that in spite of the ancient mothers' scandalous disrespect for Jewish uniqueness, some 40 percent of all the Ashkenazis in the world descend from four matriarchs (as in the Bible). *Haaretz*, as always, reported the discovery faithfully and extensively. *Maariv*, a more popular daily, added that those ancient grandmothers "were born about 1,500 years ago in Eretz Israel, from whence their families migrated to Italy, later to the Rhine and the Champagne regions."[42]

A summary of this reassuring dissertation by Doron Behar about "Ashkenazi mitochondrial DNA" was published in the *American Journal of Human Genetics*.[43] Its supervisor was Karl Skorecki, a veteran researcher in Jewish genetics. This Orthodox professor, who came to the Technion's medical

---

41   Tamara Traubman, "The Ancient Jewish Males Have Origins in the Middle East: The Origin of the Females Is Still a Mystery," *Haaretz*, 16 May 2002.

42   Tamara Traubman, "40% of the Ashkenazis Descend rrom Four Mothers," *Haaretz*, January 14, 2006; Alex Doron, "40% of the Ashkenazis: Descendants of Four Mothers from the 6th Century," *Maariv*, January 3, 2006.

43   Doron M. Behar et al., "The Matrilineal Ancestry of Ashkenazi Jewry: Portrait of a Recent Founder Event," *American Journal of Human Genetics* 78 (2006), 487–97.

school from the University of Toronto, had earlier attracted attention when he discovered the amazing "seal of priesthood." Skorecki himself is of course also a *cohen*, and an incident at his synagogue in Canada in the 1990s prompted him to investigate his "aristocratic" origin. Fortunately, he was invited by Rabbi Yaacov Kleiman, who as well as being a *cohen* himself, was also the director of the Center of Cohanim in Jerusalem, to investigate the origin of all those named Cohen in our time.[44] The Center of Cohanim is an institution that is preparing for the construction of the Third Temple in Jerusalem. For this purpose, it trains the future priests who would serve in the temple when the Al-Aqsa mosque is demolished and the Jewish temple rises in its place. The center must have been well endowed financially to be able to fund the wished-for research.

This story might seem esoteric and fantastic, but given the "ethnic" realities of the late twentieth century, it grew into a "solid" science that attracted unusual attention and created a large following in Israel and the Jewish world. The *cohanim*—the ancient blood-aristocracy descended from Aaron, the brother of Moses—became unexpectedly popular in the age of molecular genetics. Sections of the genome called haplotypes (defined as a group of alleles of different genes on a single chromosome that are linked closely enough to be inherited, usually as a unit) were supposedly found to be distinctive among more than 50 percent of the men surnamed Cohen. Scientists from Britain, Italy and Israel participated in Skorecki's investigation, and its findings were published in the prestigious British journal *Nature*.[45] It proved beyond question that the Jewish priesthood was indeed founded by a common ancestor thirty-three centuries ago. The Israeli press hastened to publish the discovery, to great genetic joy.

The amusing aspect of this story is that the "priestly gene" could just as easily be a "non-Jewish gene." Judaism is inherited from the mother, so it would not be far-fetched to assume that since the nineteenth century a good many non-believing *cohanim* have married "gentile" women, although the Halakhah forbids them to do so. These men may well have fathered "non-Jewish" offspring, who, according to Skorecki's research, would bear the "genetic seal" of the *cohanim*. But Jewish scientists are not expected to consider minor details, especially as God is no longer involved—in this era of enlightened rationalism, pure Jewish science has replaced the ancient Jewish faith, with its burden of prejudices.

44   The rabbi's book begins with the crucial event at the Canadian synagogue that led Professor Skorecki to take an interest in the genetics of the *cohanim*. Yaakov Kleiman, *DNA and Tradition: The Genetic Link to the Ancient Hebrew*, Jerusalem, New York: Devora Publishing, 2004, 17. Skorecki himself wrote the introduction and dubbed the book "masterful."

45   K. Skorecki et al., "Y-Chromosomes of Jewish Priests," *Nature* 385 (1997).

While the media celebrated the discovery and overlooked the potential contradiction in the thesis of the Jewish priestly gene, nobody asked why a costly biological investigation was devoted to the search for a hereditary religious caste. Similarly, no newspaper bothered to publish the findings of Professor Uzi Ritte, of the Department of Genetics at the Hebrew University in Jerusalem, who had examined those same priestly haplotypes on the Y-chromosome and found nothing distinctive about them.[46]

Once again, the public's veneration of the "hard" sciences paid off. Laymen have no reason to doubt the truth of information derived from what is perceived to be a precise science. Like the field of physical anthropology in the late nineteenth and early twentieth centuries, which released dubious scientific discoveries to the race-hungry public, the science of molecular genetics at the end of the twentieth and beginning of the twenty-first century feeds fragmentary findings and half-truths to the identity-seeking media. Yet so far, no research had found unique and unifying characteristics of Jewish heredity based on a random sampling of genetic material whose ethnic origin is not known in advance. By and large, what little is known about the methods of selecting test subjects seems very questionable. Moreover, the hasty findings are all too often constructed and supported by historical rhetoric unconnected to the research laboratories. The bottom line is that, after all the costly "scientific" endeavors, a Jewish individual cannot be defined by any biological criteria whatsoever.

This is not to preclude the potential contribution of genetic anthropology in uncovering important aspects of human history, and importantly in the fight against disease. Most probably, the investigation of DNA, a relatively young science, has a brilliant future. But in a state in which the law prevents marriage between a "Jew" and a "non-Jew," we should be very wary about research that seeks genetic markers common to the "chosen people." Like similar investigations carried out by Macedonian racists, Lebanese Phalangists, Lapps in northern Scandinavia, and so on,[47] such Jewish-Israeli research cannot be entirely free from crude and dangerous racism.

---

46 Falk, *Zionism and the Biology of the Jews*, 189. On the methods used by various scientists, see the article by John P. A. Ioannidis, "Why Most Published Research Findings Are False," *PLos Med* 2(8) (2005): e124.

47 On the Macedonian genes, see for example Antonio Arnaiz-Villena et al., "HLA Genes in Macedonians and the Sub-Saharan Origins of the Greeks," *Tissue Antigens* 57: 2 (2001), 118–27. On the "Case of the Jews," see the instructive article by Katya Gibel Azoulay, "Not an Innocent Pursuit: The politics of a 'Jewish' Genetic Signature," *Developing World Bioethics* 3: 2 (2003), 119–26; and also Avshalom Zoossmann-Diskin et al., "Protein Electrophoretic Markers in Israel: Compilation of Data and Genetic Affinities," *Annals of Human Biology* 29: 2 (2002), 142–75.

In 1940 the philosopher Walter Benjamin told a story about a famous chess-playing automaton (known as the Turk) that used to astonish audiences with its clever moves. Underneath the table hid a hunchbacked dwarf who actually played the game. In Benjamin's analogy, the automaton represented materialistic thinking, and the hidden dwarf theology—meaning that in the age of modern rationalism, religious faith had to stay hidden.[48]

This image may be applied to the culture of biological science in Israel, and the public arena that it periodically furnishes with novelties: the genetic robot appears to be making the moves on the chessboard, while the little hunchback—the traditional idea of race—is obliged to hide because of the politically correct world discourse, yet continues to dupe and conduct the thrilling chromosome show.

In a state that defines itself as Jewish yet does not present distinguishing cultural markers that might define a worldwide secular Jewish existence—except for some depleted, secularized remnants of religious folklore—the collective identity needs a misty, promising image of an ancient biological common origin. Behind every act in Israel's identity politics stretches, like a long black shadow, the idea of an eternal people and race.

FOUNDING AN *ETHNOS* STATE

In 1947 the UN General Assembly resolved by a majority vote to establish a "Jewish state" and an "Arab state" in the territory that had previously been known as "Palestine/Eretz Israel."[49] At that time, many thousands of displaced Jewish persons were wandering in Europe, and the small community that had been created by the Zionist settlement enterprise was supposed to take them in. The United States, which before 1924 had taken in many of the Yiddish Jews, now refused to open its gates to the broken remnants of the great Nazi massacre. So did the other rich countries. In the end, it was easier for these countries to solve the troublesome Jewish problem by offering a faraway land that was not theirs.

The governments that voted for the resolution did not concern themselves with the precise meaning of the term "Jew," and did not imagine what it would come to mean as the new state consolidated. At the time, the Zionist elite—which had aspired and struggled to achieve a Jewish sovereignty—would have been unable to define clearly who was a Jew and who a gentile. Physical

---

48   Walter Benjamin, "On the Concept of History," in *Selected Writings*, vol. 4, Cambridge, MA: The Belknap Press of Harvard University Press, 2003, p. 389.

49   See the declaration available at www.knesset.gov.il.

anthropology and, later, imported molecular genetics also failed to come up with a scientific yardstick by which to determine the origin of an individual Jew. Let us not forget that the Nazis themselves—despite their biological race doctrine, the jewel in their ideological crown—had been unable to do this, and so they ended up having to categorize Jews on the basis of bureaucratic documentation.

The first important mission to be undertaken by the new state was the removal, as best it could, of those who definitely did not regard themselves as Jews. The Arab states' stubborn refusal to accept the UN's partition resolution of 1947, and their joint assault on the young Jewish state, actually helped it to consolidate. Of the approximately 900,000 Palestinians who should have remained in Israel and the additional territories it had seized in its military victory, some 730,000 fled or were expelled—more than the total number of Jews in the country at that time (630,000).[50] More significant for the country's future was the ideological principle that it was the historical patrimony of the "Jewish people," so that the state could without compunction refuse to allow the hundreds of thousands of refugees to return to their homes and fields when the fighting was over.

This partial cleansing did not entirely solve the identity problems in the new state. About 170,000 Arabs remained within its boundaries, and many of the displaced people who arrived from Europe brought their non-Jewish spouses. The 1947 UN resolution had clearly stated that the minorities remaining in both of the new states should have civil rights, and made this a condition of admitting them to the organization. Israel therefore had to grant citizenship to the Palestinians who remained. It expropriated more than half their land, and kept them under military government and harsh restrictions until 1966, but legally they were Israeli citizens.[51]

The Proclamation of Independence, the State of Israel's founding charter, reflected this ambivalence. On the one hand, it met the UN requirements regarding the state's democratic character—it promised "complete equality of social and political rights to all its inhabitants irrespective of religion, race or sex; [and] freedom of religion, conscience, language, education and culture." On the other hand, it would embody the Zionist vision of its founders—

50   On the origin of the Palestinian refugee problem, see Benny Morris, *The Birth of the Palestinian Refugee Problem Revisited*, Cambridge: Cambridge University Press, 2003; Ilan Pappe, *The Ethnic Cleansing of Palestine*, Oxford: Oneworld Publications, 2007; see also Dominique Vidal, *Comment Israël expulsa les Palestiniens (1947–1949)*, Paris: L'Atelier, 2007.

51   On the politics of land expropriation in Israel, see the impressive book of Oren Yiftachel, *Ethnocracy: Land and Identity Politics in Israel/Palestine*, Philadelphia: University of Pennsylvania Press, 2006.

to implement "the right of the Jewish people to national rebirth in its own country" through "the establishment of a Jewish state in Eretz-Israel." How was this ambivalent? The following pages will try to answer this question.

Every large human group that thinks of itself as a people, even if it never was one and its past is entirely imaginary, has the right to national self-determination. Indeed, struggles for political independence have created more nations than nations have fought national struggles. It is well known that any attempt to deny a human group its self-determination only intensifies its demand for sovereignty and enhances its collective identity. This does not, of course, give a particular group that sees itself as a people the right to dispossess another group of its land in order to achieve its self-determination. But that is precisely what happened in Mandatory Palestine in the first half of the twentieth century (in 1880 there were in Palestine 25,000 Jews and 300,000 Arabs, and in 1947 there were still just 650,000 Jews and 1.3 million Palestinians). Nevertheless, the project of Zionist settlement that took in the persecuted and excluded Jews and that then became independent Israel could have devised its constitutional foundations so that in time they would become genuinely democratic. This would have meant applying the principle of equality to all its citizens, rather than to its Jews alone.

In the first chapter of this book I argued that not only is there no inherent contradiction between nationalism and democracy, but that in fact they complement each other. So far, there has been no modern democracy—that is, a state of which the sovereign is the citizenry—without there being some national or multinational framework that contains and expresses this sovereignty. The strength of the national identity derives from the consciousness that all the state's citizens are equal. It would not be wrong to say that the terms "democracy" and "national identity" usually overlap, encompassing the same historical process.

The choice of the new state's name, and the ensuing debate around it, offer a glimpse into the camera obscura of Jewish rebirth. The ancient kingdom of Israel under the Omride dynasty did not, in the religious tradition, have a good reputation, and so there was some searching of the heart in regard to calling the state "Israel." There were also supporters for "State of Judea," to be a direct successor to the House of David and the Hasmonean kingdom, and for "State of Zion," in honor of the movement that conceived it. But if the state were named "Judea," then all its citizens would be called Judeans, meaning Jews, and if it were named "Zion," its citizens would be called Zionists. The former would have infringed on the identity of Jewish believers throughout the world, and the Arab citizens would have become Jewish citizens with full civil rights (as

Ber Borochov and the young Ben-Gurion had hoped long before). In the latter case, the world Zionist movement would probably have had to disband after independence, and the Arab citizens would have been classified as Zionists.

There was no choice but to call the new state "Israel." Ever since then, all its citizens, Jews and non-Jews alike, have been called Israelis. As we shall see, the state would not be content with the Jewish hegemony expressed by the name "Israel," by its flag, its anthem and its state emblems. Because of its ethnocentric nationalist character, it would refuse to belong, formally and effectively, to all its citizens. It had been created expressly for the "Jewish people," and although a major part of this *ethnos* has failed to implement its right to self-determination within its borders, the state has always insisted that it belongs to this *ethnos*.

What is the Jewish *ethnos*? We have surveyed Jewry's possible historical origins and, beginning in the second half of the nineteenth century, the essentialist construction of a "people" out of the vestiges and memories of this variegated Jewry. But who would be included among the authorized proprietors of the Jewish state that was being "reestablished" after two thousand years in "Israel's exclusive land"? Would it be anyone who saw himself or herself as a Jew? Or any person who became an Israeli citizen? This complex issue would become one of the main pivots on which identity politics in Israel would revolve.

To understand this development, we must go back to the eve of the Proclamation of Independence. In 1947 it had already been decided that Jews would not be able to marry non-Jews in the new state. The official reason for this civil segregation—in a society that was predominantly secular—was the unwillingness to create a secular-religious split. In the famous "status quo" letter that David Ben-Gurion, as head of the Jewish Agency, co-signed with leaders of the religious bloc, he undertook, inter alia, to leave the laws of personal status in the new state in the hands of the rabbinate.[52] For reasons of his own, he also supported the religious camp's firm opposition to a written constitution. Ben-Gurion was an experienced politician, skilled at getting what he wanted.

In 1953 the political promise to bar civil marriage in Israel was given a legal basis. The law defining the legal status of the rabbinical courts determined that they would have exclusive jurisdiction over marriage and divorce of Jews in Israel. By this means, the dominant socialist Zionism harnessed the principles of the traditional rabbinate as an alibi for its fearful imaginary that was

---

52   See the letter in the annex to the article by Menacem Friedman, "The history of the Status-Quo: Religion and State in Israel," in *The Transition from "Yishuv" to State 1947–1949: Continuity and Change*, Varda Pilowsky (ed.), Haifa: Herzl Institute, 1990 (in Hebrew), 66–7.

terrified of assimilation and "mixed marriage."[53]

This was the first demonstration of the state's cynical exploitation of the Jewish religion to accomplish the aims of Zionism. Many scholars who have studied the relations between religion and state in Israel have described them as Jewish nationalism submitting helplessly to the pressures applied by a powerful rabbinical camp and its burdensome theocratic tradition.[54] It is true there were tensions, misunderstandings and clashes between secular and religious sectors in the Zionist movement and later in the State of Israel. But a close examination reveals that nationalism needed the religious pressure, and often invited it in order to carry out its agenda. The late Professor Yeshayahu Leibowitz was more perceptive than most when he described Israel as a secular state in religious cohabitation. Given the great difficulty of defining a secular Jewish identity, and the highly uncertain boundaries of this impossible entity, it had no choice but to submit to the rabbinical tradition.[55]

It must be stated, however, that a secular Israeli culture soon began to emerge, and surprisingly fast. Although some of its features—such as festivals, holidays and symbols—derived from Jewish sources, this culture could not serve as a common foundation for the "worldwide Jewish people." With its distinctive elements—from language, music and food to literature, the arts and cinema—the new culture began to demarcate a new society, quite different from what those who are known as Jews and their children experience in London, Paris, New York and Moscow. Members of the "Jewish people" around the world do not speak, read or write in Hebrew, are not imprinted by Israel's urban or rural landscapes, do not experience the divisions, tragedies and joys of Israeli society, don't even know how to cheer their football teams, don't grumble about the country's Income Tax and don't eulogize the party leaders, who invariably let down the "people of Israel."

Consequently, the attitude that emerged in Zionist ideology toward the young Israeli culture was equivocal. Here was an adored infant who was not

---

53   The educational system in Israel is likewise almost totally divided. There are hardly any schools attended by both Judeo-Israelis and Palestino-Israelis. The separation is not due to concern for Palestinian cultural autonomy and preservation of memory—the educational system and curricula are wholly subordinate to the Israeli Ministry of Education. The kibbutz movement, the jewel in Israeli socialism's crown, has also always practiced such segregation. Arabs were not accepted by the kibbutzim, nor have they ever been integrated in other Jewish communal frameworks.

54   See for example Gershon Weiler, *Jewish Theocracy*, Leiden: Brill, 1988.

55   On this subject see also Baruch Kimmerling, "The Cultural Code of Jewishness: Religion and Nationalism," in *The Invention and Decline of Israeliness: State, Society, and Military*, Berkeley: University of California Press, 2001, 173–207.

entirely legitimate, a bastard child to be cherished without looking closely at its distinctive features, which were fascinating but unprecedented in history and tradition. These modern features—which both derived from tradition and rejected it, which included elements of identity taken from both East and West and also erased them—formed a new and unfamiliar symbiosis. This secular culture is hard to define as entirely Jewish, for three main reasons:

1) the discrepancy between it and all the Jewish religious cultures, past and present, is too conspicuous;
2) the Jews of the world are not familiar with it and have no share in its rich variety and evolution;
3) non-Jews in the State of Israel, whether Palestino-Israelis, Russian immigrants, or even foreign workers residing in it, know its nuances far better than Jews elsewhere in the world, and increasingly experience it, even while preserving their own distinctions.

Zionist thinking has always been careful not to call the new Israeli society a people, much less a nation. Just as in the past it refused, in contrast to the popular Bund party, to define the large Yiddish population as a distinctive Eastern European people, it has refused to acknowledge the Jewish-Israeli entity, which manifests the attributes of a people, or even a nation, by any criterion—language, mass culture, territory, economy, sovereignty, and so on. The specific historical character of this new people has been denied time and again by its founders and shapers. It is perceived by Zionism, as it is by Arab nationalism, as "neither a people nor a nation," but as those segments of world Jewry that intend to "make aliyah to" (or invade) "Eretz Israel" (or Palestine).

But the main unifying basis for international Jewry, apart from the painful memory of the Holocaust—which unfortunately grants anti-Semitism a permanent, if indirect, say in defining the Jew—remains the old, depleted religious culture (with the genetic demon slithering quietly behind). There has never been a secular Jewish culture common to all the Jews in the world, and the well-known argument of Rabbi Yeshaiahu Karelitz—that "the [secular-Jewish] cart is empty"—was and remains correct. But in his traditionalist naiveté, the great rabbinical scholar expected the empty secular cart to make way for the loaded religious cart. He failed to see that modern nationalism had cleverly succeeded in lightening the payload of the heavy cart and diverting it to its own destination.

As in such countries as Poland, Greece and Ireland before the Second World War, or even today's Estonia and Sri Lanka, the Zionist identity contains a very distinctive blend of ethnocentric nationalism with traditional religion, where the religion becomes an instrument serving the leaders of the imaginary *ethnos*. Liah Greenfeld described these particular types of problematic nationalism as follows:

> ... religion being no longer the expression of the revealed truth and inner personal conviction, but an outward sign and symbol of their collective distinctness ... What is of greater moment is that, when valued chiefly for this external—and mundane—function, religion becomes an ethnic characteristic, an ascriptive, unalterable attribute of a collectivity, and, as such, a reflection of necessity, rather than personal responsibility and choice; that is to say, in the final analysis, a reflection of race.[56]

In later years, when the socialist ethos and myth of secular Zionism sank under the financial impact of the free market, far more layers of religious paint would be needed to decorate the fictitious *ethnos*. But even then, toward the end of the twentieth century, Israel would not become a more theocratic state. While the religious elements in the dynamics of Israeli politics have been growing stronger, so has the modernization of these very elements; they become progressively more nationalistic and hence much more racist. The lack of separation between the rabbinate and the state never reflected the real strength of the faith, whose authentic religious impulse has in fact waned over the years. The absence of separation has been a direct product of the endemic weakness of the insecure nationalism, which was forced to borrow the bulk of its imagery and symbols from the traditional religion and its texts, thereby becoming its hostage.

Just as Israel was unable to decide on its territorial borders, it did not manage to draw the boundaries of its national identity. From the start it hesitated to define the membership of the Jewish *ethnos*. To begin with, the state appeared to accept an open definition that a Jew was any person who saw himself or herself as a Jew. In the first census, held on November 8, 1948, residents were asked to fill out a questionnaire in which they stated their nationality and religion, and these were what served as the basis for civil registration. In this way the young state managed quietly to Judaize many spouses who were not Jews. In 1950, newborn children were registered on a separate page without reference to nationality and religion—but there were two such forms, one in Hebrew and one in Arabic, and whoever filled out a Hebrew form was assumed to be a Jew.[57]

Also in 1950, Israel's parliament—the Knesset—passed the Law of Return.

---

56 Liah Greenfeld, "The Modern Religion," in *Nationalism and the Mind: Essays on Modern Culture*, Oxford: Oneworld Publications, 2006, 109.

57 On this subject see Yigal Elam, *Judaism as a Status Quo*, Tel Aviv: Am Oved, 2000 (in Hebrew), 16.

This was the first basic law that gave legal force to what the Proclamation of Independence had declared. This law declared: "Every Jew has the right to come to this country as an *oleh* [immigrant]" unless he "(1) is engaged in an activity directed against the Jewish people; or (2) is likely to endanger public health or the security of the State." Then in 1952 came the law that granted automatic citizenship on the basis of the Law of Return.[58]

Beginning in the late 1940s, the world rightly viewed Israel as a refuge for the persecuted and the displaced. The systematic massacre of the Jews of Europe and the total destruction of the Yiddish-speaking people drew widespread public sympathy for the creation of a state that would be a safe haven for the remnant. In the 1950s, provoked by the Israeli-Arab conflict but also by the rise of authoritarian Arab nationalism, semireligious and not especially tolerant, hundreds of thousands of Arab Jews were driven from their homelands. Not all were able to reach Europe or Canada; some went to Israel, whether or not they wished to go there. The state was gratified and even sought to attract them (though it viewed with unease and contempt the diverse Arab cultures they brought with their scanty belongings).[59] The law that granted the right of immigration to every Jewish refugee who was subject to persecution on account of faith or origin was quite legitimate in these circumstances. Even today such a law would not conflict with the basic principles in any liberal democracy, when many of the citizens feel kinship and a common historical destiny with people close to them who suffer discrimination in other countries.

Yet the Law of Return was not a statute designed to make Israel a safe haven for those who were persecuted in the past, present or future because people hated them as Jews. Had the framers of this law wished to do so, they could have placed it on a platform of humanist principle, linking the privilege of asylum to the existence and threat of anti-Semitism. But the Law of Return and the associated Law of Citizenship were direct products of an ethnic nationalist worldview, designed to provide a legal basis for the concept that the State of Israel belongs to the Jews of the world. As Ben-Gurion declared at the start of the parliamentary debate on the Law of Return: "This is not a Jewish state only because most of its inhabitants are Jews. It is a state for the Jews wherever they may be, and for any Jew who wishes to be here."[60]

Anyone who was included in "the Jewish people"—including such notables as Pierre Mendes-France, the French prime minister in the early 1950s;

---

58   Available at www.knesset.gov.il/laws/special/heb/chok_hashvut.htm.
59   On this immigrant absorption, see Yehouda Shenhav, *The Arab Jews: A Postcolonial Reading of Nationalism, Religion, and Ethnicity*, Stanford: Stanford University Press, 2006.
60   In *Divray Haknesset* ("Protocols of the Knesset") 6, 1950, 2035.

Bruno Kreisky, the Austrian chancellor in the 1970s; Henry Kissinger, the US secretary of state at that time; or Joe Lieberman, the Democratic candidate for vice president of the United States in 2000—was a potential citizen of the Jewish state, and their right to settle there was guaranteed by the Law of Return. A member of the "Jewish nation" might be a full citizen with equal rights in some liberal national democracy, might even be the holder of an elected position in it, but Zionist principle held that such a person was destined, or even obliged, to migrate to Israel and become its citizen. Moreover, immigrants could leave Israel immediately after arrival, yet keep their Israeli citizenship for the rest of their lives.

This privilege, which was not extended even to close family members of non-Jewish Israeli citizens, should have included a clear definition of who was truly qualified to enjoy it. But neither the Law of Return nor the Law of Citizenship—which ensured the continued official status of the Zionist Federation and the Jewish National Fund in Israel, further consolidating Israel as the state of world Jewry—includes such a definition. The question hardly came up during the first decade of the state's existence. The society that was taking shape and tripling its population was engaged in creating a common cultural foundation for the masses of immigrants, and the really urgent question was: How does one become an Israeli?

The political failure and the forced withdrawal from the Sinai Peninsula in 1956 cooled the overheated atmosphere that prevailed after the military victory in the Suez war. In March 1958, during this calmer period in the national mood, Minister of the Interior Israel Bar Yehudah, a faithful representative of the Zionist left (as a leader of Ahdut Ha'avodah), instructed his office that "a person declaring sincerely that he is a Jew will be registered as a Jew, and no further proof will be required."[61] The representatives of the national-religious camp were predictably furious. The astute Prime Minister Ben-Gurion, knowing full well that it would be impossible in an immigrant state to determine on a purely voluntary basis who was a Jew, soon overturned the secular gesture of his minister of the interior, and ambiguous order was restored. The Ministry of the Interior was then handed to the Orthodox camp, which went back to registering people as Jews on the basis of their mother's "identity."

The nature of Jewish nationalism, enshrined in the laws of the state, was cast into sharp focus four years later. In 1962 Shmuel Oswald Rufeisen, known as "Brother Daniel," petitioned the High Court of Justice (the Supreme Court) to instruct the state to recognize him as a Jew by nationality. Rufeisen was born

---

61   Elam, *Judaism as a Status Quo*, 12.

to a Jewish family in Poland in 1922, and as a teenager joined a Zionist youth movement. He fought as a partisan against the Nazi occupation and saved the lives of many Jews. At some point he hid in a monastery, where he converted to Christianity. After the war he studied for the priesthood, and in order to go to Israel he became a Carmelite monk.[62] In 1958 he went to Israel because he wished to take part in the Jewish destiny and still saw himself as a Zionist. Having given up his Polish citizenship, he applied to become an Israeli citizen on the basis of the Law of Return, arguing that although he was a Catholic by religion, he was still a Jew by "nationality." When his application was rejected by the Ministry of the Interior, he petitioned the High Court of Justice. By a four-to-one decision, the court rejected his petition to be given Israeli citizenship on the basis of the Law of Return. He was, however, granted an Israeli identity card, which stated, "Nationality: Not clear."[63]

Ultimately, Brother Daniel's betrayal of Judaism by joining the religion of the Nazarene overcame the deterministic biological imaginary. It was categorically decided that there was no Jewish nationality without its religious shell. Ethnocentric Zionism needed the Halakhic precepts as its principal criteria, and the secular judges understood this national-historical necessity very well. Another effect that this decision had on the concept of identity in Israel was to deny the right of the individual to declare himself a Jew—now, only the sovereign judicial authority could determine the "nationality" of a citizen living in his own country.[64]

Another important test case for the definition of a Jew took place toward the end of the decade. In 1968 Major Binyamin Shalit petitioned the High Court of Justice to order the minister of the interior to register his two sons as Jews. Unlike Brother Daniel, the mother of these boys was not a born Jew but a Scottish gentile. Shalit, a well-regarded officer in Israel's victorious army, argued that his sons were growing up as Jews and wished to be considered full citizens in the state of the Jewish people. By what seemed a miracle, five of the nine judges who heard the petition decided that the boys were Jewish by nationality, if not by religion. But this exceptional decision shook the entire political structure. This was after the Six-Day War of 1967, when Israel had captured a large non-Jewish population, and the opposition to mingling with gentiles had actually grown more rigid. In 1970, under pressure from the reli-

---

62 On this unique and heroic figure, see Nechama Tec, *In the Lion's Den: The Life of Oswald Rufeisen*, New York: Oxford University Press, 1990.
63 Ibid., 231.
64 On the judges' different positions, see Ron Margolin, (ed.), *The State of Israel as a Jewish and Democratic State*, Jerusalem: The World Union for Jewish Studies, 1999 (in Hebrew), 209–28.

gious camp, the Law of Return was amended to include, finally, a full and exact definition of who is an authentic member of the people of Israel: "A Jew is one who was born to a Jewish mother, or converted to Judaism and does not belong to another religion." After twenty-two years of hesitation and questioning, the instrumental link between the rabbinical religion and the essentialist nationalism was now well and truly welded.

Needless to say, many secular supporters of nationalism would have preferred more flexible or scientific criteria by which to define Jews—for example, accepting cases where the father was a Jew, or finding some genetic marker to reveal a person's Jewishness. But in the absence of looser criteria or a reliable scientific one, the Jewish Israeli majority resigned itself to the Halakhic verdict. To them, the rigid tradition was preferable to a serious blurring of the Jewish distinction and to turning Israel into a mere liberal democracy belonging to all its citizens. Not all Israelis, of course, accepted the strict definition of their Jewishness.

After the amendment to the Law of Return, one person petitioned to change the nationality stated on his identity card from Jewish to Israeli. Georg Rafael Tamarin was a lecturer in education at Tel Aviv University. He had come to Israel from Yugoslavia in 1949, and declared himself to be a Jew. In the early 1970s he applied to have his nationality changed from Jewish to Israeli for two reasons: one, that the new criterion for defining a Jew had become, in his opinion, a "racial-religious" one; and two, that the establishment of the State of Israel had created an Israeli nationality, to which he felt he belonged. His petition was rejected by a unanimous vote; the judges decided that he had to remain a Jew by nationality, as an Israeli nationality did not exist.[65]

Curiously, the president of the Supreme Court, Justice Shimon Agranat, Israel Prize laureate, did not simply base his decision on the Proclamation of Independence. He also proceeded to explain why there was a Jewish nation but absolutely not an Israeli one. Agranat's conceptualization of nationhood and nationality was inconsistent, as it rested entirely on subjective aspects yet refused to allow individual choice, and it reflected the dominant ideology in Israel. He cited as proof of the existence of a Jewish nation the emotion and tears of the Israeli paratroopers who captured the Western Wall, thus showing himself influenced more by journalistic stories than by books of history and

---

65 "Tamarin versus the State of Israel" in the High Court of Justice, decision 630/70, January 20, 1972. Tamarin based his petition on the work of the French sociologist Georges Friedmann, *The End of the Jewish People?*, New York: Doubleday, 1967. The conclusion of this highly pro-Israel book is that an Israeli nation is gradually taking shape whose features differ from those of historical Jewry.

political philosophy—though this did not prevent him from flaunting his scholarship throughout the written decision.

Despite the narrow definition of the Jew in the Law of Return, the state's pragmatic needs were too strong to exclude other "white" immigrants. Following a wave of anti-Semitism in Poland in 1968, many of the families who emigrated from there had one non-Jewish partner. In the second half of the twentieth century, both in the Soviet Union and the Communist bloc and in the liberal-democratic countries, there were numerous "mixed marriages," which promoted assimilation in the various national cultures. (This phenomenon led Golda Meir, Israel's truculent prime minister, to declare that a Jew who married a gentile was in effect joining the six million victims of the Nazis.)

This grave situation forced the lawmakers to balance the narrow definition of the Jew by widening significantly the right of aliyah—immigration to Israel. Clause 4a was added to the Law of Return. Dubbed the "grandchild clause," it enabled not only Jews but also their "non-Jewish" children, grandchildren and spouses to immigrate to Israel. It was enough for one grandparent to qualify as a Jew for the offspring to become citizens of Israel. This important clause would later open the door to the huge influx of immigrants that began in the early 1990s, with the fall of Communism. This immigration, which had no ideological dimension—Israel had begun in the 1980s to urge the United States not to accept Soviet Jewish refugees—meant that more than 30 percent of the newcomers could not be registered as Jews on their identity cards.

While nearly three hundred thousand new immigrants were not classified as members of the Jewish people ("an assimilatory time-bomb," as the Israeli press described it), this did not prevent the continued intensification of ethnocentric identity—an intensification that had begun in the late 1970s. Paradoxically, the rise of the Likud party, led by Menahem Begin, strengthened two processes that had been evident in Israel's political culture for some time: liberalization and ethnicization.

The decline of Zionist socialism, whose Eastern European origins had not been especially tolerant or pluralistic, and the coming to power of a popular right-wing party, disliked by most Israeli intellectuals, gave greater legitimacy to political and cultural confrontation. Israel became accustomed to periodic power changes, such as it had not known during the first thirty years of its existence. The tradition of protest and criticism also changed. The first war in Lebanon showed that it was possible to attack the government even while battles raged, and yet not to be denounced as a traitor.

At the same time, the gradual shrinking of the socialist-Zionist welfare state and the rise of economic neoliberalism loosened somewhat the constraints of the state supra-identity. When the omnipotent national state became a limited-liability institution, alternative sub-identities, especially ethnic and communal ones, grew stronger. This was a global process, not confined to Israel, and will be discussed further.

Though Israeli culture continued to develop and flourish during the first twenty years of power over the territories seized in 1967—two decades that passed fairly quietly—prospects for the consolidation of an Israeli civil identity were weakened. The policy of massive settlement in the West Bank and the Gaza Strip was conducted in an undisguisedly apartheid manner—while encouraging its citizens to settle in the occupied territories, Israel did not legally annex most of them, so as to avoid being responsible for the local inhabitants. This led to the creation of a state-subsidized "masters' democracy" in the new spaces, reinforcing a lordly ethnocentric consciousness even in Israel's relatively democratic circles.

Another factor that heightened the exclusionary essentialist tendency in the Jewish population, especially in its tradition-minded and socioeconomically weaker sectors, was the eruption into the public arena and audio-visual media of Palestino-Israeli figures of a new kind, who dared to claim their right to an equal share in the joint homeland. Fear of losing the Zionist privileges that had been granted because of the "Jewish" nature of the state exacerbated a selfish "ethnic" exclusivity among the masses, especially the "eastern Jews" or "Russian Jews," who had not been sufficiently acculturated by Israel and hence were economically underrewarded. These groups felt especially threatened by the growing demands for equality coming from representatives of the Arab population.

"JEWISH AND DEMOCRATIC"—AN OXYMORON?

The liberalization and ethnicization of the 1980s gave rise, among other developments, to a new Arab-Jewish party—more radical in its criticism than the traditional Communist Party, which had previously represented the Arab protest, and far more challenging in its attitude to the identity politics of the State of Israel. The Progressive List for Peace, led by Mohammed Mi'ari, expressed a different kind of criticism about the character of the State of Israel, including calls for its de-Zionization. This was just the start. When elections for the Knesset approached, the parliamentary elections committee disqualified the new party, as well as the far-right party led by Rabbi Meir Kahane. The Supreme Court, which was becoming the stronghold of Israeli liberalism, overruled the disqualification, and both lists were allowed to run.

Unlike earlier Palestino-Israeli movements, such as al-Ard in the 1960s and Sons of the Village in the 1970s, the Progressive List, with retired Major General Mattityahu Peled as the number two on its list, won two seats in the 120-seat house in 1984. The new Knesset reacted to this modest achievement in 1985 by passing, by a large majority and with no opposition, a new amendment to the Basic Law: The Knesset.[66] Clause 7a stated that a party would not be allowed to run for the Israel parliament if its platform included one of the following: "(1) negation of the existence of the State of Israel as the state of the Jewish people; (2) negation of the democratic character of the State; (3) incitement to racism."

Despite the new law, again thanks to the intervention of the Supreme Court, the Progressive List for Peace was able to run. Subsequently, more Arab parties appeared that, without defying the law, kept challenging the Israeli public with questions about the nature of the state. A whole generation of Palestinian intellectuals—too young to have experienced the Nakbah and the military government, and who had undergone Israelization by adopting Hebrew culture in addition to their own Arab culture—began to voice with growing confidence their dissatisfaction with the political state of affairs. They pointed out that the State of Israel—into which they had been born, in which they constituted one-fifth of the population, and of which they were formally full citizens—insisted that it was not their state but belonged to a different people, most of whom remained overseas.

An outstanding early figure in this protest against Jewish exclusivity was the writer and translator Anton Shammas. A gifted bilingual intellectual and the author of the novel *Arabesques*, which deals with his divided national identity, he issued a challenge to Israeli society: let us all be multicultural Israelis, and create a common national identity that will not erase our identities of origin but aim for an Israeli symbiosis between the Jewish and Arab citizens of the state.[67] A. B. Yehoshua, one of Israel's leading writers and a typical representative of the Zionist left, rejected the proposal with characteristic self-assurance: Israel must remain the state of the dispersed Jewish people, and must not become the state of all its citizens. "The Law of Return is the moral basis of Zionism," he argued, and the dangerous proposal to create a dual identity in the Jewish state should be rejected. The established author was horrified by the very idea of becoming a Jewish-Israeli (analogous to the

---

66   See the article of Amos Ben Vered in *Haaretz*, August 2, 1985.
67   See his articles, "The New Year for the Jews," *Ha'hir*, September 13, 1985; "The Blame of the Babushka," *Ha'hir*, January 24, 1986; and "We (Who Is That?)," *Politika*, October 17, 1987, 26–7.

defective Jewish-Americans). He wanted to be a "nonhyphenated" whole Jew, and if this displeased a "new Israeli" like Anton Shammas, he should pack his belongings and move to the future national Palestinian state.[68]

This was perhaps the last time that a well-known Palestino-Israeli intellectual proposed a joint cultural life in a pluralistic but egalitarian liberal democracy. The negative response of the Israeli Zionist left, as well as the intifada that erupted at the end of 1987, made such proposals even rarer. While Israeli Palestinians expressed solidarity with the national liberation struggle of the Palestinians in the occupied territories, they were so far not calling for national territorial separation. But pride in the oppressed Palestinian culture and the desire to preserve it at all costs led many to call for Israel to become a consociational, or multicultural, democracy. The single unifying demand was for Israel to become theirs, so that they could belong to it.

The debate concerning "the state of the Jewish people" was heating up. In the 1990s, with the subject of post-Zionism engaging various intellectual circles, the definition of the State of Israel became one of the key issues. In the past, anti-Zionism had been equated with the denial of Israel's right to exist, and the one principle that all Zionists agreed on was that Israel must remain the exclusive state of all the Jews in the world. Now, post-Zionism supported full recognition of the State of Israel within the 1967 borders, but combined it with the uncompromising demand that it become the state of all Israeli citizens.

Following the Oslo Accords in 1993, and especially the outbreak of the Second Intifada in 2000, the territorial myth of the "entire Land of Israel" as the patrimony of the Jewish people began to dissipate. But the process was accompanied by the insistence on the Jewish people's exclusive claim to the State of Israel. A large portion of the former territory-minded right wing grew into a rigid and racist right wing, while the center-liberal camp entrenched itself in its Zionist positions and sought to legitimize them juridically and philosophically.

In 1988 Justice Meir Shamgar, president of the Supreme Court and an Israel Prize laureate, declared that "the existence of the State of Israel as the state of the Jewish people does not conflict with its democratic character, just as the Frenchness of France does not conflict with its democratic character."[69] This absurd comparison—all the citizens of France, old or new, are identified

---

68   Abraham B. Yehoshua, "Reply to Anton," in *The Wall and the Mountain*, Tel Aviv: Zmora, Bitan, 1989 (in Hebrew), 197–205.
69   Moshe Neuman versus the president of the central electoral commission, decision (4) 177, 189.

as French, and no non-French citizens qualify as hidden partners in its sovereignty—marked the start of a juridical process embellished with a colorful
range of ideas.

In 1992 two of the Basic Laws—Human Dignity and Liberty, and Freedom
of Occupation—already contained the categorical statement that Israel is
a "Jewish and democratic state." The Basic Law concerning political parties,
passed that same year, also decreed that a party that denied the existence of
Israel as a Jewish and democratic state would be barred from taking part in the
elections.[70] Paradoxically, this meant that henceforth it would not be possible
to transform the Jewish state into an Israeli democracy by a liberal-democratic
process. The dangerous aspect of this legislation was that it did not make clear
exactly what made a state—a sovereign political body that is supposed to serve
its citizens—a Jewish one, and what might threaten or undo it as such.

It was Professor Sammy Smooha, a sociologist at Haifa University, who
meticulously exposed the problematics and anomalies of a democracy that
called itself Jewish. In 1990 he borrowed from Juan José Linz, a political
sociologist at Yale University, the term "ethnic democracy" and applied it to
Israel.[71] Over the years, he developed and perfected a groundbreaking analysis
that placed Israel very low in the hierarchy of democratic regimes. Methodically
comparing it with liberal, republican, consociational and multicultural democracies, he concluded that Israel did not fit into any of these categories. Instead,
it could be classified, along with states like Estonia, Latvia and Slovakia, as an
"incomplete democracy" or a "low-grade democracy."

Liberal democracy represents the whole society that exists within its
boundaries, with complete equality between all the citizens, irrespective of
their origins or cultural affiliations. It functions primarily as a night watchman,
guarding rights and laws, and its involvement in the cultural formation of its
citizens is scanty and minimal. Most of the Anglo-Saxon and Scandinavian
states exemplify this model to a greater or lesser extent. Republican democracy resembles this model in the complete equality of its citizens, but it is
much more involved in the cultural formation of its national collective. Such
a state is less tolerant of secondary cultural identities and seeks to assimilate
them into one overarching culture—France is the most prominent example of
this category. The consociational, or associative, democracy formally recognizes cultural-linguistic groups, institutionally ensures their equal standing

---

70   See www.knesset.gov.il/laws/special/heb/yesod1.pdf and www.knesset.gov.il/elections
16/heb/laws/party_law.htm#4.
71   Sammy Smooha, "Minority Status in an Ethnic Democracy: The Status of the Arab
Minority in Israel," *Ethnic and Racial Studies* 13 (1990), 389–413.

in government, with the right of veto in joint decisions, while fostering the full autonomy of each and every group—Switzerland, Belgium and contemporary Canada best exemplify this model. The multicultural democracy, on the other hand, plays a less formal role in sustaining the different cultural groups in its system. But it respects them, avoids harming them, and grants communal rights to minorities, making no attempt to impose one particular culture. Great Britain and the Netherlands are the leading examples in this category. The most important quality in this catalogue, shared by all these regimes, is that they see themselves as representing all the citizens in their states—including societies with a hegemonic cultural-linguistic group as well as minorities.

In Smooha's opinion, Israel cannot be included in any of the above categories, if only because it does not see itself as the political embodiment of the civil society within its boundaries. Not only was Zionism the official ideology that dominated the Jewish state at its birth, but its citizens are expected to continue to fulfill its particularist aims till the end of time. While a kind of democracy does exist within the pre-1967 boundaries of Israel—with civil rights, freedom of expression and political association, and periodic free elections—the absence of basic civil and political equality sets its apart from the flourishing democracies of the West.

Despite Smooha's efforts to avoid an overly normative judgment, his analysis implied a radical criticism of the State of Israel, though his political conclusions were far more moderate than might have been expected. As he saw it, there was little real likelihood that Israel would become a state of all its citizens. Therefore, the most reasonable prospect was an improved ethnic democracy, in which discrimination was minimized but the exclusionary core was preserved: "The best solution for the Arabs of Israel would, of course, be a 'consociational,' namely, a binational, state; but the opposition of the Jews to such an option, which would eliminate the Jewish state, would be total, so that its implementation would be a terrible injustice to most of the population."[72]

We may or may not accept Smooha's conceptual scheme—a consociational democracy like Switzerland, for example, is not exactly a multinational state— or his idea that ending discrimination against a subordinate minority would be "a terrible injustice" to the dominant majority. But there is no denying that the Haifa scholar was the first Israeli academic to pry open the Pandora's box that is Israel's politics of identity. There had been a significant lack of theoretical

---

72 See also Sammy Smooha, "The Regime of the State of Israel: Civic Democracy, Non-Democracy or an Ethnic Democracy?," *Israeli Sociology* 2: 2 (2000, in Hebrew), 620. See also "The Model of Ethnic Democracy: Israel as a Jewish and Democratic State," *Nation and Nationalism* 8: 4 (2002), 475–503.

analysis in this field, and Smooha's essays displayed exceptional critical insight. It goes without saying that this breakthrough attracted a good many responses from Zionist intellectuals as well as from post-Zionists and Palestino-Israelis.[73]

Responding to Smooha's critique, and even more so to the "Jewish" legislation of the early 1990s, some of Israel's leading scholars, traditional and liberal alike, tried to prove that Israel was a normative democracy. The following spectrum of opinions represents some of the most prominent, all of them, not accidentally, laureates of the Israel Prize—this being the highest honor paid by the state to its outstanding figures in the humanities and sciences, and thereby to its own position. As the Israel Prize laureates form a major hub in the world of Israeli culture, their views reflect the essence of the national ideology and reveal its character.

For example, Eliezer Schweid, professor of Jewish philosophy at the Hebrew University in Jerusalem, could see no contradiction in the phrase "a Jewish and democratic state." Israel had been established "in order to restore to the Jewish people the basic democratic rights it had been denied through many generations in exile ... There is no moral reason why the Jewish people should forgo this right in the state it has built for itself with its own hands, invested tremendous creative energy in it, spilt its blood for it, developed its economy, society and culture."[74] As Schweid saw it, talking about a contradiction between Judaism and democracy was senseless, because "the Jewish religion and Jewish nationalism contain the ethical sources which defined human rights and the idea of the social pact that forms constitutional democracy." Moreover, if Israel did not exist as the state of the Jewish people, there was no point in maintaining its existence.

Professor Shlomo Avineri of the Hebrew University, a former director-general of the foreign ministry, thought that Israel as a "Jewish state" was immeasurably superior to the French republic, which assimilates and erases identities. Israel's tolerance resembles that of Britain, he said, and is even superior to it in many ways. For example, the absence of civil marriage and the preservation of communal-confessional marriage, which had existed under Ottoman rule, together with the separation practiced in education, indicated that there was in fact in Israel a broad cultural autonomy for its non-Jewish citizens: "Without ever having decided this, the State of Israel recognizes the

---

73   On Smooha and the reactions to his analyses, see Eyal Gross, "Democracy, Ethnicity and Legislation in Israel: Between the 'Jewish State' and the 'Democratic State,'" *Israeli Sociology* 2: 2 (2000), 647–73.

74   Eliezer Schweid, "Israel: 'a Jewish State' or 'a State of the Jewish people'?" in *Zionism in a Post-Modernist Era*, Jerusalem: The Zionist Library, 1996 (2000, in Hebrew), 116.

right of the Arab citizens to equality not only as individuals, but as a group."[75] Therefore, the Jerusalem professor opined, the Jewish state ought to keep its emblems, national flag, anthem and Jewish laws—especially the Law of Return, which does not differ from any other immigration laws—so as to create a legal separation between the Jewish majority and the minorities that live in its midst and alongside it, and still be a worthwhile multicultural democracy. After all, a similar situation is found in the world's most liberal states.

Surely the professor of political science—even though his area of expertise was German philosophy—must have known the famous 1954 decision of the US Supreme Court in Brown v. Board of Education of Topeka, which determined that "separate but equal" cannot be "equal," and is therefore a violation of the Fourteenth Amendment to the Constitution, which states that all US citizens are equal. This historical decision fueled the civil rights struggles and eventually led to a thorough change in identity politics in the United States, yet evidently it did not get through to the Zionist mind of the senior scholar in Jerusalem—the city, not incidentally, that was supposed to be Israel's "unified" capital, where tens of thousands of Palestinians, annexed in 1967, live as permanent residents but not citizens, and thus have no share in the sovereign power over them.

It was the same for Asa Kasher, a professor of philosophy at Tel Aviv University and, like the others, a laureate of the Israel Prize—in this case, for his writings on morality. He argued that Israel did not differ from the best democracies in the world and that there was no inherent contradiction in the phrase "Jewish and democratic." As he saw it, the problems of a democratic national state were not unique to Israel: "In Spain there are the Basques, in the Netherlands the Frisians, in France the Corsicans. In this respect, the State of Israel, where 20 percent of the population belong to a different nation, is not exceptional."[76] Hence, the State of Israel is democratic in its "practical ideal" and should not be called upon to become expressly a state of all its citizens. Naturally the sense of belonging felt by the majority differs from that of the minority, but that is the way of the modern nation-states.

Apparently Asa Kasher, for all his wide scholarship, did not know that while the Castilian language and culture predominate in Spain, the state belongs to all Spaniards, be they Castilian, Catalan, Basque or something else.

---

75   Shlomo Avineri, "National Minorities in the National Democratic State," in *The Arabs in Israeli Politics: Dilemmas of Identity*, Eli Rekhes (ed.), Tel Aviv: Moshe Dayan Center, 1998 (in Hebrew), 24.

76   Asa Kasher, "The Democratic State of the Jews," in *The State of Israel: Between Judaism and Democracy*, Yossi David (ed.), Jerusalem: Israeli Democracy Institute, 2000 (in Hebrew), 116.

No Spanish government would survive long if it announced that it was the state of the Castilians rather than of all Spaniards. The French republic does not belong solely to the mainland Catholic citizens but also to the people of Corsica, just as it belongs to French Jews, Protestants and even Muslims. Yet for a Jewish philosopher living in Israel, this difference in national definitions was too trivial to consider, since the "Jewish people's democracy" is equal in its fine moral stature to any Western society.

Prominent among those who offered a theoretical underpinning to the definition of Israel as a democratic state of the Jewish people were a number of jurists. Since the Basic Laws had begun to insert the term "Jewish" into their wording, various judges and professors of law felt it their duty to provide a well-grounded defense of the new legislation. Papers piled up in the effort to convince the skeptics that it was possible for a state to adhere to the Jewish tradition yet treat its non-Jews as completely equal. The impression gained from their writings was that their concept of equality was another way of saying "indifference."

For retired Justice Haim Hermann Cohen, former deputy president of the Supreme Court and minister of justice, as well as an Israel Prize laureate, the issue was straightforward: "The genes of our forefathers are in us, whether we like it or not. A man who respects himself strives to discover not only where he stands and where he is heading, but also where he came from. The heritage of Israel, in the broadest sense of the word, is the legacy that the state has inherited by its very nature, and it makes it a Jewish state by its very nature."[77]

This statement does not mean that Haim Cohen was a racist. He had always been a liberal judge—in the Rufeisen case, his was the voluntarist dissenting opinion—and he also knew that the "biological-genetic continuity was very questionable." But making a considerable effort to define the non-religious Jewishness of his state, he asserted: "A Jewish identity does not mean a biological-genetic continuity—more important is the spiritual-cultural continuity. The former defines the state as the state of the Jews; the latter as a Jewish state. The two identities are not contradictory—they complement each other, and may also be mutually dependent and conditional."[78]

It must have been this conditionality that led Cohen to include in the Jewish continuity and the heritage of Israel not only the Bible, the Talmud and its parables but also the work of Spinoza, the philosopher who had quit Judaism and was ostracized by its followers. Yet while struggling mightily to

---

77   Haim Cohen, "The Jewishness of the State of Israel," *Alpayim* 16 (1998), 10
78   Ibid., 21.

characterize Jewish democracy, he made no reference to the 20 percent of its citizens who are Arab, nor to the 5 percent meticulously registered by the Ministry of the Interior as non-Jews, even though they speak Hebrew and pay their taxes.

Aharon Barak, a former president of the Supreme Court and yet another Israel Prize laureate, was also thought of as one of the most liberal and scholarly judges in the history of Israeli law. Addressing the Thirty-fourth Zionist Congress in 2002, he spoke about "the values of Israel as a Jewish and democratic state."[79] What were the state's Jewish norms? A combination of Halakhic and Zionist elements. The world of the Halakhah is "an endless ocean," while the world of Zionism is the language, the national symbols, the flag, the anthem, the festivals and the Law of Return—yet Israel also "liberates state lands for Jewish settlement." What were the state's democratic values? The separation of powers, the rule of law, and the protection of human rights, including the rights of the minority. It was necessary to seek a synthesis and a balance between the two sets of values: "Giving Jews the right to immigrate does not discriminate against those who are not Jews. It recognizes a non-discriminatory difference. But a person who lives in our national home is entitled to equality, irrespective of religion and nationality."[80] That was why the judge strove to do justice to the Arab minority, being much more aware than other jurists that equality is the heart of modern democracy.

Is there equality in the state when one of its values is "liberating state lands for Jewish settlement"? Supreme Court Justice Barak did not have to answer this question to the participants of the Zionist Congress in Jerusalem. Nor was his audience astonished, since on an earlier occasion the democratic judge defined the character of the State of Israel in similar terms: "A Jewish state is one for which Jewish settlement in its fields, cities and villages comes before anything else ... A Jewish state is one in which Hebrew Law plays an important part, and in which the laws of marriage and divorce of Jews are based on the Torah."[81] In other words, for the secular liberal Aharon Barak, Israel is Jewish thanks to such projects as the famous "Judaization of the Galilee," which rests on the long-standing judicial segregation of Jews and non-Jews.

Daniel Friedman was not a judge, but he was appointed minister of justice by Prime Minister Ehud Olmert. Prior to that, he had been a law professor at Tel Aviv University, and had of course received the Israel Prize. Responding to an article of mine in 2000, after thirteen Palestino-Israelis had been killed

---

79   Available at www.nfc.co.il/archive/003-D-1202-00.html?tag=21-53-48#PTEXT1767.
80   Ibid.
81   See in Margolin (ed.), *The State of Israel*, 11.

by the police during unarmed protests, he expressed profound amazement at the argument that "the very definition of the state as a Jewish one implies a nonegalitarian element."[82] Most states are national states, he argued, so why can't Israel be one? How is Israel different from England? "In England there is a Jewish minority and a Muslim minority who enjoy equal rights. Nevertheless, they cannot complain that England is the country of English people, associated with the Anglican Church, and that the dominant language, in which alone it is possible to act in the public sphere, is English. The minorities cannot demand the appointment of a Jewish or Muslim monarch, nor equal status for a different language."[83]

Evidently we cannot expect an Israeli professor of law, eager to prove that his state is a perfect democracy, to employ more precise terminology. Although it is true that the word "England" is often used as synonymous with Britain, such carelessness is out of place in a complex discussion about nation and nationality. Since 1801 England has been part of the United Kingdom, incorporating Scotland, Wales and (since Irish independence in 1922) Northern Ireland. The historical and cultural background of the joint realm is ecclesiastical, but Christian England does not intervene in the marital choice of a Jew who lives there, who may wish to marry a Christian Scot, or even a Muslim of Pakistani origin. Needless to say, England is not the state of the world Anglicans, as Professor Friedman's Israel is the state of the Jews of the world—nor is it even the state of the English, even though English is the official language in the kingdom. A Jew cannot be the monarch of Great Britain, but neither can an Englishman who is not a member of the royal family. In any case, the hegemon in Britain is not the reigning monarch but parliament, and Michael Howard, the son of a Romanian Jewish immigrant and leader of the Conservative Party in the early twenty-first century, might have become British prime minister (instead of making aliyah to Israel).

Britain is the state of all its citizens—English, Scottish, Welsh, Northern Irish, Muslims who immigrated and became citizens, even Orthodox Jews who acknowledge only the divine sovereign. In the eyes of the law, they are all Britons, and the kingdom belongs to all its citizens. Were England to declare that Britain is the state of the English, as Israel is of the Jews, then even before the children of Pakistani immigrants begin to protest, the Scots and the Welsh would break up the United Kingdom. Furthermore, Britain is a multicultural country, and its principal minorities have long enjoyed considerable autonomy.

82   Shlomo Sand, "To Whom Does the State Belong?," *Haaretz*, October 10, 2000.
83   Daniel Friedman, "Either Confrontation or Integration," *Haaretz*, October 17, 2000.

For Daniel Friedman, however, the Arab citizens of Israel parallel newly naturalized immigrants, rather than the Scots and the Welsh in England.

Other jurists have written in defense of the "state of the Jewish people," but let us examine only one other, who, together with a historian, wrote a whole book on the subject. In 2003 Amnon Rubinstein, professor of law, former minister of education and of course Israel Prize laureate, coauthored a book with Alexander Yakobson entitled *Israel and the Nations*, which may be the most serious critique so far of post-Zionism.[84]

Rubinstein and Yakobson were not satisfied with the functioning of the "Jewish democracy." Not only did they expressly call for the enlargement of human rights and equality in Israel, but their argumentation tried very hard to rest on universal norms. At the same time, they both firmly asserted that there was no contradiction between the state being Jewish *and* democratic. The problems of Israel are normative in the free world, they said, and may be rationally solved by improving the methods of governance and the foundations of the law. The authors set out from the familiar assumption that, as every people has a right to self-determination, so does the "Jewish people." Moreover, no state is wholly neutral culturally, and there is no reason to expect only Israel to be so.

Rubinstein and Yakobson argued that, since the UN recognized in 1947 the right of the Jews to self-determination, the Jewish state must be preserved until the last Jew "makes aliyah." They did not claim this right for the Jewish Israeli people that had come into being in the Near East—they did not recognize any Israeli national entity. But reality can be problematic for Zionist legal theoreticians: in the early twenty-first century, Jews are nowhere barred from leaving their countries, and still they refuse to implement their right to national sovereignty. Migration to Israel has been reversed; as of the time of writing, more people are leaving Israel than are entering.[85]

Rubinstein's advantage in the book he coauthored with Yakobson was that, unlike the other Zionist thinkers and jurists, he was aware that, as a nation-state, Israel could not be compared to liberal democracies in the West, and therefore he took most of his analogies from Eastern European countries. The authors happily drew on the concepts of nationality on the Hungarian political right, in Ireland and Greece before their constitutional reforms, in Germany before the 1990s, in Slovenia after the fall of Yugoslavia. The examples cited to

---

84   Alexander Yakobson and Amnon Rubinstein, *Israel and the Family of Nations: The Jewish Nation-State and Human Rights*, New York: Routledge, 2008.

85   See Gad Lior, "More Emigrants than Immigrants," *Yediot Ahronot*, April 20, 2007 (in Hebrew).

justify Israel's ethnocentric policy prompt one to ask if the two authors would be willing to live as Jews in one of the Eastern European states they praise, or would they rather settle in a more normative, liberal democracy?

Throughout the book, the genuine attachment that many Jews feel for Israel is presented as a national consciousness. This lack of discrimination between, on the one hand, an attachment based largely on painful memories and post-religious sensibility with a touch of tradition and, on the other hand, desire for national sovereignty diminishes the work. Unfortunately, the authors seem unaware that nationality is not merely a sense of belonging to some collective body; it is more than a feeling of solidarity and a common interest, for otherwise Protestants would be a nation, and so would cat lovers. A national consciousness is primarily the wish to live in an independent political entity. It wants its subjects to live and be educated by a homogeneous national culture. That was the essence of Zionism at its inception, and so it remained for most of its history until recent times. It sought independent sovereignty and achieved it. There have been other Jewish solidarities, but most of them were not national, and some were even expressly antinational.

But since the Jewish masses are not keen to live under the Jewish sovereignty, the Zionist arguments have had to be stretched beyond all national reason. The weakness of today's Zionist rationale lies in its failure to acknowledge this complex reality, in which Jews may be concerned about the fate of other Jews, yet have no wish to share a national life with them. Another serious flaw in Rubinstein and Yakobson's book, which is common to all the advocates of the "Jewish democracy," concerns their understanding of modern democracy, and this calls for a brief analysis of this controversial conceptual system.

Today there are many definitions of democracy, some complementary, some conflicting. Between the end of the eighteenth century and the middle of the twentieth, it mainly denoted government by the people, as opposed to all the premodern regimes in which the sovereign ruled over his or her subjects by the grace of God. Since the Second World War, and especially since the Cold War, the term has been used in the West to denote liberal democracies, which of course did not stop the socialist states from seeing themselves as popular democracies of even higher quality than the Western parliamentary variety.

This persistent ideological confusion calls for an analytical and historical separation between liberalism and democracy. Liberalism was born in the heart of the Western European monarchies, which it proceeded to curb by creating parliaments, political pluralism, separation of powers, and the rights of subjects vis-à-vis arbitrary power, as well as certain individual rights that no society in history had ever known. Nineteenth-century Britain is a good example of a liberal regime that was not at all democratic. The franchise was still limited to a small elite, and the great majority of the people v ere not yet allowed into the sphere of modern politics.

By contrast, the modern idea of democracy—namely, the principle that the entire people must be its own sovereign—burst into the historical arena as an intolerant tempest with marked antiliberal qualities. Its early spokesmen were Maximilien Robespierre and Saint-Just and other Jacobins in the great French Revolution. They sought to advance the principle of universal franchise and political equality, but did so through extremely authoritarian, even totalitarian, means. Only toward the end of the nineteenth century, for reasons too complex to cover here, did there begin to spread a liberal democracy that recognized the principle of the people's sovereignty while maintaining the rights and freedoms previously achieved by advancing liberalism. It expanded and consolidated them as the foundations of today's political culture.

The liberal democracies that arose in North America and in Europe were all national ones, and far from perfect in their early phases. Some did not extend the vote to women; in others, the voting age was quite advanced. In some countries certain social sectors had double votes. Both the "ethnic" and the "non-ethnic" nation-states were slow to extend the vote to all their inhabitants equally. But unlike the handful of democracies that existed in the ancient Greek world, modern democracies were born with a distinctive birthmark: a universal tension dictated their progress and forced them to advance in the direction of ever-increasing civil equality, to be implemented within the boundaries of the national state. "Man"—a category never quite known in the ancient world— joined "citizen," "nation" and "state" as a key term in the central discourse of modern politics. Thus for any state to be a democracy, sovereignty and equality for all human beings living together in civil society became the minimum requirement. At the same time, the extent of rights and freedoms guaranteed to individuals and minority groups, just like the separation of powers and an independent judiciary, testifies to the liberal qualities of the democracy.

Can Israel be defined as a democratic entity? It certainly bears many liberal features. Inside pre-1967 Israel the freedoms of expression and association are broad even in comparison with those in Western democracies, and the Supreme Court has repeatedly reined in governmental arbitrariness. Amazingly, even in times of intense military conflicts, pluralism has been maintained no less than in several liberal democracies in wartime.

But Israeli liberalism has its limitations, and civil rights violations are commonplace in the Jewish state. There is no civil marriage, no civil burial in public cemeteries, no public transportation on Saturdays and Jewish festivals, not to mention the trampling of the land-ownership rights of the Arab citizens. These expose a very un-liberal aspect of Israeli legislation and its everyday culture. Moreover, the more than forty-year domination of a whole nation, depriving it of all rights, in the territories occupied since 1967 has prevented the consolidation and expansion of genuine liberalism within Israel's jurisdiction. Nevertheless, despite the serious flaws in the area of individual rights, basic liberties are maintained, as well as the main democratic principle of periodic general elections, and the government is elected by all the citizens. May Israel not, therefore, qualify as a classic democracy, ruling—albeit belatedly—over a colonial region, as the European powers did in the past?

It should also be noted that the difficulty in characterizing Israel as a democracy does not lie in the fact that the Sabbath and the Jewish festivals are its main days of rest, nor even that the symbols of the state derive from Jewish tradition. For that matter, the historical and emotional attachment between Jewish Israeli society and Jewish communities in other countries does not preclude a democratic regime in Israel. If in the United States various cultural-linguistic communities maintain close contacts with their lands of origin, if Castilian is hegemonic in Spain, and if in secular France several of the holidays stem from the Catholic tradition, there is no reason why the cultural-symbolic setting in Israel cannot be Jewish. Of course, in a normative democracy where there are cultural and linguistic minority groups, it is advisable to include civil symbols and festivals shared by all the citizens. Not surprisingly, no such attempt has been made in the Jewish state. The peculiar character of Israel's supra-identity, whose primeval code was inherent in Zionism from the start, is what makes it doubtful that a "Jewish" state can also be democratic.

The Jewish nationalism that dominates Israeli society is not an open, inclusive identity that invites others to become part of it, or to coexist with it on a basis of equality and in symbiosis. On the contrary, it explicitly and culturally segregates the majority from the minority, and repeatedly asserts that the state belongs only to the majority; moreover, as noted earlier, it promises eternal proprietary rights to an even greater human mass that does not choose to live in it. In this way, it excludes the minority from active and harmonious participation in the sovereignty and practices of democracy, and prevents that minority from identifying with it politically.

When a democratic government looks at the electorate, it is supposed to see in the first place nothing but citizens. It is elected by them, funded by them and in principle is expected to serve them. The general welfare must include, if only theoretically, all the citizens. Only in the second, or even third, place can a democratic government, if it is also liberal, acknowledge the various cultural subgroups and act to restrain the strong ones and defend the weak ones, to moderate their relationships as much as possible, and to avoid harming their identities. Democracy need not be culturally neutral, but if there is a state supra-identity that directs the national culture, it must be open to all or at least seek to be so, even if the minority insists on staying out of the hegemonic national bear-hug. In all the existing kinds of democracy, it is the cultural minority that seeks to preserve its distinction and identity vis-à-vis the mighty majority. Its smaller size also entitles it to certain privileges.

In Israel the situation is reversed: the privileges are reserved for the Jewish majority and its "kinfolk who are still wandering in exile." This occurs through numerous mechanisms: the law of absentee properties and the law of land purchase, passed in the early days of the state; the Law of Return, the law of marriage and divorce and the various statutes and orders that employ the concept of "ex-military" to discriminate—by means of privileges and allocation of funds excluding the Palestino-Israelis (who are not conscripted)—and that preserve the bulk of public resources for the Jewish population. By a series of measures ranging from the generous "absorption grants" given to "new immigrants" to the fat subsidies given to the settlers in the occupied territories (who vote in the general elections even though they reside outside the state's borders), Israel openly favors the "biological descendants" of the ancient kingdom of Judea.

If the word "Jewish" were replaced by the word "Israeli," and if the state thus became open and accessible to all the citizens, who would then be able to navigate its identity landscape at will, it might be possible to take a softer line and begin to treat Israel as a political entity heading toward an eventual status of democracy. But such freedom of movement has been permanently prohibited in Israel. The Ministry of the Interior determines the "nationality" of every citizen, who may neither choose it nor change it, except by converting to Judaism and becoming officially a Jewish believer. The Jewish state takes pains to register its authorized proprietors, the Jews, on their identity cards and/or in the population registry. It also meticulously defines the "nationality" of other, non-Jewish citizens, sometimes absurdly: an Israeli who was born before 1989 to a non-Jewish mother in, say, Leipzig may still be registered as having "East German" nationality.

Nevertheless, the concept of "Jewish democracy" might still be plausible if there were evidence of a historical trend toward the loosening of the ethnocentric fetters and a conscious effort to consolidate Israelization. Despite the exclusive starting points—imported into Mandatory Palestine by the Eastern European

Zionists and hardened in the course of the colonization—the concept of democracy could have been advanced by efforts to make the identity morphology increasingly civil. But the absence of such a trend in the general culture—as well as in the educational and legislative systems—and the determined opposition of the political, judicial and intellectual elites to any wider universalization of the dominant identity inside the "Jewish state" impedes any theoretical goodwill effort to classify Israel as a democracy. The essentialist outlook that depends on the definitions of Jew and non-Jew, and the definition of the state by way of this outlook, together with the stubborn public refusal to allow Israel to be a republic of all Israeli citizens, constitute a deep-rooted barrier to any kind of democracy.

Therefore, although we are not in the field of zoology, and the precise terminology is less demanding than it is in the life sciences, Israel must still be described as an "ethnocracy."[86] Better still, call it a Jewish ethnocracy with liberal features—that is, a state whose main purpose is to serve not a civil-egalitarian *demos* but a biological-religious *ethnos* that is wholly fictitious historically, but dynamic, exclusive and discriminatory in its political manifestation. Such a state, for all its liberalism and pluralism, is committed to isolating its chosen *ethnos* through ideological, pedagogical and legislative means, not only from those of its own citizens who are not classified as Jews, not only from the Israeli-born children of foreign workers, but from the rest of humanity.

ETHNOCRACY IN THE AGE OF GLOBALIZATION

Although it has experienced many upheavals, Israel has existed as a liberal ethnocracy for more than sixty years. The liberal features have grown stronger over the years, but the state's ethnocentric foundation remains an obstacle to their development. Furthermore, the effective myths that guided the construction of the national state may give rise to a future challenge to its very existence.

The myth of the historical claim to Eretz Israel, which fortified the self-sacrificing endeavors of the first Zionist settlers and legitimized the acquisition of the territorial base for the future state, led it after nineteen years of independence to become immured in an oppressive colonialist situation from

---

86   It was Nadim Rouhana, As'ad Ghanem and Oren Yiftachel who began to apply the terms "ethnic state" and "ethnocracy" to Israel. See Nadim N. Rouhana, *Palestinian Citizens in an Ethnic Jewish State: Identities in Conflict*, New Haven: Yale University Press, 1997; As'ad Ghanem, "State and Minority in Israel: The Case of Ethnic State and the Predicament of Its Minority," *Ethnic and Racial Studies* 21: 3 (1998), 428–47; and Oren Yiftachel, *Ethnocracy: Land and Identity Politics in Israel/Palestine*.

which it is still unable to extricate itself. The occupation in 1967 led many Zionists, secular and religious alike, to view the new territories as the heart of the ancestral land. On the purely mythological level they were right—the imaginary spaces in which Abraham, David and Solomon lived were not Tel Aviv, the coast and the Galilee, but Hebron, Jerusalem and the mountains of Judea. For ethnic reasons, the supporters of the "whole Eretz Israel" rejected any idea of merging on an equal basis with the inhabitants of these territories. The partial but decisive removal of many of the local people, such as was carried out in 1948 on the coastal plain and in the Galilee, was not possible in 1967. Yet it remained an unspoken wish. A formal annexation of the new territories was avoided, as it would have led to a binational state and nullified the chances of maintaining a state with a Jewish majority.

It took the political elites in Israel forty years to diagnose the situation, and to comprehend that in an advanced technological world, control over bits of land is not always a source of power. Up to the time of writing, Israel has not yet produced a bold leadership capable of splitting up "Eretz Israel." All the governments have supported and encouraged the settlements, and not one has so far tried to dismantle those that floursih in the heart of the "biblical homeland."[87] However, even if Israel abandoned the territories taken in 1967, the inherent contradiction in its very composition would still not be resolved, and another myth, even more firmly hard-wired than the territorial one, would continue to haunt it.

The myth of the Jewish *ethnos* as a self-isolating historical body that always barred, and must therefore go on barring, outsiders from joining it is harmful to the State of Israel, and may cause it to disintegrate from within. Maintaining an exclusionary "ethnic" entity, and discriminating against one-quarter of the citizens—Arabs and those who are not considered Jews in accordance with misguided history and the Halakhah—leads to recurring tensions that may at some point produce violent divisions that will be difficult to heal. For Palestino-Israelis, every stage in their interaction with everyday Israeli culture accelerates their political alienation, however paradoxical this may sound. Social encounters and a closer acquaintance with Israeli cultural and political values and opportunities that today are reserved only for those defined as Jews heighten the desire for greater equality and more active political participation. That is why the so-called Arabs of 1948 are increasingly opposed to the existence

---

87   The national attachment to Gaza never equaled the sense of proprietorship toward Hebron and Bethlehem. On the inability of Israel's political elites to achieve a peace accord, see the valuable book by Lev Luis Grinberg, *Politics and Violence in Israel/Palestine*, New York, Routledge, 2009.

of Israel as an exclusively Jewish state, and there's no telling how far this opposition may develop, or how it may be halted.

The complacent assumption that this growing and strengthening populace will always accept its exclusion from the political and cultural heart is a dangerous illusion, similar to the blindness of Israeli society to the colonialist domination in Gaza and the West Bank before the First Intifada. But whereas the two Palestinian uprisings that broke out in 1987 and 2000 exposed the weakness of Israel's control over its apartheid territories, their threat to the existence of the state is negligible compared with the potential threat posed by the frustrated Palestinians living within its borders. The catastrophic scenario of an uprising in the Arab Galilee, followed by iron-fisted repression, may not be too far-fetched. Such a development could be a turning-point for the existence of Israel in the Near East.

No Jew who lives today in a liberal Western democracy would tolerate the discrimination and exclusion experienced by the Palestino-Israelis, who live in a state that proclaims it is not theirs. But Zionist supporters among the Jews around the world, like most Israelis, are quite unconcerned, or do not wish to know, that the "Jewish state," because of its undemocratic laws, could never have been part of the European Union or one of America's fifty states. This flawed reality does not stop them from expressing solidarity with Israel, and even regarding it as their reserve home. Not that this solidarity impels them to abandon their national homelands and emigrate to Israel. And why should they, seeing that they are not subjected to daily discrimination and alienation of the kind that Palestino-Israelis experience daily in their native country?

In recent years the Jewish state has become less interested in large-scale immigration. The old nationalist discourse that revolved around the idea of aliyah has lost much of its appeal. To understand current Zionist politics, replace the word "aliyah" with "diaspora." Today Israel's strength no longer depends on demographic increase, but rather on retaining the loyalty of overseas Jewish organizations and communities. It would be a serious setback for Israel if all the pro-Zionist lobbies were to immigrate en masse to the Holy Land. It is much more useful for them to remain close to the centers of power and communications in the Western world—and indeed they prefer to remain in the rich, liberal, comfortable "diaspora."

At the end of the twentieth century, the weakening of the nation-state in the Western world indirectly presented contemporary Zionism with new advantages. Economic, political and cultural globalization has significantly eroded classical nationalism, but it has not done away with the basic need for identity and alternative collective associations. The post-industrial context in the wealthy West, with its tremendous movement of material and cultural commerce, has not stopped people from seeking tangible social frameworks. And as the omnipotent state of the twentieth century gradually declines, the search for sub-identities—whether neoreligious, regional, ethnicist, communal or even sectist—has become prominent in the changing morphological fabric of the new world, and it's not clear where this development is heading.

Amid all these developments, Jewish "ethnicity" has enjoyed a resurgence. In the United States this has been a noticeable fashion for some time. As a typical immigrant state, the liberal and pluralistic American superpower has always left a generous margin for legitimate sub-identities. Mass nationalization in the US never sought to erase previous cultural layers or remnants of old beliefs (other than those it had exterminated at the start). In the presence of the Anglo-American, Latin American or African American, a descendant of Eastern European Jewry had to identity himself or herself as Jewish American. The person may not have preserved elements of the great Yiddish culture, but the need to belong to a particular community meant finding a focus of identity amid the sweeping cultural vortex.

As the Yiddish culture lost its vitality, Israel increased in importance for many American Jews, and the number of Zionists increased. If, during the Second World War, American Jewry behaved rather apathetically toward the mass slaughter in Europe, it responded with sympathy and support for Israel, especially following Israel's victory in the 1967 war. In Europe, with the rise of the European Union and the weakening of the nation-states within it, the Jewish institutions in London and Paris also experienced a transnational ethnicization, and the State of Israel learned to derive maximum political benefit from this worldwide network of Jewish power.

Since the late 1970s, the perpetuation of the Jewish *ethnos* state has paid handsome dividends, and the closer Brooklyn came to Jerusalem, the further was Arab Nazareth removed from the heartbeat of Jewish-Israeli politics. That is why any project that proposed turning Israel into a republic of its citizens has come to seem like a fantasy. Jewish-Israeli blindness regarding the democratic radicalization of the Palestino-Israeli community, especially its younger and educated elements, has always been based on plain material interest. It not only rested on the weighty mythological past and was sustained by simple ignorance—it has also been reinforced by the profit and power derived from the existence of the overseas *ethnos*, which is content to subsidize it.

But there's a fly in the ointment. Although the globalization of the late twentieth century was accompanied by increased pro-Zionist ethnicization among the established Jewish communities, the runaway assimilation at ground level has continued to mix Jews with those who live beside them, who attend the same universities and who share the same workplace. The impact of everyday cultures, local and global, is stronger than the synagogue and the Zionist Sabbath folklore. Consequently the demographic power base of the Jewish establishment is steadily eroding. Comfortable Jewish life in the "diaspora," the irresistible power of young love, and the welcome decline in anti-Semitism are all taking their toll. Surveys indicate that not only is mixed marriage on the rise, but support for Israel among Jewish families under thirty-five is declining. Only among the over-sixties is solidarity with Israel stable and popular. These data suggest that the inflow of power from Israel's "transnational diaspora" may not last forever.[88]

Nor should Israel assume that the support of the mighty West will never falter. The neocolonialism of the early twenty-first century—exemplified in, for instance, the conquest of Iraq and Afghanistan—has intoxicated the power elites in Israel, but for all the rising globalization, the West is still far away while Israel is situated in the Near East. The violent reaction to the humiliation of the East will fall not on the remote metropolis but on its forward outpost. The fate of the self-segregating *ethnos* state in a corner of the Arab and Muslim world is uncertain. In the present historical stage, as is usually the case, we cannot see the future, but there are good reasons to fear it.

For example, the peace camp must consider that a compromise accord with a Palestinian state, if achieved, may not only end a long and painful process, but start a new one, no less complex, inside Israel itself. The morning after may be no less painful than the long nightmare preceding it. Should a Kosovo erupt in the Galilee, neither Israel's conventional military might, nor its nuclear arsenal, nor even the great concrete wall with which it has girdled itself will be of much use. To save Israel from the black hole that is opening inside it, and to improve the fragile tolerance toward it in the surrounding Arab world, Jewish identity politics would have to change completely, as would the fabric of relations in the Palestino-Israeli sphere.

The ideal project for solving the century-long conflict and sustaining the closely woven existence of Jews and Arabs would be the creation of a democratic binational state between the Mediterranean Sea and the Jordan River. To ask the Jewish Israeli people, after such a long and bloody conflict, and in view of the tragedy experienced by many of its immigrant founders in the twentieth century, to become overnight a minority in its own state may not be the smartest

---

88 See the article by Shmuel Rozner, "Mixed Marriages Create Two Jewish Peoples," *Haaretz*, December 29, 2006; and also the reports in *Yediot Ahronot*, August 31, 2007.

thing to do. But if it is senseless to expect the Jewish Israelis to dismantle their own state, the least that can be demanded of them is to stop reserving it for themselves as a polity that segregates, excludes, and discriminates against a large number of its citizens, whom it views as undesirable aliens.

The Jewish supra-identity must be thoroughly transformed and must adapt to the lively cultural reality it dominates. It will have to undergo a process of Israelization, open to all citizens. It is too late to make Israel into a uniform, homogeneous nation-state. Therefore, in addition to an Israelization that welcomes the "other," it must develop a policy of democratic multiculturalism—similar to that of the United Kingdom or the Netherlands—that grants the Palestino-Israelis not only complete equality but also a genuine and firm autonomy. Their culture and institutions must be preserved and nurtured at the same time as they are brought into the centers of power of the hegemonic Israeli culture. Palestino-Israeli children should have access, if they wish it, to the heart of Israeli social and productive centers. And Jewish-Israeli children must be made aware that they are living in a state in which there are many "others."

Today this forecast seems fantastic and utopian. How many Jews would be willing to forgo the privileges they enjoy in the Zionist state? Would the Israeli elites be capable, following this cultural globalization, of undergoing a mental reformation and adopting a more egalitarian temperament? Do any of them really want to institute civil marriage and to separate the state entirely from the rabbinate? Could the Jewish Agency cease to be a state institution and become a private association for the fostering of cultural ties between the Jews of Israel and Jewish communities around the world? And when will the Jewish National Fund stop being a discriminatory ethnocentric institution, and return the 130,000 hectares of "absentee" lands that were sold to it by the state for a symbolic amount—more specifically, return them to the seller at that same symbolic price so that they may serve as the primary capital from which to compensate the Palestinian refugees?

Furthermore, will anyone dare to repeal the Law of Return, and to offer Israeli citizenship only to those Jews who are fleeing persecution? Will it be possible to deny a New York rabbi on a brief visit to Israel his automatic right to become an Israeli citizen (usually done on the eve of general elections) before he returns to his native country? And what's to stop such a Jew, assuming he is a fugitive (though not because of criminal acts), from living a contented Jewish religious life in an Israeli republic of all its citizens, just as he does in the United States?

And now the last, perhaps the hardest, question of them all: To what extent is Jewish Israeli society willing to discard the deeply embedded image of the "chosen people," and to cease isolating itself in the name of a fanciful history or dubious biology and excluding the "other" from its midst?

There are more questions than answers, and the mood at the end of this book, much as was the case in the personal stories at its start, is more pessimistic than hopeful. But it is appropriate for a work that has hung question marks over the Jewish past to conclude with a short, impertinent questionnaire about the uncertain future.

In the final account, if it was possible to have changed the historical imaginary so profoundly, why not put forth a similarly lavish effort of the imagination to create a different tomorrow? If the nation's history was mainly a dream, why not begin to dream its future afresh, before it becomes a nightmare?

Afterword: A People without a Land, a Land without a People? *Some Replies to My Critics*

And the diasporas that dissolve by regrouping in Israel do not yet make up a people, simply a population and a scattering of human beings, with no language, education or roots, without being fuelled by the vision of a nation.
—David Ben-Gurion, *Rebirth and Destiny of Israel*, 1950

I wrote *The Invention of the Jewish People* in Hebrew, and naturally its first reviews were in that language. The publication of the book in French and then in English gave rise to further rounds of responses, and I will not be able in the context of these pages to present a sufficient spectrum of arguments and defenses to deal with them all. In particular, I feel rather disarmed in the face of the claim that everything I wrote is both already familiar and completely false. And for this reason I have chosen to focus on certain key objections that have been raised to the disturbing meta-narrative that my book outlines.

First of all, and to ward off misunderstanding: far from it having been my intention to write a history of the Jews, I basically set out to criticize historiographical concepts and constructions that have long been prevalent in this subject area. I then proposed certain criteria that make it possible to define the concept of nationality that served as cradle-song to the State of Israel, and to which historians have contributed so much. Zionist colonization could certainly not have been undertaken without an ideological preparation that gave rise to the blossoming and crystallization of myths. It is also necessary to emphasize that the historical construction that has fuelled our national myths is not the speciality of the Zionist enterprise, but forms an intrinsic part of the formation of collective consciousness throughout the modern world. Everyone knows today that a national memory cannot be born without the devoted involvement of "certified commemorators."

"THE JEWS HAVE ALWAYS EXISTED AS A PEOPLE"

Resort to the fluid term "people" has been common enough in the modern age. If in a distant past this word was applied to religious groups such as "the people of Israel," "the Christian people," or "the people of God," in modern times its use has served more to designate human collectivities that have secular cultural and linguistic elements in common. In a general sense, before the rise of printing, books, newspapers and state education, it is very hard to use the concept of "people" to define a human group. When the lines of communication between tribes or villages were weak and unreliable, when the medley of dialects varied between one valley and the next, when the restricted vocabulary available to the farmer or shepherd extended to little more than his work and his religious beliefs, the reality of the existence of peoples in this sense can be seriously questioned. To define an illiterate society of agricultural producers as a "people" has always struck me as problematic, and as bearing the hallmark of a disturbing anachronism.

The definition of the Hasmonean kingdom as a nation-state, then, as we find in the Zionist history textbooks, raises a smile. A society whose rulers, established in the capital, spoke Aramaic, while the majority of their subjects expressed themselves in a range of Hebrew dialects, and where the kingdom's merchants conducted their business in the Greek *koine*, in no way amounted to a nation, and we can seriously question whether it can be defined as a people.

Historians, always dependent on the written word as transmitted by one-time centres of intellectual power, have been rashly inclined to generalize and apply to societies as a whole the identities of a thin stratum of "elites" whose doings are recorded in written documents. In kingdoms and principalities endowed with an administrative language, the degree of identification with the administrative apparatus was, for the great majority of their subjects, most often close to zero. If any form of ideological identification with the kingdom could exist, it was one that linked it to the landed nobility and the urban elites who accepted the rulers and provided a basis for their power.

Before the rise of modernity, there was no class of individuals whose task it was to express or represent the opinion of the "people." With the exception of the monarchy's chroniclers or historians, the only intellectuals concerned with broadcasting and developing an identity among the broad strata of the population were members of the clergy. The degree of relative autonomy that these managed to obtain in relation to governments depended on the strength of religious faith and its foundation. The power of the "agents" of religion depended both on the level of ideological solidarity and on the intensity of communication that existed between them: on the one hand they maintained the faith, while they were on the other hand the only ones to shape and transmit a collective memory. This is why the Berbers who had converted to Judaism in the Atlas Mountains knew more about the Exodus from Egypt and the tablets given to Moses in Sinai than they did about the prince who ruled them from a distant capital; just as in the kingdom of France, peasants were more familiar with the Nativity story than with the name of their king.

Five hundred years ago, there was no French people, no more than there was an Italian or Vietnamese people, and in the same way, no more was there a Jewish people scattered across the world. There certainly did exist, founded on religious ritual and faith, an important Jewish identity, of various strengths according to context and circumstance; the more removed the community's cultural components were from religious practice, the more they resembled the cultural and linguistic practices of its non-Jewish environment. The considerable differences in daily life between the different Jewish communities forced Zionist historians to emphasize a single "ethnic" origin: the majority of Jewish populations, if not all of them, supposedly derived from a single source, that of the ancient Hebrews. Certainly, the majority of Zionists did not believe in a pure race—as I explained in this book, the Jewish religion did not permit such an idea—and yet almost all these historians referred to a common biological origin as the decisive criterion for membership of a single people. Just as the French were persuaded that their ancestors were the Gauls, and the Germans cherished the idea that they descended directly from the Aryan Teutons, so the Jews had to know that they were the authentic descendants of the "children of Israel" who came out of Egypt. Only this myth of Hebrew ancestors could justify the right that they claimed over Palestine. Many people are still convinced of this today. Everyone knows that, in the modern world, membership of a religious community does not provide ownership rights to a territory, whereas an "ethnic" people always have a land they can claim as their ancestral heritage.

This is why, in the eyes of the first Zionist historians, the Bible ceased to be an impressive theological text and became a book of secular history, whose teaching is still dispensed to all Jewish Israeli pupils in specially designated lessons, from the first year of elementary school to graduation from high school. According to this teaching, the people of Israel were no longer made up of those chosen by God, but became a nation issuing from the seed of Abraham. And so when modern archaeology began to show that there had not been an Exodus from Egypt, and that the great, unified monarchy of David and Solomon never existed, it met with a bitter and embarrassed reaction from the secular Israeli public; some people did not even flinch from accusing the "new archaeologists" of "Bible denial."

EXILE AND HISTORICAL MEMORY

The secularization of the Bible was conducted in parallel with the nationalization of the "Exile." The myth that recounted the expulsion of the "Jewish people" by the Romans became the supreme justification for claiming historical rights over a Palestine that Zionist rhetoric transformed into the "Land of Israel." We have here a particularly astonishing example of the molding of a collective memory. Thus, even though all specialists in ancient Jewish history know that the Romans did not deport the population of Judea (there is not even the slightest work of historical research on this subject), other, less qualified individuals have been, and largely remain, convinced that the ancient "People of Israel" were forcibly uprooted from their homeland, as is solemnly stated in the Declaration of Independence of the State of Israel.

Zionist historians seized on the term "Exile" (*Gola* or *Galout* in Hebrew), which in Judaic religion expressed a rejection of Christian salvation, and gave it a physical or political sense. With a certain panache, they transformed the deep metaphysical and theological opposition of "Exile–Redemption" into "Exile–Homeland." Over the centuries, Jews ardently longed for Zion, their holy city, but it never occurred to them, not even to those living close by, to go and settle there in their earthly life.[1] It is certainly hard to live at the heart of a holy place, all the more so when the small minority who did live there were well aware how they continued to live in exile: only the coming of the Messiah would allow them to reach the metaphysical Jerusalem—along with all the dead, we should not forget.

This is the point to make a certain clarification: quite contrary to what various critics have claimed, I did not write this book in order to challenge the historical rights of Jews to Zion.[2] I still naively believed, a few years ago, that the Exile had indeed taken place in the early years of the Christian era; but I never thought that two thousand years of absence conferred rights to the land, whereas twelve hundred years of presence gave none to the local population.

It would never occur to anyone to deny the existence of the United States because indigenous peoples were robed of their lands when the nation was formed. No one would claim that the Norman conquerors should be expelled from the British Isles or the Arabs brought back to Spain. If we want to avoid

---

1   It seems to me that Simon Schama, who wrote that my "book fails to sever the remembered connection between the ancestral land and Jewish experience," misunderstood my analysis of the historical affinity of Jews to their Holy Land. See his review in the *Financial Times*, November 13, 2009.

2   See for example Patricia Cohen, "Book Calls Jewish People an 'Invention,'" *"New York Times*, November 24, 2009.

transforming the world into a giant mental hospital, we must resist the urge to redistribute populations according to some historical model. Israel can today claim the right to exist only by accepting that a painful historical process led to its creation, and that any attempt to challenge this fact will produce new tragedies.

ARE THE PALESTINIANS THE DESCENDANTS OF THE ANCIENT JEWS?

What happened to the population of Judea if it did not undergo exile? I have been accused of claiming that the Palestinians of today are its direct descendants. This is certainly not an idea that I came up with; in my book I cited the declarations of prominent Zionist leaders, including David Ben-Gurion, Yitzhak Ben-Zvi and Israel Belkind, who all believed that the "fellahs" they encountered in the early days of colonization were descended from the ancient Jewish people, and that the two populations had to be reunited. They knew perfectly well that there was no exile in the first century CE, and they logically concluded that the great mass of the Jews had converted to Islam with the arrival of Arab forces in the early seventh century. David Ben-Gurion later went on to express a totally different position, when he helped to draft the Declaration of Independence of the state of Israel, without ever explaining this reversal.

For my own part, I believe that today's Palestinians derive from a variety of origins, just like all contemporary peoples. Each conqueror left his mark in the region: Egyptians, Persians and Byzantines all fertilized the local women and many of their descendants must be there still. And yet, though this is not so important in my view, I believe that the young Ben-Gurion was correct—if imprecise—it is quite likely that an inhabitant of Hebron is closer in origin to the ancient Hebrews than are the majority of those across the world who identify themselves as Jews.

THE LAST RESORT: A JEWISH DNA

After exhausting all the historical arguments, several critics have seized on genetics. The same people who maintain that the Zionists never referred to a race conclude their argument by evoking a common Jewish gene. Their thinking can be summed up as follows: "We are not a pure race, but we are a race just the same." In the 1950s there was research in Israel on characteristic Jewish fingerprints, and from the 1970s, biologists in their laboratories (sometimes also in the USA) have sought a genetic marker common to all Jews. I reviewed in my book their lack of data, the frequent slipperiness of their conclusions, and their ethno-nationalist ardor, which is unsupported by any serious scientific findings. This attempt to justify Zionism through genetics is reminiscent of the procedures of late nineteenth-century anthropologists who very scientifically set out to discover the specific characteristics of Europeans.

As of today, no study based on anonymous DNA samples has succeeded in identifying a genetic marker specific to Jews, and it is not likely that any study ever will. It is a bitter irony to see the descendants of Holocaust survivors set out to find a biological Jewish identity: Hitler would certainly have been very pleased! And it is all the more repulsive that this kind of research should be conducted in a state that has waged for years a declared policy of "Judaization of the country" in which even today a Jew is not allowed to marry a non-Jew.

CONVERTS, KHAZARS AND HISTORIANS

Scarcely any scholarly criticism has contradicted my assertion that there was no forced exile of a Jewish people in the first or second centuries CE, and most critics are perfectly well aware that the Bible is not a book of history. But the section of my book devoted to the subject of the Khazars has attracted many critics: "We all read about the Khazars as children … It's a worn-out and unfounded myth … The anti-Semitic writer Arthur Koestler invented it … The Arabs have been saying this for a long time …" etc. What is particularly striking about these responses is that they come from critics who have hardly a word to say on the conversions that the Hasmoneans imposed on their neighbors, nor on the massive conversions conducted in antiquity around the Mediterranean basin,[3] nor on Adiabene in Mesopotamia, nor on the conversion of the Himyar kingdom in the south of the Arabian peninsula, nor on the Judaized Berbers of North Africa.

Contrary to modern conceptions, from the second century BCE to the early fourth century CE Judaism was a proselytizing religion, dynamic and expanding, and no data today can refute this. The communitarian withdrawal was a much later phenomenon, when the persistence of Jewish minorities within the now dominant Christian and Islamic worlds was conditional on the complete cessation of any Jewish proselytizing. But in the "pagan" regions, Judaism continued to attract new followers, which leads us to the subject of the Khazars.

---

3   An exception is Martin Goodman, who naively adopts the Zionist myth that explains the demographic growth of the Jews in the ancient world on the basis that they were the only group who prohibited abortions and didn't kill their children. See his review "Secta and Natio," *Times Literary Supplement*, February 26, 2010. Much more interesting about this subject is the article of Maurice Sartre, «A-t-on inventé le peuple juif?», *Le Débat, Histoire, Politique, Société*, 158, January 2010, 177–184.

The Khazar kingdom was the last to be converted to Judaism, most likely in the eighth century CE; this much is beyond dispute, but the anger of Zionist historians was aroused by the attempt to connect the very substantial Jewish presence in Eastern Europe with the break-up of the Khazar kingdom and the emigration of its Jewish subjects into the Ukraine, Russia, Poland and Hungary. It is important to bear in mind, however, that the thesis maintaining that the strong demographic Jewish presence in these regions would be incomprehensible without the existence of a Jewish Khazar kingdom was not invented by Arthur Koestler, whose only problem was that he was rather late in publishing his book *The Thirteenth Tribe*. In actual fact, through to the 1960s almost all historians, including Zionist ones, supported this position and I cite a number of these in my book.[4]

Ben-Zion Dinur, the father of Israeli historiography as well as a former minister of education, called Khazaria "a Diaspora mother, the mother of one of the greatest of the Diasporas—of Israel in Russia, Lithuania and Poland." According to the American Jewish historian Salo Baron, who didn't hide his sympathies for Israel:

> Before and after the Mongol upheaval, the Khazars sent many offshoots into the unstudied Slavonic lands, helping ultimately to build up the great Jewish centers of Eastern Europe ... During the half millennium (740–1250) of its existence, however, and its aftermath in the Eastern European communities, this noteworthy experiment in Jewish statecraft doubtless exerted a greater influence on Jewish history than we are as yet able to envisage. From Khazaria Jews began drifting into the open steppes of Eastern Europe, during both the period of their country's affluence and that of its decline.

When the great historian Marc Bloch had to come up with a definition of the Jews, he described them as "a group of co-religionists originally brought together from every corner of the Mediterranean, Turco-Khazar, and Slav worlds."[5] The most important work demonstrating that the origin of the majority of Eastern European Jews lies in the Turkic and Slav tribes of the Khazar kingdom is that of Abraham Polak, professor and founder of the department of Middle Eastern history at the University of Tel Aviv. As far as the "Khazar problem" is concerned, the difference between Zionists and non-Zionists is that the latter put forward the very unlikely thesis that the mass of Jews in the Khazar kingdom came from "Eretz Israel," and sought to preserve in their new land the principle of Abrahamic descent.

---

4 This is the reason I was quite surprised by critics who accused me of ignoring the fact that Zionist scholars had always known and written about the Khazars. See for example Israel Bartal, "Inventing an Invention," *Haaretz*, July 6, 2008.

5 Marc Bloch, *Strange Defeat*, New York: Norton, 1999, 3.

Perhaps these historians are all mistaken. But in any case, the connection between the converted Jews of the great Khazar kingdom and the development of the "Yiddish people" in Eastern Europe has not been the object of serious study since the writings of Abraham Polak in the 1940s. No new historical discovery has seen the light, no research has been undertaken since then to show or explain how, from the small Jewish minority in Western Germany, a mass emigration was in a position to generate, by the early eighteenth century, a presence of over three-quarters of a million Jews in the Polish-Lithuanian commonwealth alone (without Russia, Eastern Ukraine, Romania, Hungary and Bohemia), a large number even before the demographic upturn of the nineteenth and twentieth centuries. The calculations of various Zionist demographers claiming that Jews multiplied ten times faster than their neighbors—in particular, because they washed their hands before meals—are completely groundless.[6] Until a new and credible thesis comes along to refute it, only the existence in the East of a medieval Jewish kingdom is able to explain this demographic "explosion," with no equivalent in any other region of the world at this time. Besides, recent philological researches have shown how the origins of the Yiddish language differ from those of the Judeo-German dialect of the West German ghettos.

However, in a time of global decolonization and the rise of the Palestinian national movement, while Israel maintained its hold over the entire area between the Mediterranean and the Jordan valley, it was no longer possible to leave room for doubt as to the origins of the conquerors of Jerusalem: all of them, or at least the great majority, had to be shown to be the descendants of the kingdoms of David and Solomon. And so the Jewish Khazars were expelled from history twice over: first by Soviet historiography in the wake of the Second World War; and second by Zionist historiography after the war of June 1967. In both cases, ideological necessity refashioned national memory.

DENYING THE EXISTENCE OF AN ISRAELI PEOPLE

I have been accused of denying the existence of the Jewish people,[7] and I have to acknowledge that this assertion, though often burdened with an evident and offensive accusatory slant that insinuates an equivalence with the outrage that is holocaust denial, is not totally unfounded. The question must be asked: Did

---

6   See Jits van Straten's excellent critique of historians and demographers such as Bernard D. Weinryb and Sergio DellaPergola in his article "Early Modern Polish Jewry: The Rhineland Hypothesis Revisited," *Historical Methods: A Journal of Quantitative and Interdisciplinary History Quarterly*, 40:1 (2007), 39–50.

7   See for example Anita Shapira, "The Jewish-People Deniers," *Journal of Israeli History*, 28:1 (2009), 63–72.

the slow emergence of ever broader and more reliable lines of communication, through which populations began to forge themselves as peoples in the context of centralizing kingdoms and early nation-states, create a Jewish people? The response is negative. With the exception of Eastern Europe, where the demographic weight and uniquely distinctive structure of Jewish life nurtured a specific form of popular culture and vernacular language, no Jewish people—as a single, cohesive entity—ever appeared. The Bund party, which represented one of the "proto-national" expressions of Eastern Europe's Jewish population, understood that the boundaries of the people whose representative and defender it set out to be coincided with those of the Yiddish tongue. It is interesting, moreover, to note that the early Zionists in Western Europe earmarked Palestine for the Jews of the Yiddish-speaking world, and not for themselves; they sought for their part to be properly English, German, French or American, and even joined passionately in the national wars of their respective countries.

If there was no such thing as a Jewish people in the past, has Zionism succeeded in creating one in modern times? Everywhere in the world where nations formed, in other words where human groups claimed sovereignty for themselves or struggled to preserve it, peoples were invented and endowed with long antecedents and distant historical origins. The Zionist movement proceeded in the same way. But if Zionism succeeded in imagining an eternal people, it did not manage to create a world Jewish nation. Today, Jews everywhere have the option to emigrate to Israel, but the majority of their number have chosen not to live under Jewish sovereignty, and prefer to retain another nationality.

If Zionism has not created a world Jewish people, and still less a Jewish nation, it has, however, given birth to two peoples, and even two new nations that it unfortunately refuses to recognize, considering them illegitimate offspring. There exists today a Palestinian people, the direct creation of colonization, that aspires to its own sovereignty and fights desperately for what is left of its homeland, and likewise an Israeli people ready to defend with total commitment its national independence. This latter, unlike the Palestinian people today, does not enjoy any recognition, even though it has its own language, a general system of education, and an artistic heritage in literature, cinema and theatre that expresses a vigorous and dynamic secular culture.

The Zionists throughout the world may donate to Israel, and exert pressure on the governments of their countries in support of Israeli policy, but most often they do not understand the language of the nation supposed to be theirs, they abstain from joining the "people who have emigrated to their homeland," and decline to send their children to take part in the wars of the Middle East. At the moment that these lines are being written, the number of Israelis immigrating to Western countries is greater than that of Zionists settling in Israel. We also know that if they had been able to choose at the time, the great majority of Jews leaving the USSR would have moved directly to the United States, as the Yiddish-speaking Jews of Eastern Europe did a century before. (Would the state of Israel have seen the light, moreover, if the United States had not closed its borders to immigrants from Central and Eastern Europe in the 1920s, a policy implacably maintained through the following decade against refugees fleeing Nazi persecution, and still in the aftermath of the Second World War toward Jews who escaped from Europe?)

The Middle East today is probably the most dangerous region in the world for those who consider themselves Jews. Among the reasons for this is the denial by Zionists of the existence of an Israeli people, whom they consider simply as the bridgehead of a "Jewish people" engaged in a colonization that must continue, and whom Zionism prefers to envelop in a self-enclosed ethnocentric ideology.

ETHNIC NATIONALITY AND THE STATE OF ISRAEL

As they take their first steps, almost all nationalities are guided by the dream of embodying the consciousness and memory of an "ethnic" people. The need to define a national group gave rise to conflicts throughout the nineteenth century, some of which continue in various places today. In the majority of liberal democratic nation-states, a civic and political conception of nationality eventually triumphed, whereas in others, an ethnocentric definition of membership in and ownership of the state has remained dominant. Zionism, born in Central and Eastern Europe, unmistakably resembles the prevailing ethno-biological and ethno-religious currents of the environment from which it originates. The contours of the nation were not seen as laid down by language, an everyday secular culture, presence on a territory and a political desire for integration in the collective. Instead, biological origin, combined with fragments of a "nationalized" religion, constituted the criterion for inclusion in the "Jewish people." It was impossible to unite this nation on the basis of a voluntary secular membership, and it is impossible to stop belonging to the "Jewish people," and these original elements are still in force today in Israel—this is the real source of the problem.

Zionist colonization reinforced this form of nationality. In its early stages there was indeed some hesitation about the boundaries of the Jewish nation;

it was envisaged at one time to include the Arabs present in Palestine, on the basis of their own "ethno-biological" origin; but as soon as they began vigorously to oppose foreign colonization, the definition of the nation was definitively refocused along ethnocentric and religious lines. Ethno-biological criteria have not been maintained so firmly in all societies issuing from colonization. (If these criteria did dominate for a long time the national definitions of Puritan colonization in North America, they were more rapidly dissolved in the new nations established in Central and South America, where Catholicism prevailed.)[8] In Israel, the 1960s saw the embryonic expression of a civic nationality; but after 1967, the subordinate position of the whole Arab population between the Mediterranean and the Jordan valley meant the definition of the imaginary Jewish "ethnos" became increasingly narrow.

Jewish ethnocentrism has continued to become more pronounced in recent years. The weakening of the territorial myth has been accompanied by the strengthening of the "Ethnos" myth; the results of the last legislative elections are an eloquent expression of this trend. In parallel, in the Western world, the retreat of classical civic nationality and the rise of enclosing forms of communitarianism, bound up with cultural globalization and the upheavals of immigration, have encouraged tendencies to withdraw into an exclusive Jewish identity. Whether religious or secular, Jewish identity as such is in no way reprehensible, and after Hitler and Nazism it would be foolish or even suspect to oppose it. However, when this identification is empty of spiritual, cultural or ethical experiences, when it leads to the isolation of Jews from their neighbors and entails their identifying with Israeli militarism and a policy that seeks to dominate another people by force, there is cause for concern.

Israel, in the early twenty-first century, defines itself as the state of the Jews and as the property of the "Jewish people," in other words of Jews living anywhere in the world, and not a possession of the ensemble of Israeli citizens residing on its soil—which is why it is appropriate to define it as an ethnocracy rather than a democracy.

Foreign workers and their families, deprived of citizenship, have absolutely no possibility of being integrated into the social body, even if they have been living in Israel for decades, even if their children were born there and speak only Hebrew. As for the quarter of the population identified by the ministry of the interior as "non-Jewish," although they have citizenship they cannot claim Israel as "their" state. It is hard to know how much longer the Israeli Arabs,

---

8   With regard to my "ignoring the centrality of settler nationalism to an understanding of the Zionist Israeli project," see Gabriel Piterberg, "Converts to Colonizers?" *New Left Review*, 2:59 (2009), 145–151.

who represent 20 per cent of the country's inhabitants, will continue to tolerate being viewed as foreigners in their own homeland. Since the state is a Jewish one and not Israeli, the more those Arab citizens are "Israelized" in terms of culture and language, the more they become anti-Israeli in their political positions—a fact that is in no way paradoxical. Is it really so difficult to imagine that one of the next "intifadas" may take place not in the occupied territories on the West Bank subjected to an apartheid-style regime, but instead break out in the very heart of the segregationist ethnocracy, which is to say, within Israeli's 1967 frontiers?

It is still possible to close one's eyes to the truth. Many voices will continue to maintain that the "Jewish people" has existed for four thousand years, and that "Eretz Israel" has always belonged to it. And yet the historical myths that were once, with the aid of a good deal of imagination, able to create Israeli society are now powerful forces helping to raise the possibility of its destruction.

Tel Aviv University, 2010.

Acknowledgments

I am deeply grateful to all my colleagues, students and friends who helped me at various stages in the writing of this book. My thanks to Yehonatan Alsheh, Nitza Erel, Yoseph Barnea, Samir Ben-Layashi, Israel Gershoni, Yael Dagan, Eik Doedtmann, Naftali Kaminski, Yuval Laor, Gil Mihaely, Uri Ram, Dan Tsahor, Amnon Yuval, Paul Wexler, and most especially to Stavit Sinai. They were the first to read parts of the manuscript, and their valuable comments helped me greatly to improve it.

The final chapters of the book were written while I stayed at the University of Aix-en-Provence in southern France, and I owe thanks to M. Bernard Cousin, the University's Vice-President, for his warm and generous hospitality. My thanks, also, to all the scholars and friends at Maison méditerranéene des sciences de l'homme, whose insights, comments and conversation shed light on areas I would not have discovered on my own.

Other friends encouraged me to keep going when I felt despondent and uncertain. I'm grateful to Houda Benallal, Michel Bilis, Roni and Dan Darin, Boas Evron, Levana Frenk, Jean-Luc Gavard, Eliho Matz, Basel Natsheh and Dominique Vidal. They all, in their different ways, gave me the strength to go on when I despaired. And there is no measuring the debt I owe my wife Varda and my daughters Edith and Liel for their heart-warming support.

My thanks also to Yael Lotan for her fine English translation, and to the staff at Verso, who labored hard to bring the book to the English-speaking public.

It goes without saying that the people who helped me, directly or indirectly, to write this book, are in no way responsible for the views expressed in it, much less for any inaccuracies that it may contain. Since no institution or fund financed it, I felt completely free in writing it, a freedom I don't think I had ever experienced before.

Index

The Khazars (Lerner), 231
The Khazars in the Light of the Soviet
  Historiography (Lior), 230 n.89, 233 n.97
Khazar Studies (Golden), 238 n.109
Khosrau II, 214
kibbutz, 4–5, 284 n.53
Kiev, 21, 105, 214, 219, 226–28, 233–34, 237, 250
Kimmerling, Baruch, 284 n.55; Zionism and
  Territory, 19 n.4
The Kingdom of the Khazars with Ehud Yaari
  (TV), 236 n.105
Kiriat Sefer, 237 n.107
Kirsh, Nurit, 273; The Teaching and Research of
  Genetics at the Hebrew University, 273 n.34
Kissinger, Henry, 288
Kitroser, Félix E., Jazaria, 238 n.111
Kivunim, 240 n.119
Klausner, Jospeh, The History of
  the Second Temple, 142, 159 n.63; In the
  Time of the Second Temple, 143 n.32
Kleiman, Rabbi Yaacov, 278; DNA and
  Tradition: The Genetic Link to the Ancient
  Hebrew, 278 n.44
Knesset, 104, 250, 280 n.49, 286, 287 n.58,
  292–93, 295 n.70
Knox, Robert, The Races of Man, 78
Koestler, Arthur, The Thirteenth Tribe, 225 n.77,
  238–41, 244
Kohn, Hans, 45–46, 48, 51, 260, 262; criticism
  of, 47; and Daniel Walden, Readings in
  American Nationalism, 47 n.34; A History of
  Nationalism in the East, 46 n.33; The Idea of
  Nationalism, 46; The Mind of Germany, 47
  n.34; Nationalism, Its Meaning and History,
  47 n.34; Nationalism and Liberty, 38 n.23;
  Prophets and Peoples, 32 n.12
Kokovtsov, Pavel, 233
Kreisky, Bruno, 288
Kumar, Krisham, The Making of English
  National Identity, 42 n.27
Kutschera, Hugo Von, Die Chasaren, 232 n.94
The Kuzari (Halevi), 213, 221
Kuzio, Taras, 47 n.35

labor: and conflict with capital, 44; division of,
  37–38, 54, 58, 60–61, 244
Land, Labor and the Origins of the Israeli-
  Palestinian Conflict (Shafir), 19 n.4
Landau, Menahem, 212 n.46, 226 n.80
language of administration, 31, 36, 57, 60, 94
Language Contact and Lexical Enrichment in
  Israeli Hebrew (Zuckermann), 107 n.90
Lavisse, Ernest, 49 n.37
Law of Return, 286–91, 293, 298, 300, 306, 312
Lazarus, Moritz, 84
Lebanon, 7, 159, 291

Lecker, Michael, 194 n.4
Leibowitz, Yeshayahu, 284
Lemche, Niels Peter, 118 n.114, 125; Ancient
  Israel, 125 n.122
Lenin, Vladimir Ilych, 2, 6, 33
Leo Baeck Institute Yearbook, 86 n.38
Lerner, Joseph Yehuda, The Khazars, 231
Letter of Aristeas, 161–63
Letters on the Old and New Judaism (Dubnow),
  90 n.44
Levine, Lee Israel, 133 n.10; Judaism and
  Hellenism in Antiquity, 155 n.54
Levinsohn, Isaac Baer (Rival), Testimony in
  Israel, 243
Lewicki, Tadeusz, 246 n.132
Libya, 199, 201, 204
Lieberman, Joe, 288
Liebeschütz, Hans, 86 n.38
The Life of Flavius Josephus, 160 n.67
Likud, 291
Lindenberger, James M., The Aramaic Proverbs
  of Ahiqar, 125 n.121
Linder, Amnon, 177 n.105
Linz, Juan Jose, 295
Lior, Yehoshua, 235 n.104; The Khazars in the
  Light of the Soviet Historiography, 230 n.89,
  233 n.97
literacy, 37, 56, 61
literate elite, 54, 58
literati, 57, 61, 67–68, 170
The Literature of History, 211 n.44, 214 n.50, 223
  n.69
Lithuania, 49, 229, 241–43, 245–47, 252
Litman, Jacob, The Economic Role of the Jews in
  Medieval Poland, 241 n.123
Living with the Bible (Dayan), 112
La Livre de ma vie (Dubnow), 88 n.43
The Lost Communities of Israel, 221 n.66
The Love of Zion (Mapu), 74 n.20
Luther, Martin, 66, 82

Maariv, 277
Machiavelli, Niccolò, 57
Mada, 274
Maimonides, 175
Maistre, Joseph de, 60
The Making of English National Identity
  (Kumar), 42 n.27
The Making of the English Working Class
  (Thompson), 45 n.31
Malik Karib Yuhamin, 193–94
Man and Land in Eretz Israel in Antiquity, 132
  n.6
Mao Zedong, 34
Mapu, Abraham, The Love of Zion, 74 n.20
Margalit, Israel, 240 n.117